Logical Foundations
of
Artificial Intelligence

Logical Foundations
of
Artificial Intelligence

Michael R. Genesereth and Nils J. Nilsson
Stanford University

Morgan Kaufmann Publishers, Inc.

Editor and President   *Michael B. Morgan*
Production Manager   *Jennifer M. Ballentine*
Cover Designer   *Irene Imfeld*
Composition   *Arthur Ogawa and Laura Friedsam*
Book Design   *Beverly Kennon-Kelley*
Copy Editor   *Lyn Dupré*
Graduate Assistant   *Jamison Gray*
Production Assistant   *Todd R. Armstrong*

Library of Congress Cataloging-in-Publication Data

Genesereth, Michael, 1948-
   Logical foundations of artificial intelligence.

   Bibliography: p.
   Includes index.
   1. Artificial intelligence.   I. Nilsson, Nils,
1933-   .   II. Title.
Q335.G37 1986   006.3   87-5461
ISBN 0-934613-31-1

         68010

Reprinted with corrections May, 1988

Morgan Kaufmann Publishers, Inc.
P.O. Box 50490, Palo Alto, CA 94303
© 1987 by Morgan Kaufmann Publishers Inc.
All rights reserved.
Printed in the United States of America

ISBN: 0-934613-31-1

90 89 88   5 4 3 2

to
Maureen
and
Karen

Acknowledgments

WE ARE GRATEFUL for the support of Stanford University and of our many colleagues and students there. The second author also thanks SRI International for many years of an excellent research environment and the Palo Alto Laboratory of the Rockwell Scientific Center for valued help.

Many people read early drafts of this book. Some suggested major changes; some spotted small but dangerous errors. We thank them all and hope that the list below doesn't leave too many of them unmentioned.

James Allen
Mario Aranha
Marianne Baudinet
Edward Brink
Peter Cheeseman
Jens Christensen
Lai-Heng Chua
Michael Dixon
David Etherington
David Fogelsong
Bob Floyd
Peter Friedland
Matthew Ginsberg
Andrew Golding
Jamie Gray

William Greene
Benjamin Grosof
Haym Hirsh
Jane Hsu
Joseph Jacobs
Leslie Pack Kaelbling
Michael Kharitonov
Donald Knuth
Kurt Konolige
Ami Kronfeld
Vladimir Lifschitz
John Lowrance
Kim McCall
Bill McClung
Andres Modet
John Mohammed

Yoram Moses
Karen Myers
Pandu Nayak
Eunok Paek
Judea Pearl
Donald Perlis
Liam Peyton
Charles Restivo
Stan Rosenschein
Dave Singhal
David Smith
Devika Subramanian
Tom Strat
Richard Waldinger
Elizabeth Wolf

Preface

THIS BOOK rests on two main assumptions. First, scientific and engineering progress in a discipline requires the invention and use of appropriate mathematical apparatus with which to express and unify good ideas. Second, symbolic logic forms a most important part of the mathematics of Artificial Intelligence (AI). Perhaps each of these assumptions needs some defense.

One might think that our first tenet should be noncontroversial. Yet in new fields, where the knowledge corpus is still mainly tied to practice and case studies, there often is substantial resistance to attempts at mathematicization. (One of us, for example, remembers hearing some electrical engineers during the 1950s complain about the irrelevance of differential equations to the study of electrical circuits and control systems!) We do not claim that knowing the mathematical ideas and techniques of a field is *all* that is needed to succeed in that field—either in research or in practice. We do note, however, that successful preparation in mature fields of science and engineering always includes a solid grounding in the mathematical apparatus of that field. This preparation provides the all-important framework needed to interpret, understand, and build the discipline.

Because the field of AI is relatively new, it is not surprising then that there are spirited debates between the "formalists" and the "experimentalists." The formalists claim that the experimentalists would progress faster if the latter had a more thorough understanding of various AI theoretical ideas. The experimentalists claim that the formalists would be more helpful if the latter were less concerned with form and more with content. Even if we were to grant that most of the advances in AI (or in any field of engineering) are inspired by experimentalists and that formalists serve mainly to "tidy up," it is nevertheless our opinion that the important new results in AI will be achieved by those researchers whose experiments are launched from the high platform of solid theory.

The theoretical ideas of older branches of engineering are captured in the language of mathematics. We contend that mathematical logic provides the basis for theory in AI. Although many computer scientists already count logic as fundamental to computer science in general, we put forward an even stronger form of the logic-is-important argument. In Chapters 1 and 2, we claim that AI deals mainly with the problem of representing and using *declarative* (as opposed to *procedural*) knowledge. Declarative knowledge is the kind that is expressed as sentences, and AI needs a language in which to state these sentences. Because the languages in which this knowledge usually is originally captured (natural languages such as English) are not suitable for computer representations, some other language with the appropriate properties must be used. It turns out, we think, that the appropriate properties include *at least* those that have been uppermost in the minds of logicians in their development of logical languages such as the predicate calculus. Thus, we think that any language for expressing knowledge in AI systems must be at least as expressive as the first-order predicate calculus.

If we are going to use a predicate-calculus–like language as a knowledge-representation language, then the theory that we develop about such systems must include parts of proof theory and model theory in logic. Our view is rather strong on this point: Anyone who attempts to develop theoretical apparatus relevant to systems that use and manipulate declaratively represented knowledge, and does so without taking into account the prior theoretical results of logicians on these topics, risks (at best) having to repeat some of the work done by the brightest minds of the twentieth century and (at worst) getting it wrong!

Given these two assumptions, then, the book develops the major topics of AI using the language and techniques of logic. These main topics are knowledge representation, reasoning, induction (a form of learning), and architectures for agents that reason, perceive, and act. We do not treat the various applications of these ideas in expert systems, natural-language processing, or vision. Separate books have been written about these application areas, and our goal here has been to concentrate on the common, fundamental ideas with which people in all these other areas ought to be familiar.

We propose the first-order predicate calculus as a language in which to represent the knowledge possessed by a reasoning agent about its world.

We imagine that the agent exists in a world of objects, functions, and relations that form the basis for a *model* of the agent's predicate-calculus sentences. We propose that deductive inference is the major reasoning technique employed by an intelligent agent. Thus, we devote Chapters 1 through 5 of the book to a brief but complete presentation of the syntax and semantics of first-order predicate calculus, of logical deduction in general, and of resolution-refutation methods in particular.

The material in Chapters 1 through 5 and in Chapters 11 and 12 (on reasoning about actions and plans) is by now almost classical in AI. Much of the rest of the book is much closer to the current research frontier. We have attempted to draw together those recent research results that we think will, in time, become classical. We suspect that ours is the first textbook that treats these ideas. These topics include nonmonotonic reasoning, induction, reasoning with uncertain information, reasoning about knowledge and belief, metalevel representations and reasoning, and architectures for intelligent agents. We think that a field advances when important ideas migrate from research papers into textbooks. We are aware of the fact (and the reader should be too) that one takes one's chances with early migrations.

We should say something about why there is almost no mention in this book of the subject of *search*. Search is usually thought to be a cornerstone of AI. (One of us, in an earlier book, acknowledged the primacy of search in AI.) Nevertheless, as its title implies, this book is not intended to be a general introduction to the entire field of AI. A discussion of search would have detracted from the emphasis on logic that we wanted this book to have. In any case, search is well treated in other books on AI.

The book is aimed at advanced college seniors and graduate students intending to study further in AI. It assumes some knowledge of ideas of computer programming, although one does not have to program in order to learn from the book. The book also assumes mathematical sophistication. The reader who has already encountered some probability theory, logic, matrix algebra, list notation, and set theory will have an easier time with some parts of the book than will people less acquainted with these topics. Some of the more advanced sections might be skipped on a first reading; they are indicated by an asterisk (*) following the section title.

Exercises are included at the end of each chapter. (Solutions to the exercises are given at the end of the book.) Some ideas not presented in the text itself are introduced in the exercises. Most of these problems have been used successfully in classes taught by the authors at Stanford. The reader who is using this book for independent study is especially encouraged to work through the exercises. Even if the reader does not do the exercises, he should at least study those the solutions of which we have worked out—treating them as additional examples of concepts introduced in the book.

We briefly discuss important citations at the end of each chapter in sections entitled "Bibliographical and Historical Remarks." References to all cited works are collected at the end of the book. With these citations, Chapters 6 through 10 and 13 especially can be considered as a thorough introduction to the literature of these advanced topics.

At least three different languages are used in this book, and we have attempted to follow rigorously certain typographical conventions to help inform the reader which language is being used. Ordinary English is set in ordinary Roman type font (with italics for emphasis). Sentences in the predicate calculus are set in a typewriter-style font. Mathematical equations and formulas are set in a mathematical italic font. An explanation of these conventions with examples is given beginning on page xvii. The authors are grateful to Donald Knuth for inventing TeX and to Leslie Lamport for developing LaTeX. We used these typesetting systems from the very first days of preparing the manuscript, and they helped us immensely in dealing with the book's complex typography.

The authors would appreciate suggestions, comments, and corrections, which can be sent to them directly or in care of the publisher.

Contents

Typographical Conventions

---

(1) Elements of a conceptualization—objects, functions, and relations—
are written in italics, as in the following example:

The extension of the *on* relation is the set $\{\langle a,b\rangle, \langle b,c\rangle, \langle d,e\rangle\}$.

(2) Expressions and subexpressions in predicate calculus are written in
boldface, "typewriter" font, as in:

$$(\forall \mathtt{x} \ \mathtt{Apple(x)}) \ \lor \ (\exists \mathtt{x} \ \mathtt{Pear(x)})$$

(3) We use lowercase Greek letters as metavariables ranging over
predicate-calculus expressions and subexpressions. The use of
these variables is sometimes mixed with actual predicate-calculus
expressions, as in the following:

$$(\phi(\alpha) \ \lor \ \mathtt{P(A)} \ \Rightarrow \ \psi)$$

Sometimes, for mnemonic clarity, we use Roman characters, in
mathematical font, as metavariables for relation constants and
object constants, as in the following sample text:

Suppose we have a relation constant P and an object constant
A such that $P(A) \Rightarrow \mathtt{P} \land \mathtt{Q(B)}$.

(4) We use uppercase Greek letters to denote sets of predicate calculus formulas, as in:

> If there exists a proof of a sentence ϕ from a set Δ of premises and the logical axioms using Modus Ponens, then ϕ is said to be *provable* from Δ (written as $\Delta \vdash \phi$).

Since clauses are sets of literals, we also use uppercase Greek letters as variables ranging over clauses, as in:

> Suppose that Φ and Ψ are two clauses that have been standardized apart.

(5) We use ordinary mathematical (not typewriter) font for writing metalogical formulas *about* predicate-calculus statements, as in:

> If σ is an object constant, then $\sigma^I \epsilon |I|$.

Sometimes, metalogical formulas might contain predicate-calculus expressions:

$$\mathtt{A}^I = a$$

(6) We use an uppercase script $\mathcal{T}$ to denote a predicate-calculus "theory."

(7) Algorithms and programs are stated in typewriter font:

```
Procedure Resolution (Gamma)
    Repeat Termination(Gamma) ==> Return(Success),
            Phi <- Choose(Gamma), Psi <- Choose(Gamma),
            Chi <- Choose(Resolvents(Phi,Psi)),
            Gamma <- Concatenate(Gamma,[Chi])
    End
```

(8) We use the notation {x/A} to denote the substitution in which the object constant A is substituted for the variable x. We use lowercase Greek letters for variables ranging over substitutions, as in:

> Consider the combination of substitutions $\sigma\rho$.

(9) Lowercase ps and qs are used to denote probabilities:

$$p(\mathtt{P} \wedge \mathtt{Q})$$

(10) Sets of possible worlds are denoted by uppercase script letters, such as $\mathcal{W}$.

(11) Vectors and matrices are denoted by boldface capital letters, such as $\mathbf{V}$ and $\mathbf{P}$.

(12) We also use boldface capital letters (and sequences of capital letters) to denote modal operators, such as $\mathbf{B}$ and $\mathbf{K}$.

CHAPTER 1
Introduction

ARTIFICIAL INTELLIGENCE (AI) is the study of intelligent behavior. Its ultimate goal is a theory of intelligence that accounts for the behavior of naturally occurring intelligent entities and that guides the creation of artificial entities capable of intelligent behavior. Thus, AI is both a branch of science and a branch of engineering.

As *engineering*, AI is concerned with the concepts, theory, and practice of building intelligent machines. Examples of machines already within the reach of AI include *expert systems* that give advice about specialized subjects (such as medicine, mineral exploration, and finance), question-answering systems for answering queries posed in restricted but large subsets of English and other natural languages, and theorem-proving systems for verifying that computer programs and digital hardware meet stated specifications. Ahead lie more flexible and capable robots, computers that can converse naturally with people, and machines capable of performing much of the world's "knowledge work."

As *science*, AI is developing concepts and vocabulary to help us to understand intelligent behavior in people and in other animals. Although there are necessary and important contributions to this same scientific goal by psychologists and by neuroscientists, we agree with the statement made by the sixteenth-century Italian philosopher Vico: *Certum quod factum* (one is certain of only what one builds). Aerodynamics, for

1

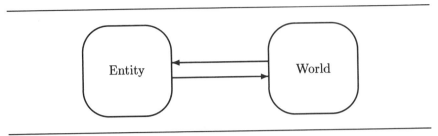

Figure 1.1   Entity and environment.

example, matured as it did because of its concern for flying machines; then it also helped us to explain and understand flight in animals. Thus, notwithstanding its engineering orientation, an ultimate goal of AI is a comprehensive theory of intelligence as it occurs in animals as well as in machines.

Note that in talking about the behavior of an intelligent entity in its environment, we have implicitly divided the world into two parts. We have placed an envelope around the entity, separating it from its environment, and we have chosen to focus on the transactions across that envelope. (See Figure 1.1.) Of course, a theory of intelligence must not only describe these transactions but must also give a clear picture of the structure of the entity responsible for those transactions. An important concept in this regard is that of *knowledge*. Intelligent entities seem to anticipate their environments and the consequences of their actions. They act as if they know, in some sense, what the results would be. We can account for this anticipatory behavior by assuming that intelligent entities themselves possess knowledge of their environments.

What more can we say about such knowledge? What forms can it take? What are its limits? How do entities use knowledge? How is knowledge acquired? Unfortunately, we cannot say much to answer these questions insofar as they pertain to natural, biological organisms. Even though we are beginning to learn how neurons process simple signals, our understanding of how animal brains—which are composed of neurons—represent and process knowledge about the world is regretfully deficient.

The situation is rather different when we turn our attention to artifacts, such as computer systems, capable of rudimentary intelligent behavior. Although we have not yet built machines approaching human levels of intelligence, nevertheless we can talk about how such machines can be said to possess knowledge. Because we design and build these machines, we ought to be able to decide what it means for them to *know* about their environments.

There are two major ways we can think about a machine having knowledge about its world. Although our ideas about the distinction between these two points of view are still being clarified, it seems that, in some of our machines, the knowledge is implicit; in other machines, it is represented explicitly.

We would be inclined to say, for example, that the mathematical knowledge built into a computer program for inverting matrices is implicit knowledge, "stored," as it is, in the sequence of operations performed by the program. Knowledge represented in this way is manifest in the actual running or execution of the matrix-inverting program. It would be difficult to extract it from the text of the computer code itself for other uses. Computer scientists have come to call knowledge represented in this way *procedural knowledge*, because it is inextricably contained in the very procedures that use it.

On the other hand, consider a tabular database of salary data. In this case, we would be inclined to say that the knowledge is explicit. Programs designed to represent their knowledge explicitly have turned out to be more versatile in performing the complex tasks that we usually think of as requiring intelligence. Particularly useful explicit representations of knowledge are those that can be interpreted as making declarative statements. We call knowledge represented in this way *declarative knowledge* because it is contained in declarations about the world. Such statements typically are stored in symbol structures that are accessed by the procedures that use this knowledge.

There are several reasons to prefer declaratively represented knowledge when designing intelligent machines. One advantage is that such knowledge can be changed more easily. To make a small change to a machine's declarative knowledge, usually we need to change just a few statements. Even small adjustments to procedural knowledge, on the other hand, may require extensive changes to the program. Knowledge represented declaratively can be used for several different purposes, even purposes not explicitly anticipated at the time the knowledge is assembled. The knowledge base itself does not have to be repeated for each application, nor does it have to be specifically designed for each application. Declarative knowledge often can be extended, beyond that explicitly represented, by *reasoning* processes that derive additional knowledge. Finally, declarative knowledge can be accessed by *introspective* programs, so that a machine can answer questions (for itself or for others) about what it knows. A price is paid for these advantages, however. Using declarative knowledge usually is more costly and slower than is directly applying procedural knowledge. We give up efficiency to gain flexibility.

It is tempting to speculate about the roles of these two kinds of knowledge in biological organisms. Many insects and other not-very-brainy creatures seem so well attuned to their environments that it is difficult to avoid saying that they have a great deal of knowledge about their worlds. A spider, for example, must use quite a bit of knowledge about materials and structures in spinning a web. Once we understand such creatures better, it seems likely that we will conclude that the knowledge they have evolved about their special niches is procedural. On the other hand, when a human mechanical engineer is consciously thinking about a new bridge design, it seems likely that he refers to declaratively represented knowledge about materials and structures. Admittedly, humans often (perhaps even usually) use procedural knowledge also. The tennis knowledge *used* by a champion player seems procedural, whereas that *taught* by an excellent teacher seems declarative. Perhaps when the distinctions between declarative and procedural knowledge are more clearly understood by computer scientists, they will indeed help biologists and psychologists characterize the knowledge of animals.

In any case, intelligent machines will need both procedural and declarative knowledge. Thus, it is difficult to see how we can study them properly without involving *all* of computer science. The most flexible kinds of intelligence, however, seem to depend strongly on declarative knowledge, and AI has concerned itself more and more with that subject. Our emphasis on declarative knowledge in this book should not be taken to imply that we think procedural knowledge unimportant. For example, when declarative knowledge is used over and over again for the same specific purpose, it would be advisable to compile it into a procedure tailored for that purpose. Nevertheless, the study of representing and using declarative knowledge is such a large and important subject in itself that it deserves book-length treatment.

The book is divided roughly into four parts. In the first five chapters, we present the main features of what is commonly called the *logicist* approach to AI. We begin by describing *conceptualizations* of the subject matter about which we want our intelligent systems to have knowledge. Then we present the syntax and semantics of the *first-order predicate calculus*, a declarative language in which we can write sentences about these conceptualizations. We then formalize the process of inference. Finally, we discuss a simple but powerful inference procedure called *resolution*, and we show how it can be used in reasoning systems.

In the next three chapters, we broaden the logical approach in various ways to deal with several inadequacies of strict logical deduction. First, we describe methods that allow *nonmonotonic reasoning*; i.e., reasoning in which tentative conclusions can be derived. Next, we discuss extensions that permit systems to learn new facts. Then, we show how to represent and reason with knowledge that is not certain.

In the next two chapters, we expand our language and its semantics by introducing new constructs, called *modal operators*, that facilitate representing and reasoning about knowledge about what other agents know or believe. Then, we show how the whole process of writing predicate-calculus sentences to capture conceptualizations can be turned in on itself at the *metalevel* to permit sentences about sentences and about reasoning processes.

In the final three chapters, we concern ourselves with agents that can perceive and act in the world. We first discuss the representation of knowledge about states and actions. Then, we show how this knowledge can be used to derive plans to achieve goals. Finally, we present a framework that allows us to relate sensory knowledge and inferred knowledge and that allows us to say how this knowledge affects an intelligent agent's choice of actions.

1.1 Bibliographical and Historical Remarks

The quest to build machines that think like people has a long tradition. Gardner [Gardner 1982] attributed to Leibniz the dream of "a universal algebra by which all knowledge, including moral and metaphysical truths, can some day be brought within a single deductive system." Frege, one of the founders of modern symbolic logic, proposed a notational system for mechanical reasoning [Frege 1879]. When digital computers were first being developed in the 1940s and 1950s, several researchers wrote programs that could perform elementary reasoning tasks, such as proving mathematical theorems, answering simple questions, and playing board games such as chess and checkers. In 1956, several of these researchers attended a workshop on AI at Dartmouth College, organized by McCarthy (who, incidentally, suggested the name *Artificial Intelligence* for the field) [McCorduck 1979]. (McCorduck's book is an interesting, nontechnical history of early AI work and workers.) Many of the important first papers about AI are contained in the collection *Computers and Thought* [Feigenbaum 1963].

From AI's very beginnings, people have pursued many approaches to the discipline. One, based on building parallel machines that could *learn* to recognize patterns, occupied many AI researchers during the 1960s and continues as one strand of what has come to be called *connectionism*. See [Nilsson 1965] for an example of some of the early work using this approach, and [Rumelhart 1986] for a collection of connectionist papers.

The computational manipulation of arbitrary symbolic structures (as opposed to operations on numbers) is at the heart of much work in AI. The idea that symbol manipulation is a sufficient process for explaining intelligence was forcefully stated in the *physical symbol system hypothesis* of Newell and Simon [Newell 1976]. The need for manipulating symbols led to the development of special computer languages. LISP, invented by McCarthy in the late 1950s [McCarthy 1960], continues to be the most popular of these languages. PROLOG [Colmerauer 1973, Warren 1977], stemming from ideas proposed by Green [Green 1969a], Hayes [Hayes 1973b], and Kowalski [Kowalski 1974, Kowalski 1979a] is rapidly gaining adherents. Much of the work in AI still is characterized mainly by the use of sophisticated symbol manipulation to perform complex reasoning tasks.

One articulation of the symbol-manipulating approach uses *production systems*, a term that has been used rather loosely in AI. Production systems derive from a computational formalism proposed by Post [Post 1943] based on string-replacement rules. The closely related idea of a *Markov algorithm* [Markov 1954, Galler 1970] involves imposing an order on the replacement rules and using this order to decide which applicable rule to apply next. Newell and Simon [Newell 1972, Newell 1973] used string-modifying production rules, with a simple control strategy, to model certain types of human problem-solving behavior. An earlier textbook by Nilsson [Nilsson 1980] used production systems as an organizing theme. More recently, the OPS family of symbol-manipulating computer-programming languages has been based on production rules [Forgy 1981, Brownston 1985]. Work on SOAR by Laird, Newell, and Rosenbloom [Laird 1987] and on *blackboard systems* by a variety of researchers [Erman 1982, Hayes-Roth 1985] can be regarded as following the production system approach.

Another important aspect of AI is *heuristic search*. Search methods are described as a control strategy for production systems in [Nilsson 1980]. Pearl's book [Pearl 1984] gave a thorough mathematical treatment of heuristic search, and his review article summarized the subject [Pearl 1987]. Lenat's work [Lenat 1982, Lenat 1983a, Lenat 1983b] on the nature of heuristics resulted in systems that exploit general heuristic properties in specific problems.

The view taken toward AI in this book follows the theme hinted at by Leibniz and Frege and then substantially elaborated and developed into specific proposals by McCarthy [McCarthy 1958 (the *advice taker* paper), McCarthy 1963]. It is based on two related ideas. First, the knowledge needed by intelligent programs can be expressed as declarative sentences in a form that is more or less independent of the uses to which that knowledge might later be put. Second, the reasoning performed by intelligent programs involves logical operations on these sentences. Good accounts of the importance of logic in AI, for representation and for reasoning, have been written by Hayes [Hayes 1977], Israel [Israel 1983], Moore [Moore 1982, Moore 1986], and Levesque [Levesque 1986].

Several people, however, have argued that logic has severe limitations as a foundation for AI. McDermott's article contained several cogent criticisms of logic [McDermott 1987a], whereas Simon emphasized the role of search in AI [Simon 1983]. Many AI researchers have stressed the importance of specialized procedures and of procedural (as opposed to declarative) representations of knowledge (see, for example, [Winograd 1975, Winograd 1980]). Minsky has claimed that intelligence in humans is the result of the interaction of a very large and complex assembly of loosely connected subunits operating much like a *society* but within a single individual [Minsky 1986].

Notwithstanding the various criticisms of logic, there does seem to be an emerging consensus among researchers that logical tools are important, at the very least, for helping us to analyze and understand AI systems. Newell [Newell 1982] made that point in his article about the *knowledge level*. The work of Rosenschein and Kaelbling on *situated automata* is a good example of an approach to AI that acknowledges the analytic utility of logic while pursuing an alternative implementational strategy [Rosenschein 1986]. The assertion that predicate calculus and logical operations can also usefully serve directly in the implementation of AI systems as a representation language and as reasoning processes, respectively, is a much stronger claim.

Several thinkers have claimed that none of the techniques currently being explored will ever achieve true, human-level intelligence. Prominent among these are the Dreyfuses, who argued that symbol manipulation operations are not the foundation of intelligence [Dreyfus 1972, Dreyfus 1981, Dreyfus 1986] (although their suggestions about what might be needed seem compatible with the claims of the connectionists). Winograd and Flores argued, mainly, that whatever mechanistic processes are involved in thinking, they are probably too complicated to be fully expressed in artificial machines designed and built by human engineers [Winograd 1986]. Searle attempted to distinguish between *real* thought and mere *simulations* of thought by rule-like computations [Searle 1980]. He also seemed to claim that computer-like machines built of silicon, for example, will not do, although machines built according to different principles out of protein might. Taking a somewhat different tack, Weizenbaum argued that, even if we could build intelligent machines to perform many human functions, it might be unethical to do so [Weizenbaum 1976].

There are several other good AI textbooks. Most of them differ from this one in that they do not emphasize logic as much as we do, and they describe applications of AI such as natural-language processing, expert systems, and vision. The books by Charniak and McDermott, Winston, and Rich are three such texts [Charniak 1984, Winston 1977, Rich 1983]. The book by Boden [Boden 1977] treats some of the philosophical issues related to AI. In addition to these books, the reader might also refer to encyclopedic collections of short articles about key ideas in AI [Shapiro 1987, Barr 1982, Cohen 1982].

Many important articles describing AI research appear in the journal *Artificial Intelligence*. In addition, there are several other relevant journals, including the *Journal of Automated Reasoning, Machine Learning*, and *Cognitive Science*. Several articles are reprinted in special collections. The American Association for Artificial Intelligence and other national organizations hold annual conferences with published proceedings [AAAI 1980]. The International Joint Council on Artificial Intelligence holds biannual conferences with published proceedings [IJCAI 1969]. Technical notes and memoranda published by the several university and industrial laboratories performing research in AI are available in microfilm from Scientific DataLink (a division of Comtex Scientific Corporation) in New York.

For an interesting summary of the opinions of several AI reseachers about the status of the field during the mid-1980s see [Bobrow 1985]. Trappl's book contains articles about the social implications of AI [Trappl 1986].

Exercises

1. *Structure and behavior.* It is common in discussing the design of artifacts to distinguish between the structure of a device (i.e., its parts and their interconnections) and its behavior (i.e., its external effects).

    a. Give a brief description of a thermostat. Describe both its external behavior and its internal structure. Explain how its structure achieves its behavior.

    b. Is it possible to determine the purpose of an artifact unambiguously, given its behavior? Provide examples to justify your answer.

    c. In his paper "Ascribing Mental Qualities to Machines," John McCarthy[McCarthy 1979b] suggests that it is convenient to talk about artifacts (such as thermostats and computers) as having mental qualities (such as beliefs and desires). For example, according to McCarthy, a thermostat *believes* it is too hot, too cold, or just right, and *desires* that it be just right. Try to adopt McCarthy's viewpoint and indicate the beliefs and desires you think an alarm clock possesses.

2. *Missionaries and cannibals.* Three missionaries and three cannibals seek to cross a river. A boat is available that can hold two people and can be navigated by any combination of missionaries and cannibals involving one or two people. If at any time the missionaries on either bank of the river or en route on the river are outnumbered by cannibals, the cannibals will indulge their anthropophagic tendencies and do away with the missionaries.

    a. Find the simplest schedule of crossings that will permit all the missionaries and cannibals to cross the river safely.

    b. State at least three facts about the world you used in solving the problem. For example, you had to know that a person can be in only one place at a time.

    c. Describe the steps that you took to solve the problem. For each step, record the facts or assumptions you used and the conclusions you drew. The purpose of this part of the problem is to get you to think about the process of solving a problem, not just to arrive at the final solution. Do just enough to get a feel for this distinction.

CHAPTER 2

Declarative Knowledge

As we have already argued, intelligent behavior depends on the knowledge an entity has about its environment. Much of this knowledge is descriptive and can be expressed in *declarative* form. The goal of this chapter is to elucidate the issues involved in formally expressing declarative knowledge.

Our approach to formalizing knowledge is much the same as that of scientists who describe the physical world; in fact, our language is similar to that used to state results in mathematics and the natural sciences. The difference is that in this book we are concerned with the issues of formalizing knowledge, rather than with discovering the knowledge to be formalized.

2.1 Conceptualization

The formalization of knowledge in declarative form begins with a *conceptualization*. This includes the objects presumed or hypothesized to exist in the world and their interrelationships.

The notion of an *object* used here is quite broad. Objects can be concrete (e.g., this book, Confucius, the sun) or abstract (e.g., the number 2, the set of all integers, the concept of justice). Objects can be primitive or composite (e.g., a circuit that consists of many subcircuits). Objects can even be fictional (e.g., a unicorn, Sherlock Holmes, Miss Right). In short, an object can be anything about which we want to say something.

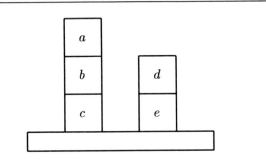

Figure 2.1   A scene from the Blocks World.

Not all knowledge-representation tasks require that we consider all the objects in the world; in some cases, only those objects in a particular set are relevant. For example, number theorists usually are concerned with the properties of numbers and usually are not concerned with physical objects such as resistors and transistors. Electrical engineers usually are concerned with resistors and transistors and usually are not concerned with buildings and bridges. The set of objects about which knowledge is being expressed is often called a *universe of discourse.*

As an example, consider the Blocks World scene in Figure 2.1. Most people looking at this figure interpret it as a configuration of toy blocks. Some people conceptualize the table on which the blocks are resting as an object as well; but, for simplicity, we ignore it here.

The universe of discourse corresponding to this conceptualization is the set consisting of the five blocks in the scene.

$$\{a, b, c, d, e\}$$

Although in this example there are finitely many elements in our universe of discourse, this need not always be the case. It is common in mathematics, for example, to consider the set of all integers, or the set of all real numbers, or the set of all *n*-tuples of real numbers, as universes with infinitely many elements.

A *function* is one kind of interrelationship among the objects in a universe of discourse. Although we can define many functions for a given set of objects, in conceptualizing a portion of the world we usually emphasize some functions and ignore others. The set of functions emphasized in a conceptualization is called the *functional basis set.*

For example, in thinking about the Blocks World, it would make sense to conceptualize the partial function *hat* that maps a block into the block on top of it, if any such block exists. The tuples corresponding to this partial function are as follows:

$$\{\langle b, a\rangle, \langle c, b\rangle, \langle e, d\rangle\}$$

When concentrating on spatial relationships, we would probably ignore functions that do not have any spatial significance, such as the *rotate* function that maps blocks into blocks according to the alphabetic order of their labels.

$$\{\langle a, b\rangle, \langle b, c\rangle, \langle c, d\rangle, \langle d, e\rangle, \langle e, a\rangle\}$$

A *relation* is the second kind of interrelationship among objects in a universe of discourse. As we do with functions, in conceptualizing a portion of the world, we emphasize some relations and ignore others. The set of relations in a conceptualization is called the *relational basis set*.

In a spatial conceptualization of the Blocks World, there are numerous meaningful relations. For example, it makes sense to think about the *on* relation that holds between two blocks if and only if one is immediately above the other. For the scene in Figure 2.1, *on* is defined by the following set of tuples.

$$\{\langle a, b\rangle, \langle b, c\rangle, \langle d, e\rangle\}$$

We might also think about the *above* relation that holds between two blocks if and only if one is anywhere above the other.

$$\{\langle a, b\rangle, \langle b, c\rangle, \langle a, c\rangle, \langle d, e\rangle\}$$

The *clear* relation holds of a block if and only if there is no block on top of it. For the scene in Figure 2.1, this relation has the following elements.

$$\{a, d\}$$

The *table* relation holds of a block if and only if that block is resting on the table.

$$\{c, e\}$$

The generality of relations can be determined by comparing their elements. Thus, the *on* relation is less general than the *above* relation since, when viewed as a set of tuples, it is a subset of the *above* relation. Of course, some relations are empty (e.g., the *unsupported* relation), whereas others consist of all n-tuples over the universe of discourse (e.g., the *block* relation).

It is worthwhile to note that, for a finite universe of discourse, there is an upper bound on the number of possible n-ary relations. In particular, for a universe of discourse of size b, there are b^n distinct n-tuples. Every n-ary relation is a subset of these b^n tuples. Therefore, an n-ary relation must be one of at most $2^{(b^n)}$ possible sets.

Formally, a *conceptualization* is a triple consisting of a universe of discourse, a functional basis set for that universe of discourse, and a relational basis set. For example, the following triple is one conceptualization of the world in Figure 2.1.

$$\langle \{a, b, c, d, e\}, \{hat\}, \{on, above, clear, table\}\rangle$$

Note that, although we have have written the *names* of objects, functions, and relations here, the conceptualization consists of the objects, functions, and relations themselves.

No matter how we choose to conceptualize the world, it is important to realize that there are other conceptualizations as well. Furthermore, there need not be any correspondence between the objects, functions, and relations in one conceptualization and the objects, functions, and relations in another.

In some cases, changing one's conceptualization of the world can make it impossible to express certain kinds of knowledge. A famous example of this is the controversy in the field of physics between the view of light as a wave phenomenon and the view of light in terms of particles. Each conceptualization allowed physicists to explain different aspects of the behavior of light, but neither alone sufficed. Not until the two views were merged in modern quantum physics were the discrepancies resolved.

In other cases, changing one's conceptualization can make it more difficult to express knowledge, without necessarily making it impossible. A good example of this, once again in the field of physics, is changing one's frame of reference. Given Aristotle's geocentric view of the universe, astronomers had great difficulty explaining the motions of the moon and other planets. The data were explained (with epicycles, etc.) in the Aristotelian conceptualization, although the explanation was extremely cumbersome. The switch to a heliocentric view quickly led to a more perspicuous theory.

This raises the question of what makes one conceptualization more appropriate than another for knowledge formalization. Currently, there is no comprehensive answer to this question. However, there are a few issues that are especially noteworthy.

One such issue is the *grain size* of the objects associated with a conceptualization. Choosing too small a grain can make knowledge formalization prohibitively tedious. Choosing too large a grain can make it impossible. As an example of the former problem, consider a conceptualization of the scene in Figure 2.1 in which the objects in the universe of discourse are the atoms composing the blocks in the picture. Each block is composed of enormously many atoms, so the universe of discourse is extremely large. Although it is in principle possible to describe the scene at this level of detail, it is senseless if we are interested in only the vertical relationship of the blocks made up of those atoms. Of course, for a chemist interested in the composition of blocks, the atomic view of the scene might be more appropriate. For this purpose, our conceptualization in terms of blocks has too large a grain.

Finally, there is the issue of *reification* of functions and relations as objects in the universe of discourse. The advantage of this is that it allows us to consider properties of properties. As an example, consider a Blocks World conceptualization in which there are five blocks, no functions, and three unary relations, each corresponding to a different color. This conceptualization allows us to consider the colors of blocks but not the properties of those colors.

$$\langle \{a, b, c, d, e\}, \{\}, \{red, white, blue\} \rangle$$

We can remedy this deficiency by *reifying* various color relations as objects in their own right and by adding a partial function—such as *color*— to relate blocks to colors. Because the colors are objects in the universe of discourse, we can then add relations that characterize them; e.g., *nice*.

$$\langle \{a, b, c, d, e, red, white, blue\}, \{color\}, \{nice\} \rangle$$

Note that, in this discussion, no attention has been paid to the question of whether the objects in one's conceptualization of the world really exist. We have adopted neither the standpoint of *realism*, which posits that the objects in one's conceptualization really exist, nor that of *nominalism*, which holds that one's concepts have no necessary external existence. Conceptualizations are our inventions, and their justification is based solely on their utility. This lack of commitment indicates the essential ontological promiscuity of AI: Any conceptualization of the world is accommodated, and we seek those that are useful for our purposes.

2.2 Predicate Calculus

Given a conceptualization of the world, we can begin to formalize knowledge as sentences in a language appropriate to that conceptualization. In this section, we define a formal language called *predicate calculus*.

All the sentences in predicate calculus are strings of characters arranged according to precise rules of grammar. For example, we can express the fact that block *a* is above block *b* by taking a relation symbol such as **Above** and object symbols **A** and **B** and combining them with appropriate parentheses and commas, as follows.

```
Above(A,B)
```

One source of expressiveness in predicate calculus is the availability of logical operators that allow us to form complex sentences from simple ones without specifying the truth or falsity of the constituent sentences. For example, the following sentence using the operator ∨ states that either block *a* is above block *b* or block *b* is above block *a*, but it makes no commitment as to which is the case.

$$\texttt{Above(A,B)} \lor \texttt{Above(B,A)}$$

The flexibility also stems from the availability of quantifiers and variables. The quantifier ∀ allows us to state facts about all the objects in our universe of discourse without enumerating them. For example, the first sentence in the following set states that every block that is on another block is above the other block. The quantifier ∃ allows us to assert the existence of an object with certain properties without identifying the object. For example, the second sentence states that there is a block that is both clear and on the table.

$$\forall x \forall y \; \texttt{On(x,y)} \; \Rightarrow \; \texttt{Above(x,y)}$$

$$\exists x \; \texttt{Clear(x)} \land \texttt{Table(x)}$$

To use a language such as predicate calculus, we need to know both its syntax and its semantics. In this section, we describe the syntax of the language in detail; as we present each construct, we informally suggest the semantics. In the next section, we define the semantics of the language formally.

The alphabet of our version of predicate calculus consists of the following *characters*. Spaces and carriage returns have no significance and are used solely for formatting.

```
A B C D E F G H I J K L M N O P Q R S T U V W X Y Z

a b c d e f g h i j k l m n o p q r s t u v w x y z

1 2 3 4 5 6 7 8 9 0 . , ( ) { } [ ] + - * / ↑

∈ ∪ ∩ = < > ≤ ≥ ⊂ ⊃ ⊆ ⊇ ¬ ∧ ∨ ∀ ∃ ⇒ ⇐ ⇔
```

There are two types of *symbols* in predicate calculus: variables and constants. Constants are further subdivided into object constants, function constants, and relation constants.

A *variable* is any sequence of lowercase alphabetic and numeric characters in which the first character is lowercase alphabetic. As we mentioned, variables are used to express properties of objects in the universe of discourse without explicitly naming them.

An *object constant* is used to name a specific element of a universe of discourse. Every object constant is a sequence of alphabetic characters or digits in which the first character is either uppercase alphabetic or numeric. The following are simple examples with obvious intended interpretations.

Confucius	Elephants	32456
Stanford	Justice	MCMXII
California	Resistor14	Twelve

A *function constant* is used to designate a function on members of the universe of discourse. Every function constant is either a functional operator (+, -, *, /, ↑, ∩, ∪) or a sequence of alphabetic characters or digits in which the first character is uppercase alphabetic. The following symbols are examples.

Age	Sin	Cardinality
Weight	Cos	President
Color	Tan	Salary

Every function constant has an associated *arity*, which indicates the number of arguments it is expected to take. For example, Sin normally takes a single argument, and ↑ takes two arguments. Symbols that stand for associative functions, such as +, take any number of arguments.

A *relation constant* is used to name a relation on the universe of discourse. Every relation constant is either a mathematical operator (=, <, >, ≤, ≥, ∈, ⊂, ⊃, ⊆, ⊇) or a sequence of alphabetic characters or digits in which the first character is uppercase alphabetic; the following symbols are examples.

Odd	Parent	Above
Even	Relative	Between
Prime	Neighbor	Nearby

Like function constants, every relation constant has an associated arity. In addition, every n-ary function constant can also be used as an $(n+1)$-ary relation constant, as we will discuss. However, the converse is not necessarily true.

Note that the type and arity of an alphanumeric constant can be determined only by the way it is used in sentences; these properties cannot be determined on the basis of the symbol's constituent characters. Different people may use the same symbol in different ways.

In predicate calculus, a *term* is used as a name for an object in the universe of discourse. There are three types of terms: variables, object constants, and functional expressions. We have already discussed variables and object constants.

A *functional expression* consists of an n-ary function constant π and n terms $\tau_1, \ldots, \tau_n$, arranged with parentheses and commas as follows.

$$\pi(\tau_1, \ldots, \tau_n)$$

For example, assuming that `Age` and `Cardinality` are both unary function constants and that `Log` is a binary function constant, the following expressions are all legal terms.

> `Age(Confucius)`
>
> `Cardinality(Elephants)`
>
> `Log(32456,2)`

Although this syntax is quite general, it is somewhat cumbersome for writing expressions involving common mathematical functions. For this reason, the class of functional expressions also is defined to include terms in any of the following *infix* forms. In each case, the operator is the function constant and the surrounding terms designate its arguments.

$(\tau_1{+}\tau_2)$	$(\tau_1{\uparrow}\tau_2)$
$(\tau_1{-}\tau_2)$	$(\tau_1{\cap}\tau_2)$
$(\tau_1{*}\tau_2)$	$(\tau_1{\cup}\tau_2)$
$(\tau_1{/}\tau_2)$	$(\tau_1{.}\tau_2)$

The use of braces designates an unordered set of elements denoted by the enclosed terms. The use of square brackets denotes a sequence.

$$\{\sigma_1, \sigma_2, \ldots, \sigma_n\}$$
$$[\sigma_1, \sigma_2, \ldots, \sigma_n]$$

From the definitions, it should be clear that functional expressions can be composed in combination with one another, as in the following examples.

> `Log(Cardinality(Elephants),2)`
>
> `(2*(A↑3))`
>
> `(Log(A)+Log(B))`

In predicate calculus, facts are stated in the form of expressions called *sentences*, or sometimes *well-formed formulas or wffs*. There are three types of sentences: atomic sentences, logical sentences, and quantified sentences.

An *atomic sentence*, or *atom*, is formed from an n-ary relation constant ρ and n terms $\tau_1, \ldots, \tau_n$, by combining them as follows.

$$\rho(\tau_1, \ldots, \tau_n)$$

Writing atomic sentences involving mathematical relations in this form can be cumbersome. For this reason, the class of atomic sentences also is defined to include expressions in any of the following infix forms.

$(\tau_1 = \tau_2)$	$(\tau_1 \in \tau_2)$
$(\tau_1 < \tau_2)$	$(\tau_1 \subset \tau_2)$
$(\tau_1 > \tau_2)$	$(\tau_1 \supset \tau_2)$
$(\tau_1 \leq \tau_2)$	$(\tau_1 \subseteq \tau_2)$
$(\tau_1 \geq \tau_2)$	$(\tau_1 \supseteq \tau_2)$

Atomic sentences involving these relations are sometimes given special names. For example, the sentence $(\tau_1 = \tau_2)$ is called an *equation*.

Function constants can also be used as relation constants, provided an expression designating the value of the function is included as the final argument. For example, the following two expressions are legal, and the facts they express are identical.

```
(Age(Confucius)=100)
```

```
Age(Confucius,100)
```

We also want to be able to express facts that cannot conveniently be expressed by atomic sentences. One often needs to express negations, disjunctions, contingencies, and so on. In predicate calculus, atomic sentences such as these can be combined with logical operators to form *logical sentences*.

A *negation* is formed using the ¬ operator. A sentence of the following form is true if and only if the embedded sentence is not true (regardless of the interpretation of the embedded sentence).

$$(\neg \phi)$$

A *conjunction* is a set of sentences connected by the ∧ operator. Each of the component sentences is called a *conjunct*. A conjunction is true if and only if each of the conjuncts is true.

$$(\phi_1 \wedge \ldots \wedge \phi_n)$$

A *disjunction* is a set of sentences connected by the ∨ operator. Each of the component sentences is called a *disjunct*. A disjunction is true if and only if at least one of the disjuncts is true. Note that more than one of the disjuncts may be true.

$$(\phi_1 \vee \ldots \vee \phi_n)$$

An *implication* is formed using the ⇒ operator. The sentence to the left of the operator is called the *antecedent*, and the sentence to the right is called the *consequent*. An implication is a statement that the consequent is true whenever the antecedent is true. By convention, whenever the antecedent is false, the implication is assumed to be true, whether or not the consequent is true.

$$(\phi \Rightarrow \psi)$$

A *reverse implication*, formed using the ⇐ operator, is just an implication with its arguments reversed. The antecedent is to the right, and the consequent is to the left.

$$(\psi \Leftarrow \phi)$$

A *bidirectional implication* or *equivalence*, formed using the ⇔ operator, is a statement that the component sentences are either both true or both false.

$$(\phi \Leftrightarrow \psi)$$

The following are all logical sentences. The intended meaning of the first is that the age of Confucius is not 100. The second states that elephants are either herbivores or carnivores. The third states that George is sick if he is at home.

```
(¬Age(Confucius,100))

((Elephants ⊂ Carnivores) ∨ (Elephants ⊂ Herbivores))

(Location(George,Home) ⇒ Sick(George))
```

With the syntax given so far, we can designate objects only by name (using an object symbol) or by description (using a functional expression). *Quantified sentences* provide a more flexible way of talking about all objects in our universe of discourse or asserting a property of an individual object without identifying that object.

A *universally quantified sentence* is formed by combining the *universal quantifier* ∀, a variable ν, and any simpler sentence ϕ. The intended meaning is that the sentence ϕ is true, no matter what object the variable ν represents.

$$(\forall \nu \ \phi)$$

The following two sentences are examples. The first states that all apples are red. The second states that every object in the universe of discourse is a red apple.

$$(\forall x \ (\text{Apple}(x) \ \Rightarrow \ \text{Red}(x)))$$

$$(\forall x \ (\text{Apple}(x) \ \wedge \ \text{Red}(x)))$$

An *existentially quantified sentence* is formed by combining the *existential quantifier* ∃, a variable ν, and any simpler sentence ϕ. The intended meaning is that the sentence ϕ is true, for at least one object in the universe of discourse.

$$(\exists \nu \ \phi)$$

Of the two sentences that follow, the first states that there is a red apple in the universe of discourse; the second states that there is an object that is either an apple or a pear.

$$(\exists x \ (\text{Apple}(x) \ \wedge \ \text{Red}(x)))$$

$$(\exists x \ (\text{Apple}(x) \ \vee \ \text{Pear}(x)))$$

A *quantified sentence* is either a universally quantified sentence or an existentially quantified sentence. The *scope* of the quantifier in a quantified sentence is the sentence embedded within the quantified sentence.

Like atomic and logical sentences, quantified sentences can be combined to form more complex sentences, as in the following examples.

$$((\forall x \ \text{Apple}(x)) \ \vee \ (\exists x \ \text{Pear}(x)))$$

$$(\forall x(\forall y \ \text{Loves}(x,y)))$$

When a quantified sentence of one type is nested within a quantified sentence of the other type, the order of nesting is extremely important.

$$(\forall x(\exists y \ \texttt{Loves(x,y)}))$$

$$(\exists y(\forall x \ \texttt{Loves(x,y)}))$$

The first sentence states that every person has some person he loves and makes no statement about whether the object of one person's love is the same as the object of another person's love. The second sentence states that there is one single person whom everybody loves, a quite different statement.

A variable can also occur as a term in a sentence without an enclosing quantifier. When used in this way, a variable is said to be *free*, whereas a variable that occurs in a sentence and in an enclosing quantifier is said to be *bound*. For example, in the following sentences, the variable x is free in the first, bound in the second, and occurs both free and bound in the third:

$$(\texttt{Apple(x)} \ \Rightarrow \ \texttt{Red(x)})$$

$$(\forall x \ (\texttt{Apple(x)} \ \Rightarrow \ \texttt{Red(x)}))$$

$$(\texttt{Apple(x)} \ \lor \ (\exists x \ \texttt{Pear(x)}))$$

If a sentence has no free variables, it is called a *closed* sentence. If it has neither free nor bound variables, it is called a *ground* sentence.

Note that the variables in quantified sentences refer to objects of a universe of discourse, not to functions or relations. Consequently, they cannot be used in functional or relational positions. We say that a language with this property is *first order*. A *second-order* language is one with function and relation variables as well. We have chosen to restrict our attention here to a first-order language both because this language allows us to prove some strong results that simply do not hold of second-order languages and because it is adequate for most purposes in AI.

Note that the parentheses around expressions involving functional, relational, and logical operators are essential to prevent ambiguities. If they were dropped indiscriminately, some terms could be interpreted in more than one way. For example, A*B+C could be the sum of a product and a constant or the product of a constant and a sum. Fortunately, such ambiguities often can be eliminated by imposing a precedence ordering on operators.

A table of precedences is given in Table 2.1. The symbol ↑ has higher precedence than * and /. The symbols * and / have higher precedence than + and -. Whenever an expression is flanked by operators of different precedence, it is associated with the operator of higher precedence; e.g., the

Table 2.1   Precedence relations ordered from high to low

$\uparrow$
$* \ / \ \cap$
$+ \ - \ \cup$
$= \ < \ > \ \le \ \ge \ \in \ \subset \ \supset \ \subseteq \ \supseteq$
$\neg$
$\wedge$
$\vee$
$\Rightarrow \ \Leftarrow \ \Leftrightarrow$
$\forall \ \exists$

expression A*B+C is the sum of a product and a constant. Whenever an expression is flanked by operators of equal precedence, it is associated with the operator on the left; e.g., the expression A*B/C is a quotient of a product and a constant. These rules of precedence are assumed throughout this book, and parentheses usually are dropped when there is no chance of ambiguity.

In addition to dropping parentheses, it is common in mathematical notation to drop the parentheses following a 0-ary function constant or relation constant. So, in the interests of simplicity, we permit this abbreviation in our language. Thus, the term F() can be written as F, and the atomic sentence R() can be written as R.

Another concession to standard notation is the abbreviation of negated atomic sentences involving mathematical operators. Rather than writing the negation operator in prefix position as indicated, the fact that the atomic sentence is negated is denoted by drawing a bar through the operator. Thus, we usually write the sentence $\phi \not\le \psi$ in place of $\neg(\phi \le \psi)$.

The preceding sections completely characterize the syntax of predicate calculus. Any sentence allowed by these rules and conventions is syntactically correct, and any sentence not specifically allowed is syntactically illegal. In later chapters, we modify the syntax slightly to allow additional types of sentences.

2.3 Semantics

In the previous section, we provided a precise definition for the syntax of predicate calculus. The treatment of semantics, however, was quite informal. In this section, we provide a precise definition of meaning called *declarative semantics*.

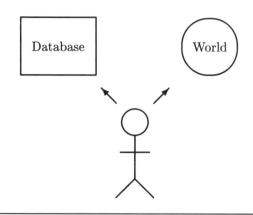

Figure 2.2   Declarative semantics.

In making our definition, we assume the perspective of the observer in Figure 2.2. We have a set of sentences and a conceptualization of the world, and we associate the symbols used in the sentences with the objects, functions, and relations of our conceptualization. We evaluate the truth of the sentences in accordance with this association, saying that a sentence is true if and only if it accurately describes the world according to our conceptualization.

Note that, in this definition of semantics, there is no dependence on the way in which the sentences of the language are expected to be used. In this respect, the approach differs radically from that taken in much of computer science, where abstract data structures are defined in terms of the operations we can perform on them.

An *interpretation* I is a mapping between elements of the language and elements of a conceptualization. We represent the mapping by the function $I(\sigma)$, where σ is an element of the language. We usually abbreviate $I(\sigma)$ to σ^I, and we represent the universe of discourse by $|I|$. For I to be an interpretation, it must satisfy the following properties.

(1) If σ is an object constant, then $\sigma^I \epsilon |I|$.

(2) If π is an n-ary function constant, then $\pi^I : |I|^n \rightarrow |I|$.

(3) If ρ is an n-ary relation constant, then $\rho^I \subseteq |I|^n$.

Note that, in describing the semantics of predicate calculus, we use symbols, such as I and σ, that are not part of the language we are describing. I, σ, and other symbols we introduce later are part of our *metalanguage* for talking *about* predicate calculus. Practice keeping firmly in mind which symbols and expressions are part of the predicate-calculus language and which are part of the metalanguage.

As an example of an interpretation, once again consider the Blocks World scene in Figure 2.1. Assume the predicate-calculus language has the five object constants A, B, C, D, and E, the function constant Hat, and the relation constants On, Above, Table, and Clear. The following mapping corresponds to our usual interpretation for these symbols.

$$\mathtt{A}^I = a$$
$$\mathtt{B}^I = b$$
$$\mathtt{C}^I = c$$
$$\mathtt{D}^I = d$$
$$\mathtt{E}^I = e$$
$$\mathtt{Hat}^I = \{\langle b, a\rangle, \langle c, b\rangle, \langle e, d\rangle\}$$
$$\mathtt{On}^I = \{\langle a, b\rangle, \langle b, c\rangle, \langle d, e\rangle\}$$
$$\mathtt{Above}^I = \{\langle a, b\rangle, \langle b, c\rangle, \langle a, c\rangle, \langle d, e\rangle\}$$
$$\mathtt{Table}^I = \{c, e\}$$
$$\mathtt{Clear}^I = \{a, d\}$$

This is the *intended interpretation*, the one suggested by the names of the constants. However, these constants can equally well be interpreted in other ways, as in the interpretation J that follows. J agrees with I on the object constants and the function constant but disagrees on the relation constants. Under this interpretation, On means *under*, Above means *below*, Table means *clear*, and Clear means *table*.

$$\mathtt{A}^J = a$$
$$\mathtt{B}^J = b$$
$$\mathtt{C}^J = c$$
$$\mathtt{D}^J = d$$
$$\mathtt{E}^J = e$$
$$\mathtt{Hat}^J = \{\langle b, a\rangle, \langle c, b\rangle, \langle e, d\rangle\}$$
$$\mathtt{On}^J = \{\langle b, a\rangle, \langle c, b\rangle, \langle e, d\rangle\}$$
$$\mathtt{Above}^J = \{\langle b, a\rangle, \langle c, b\rangle, \langle c, a\rangle, \langle e, d\rangle\}$$
$$\mathtt{Table}^J = \{a, d\}$$
$$\mathtt{Clear}^J = \{c, e\}$$

For reasons that will become clear, it is useful to interpret variables in sentences separately from other symbols. A *variable assignment U* is a function from the variables of a language to objects in the universe of discourse.

The following partial assignment is an example. (We use the abbreviation σ^U for $U(\sigma)$.) The variable x is assigned block a; variable y also is assigned block a; and variable z is assigned block b.

$$\mathbf{x}^U = a$$

$$\mathbf{y}^U = a$$

$$\mathbf{z}^U = b$$

An interpretation I and a variable assignment U can be combined into a joint assignment T_{IU} that applies to terms in general. In particular, the assignment of each nonvariable symbol corresponds to the interpretation I; the assignment of each variable corresponds to the variable assignment U; and the assignment of an expression is the result of applying the function corresponding to the function constant to the objects designated by the terms.

Given an interpretation I and a variable assignment U, the *term assignment T_{IU}* corresponding to I and U is a mapping from terms to objects, defined as follows.

(1) If τ is an object constant, then $T_{IU}(\tau) = I(\tau)$.

(2) If τ is a variable, then $T_{IU}(\tau) = U(\tau)$.

(3) If τ is a term of the form $\pi(\tau_1, \ldots, \tau_n)$ and $I(\pi) = g$ and $T_{IU}(\tau_i) = x_i$, then $T_{IU}(\tau) = g(x_1, \ldots, x_n)$.

As an example, consider the term assignment corresponding to the interpretation I and the variable assignment U defined previously. Under this assignment, the term Hat(C) designates the block b. I maps C to block c and the tuple $\langle c, b \rangle$ is a member of the function designated by Hat. The term Hat(z) designates block a, since U maps z to b, and the tuple $\langle b, a \rangle$ is in the set of tuples designated by Hat.

The notions of interpretation and variable assignment are important because they allow us to define a relative notion of truth called *satisfaction*. The definition differs from one type of sentence to another and is presented case by case in the following paragraphs. By convention, the fact that a sentence ϕ is satisfied by an interpretation I and a variable assignment U is written $\models_I \phi[\mathrm{U}]$. In this case, we say that the sentence ϕ is *true* relative to the interpretation I and the assignment U.

An interpretation and variable assignment satisfy an equation if and only if the corresponding term assignment maps the equated terms into the same object. When this is the case, the two terms are said to be *coreferential*.

(1) $\models_I (\sigma{=}\tau)[U]$ if and only if $T_{IU}(\sigma) = T_{IU}(\tau)$.

An interpretation I and a variable assignment U satisfy an atomic sentence other than an equation if and only if the tuple formed from the objects designated by the terms in the sentence is an element of the the relation designated by the relation constant.

(2) $\models_I \rho(\tau_1,\ldots,\tau_n)[U]$ if and only if $\langle T_{IU}(\tau_1),\ldots,T_{IU}(\tau_n)\rangle \epsilon I(\rho)$.

For example, consider interpretation I as defined in the previous section. Since the object constant A designates block a and B designates b, and the tuple $\langle a, b \rangle$ is a member of the set designated by the relation constant On, it is the case that $\models_I$ On(A,B)[U]. Thus, we can say that On(A,B) is true under this interpretation.

If the mapping of the relation symbol On were changed to the value in interpretation J (where On designates the *under* relation), then the sentence On(A,B) would not be satisfied. Tuple $\langle a, b \rangle$ is not a member of that relation, and thus On(A,B) would be false under that interpretation.

These examples illustrate the dependence of satisfiability on interpretation. Under some interpretations, a sentence can be true; under other interpretations, it can be false.

The satisfiability of logical sentences depends on the logical operator involved. The negation of a sentence is satisfied if and only if the sentence itself is not satisfied. A conjunction is satisfied if and only if all the conjuncts are satisfied. A disjunction is satisfied if and only if at least one of the disjuncts is satisfied. Note the inclusive sense of disjunction being assumed here. A unidirectional implication is satisfied if and only if the antecedent is false or the consequent is true. A bidirectional implication is satisfied if and only if the two component implications are satisfied.

(3) $\models_I (\neg\phi)[U]$ if and only if $\not\models_I \phi[U]$.

(4) $\models_I (\phi_1 \wedge \ldots \wedge \phi_n)[U]$ if and only if $\models_I \phi_i[U]$ for all $i = 1,\ldots,n$.

(5) $\models_I (\phi_1 \vee \ldots \vee \phi_n)[U]$ if and only if $\models_I \phi_i[U]$ for some i, $1 \leq i \leq n$.

(6) $\models_I (\phi{\Rightarrow}\psi)[U]$ if and only if $\not\models_I \phi[U]$ or $\models_I \psi[U]$.

(7) $\models_I (\phi{\Leftarrow}\psi)[U]$ if and only if $\models_I \phi[U]$ or $\not\models_I \psi[U]$.

(8) $\models_I (\phi{\Leftrightarrow}\psi)[U]$ if and only if $\models_I (\phi{\Rightarrow}\psi)[U]$ and $\models_I (\phi{\Leftarrow}\psi)[U]$.

A universally quantified sentence is satisfied if and only if the enclosed sentence is satisfied for all assignments of the quantified variable. An existentially quantified sentence is satisfied if and only if the enclosed sentence is satisfied for some assignment of the quantified variable.

(9) $\models_I (\forall\nu\phi)[U]$ if and only if for all $d \in |I|$ it is the case that $\models_I \phi[V]$ where $V(\nu) = d$ and $V(\mu) = U(\mu)$ for $\mu \neq \nu$.

(10) $\models_I (\exists\nu\phi)[U]$ if and only if for some $d \in |I|$ it is the case that $\models_I \phi[V]$ where $V(\nu) = d$ and $V(\mu) = U(\mu)$ for $\mu \neq \nu$.

If an interpretation I satisfies a sentence ϕ for all variable assignments, then I is said to be a *model* of ϕ, written $\models_I \phi$. For example, interpretation I from our Blocks World example is a model of the sentence On(x,y) $\Rightarrow$ Above(x,y). Consider the variable assignment U that maps x into block a and y into block b. Under this variable assignment and interpretation I, the sentence On(x,y) and the sentence Above(x,y) are both satisfied. Therefore, by the definition of satisfaction, they satisfy the implication as well. As an alternative, consider the variable assignment V that maps both x and y into block a. Under this variable assignment, Above(x,y) is not satisfied—but neither is On(x,y). Therefore, once again the implication is satisfied.

Obviously, a variable assignment has no effect on the satisfaction of a sentence that contains no free variables (e.g., a ground sentence or a closed sentence). Consequently, any interpretation that satisfies a ground sentence for one variable assignment is a model of that sentence.

A sentence is said to be *satisfiable* if and only if there is *some* interpretation and variable assignment that satisfy it. Otherwise, it is *unsatisfiable*. A sentence is *valid* if and only if it is satisfied by *every* interpretation and variable assignment. Valid sentences are those that are true by virtue of their logical form and thus provide no information about the domain being described. The sentence P(A) ∨ ¬P(A) is valid, because any interpretation satisfies either P(A) or ¬P(A).

We can easily extend the definitions in this section to sets of sentences as well as individual sentences. A set Γ of sentences is satisfied by an interpretation I and a variable assignment U (written $\models_I \Gamma[U]$) if and only if every member of Γ is satisfied by I and U. An interpretation I is a model of a set Γ of sentences (written $\models_I \Gamma$) if and only if it is a model of every member of the set. A set of sentences is satisfiable if and only if there is an interpretation and variable assignment that satisfies every element. Otherwise, it is unsatisfiable or *inconsistent*. A set of sentences is valid if and only if every element is valid.

Unfortunately, our definition of satisfaction is somewhat disturbing in that it relativizes the notion of truth to one's interpretation. As a result, different individuals with different interpretations may disagree on the truth of a sentence.

It is generally true that, as one writes more sentences, the number of possible models decreases. This raises the question of whether it is possible for an individual to define his symbols so thoroughly that no interpretation is possible except the one he intended. As it turns out, there is no way in general of ensuring a unique interpretation, no matter how many sentences we write down.

The concept of elementary equivalence is important in this regard. It means that two interpretations cannot be distinguished by sentences in predicate calculus. More precisely, two interpretations I and J are *elementarily equivalent* ($I \equiv J$) if and only if $\models_I \phi$ implies and is implied by $\models_J \phi$ for any sentence ϕ.

Consider the two interpretations I and J defined as follows. I's universe of discourse consists of the real numbers, and I maps the relation symbol R into the *greater than* relation on reals. J's universe of discourse consists of the rational numbers, and J maps R into the *greater than* relation on rationals. As it turns out, I and J are elementarily equivalent. Despite the fact that the two universes are of different cardinality, there is no sentence that is satisfied by one interpretation that is not also satisfied by the other.

Along with the problem of ambiguity in the definition of symbols, there is the parallel issue of the definability of the elements in a conceptualization (i.e., the objects, functions, and relations). An element x of a conceptualization is *definable* in terms of elements $x_1, \ldots, x_n$ if and only if there is a first-order sentence ϕ with nonlogical symbols $\sigma_1, \ldots, \sigma_n$ and σ for which every model over the conceptualization that maps σ_i into x_i also maps σ into x.

For example, it is possible to define the *clear* relation in terms of the *on* relation. Given an interpretation I that maps the symbol On into the *on* relation, we can define the *clear* relation using the single sentence ¬∃x On(x,y). An object is clear if and only if no object is on top of it.

Unfortunately, not every relation on a universe of discourse is definable with every interpretation. For any interpretation with an infinite universe of discourse, there are uncountably many relations, but the language of predicate calculus has only a countable number of finite sentences. As a result, some relations must necessarily be left out.

For example, the relation *on* cannot be defined in terms of *clear*. With a fixed interpretation for Clear, the sentence ¬∃x On(x,y) constrains the set of possible interpretations for On but does not make it unique.

Before we examine specific examples, it is worth pausing briefly to consider the relevance of these ideas to representing knowledge in machines. As we already mentioned, the first step in encoding declarative knowledge is conceptualizing the application area. We then select a vocabulary of object constants, function constants, and relation constants. We associate these constants with the objects, functions, and relations in our conceptualization. We can then begin to write sentences that constitute the machine's declarative knowledge.

Of course, in designing a useful machine, we try to write sentences we believe to be true; i.e., ones that are satisfied by our intended interpretation. The intended interpretation is then a model of the sentences we write. Notice that, if our beliefs are incorrect, the sentences we write may not be true in reality.

Note also that, in describing an application area, we seldom start with a complete conceptualization. For example, we rarely have lists of tuples for every function and relation. Rather, we start with an idea of a conceptualization and attempt to make it precise by writing more and more sentences.

2.4 Blocks World Example

As an example of expressing knowledge in predicate calculus, once again consider the Blocks World scene in Figure 2.1. We assume a conceptualization of the scene as five objects and the relations *on, clear, table,* and *above*. For our predicate-calculus vocabulary, we use the five object constants A, B, C, D, and E and the relation constants On, Clear, Table, and Above. In using these symbols to encode facts about our conceptualization, we assume the standard interpretation, *I*.

The sentences that follow encode the essential information about this scene. Block *a* is on block *b*; block *b* is on block *c*; and block *d* is on block *e*. Block *a* is above *b* and *c*; *b* is above *c*; and *d* is above *e*. Finally, block *a* is clear, and so is block *d*. Block *c* is on the table, and so is block *e*.

On(A,B)	Above(A,B)	Clear(A)
On(B,C)	Above(B,C)	Clear(D)
On(D,E)	Above(A,C)	Table(C)
	Above(D,E)	Table(E)

Note that all these sentences are true under the intended interpretation. Since A designates block *a* and B designates block *b*, and block *a* is on block *b*, the first sentence in the first column is true. Since D designates block *d* and E designates block *e*, and the pair $\langle d, e \rangle$ is a member of the relation designated by the symbol Above, the last sentence in the second column is true. For similar reasons, the other sentences are true as well.

In addition to encoding simple sentences, we can encode more general facts. In the Blocks World, if one block is on another, then that block is above the other. Furthermore, the *above* relation is transitive; if one block is above a second and the second is above a third, then the first also is above the third.

$$\forall x \forall y \ (On(x,y) \Rightarrow Above(x,y))$$

$$\forall x \forall y \forall z \ (Above(x,y) \land Above(y,z) \Rightarrow Above(x,z))$$

One advantage to writing such general sentences is economy. If we record *on* information for every object and encode the relationship between the *on* relation and the *above* relation, there is no need to record any *above* information explicitly.

Another advantage is that these general sentences apply to Blocks World scenes other than the one pictured here. It is possible to create a Blocks World scene in which none of the specific sentences we have listed is true, but the general sentences are still correct.

Of course, there are other true sentences one can write about the Blocks World. Many of these sentences are redundant in that they are entailed by the preceding sentences. This notion of logical entailment is defined more precisely in the next chapter.

2.5 Circuits Example

Figure 2.3 is a schematic diagram for a digital circuit called a full adder. Let us consider how we might conceptualize a circuit of this sort and describe its structure as a set of sentences in predicate calculus.

We can think of the circuit f_1 as a composite component, consisting of subcomponents called "gates." There are two *xor* gates x_1 and x_2, two *and* gates a_1 and a_2, and an *or* gate o_1. Each device has a number of ports through which data flow. The input ports are on the left side of the box designating the device; the output ports are on the right side. Thus, the universe of discourse consists of 26 objects: 6 components and 20 ports.

We can use functions to associate ports with components. The binary function *input* maps an integer and a component into the corresponding input port. The binary function *output* maps an integer and a component into the corresponding output port. Thus, we can think about the first input of the adder, or about its second output, and so forth.

The solid lines connecting ports to other ports depict wires, which transmit data between components. We could conceptualize these wires as objects like gates, with inputs and outputs of their own; but this would not answer the question of how to encode the relationship between the inputs

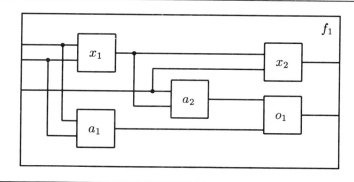

Figure 2.3   A full adder.

and outputs of those wires and the ports to which they are connected. Instead, let us ignore the presence of wires and think about the connectivity of a circuit using a single binary relation that associates ports with the ports to which they are connected. For example, the third input of f_1 is connected to the first input of a_2. We assume that connectivity is unidirectional, from left to right.

To describe the structure of f_1 in predicate calculus, we need to choose symbols that designate the elements of our conceptualization. The following vocabulary suffices.

- `F1, X1, X2, A1, A2, O1` designate the six components.

- `Adder(x)` means that `x` is an adder.

- `Xorg(x)` means that `x` is an *xor* gate.

- `Andg(x)` means that `x` is an *and* gate.

- `Org(x)` means that `x` is an *or* gate.

- `I(i,x)` designates the ith input port of device `x`.

- `O(i,x)` designates the ith output port of device `x`.

- `Conn(x,y)` means that port `x` is connected to port `y`.

Given this vocabulary, we can describe our conceptualization of the circuit with the following predicate-calculus sentences. The first six sentences indicate the types of the components. The remaining sentences capture their connectivity.

$$\text{Adder(F1)}$$

$$\text{Xorg(X1)}$$

$$\text{Xorg(X2)}$$

$$\text{Andg(A1)}$$

$$\text{Andg(A2)}$$

$$\text{Org(A3)}$$

$$\text{Conn(I(1,F1),I(1,X1))}$$

$$\text{Conn(I(2,F1),I(2,X1))}$$

$$\text{Conn(I(1,F1),I(1,A1))}$$

$$\text{Conn(I(2,F1),I(2,A1))}$$

$$\text{Conn(I(3,F1),I(2,X2))}$$

$$\text{Conn(I(3,F1),I(1,A2))}$$

```
Conn(O(1,X1),I(1,X2))

Conn(O(1,X1),I(2,A2))

Conn(O(1,A2),I(1,O1))

Conn(O(1,A1),I(2,O1))

Conn(O(1,X2),O(1,F1))

Conn(O(1,O1),O(2,F1))
```

We can describe the state of a circuit such as f_1 by enlarging our conceptualization to include high and low values (i.e., bits) and a relation that associates a port with the value on that port. These additional conceptual elements suggest the following vocabulary.

- V(x,z) means that the value on port x is z.

- 1 and 0 designate high and low signals, respectively.

Using this vocabulary, we can assert specific values for the ports in the circuit. For example, the following sentences assert that the inputs to the circuit are high, low, and high, respectively, and that the outputs are low and high.

```
V(I(1,F1),1)

V(I(2,F1),0)

V(I(3,F1),1)


V(O(1,F1),0)

V(O(1,F1),1)
```

We also can use this vocabulary to describe the general behavior of the components in the circuit. The first two sentences that follow capture the behavior of an *and* gate; the second pair of sentences describes the behavior of an *or* gate; and the third pair describes an *xor* gate. The final sentence describes the behavior of an ideal connection.

```
∀x (Andg(x) ∧ V(I(1,x),1) ∧ V(I(2,x),1) ⇒ V(O(1,x),1))

∀x∀n (Andg(x) ∧ V(I(n,x),0) ⇒ V(O(1,x),0))


∀x∀n (Org(x) ∧ V(I(n,x),1) ⇒ V(O(1,x),1))

∀x (Org(x) ∧ V(I(1,x),0) ∧ V(I(2,x),0) ⇒ V(O(1,x),0))


∀x∀z (Xorg(x) ∧ V(I(1,x),z) ∧ V(I(2,x),z) ⇒ V(O(1,x),0))
```

$$\forall x \forall y \forall z \ (\texttt{Xorg(x)} \land \texttt{V(I(1,x),y)} \land \texttt{V(I(2,x),z)} \land \texttt{y} \neq \texttt{z}$$
$$\Rightarrow \texttt{V(O(1,x),1))}$$

$$\forall x \forall y \forall z \ (\texttt{Conn(x,y)} \land \texttt{V(x,z)} \Rightarrow \texttt{V(y,z))}$$

Notice that these sentences completely characterize the digital structure and behavior of f_1. To describe additional properties, we would have to expand or modify our conceptualization and vocabulary. For example, we might want to express the fact that a_1 is malfunctioning. To do this, we would have to add an additional relation and phrase an appropriate sentence. Asserting that a connection is malfunctioning is a little more complicated, because connections are not objects. To express such information, we would need to reify connections. For the circuit in Figure 2.3, this would lead to 12 new objects; to relate these new connection objects to the ports they connect, we would have to extend the binary connectivity relation into a ternary relation that associates a port, the port to which it is connected, and the corresponding connection. In formalizing knowledge, it is always important to recognize the need for a new conceptualization and a new vocabulary when appropriate.

2.6 Algebraic Examples

Using predicate calculus, we can express the definitions and properties of common mathematical functions and relations, as illustrated by the examples in this section.

The following sentences express the associativity, commutativity, and identity properties of the + function. The first sentence states that the number obtained by adding x to the result of adding y to z is the same as the number obtained by adding to z the result of adding x and y. The second sentence states that the order of addition is unimportant. The third sentence states that 0 is an identity for +.

$$\forall x \forall y \forall z \ \texttt{x+(y+z)=(x+y)+z}$$

$$\forall x \forall y \ \texttt{x+y=y+x}$$

$$\forall x \ \texttt{x+0=x}$$

In its usual interpretation, the $\leq$ symbol is used to denote a partial order; i.e., one that is reflexive, antisymmetric, and transitive. The first sentence that follows asserts that the relation holds of any object and itself. The second sentence asserts that, if the relation holds between object x and object y and between y and x, then x and y must be equal. The third sentence states that the relation holds between object x and object z if it holds between object x and object y and also between object y and object z.

$$\forall x \ x \leq x$$

$$\forall x \forall y \ x \leq y \ \wedge \ y \leq x \ \Rightarrow \ x = y$$

$$\forall x \forall y \forall z \ x \leq y \ \wedge \ y \leq z \ \Rightarrow \ x \leq z$$

We can characterize functions and relations on sets in a similar manner. For example, given the membership relation $\in$, we can define the intersection function $\cap$, as follows. An object is a member of the intersection of two sets if and only if it is a member of both sets.

$$\forall s \forall t \forall x \ (x \in s \ \wedge \ x \in t) \ \Leftrightarrow \ x \in s \cap t$$

The following sentences express the associativity, commutativity, and idempotence of the intersection function. All three properties can be proved from the preceding definition.

$$\forall r \forall s \forall t \ r \cap (s \cap t) = (r \cap s) \cap t$$

$$\forall s \forall t \ s \cap t = t \cap s$$

$$\forall s \ s \cap s = s$$

If the sentences in this section look familiar, that is as it should be. Predicate calculus was originally developed to express mathematical facts, and it is in common use today.

2.7 List Examples

If $\tau_1, \ldots, \tau_n$ are legal terms in our language, then a *list* is a term of the following form, where n is any integer greater than or equal to zero.

$$[\tau_1, \ldots, \tau_n]$$

The primary use of lists is the representation of sequences of objects. For example, if we use numerals to designate numbers, we can use the following list to designate the sequence consisting of the first three integers in ascending order.

$$[1, 2, 3]$$

Because lists are themselves terms, we can nest lists within lists. For example, the following term is a list of all permutations of the first three positive integers.

$$[[1,2,3],[1,3,2],[2,1,3],[2,3,1],[3,1,2],[3,2,1]]$$

To talk about lists of arbitrary length, we use the binary functional operator "." in infix form. In particular, a term of the form $\tau_1 . \tau_2$ designates a sequence in which τ_1 is the first element and τ_2 is the rest of the list. With this operator, we can rewrite the list [1,2,3] as follows.

$$(1.(2.(3.[])))$$

The advantage of this representation is that it allows us to describe functions and relations on lists without regard to length.

As an example, consider the definition of the binary relation **Member**, which holds of an object and a list if the object is a top-level member of the sequence denoted by the list. Using the "." operator, we can describe the **Member** relation as follows. Obviously, an object is a member of a sequence if it is the first element; however, it is also a member if it is member of the rest of the list.

∀x∀l Member(x,x.l)

∀x∀y∀l Member(x,l) ⇒ Member(x,y.l)

We also can define functions to manipulate lists in different ways. For example, the following axioms define a function called **Append**. The value of **Append** is a sequence consisting of the elements in the sequence supplied as its first argument followed by the elements in the sequence supplied as its second argument. Thus, Append([1,2],[3,4]) denotes the same sequence as the list [1,2,3,4].

∀m Append([],m)=m

∀x∀l∀m Append(x.l,m)=(x.Append(l,m))

Of course, we can also define relations that depend on the structure of the elements of a sequence. For example, the **Among** relation is true of an object and a sequence if the object is a member of the sequence, if it is a member of a sequence that is itself a member of the sequence, and so on.

∀x Among(x,x)

∀x∀y∀z (Among(x,y) ∨ Among(x,z)) ⇒ Among(x,y.z)

Lists are an extremely versatile representational device, and the reader is encouraged to become as familiar as possible with the techniques of writing definitions for functions and relations on lists. As is true of many tasks, practice is the best approach to gaining skill.

2.8 Natural-Language Examples

As a final example of using predicate calculus, consider the task of formalizing the information in the following English sentences. We assume that the conceptualization underlying all the sentences is the same. The universe of discourse is the set of all plants. There is a unary relation for being a mushroom, another for being purple, and a third for being poisonous. We designate these relations with the unary relation symbols Mushroom, Purple, and Poisonous. Each English sentence is followed by one or more translations into predicate calculus. Where more than one translation is given, the alternatives are logically equivalent.

All purple mushrooms are poisonous.

∀x Purple(x) ∧ Mushroom(x) ⇒ Poisonous(x)

∀x Purple(x) ⇒ (Mushroom(x) ⇒ Poisonous(x))

∀x Mushroom(x) ⇒ (Purple(x) ⇒ Poisonous(x))

The use of the word *all* in this sentence is a clear indication that it is universally quantified. The equivalence of the three sentences should be obvious. The first states that, if an object is a mushroom and purple, then it is poisonous. The second states that, if an object is purple, then, if it is also a mushroom, it is poisonous. The third sentence states that, if an object is a mushroom, then, if it is also purple, it is poisonous. All three statements assert the poisonous quality of any purple mushroom.

A mushroom is poisonous only if it is purple.

∀x Mushroom(x) ∧ Poisonous(x) ⇒ Purple(x)

∀x Mushroom(x) ⇒ (Poisonous(x) ⇒ Purple(x))

Here we have the converse of the relationship in the preceding sentence. The argument for equivalence is the same as for the preceding sentence.

(Caution: A conceptualization of the world in which this is a true sentence may be hazardous to your health!)

> *No purple mushroom is poisonous.*
>
> ∀x ¬(Purple(x) ∧ Mushroom(x) ∧ Poisonous(x))
>
> ¬(∃x Purple(x) ∧ Mushroom(x) ∧ Poisonous(x))

The use of the word *no* here indicates that something is not true. The fact that, for all objects, something is not true (as suggested by the first rendition) is equivalent to the lack of existence of an object for which it is true (as suggested by the second).

> *There is exactly one mushroom.*
>
> ∃x Mushroom(x) ∧ (∀z z≠x ⇒ ¬Mushroom(z))

The easiest way to encode information about the number of objects having a property is to state the cardinality of the set of all objects having that property. Although the specified conceptualization includes neither this set nor the cardinality function, it is possible to express that there is only one mushroom using the equality relation. Note that the fact can be stated even though the identity of the individual mushroom is unknown.

2.9 Specialized Languages

One of the disadvantages of predicate calculus as a knowledge-representation language is that, like English, it is sometimes cumbersome. For this reason, AI researchers often prefer specialized languages, many of them graphical. In this section, we present a few examples and address their strengths and weaknesses for encoding declarative knowledge.

A *binary table*, is an example of a sentence in a graphical language. As our alphabet, we take the set of all uppercase and lowercase letters, the digits, and both horizontal and vertical lines. The symbols are the

π	τ_1	$\cdots$	τ_n
σ_1	α_{11}	$\cdots$	α_{1n}
$\vdots$	$\vdots$	$\ddots$	$\vdots$
σ_m	α_{m1}	$\cdots$	α_{mn}

Figure 2.4   The form of a binary table.

same as those in predicate calculus, except that we divide all symbols into object constants and binary function constants only. A legal sentence in the table language is a two-dimensional configuration of symbols in the form shown in Figure 2.4, where π is a binary function constant and the symbols $\sigma_1, \ldots, \sigma_m$ and $\tau_1, \ldots, \tau_n$ and $\alpha_{11}, \ldots, \alpha_{mn}$ are all object constants.

An interpretation I satisfies a sentence in the table language if and only if each entry in the table designates the value of the function designated by the function constant in the upper-left corner applied to the objects designated by the corresponding row and column labels.

$$\pi^I(\sigma_i^I, \tau_j^I) = \alpha_{ij}^I$$

Figure 2.5 presents a legal binary table, assuming that the symbol Score is a binary function constant and the other symbols in the table are all object constants.

Suppose that I is an interpretation that maps the symbols Gauss, Herbrand, and Laurent into the students with those names. It maps the symbols Quiz1, Quiz2, Quiz3, and Final into four tests taken by those students. It maps sequences of digits into the corresponding base-10 integers. It maps the function constant Score into a function that maps a student and a test into the student's score on that test. Then I satisfies this table if and only if under this mapping the indicated scores are correct; e.g., Gauss got a 94 on the second quiz.

The language of binary tables is excellent for expressing information about binary functions; it does not work at all for other types of information. Of course, there are many other types of tables, some with multiple labels on rows, some with multiple labels on columns, some with more complex entries.

Another specialized language, explored in the early days of AI, is the semantic net. A *semantic net* is a directed graph with labeled nodes and arcs. The alphabet consists of all uppercase and lowercase letters, the digits, nodes, and directed arcs of arbitrary length and direction. The symbols of the language are the same as in predicate calculus, and they are divided into object constants and binary relation constants. A two-dimensional configuration of elements from this alphabet is a legal labeled directed graph if and only if each node has an associated object constant

Score	Quiz1	Quiz2	Quiz3	Final
Gauss	92	94	89	100
Herbrand	86	79	92	85
Laurent	52	70	45	68

Figure 2.5 **Knowledge encoded in a binary table.**

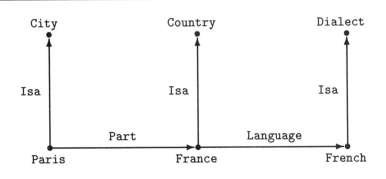

Figure 2.6   A semantic net.

written near it, each arc has an associated binary relation constant written near it, and each arc begins at a node and ends at a node. Figure 2.6 is an example of a semantic net, provided that the symbols Isa, Part, and **Language** are all binary relation constants and that the other symbols are all object constants.

An interpretation satisfies a semantic net if and only if the relation designated by the label on each arc holds of the objects designated by the labels on the nodes the arc connects. This particular semantic net is satisfied by the standard interpretation, since Paris is a city in France, France is a country, and the language in France is the French dialect.

A semantic net is particularly good for representing binary relations and, consequently, unary functions. Nonbinary relations can be handled by using arcs with more than two endpoints.

The language of frames is another language that has received considerable attention in the AI community, as much for its semantic richness (discussed later) as for its syntax. There are numerous frame languages and considerable variation in detail from one language to another. However, the following definition is consistent with the majority of these languages.

The alphabet of our frames language consists of uppercase and lowercase letters, digits, the colon character, and both horizontal and vertical lines. The symbols of the frames language are the same as those in predicate calculus and are divided into object constants, unary function constants, and binary relation constants. Each sentence is a structured object in the form of a frame (see Figure 2.7), where the symbol in the upper-left corner is an object constant, the symbols before the colons are function or relation constants, and the symbols after the colons are object constants. The sentences in the language are called *frames*; the symbol in the upper-left corner is the frame's *name*; the symbols before the colons are commonly termed *slots*; and the symbols after the colons are called *values*.

$$
\begin{array}{|ll|}
\hline
\alpha & \\
\hline
\rho_1: & \beta_1 \\
\vdots & \vdots \\
\rho_n: & \beta_n \\
\hline
\end{array}
$$

Figure 2.7   The general form of a frame.

An interpretation satisfies a sentence in the frames language if and only if the object designated by the value of each slot is the same as the object obtained by applying the function designated by the slot to the object designated by the frame name.

$$\langle \alpha^I, \beta_i^I \rangle \in \rho_i^I$$

Figure 2.8 shows two examples of knowledge encoded in frames. Jones is a freshman advised by Tversky and is in the psychology department. Tversky is a faculty member in the psychology department and advises Jones and Thorndyke.

One problem common to specialized languages such as tables, semantic nets, and frames is an inability to handle partial information. For example, there is no way in the table language to state the fact that either Herbrand or Laurent got a 90 on the first quiz without saying which of them did. There is no way in a semantic net to say that Paris is in some country without saying which one. There is no way in the frame language to say that Tversky is *not* Jones's advisor without saying who is.

In fairness to the language of semantic nets, it should be pointed out that various extensions have been proposed that allow one to express logical combinations of facts or quantified facts. However, these extensions compromise the simplicity of the language to a large extent.

In fairness to the frames language, it should be pointed out that the original idea of frames included provision for the association of procedural

Jones	
Isa:	Freshman
Dept:	Psychology
Advisor:	Tversky

Tversky	
Isa:	Faculty
Dept:	Psychology
Advisees:	{Jones,Thorndyke}

Figure 2.8   Knowledge encoded in frames.

knowledge with the declarative knowledge stored as slot values. This allows us to express knowledge beyond that we discussed. Unfortunately, it does not allow us to express this knowledge in declarative form.

In fairness to all these specialized languages, it should be noted that partial information always can be captured by defining new relations. For example, we can change the *score* function illustrated in Figure 2.5 to be a binary function from students and quizzes to *sets* of scores, with the idea that the actual score is a member of the set so designated. This would allow one to state that Herbrand got either an 80 or a 90 by recording the set {80,90} as his score. Representing other partial information is more difficult but still is possible. This approach has the disadvantage that the new conceptualizations are quite cumbersome; and, as a result, the specialized languages lose much of their perspicuity.

The language of predicate calculus addresses the problem of partial information head on by providing logical operators and quantifiers that allow us to express partial information. As a result, there is no need (in principle) either to encode declarative knowledge in procedural form or to change one's conceptualization of the world.

The primary disadvantage of predicate calculus is that it is less succinct than are specialized languages for many kinds of knowledge. On the other hand, no single specialized language is ideal for expressing all facts. For some kinds of information, tables are best. For other information, semantic nets or frames are best. For yet other information, bar graphs or pie charts or color or animation may be best.

Of course, we can easily define specialized languages such as tables, semantic nets, and frames in terms of predicate calculus. Having done so, we can use those languages where they are appropriate; where they fail, we can fall back on the expressive power of the full predicate calculus.

For these reasons, we have chosen to use predicate calculus in this text. The approach also has the pedagogical benefit of allowing us to compare and analyze different languages within a single common framework. Also, it is possible to describe inference procedures for just one language and have them apply automatically to these other languages as well.

2.10 Bibliographical and Historical Remarks

Although we stress in this book languages and reasoning methods for declarative representations of knowledge, the difficult problem for AI is the conceptualization of a domain. Every AI application begins with a particular conceptualization, and the reader should become familiar with several examples of these in order to gain an appreciation for this aspect of AI.

Conceptualizations used by expert systems usually are sharply limited to a small set of objects, functions, and relations. Typical examples are those used by MYCIN [Shortliffe 1976], PROSPECTOR [Duda 1984], and DART [Genesereth 1984]. Inventing conceptualizations for broader domains that include common, everyday phenomena has proved quite difficult. Among the attempts to formalize commonsense knowledge are those of Hayes [Hayes 1985a] and those reported in [Hobbs 1985a, Hobbs 1985b]. The problem of grain size in conceptualizations has been studied by Hobbs [Hobbs 1985c]. Probably the most ambitious attempt to capture a large body of general knowledge in a representation that is independent of its many possible later uses is the CYC project of Lenat and colleagues [Lenat 1986].

Our treatment of the predicate calculus in this book is based on that of Enderton [Enderton 1972]. Other good textbooks on logic are those of Smullyan [Smullyan 1968] and Mendelson [Mendelson 1964]. A book by Pospesel [Pospesel 1976] is a good elementary introduction with many examples of English sentences represented as predicate-calculus sentences.

Semantic networks have a long tradition in AI and in cognitive psychology. In psychology, they have been used as models of memory organization [Quillian 1968, Anderson 1973]. In AI, they have been used more or less as a predicate-calculus–like declarative language [Simmons 1973, Hendrix 1979, Schubert 1976, Findler 1979, Duda 1978].

Closely related to semantic networks are languages that use frames. Following a key paper on frames by Minsky [Minsky 1975], several frame-based languages were developed, including KRL [Bobrow 1977, 1979, Lehnert 1979], FRL [Goldstein 1979], the UNITS [Stefik 1979], and KL-ONE [Brachman 1985c].

Comparisons between frames and semantic networks on the one hand and ordinary predicate calculus on the other have been discussed by Woods [Woods 1975], Brachman [Brachman 1979, 1983c], Hayes [Hayes 1979a], and Nilsson [Nilsson 1980, Chapter 9]. Although many versions of semantic networks do not have the full expressive power of first-order predicate calculus, they do carry extra indexing information that makes many types of inferences more efficient. (However, see [Stickel 1982, 1986, Walther 1985] for examples of how similar indexing can be achieved in implementations of systems that perform inferences on predicate-calculus expressions.) There also are relations between semantic network representations and so-called *object-oriented programming* methods [Stefik 1986]. Some representation systems have used semantic-network–style representations to express taxonomic information, and ordinary predicate calculus to express other information [Brachman 1983a, 1983b, 1985a].

For the same reasons that logical languages are important for representing information in AI programs, they also are attractive target languages into which to attempt translations of natural-language sentences in systems that perform natural-language processing. A volume edited by Grosz et al. contains several important papers on this topic [Grosz 1986].

Exercises

1. *Grain size.* Consider a conceptualization of the circuit in Figure 2.3 in which there are just six objects: the full adder and its five subcomponents. Devise a relational basis set that allows you to define the connectivity of the circuit.

2. *Reification.* Devise a conceptualization of the circuit in Figure 2.3 that allows you to express properties of connections, such as *broken* and *intermittent.*

3. *Syntax.* For each of the following examples, indicate whether or not it is a syntactically legal sentence in predicate calculus.

   a. 32456 > 32654

   b. 32456 > France

   c. p ∨ q

   d. Likes(Arthur,France ∧ Switzerland)

   e. ∀x Neighbor(France,Switzerland) ⇒ Prime(x)

   f. ∀country Neighbor(France,country)

   g. ∀x∃x Neighbor(x,x)

   h. (∀x P(x)) ⇒ (∃x P(x))

   i. (∀p p(A)) ⇒ (∃p p(A))

   j. (P(0) ∧ (∀x P(x) ⇒ P(x+1))) ⇒ (∀x P(x))

4. *Groups.* Recall that a group is a set with a binary function and a distinguished element such that (a) the set is closed under the function, (b) the function is associative, (c) the distinguished element is an identity for the function, and (d) each element has an inverse. Express these properties as sentences in predicate calculus.

5. *Lists.* Write the axioms defining the function Reverse, whose value is the reverse of the list supplied as its argument.

6. *Translation.* Use the following vocabulary to express the assertions in the following sentences.

   • Male(x) means that the object denoted by x is male.

   • Female(x) means that x is female.

   • Vegetarian(x) means that x is a vegetarian.

   • Butcher(x) means that x is a butcher.

a. No man is both a butcher and a vegetarian.

b. All men except butchers like vegetarians.

c. The only vegetarian butchers are women.

d. No man likes a woman who is a vegetarian.

e. No woman likes a man who does not like all vegetarians.

7. *Reverse translation.* Translate the following predicate-calculus sentences into colloquial English. You can assume that all constants have their obvious meanings.

a. ∀x Hesitates(x) ⇒ Lost(x)

b. ¬∃x Business(x) ∧ Like(x,Showbusiness)

c. ¬∀x Glitters(x) ⇒ Gold(x)

d. ∃x∀t Person(x) ∧ Time(t) ∧ Canfool(x,t)

8. *Interpretation and satisfaction.* For each of the following sentences, give interpretations to the symbols such that the sentence makes sense and represents the world accurately (i.e., you believe it to be true).

a. 2 > 3

b. ¬P ⇒ ¬Q

c. ∀x∀y∀z R(x,y,z) ⇒ R(y,z,x)

9. *Interpretation and satisfaction.* For each of the following three sentences, give an interpretation that makes that sentence false but makes the other two sentences true.

a. P(x,y) ∧ P(y,z) ⇒ P(x,z)

b. P(x,y) ∧ P(y,x) ⇒ x=y

c. P(A,y) ⇒ P(x,B)

10. *Satisfiability.* Say whether each of the following sentences is unsatisfiable, satisfiable, or valid.

a. P ⇒ P

b. P ⇒ ¬P

c. ¬P ⇒ P

d. P ⇔ ¬P

e. P ⇒ (Q ⇒ P)

11. *Definability.* Define the *above* relation in terms of the *on* relation, and define *on* in terms of *above*.

12. *Tables.* The tables language described in this chapter is ideal for expressing information about binary *functions*. Invent a table language appropriate for expressing binary *relations* and use it to encode the following information. Be sure that you can encode this information without changing the underlying conceptualization.

    a. The facts in Figure 2.6.

    b. The facts in Figure 2.8.

13. *Frames.* Consider the frames language defined in the text.

    a. Explain why you cannot express the facts in Figure 2.5 in this language without changing the underlying conceptualization.

    b. Express the facts in Figure 2.6 in the frames language.

14. *Pie charts and layered bar graphs.* The following illustrations are examples of the same knowledge encoded in two different languages. Both are good for expressing the relative proportions of a total quantity in a set of subcategories.

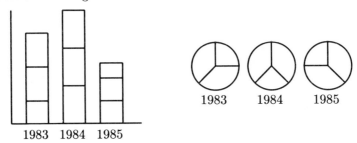

    a. What information expressed by the layered bar graph is not captured in the pie chart?

    b. Devise a graphical extension of the pie-chart language that allows us to express this additional information.

CHAPTER 3

Inference

INFERENCE IS THE PROCESS of deriving conclusions from premises. For example, from the premise that Art is either at home or at work and the premise that Art is not at home, we can conclude that he must be at work. The ability to perform inferences of this sort is an essential part of intelligence.

We begin this chapter with a discussion of inference and inference procedures in general. We then narrow our discussion by defining the criteria of soundness and completeness. Finally, we present a procedure that satisfies these criteria.

3.1 Derivability

Inference is typically a multistep process. In some cases, we can derive a conclusion from a set of premises in a single step. In other cases, we first need to derive intermediate conclusions.

Each step in this process must be sanctioned by an acceptable *rule of inference*. A rule of inference consists of (1) a set of sentence patterns called *conditions*, and (2) another set of sentence patterns called *conclusions*. Whenever we have sentences that *match* the conditions of the rule, then it is acceptable to infer sentences matching the conclusions.

Modus ponens (MP) is an example. The sentence patterns above the line in the following display are the conditions, and the sentence pattern below the line is the sole conclusion. The significance of this rule is that, whenever sentences of the form $\phi \Rightarrow \psi$ and ϕ have been established, then it is acceptable to infer the sentence ψ as well.

$$\phi \Rightarrow \psi$$
$$\phi$$
$$\overline{\qquad}$$
$$\psi$$

Suppose, for example, that we believe the sentence `On(A,B)` and we also believe the sentence `On(A,B)` $\Rightarrow$ `Above(A,B)`. Then, modus ponens allows us to infer the sentence `Above(A,B)` in a single step.

Modus tolens (MT) is the reverse of modus ponens. If we believe that ϕ implies ψ and we believe that ψ is false, then we can infer that ϕ must be false as well.

$$\phi \Rightarrow \psi$$
$$\neg\psi$$
$$\overline{\qquad}$$
$$\neg\phi$$

And elimination (AE) states that, whenever we believe a conjunction of sentences, then we can infer each of the conjuncts. In this case, note that there are multiple conclusions.

$$\phi \wedge \psi$$
$$\overline{\qquad}$$
$$\phi$$
$$\psi$$

And introduction (AI) states that, whenever we believe some sentences, we can infer their conjunction.

$$\phi$$
$$\psi$$
$$\overline{\qquad}$$
$$\phi \wedge \psi$$

Universal instantiation (UI) allows us to reason from the general to the particular. It states that, whenever we believe a universally quantified sentence, we can infer an instance of that sentence in which the universally quantified variable is replaced by any appropriate term.

$$\forall\nu\ \phi$$
$$\overline{\qquad}$$
$$\phi_{\nu/\tau} \quad \text{where } \tau \text{ is free for } \nu \text{ in } \phi$$

For example, consider the sentence $\forall$y `Hates(Jane,y)`. From this premise, we can infer that Jane hates Jill; i.e., `Hates(Jane,Jill)`. We also can infer that Jane hates herself; i.e., `Hates(Jane,Jane)`. We can even infer than Jane hates her mother; i.e., `Hates(Jane,Mom(Jane))`.

In addition, we can use universal instantiation to create conclusions with free variables. For example, from $\forall$y `Hates(Jane,y)`, we can infer

Hates(Jane,y). In doing so, however, we have to be careful to avoid conflicts with other variables in the quantified sentence. This is the reason for the constraint on the replacement term. As an example, consider the expression ∀y∃z Hates(y,z); i.e., everybody hates somebody. From this expression, it makes sense to infer ∃z Hates(Mom(x),z); i.e., everybody's mother hates somebody. However, we do not want to infer ∃z Hates(Mom(z),z); i.e., there is someone who is hated by his mother.

We can avoid this problem by obeying the restriction on the universal instantiation rule. We say that a term τ is *free* for a variable ν in an expression ϕ if and only if ν does not occur within the scope of a quantifier of some variable in τ. For example, the term Mom(x) is free for y in ∃z Hates(y,z). However, the term Mom(z) is not free for y, since y occurs within the scope of a quantifier of z. Thus, we cannot substitute Mom(z) for y in this sentence, and we avoid the problem we have just described.

Existential instantiation (EI) allows us to eliminate existential quantifiers. Like universal instantiation, this rule states that we can infer an instance of the quantified sentence in which the existentially quantified variable is replaced by a suitable term.

$$\frac{\exists \nu\ \phi}{\phi_{\nu/\pi(\nu_1,\dots,\nu_n)}}$$

where π is a new function constant
where $\nu_1, \dots, \nu_n$ are the free variables in ϕ

For example, if we have the premise ∃z Hates(y,z) and if Foe is a new function constant, we can use existential instantiation to infer the sentence Hates(y,Foe(y)). The term Foe(y) here is a term designating the person y hates.

The mention of free variables in the replacement term is intended to capture the relationship between the value of the existentially quantified variable and the values for the free variables in the expression. Without this restriction, we would be able to instantiate the sentence ∀x∃y Hates(x,y) and the sentence ∃y∀x Hates(x,y) in the same way, despite their very different meanings.

Of course, when there are no free variables in an expression, the variable can be replaced by a function of no arguments or, equivalently, by a new constant. For example, if we have the sentence ∃y∀x Hates(x,y), and Mike is a new object constant, we can infer ∀x Hates(x,Mike); i.e., everyone hates Mike.

Note that, in performing existential instantiation, it is extremely important to avoid object and function constants that have been used already. Without this restriction, we would be able to infer Hates(Jill,Jill) from the somewhat weaker fact ∃z Hates(Jill,z).

Although these rules cover many cases of inference, they are not by themselves exhaustive. Later, we define a criterion of exhaustiveness and present rules that satisfy our criterion.

Given any set of inference rules, we say that a conclusion ϕ is *derivable* from a set of premises Δ if and only if (1) ϕ is a member of Δ, or (2) ϕ is the result of applying a rule of inference to sentences derivable from Δ. A *derivation* of ϕ from Δ is a sequence of sentences in which each sentence either is a member of Δ or is the result of applying a rule of inference to elements earlier in the sequence.

As an illustration of these concepts, consider the following problem. We know that horses are faster than dogs and that there is a greyhound that is faster than every rabbit. We know that Harry is a horse and that Ralph is a rabbit. Our job is to derive the fact that Harry is faster than Ralph.

First, we need to formalize our premises. The relevant sentences follow. Note that we are adding two facts about the world not stated explicitly in the problem: that greyhounds are dogs and that our speed relationship is transitive.

$\forall x \forall y$ Horse(x) $\wedge$ Dog(y) $\Rightarrow$ Faster(x,y)

$\exists y$ Greyhound(y) $\wedge$ ($\forall z$ Rabbit(z) $\Rightarrow$ Faster(y,z))

$\forall y$ Greyhound(y) $\Rightarrow$ Dog(y)

$\forall x \forall y \forall z$ Faster(x,y) $\wedge$ Faster(y,z) $\Rightarrow$ Faster(x,z)

Horse(Harry)

Rabbit(Ralph)

Our goal is to show that Harry is faster than Ralph. In other words, starting with the preceding sentences, we want to derive the following sentence:

Faster(Harry,Ralph)

The derivation of this conclusion goes as shown below. The first six lines correspond to the premises just formalized. The seventh line is the result of applying existential instantiation to the second sentence. Because there are no free variables, we replace the quantified variable by the new object constant Greg. The eighth and nine lines come from and elimination. The tenth line is a universal instantiation of the ninth line. In the eleventh line, we use modus ponens to infer that Greg is faster than Ralph. Next, we instantiate the sentence about greyhounds and dogs and infer that Greg is a dog. Then, we instantiate the sentence about horses and dogs; we use and introduction to form a conjunction matching the antecedent of this instantiated sentence; and we infer that Harry is faster than Greg. In the final sequence, we instantiate the transitivity sentence, again form the necessary conjunction, and infer the desired conclusion.

1. $\forall x \forall y$ Horse(x) $\wedge$ Dog(y) $\Rightarrow$ Faster(x,y) $\qquad \Delta$
2. $\exists y$ Greyhound(y) $\wedge$ $\qquad \Delta$
   ($\forall z$ Rabbit(z) $\Rightarrow$ Faster(y,z))
3. $\forall y$ Greyhound(y) $\Rightarrow$ Dog(y) $\qquad \Delta$
4. $\forall x \forall y \forall z$ Faster(x,y) $\wedge$ Faster(y,z) $\qquad \Delta$
   $\Rightarrow$ Faster(x,z)
5. Horse(Harry) $\qquad \Delta$
6. Rabbit(Ralph) $\qquad \Delta$
7. Greyhound(Greg) $\wedge$ $\qquad$ 2, EI
   ($\forall z$ Rabbit(z) $\Rightarrow$ Faster(Greg,z))
8. Greyhound(Greg) $\qquad$ 7, AE
9. $\forall z$ Rabbit(z) $\Rightarrow$ Faster(Greg,z) $\qquad$ 7, AE
10. Rabbit(Ralph) $\Rightarrow$ Faster(Greg,Ralph) $\qquad$ 9, UI
11. Faster(Greg,Ralph) $\qquad$ 10, 6, MP
12. Greyhound(Greg) $\Rightarrow$ Dog(Greg) $\qquad$ 3, UI
13. Dog(Greg) $\qquad$ 12, 8, MP
14. Horse(Harry) $\wedge$ Dog(Greg) $\qquad$ 1, UI
    $\Rightarrow$ Faster(Harry,Greg)
15. Horse(Harry) $\wedge$ Dog(Greg) $\qquad$ 5, 13, AI
16. Faster(Harry,Greg) $\qquad$ 14, 15, MP
17. Faster(Harry,Greg) $\wedge$ Faster(Greg,Ralph) $\qquad$ 4, UI
    $\Rightarrow$ Faster(Harry,Ralph)
18. Faster(Harry,Greg) $\wedge$ Faster(Greg,Ralph) $\qquad$ 16, 11, AI
19. Faster(Harry,Ralph) $\qquad$ 17, 19, MP

The main thing to note about this derivation is that it is completely mechanical. Each conclusion follows from previous conclusions by a mechanical application of a rule of inference. On the other hand, in producing this derivation, we rejected numerous alternative inferences. Making these choices intelligently is one of the key problems in automating the process of inference.

3.2 Inference Procedures

The definition of derivability in the previous section is underconstrained. In the process of deriving a conclusion, we often have a choice of inferences to consider. An inference procedure is a way of making this choice.

In what follows, we use the word *database* to denote a finite sequence of sentences. In trying to prove a given sentence, we begin with an initial database containing the premises for the problem; we perform an inference step, leading to a new database; then we iterate this procedure until the desired sentence is obtained. In this way, step by step, the process of inference implicitly defines a sequence of databases.

As an example, consider the database sequence that follows. The initial database consists of just four sentences; and each succeeding database contains an additional sentence, obtained by applying modus ponens to elements in the preceding database. In the first step, we derive the new sentence Q from the first two sentences in the initial database. In the second step, the first and third sentences are used to obtain the new sentence R.

P		P		P
P ⇒ Q		P ⇒ Q		P ⇒ Q
P ⇒ R	⟶	P ⇒ R	⟶	P ⇒ R
Q ⇒ S		Q ⇒ S		Q ⇒ S
		Q		Q
				R

On the other hand, we could equally well have interchanged the order of the two inferences, leading to the following history:

P		P		P
P ⇒ Q		P ⇒ Q		P ⇒ Q
P ⇒ R	⟶	P ⇒ R	⟶	P ⇒ R
Q ⇒ S		Q ⇒ S		Q ⇒ S
		R		R
				Q

An *inference procedure* is a function *step* that maps an initial database d from the set $\mathcal{D}$ of all databases and a positive integer n into the database for the n-th step of inference.

$$step : \mathcal{D} \times N \longrightarrow \mathcal{D}$$

Obviously, the value of an inference procedure on its first step is required to be the initial database.

$$step(\Delta, 1) = \Delta$$

Other than this, there are no constraints on the definition of an inference procedure. For example, we can define a procedure that produces the first sequence shown above, and we can define a different inference procedure that produces the second sequence. We can even define a procedure that deletes sentences from our database.

This definition is quite general, and there are some special cases that deserve attention. First, we look at Markov inference procedures; then we turn to incremental inference procedures.

In a *Markov inference procedure*, the choice of database on each step is determined entirely by the database for the last step. Consequently, we can formalize a Markov inference procedure as a function *next* from databases to databases that maps each database produced during inference into its successor.

$$next : \mathcal{D} \longrightarrow \mathcal{D}$$

Given a Markov inference procedure named *next*, it is easy to define the corresponding inference procedure *step*. The value on the first step is just the initial database. Thereafter, the value is the result of applying *next* to the preceding database.

$$step(\Delta, n) = \begin{cases} \Delta & \text{if } n = 1 \\ next(step(\Delta, n - 1)) & \text{otherwise} \end{cases}$$

Because the choice of database on each step of inference is determined entirely by the previous database, we can ignore all other information about history. Consequently, Markov inference procedures are simpler to understand and easier to implement than are many non-Markov procedures.

Although there is no explicit dependence on history in a Markov inference procedure, it is possible to define some history-based procedures by exploiting the information about history implicit in the order of sentences in each database. We present an example of this in Chapter 10.

Unfortunately, not every inference procedure can be formalized in this way. As an example, consider an inference procedure that uses modus ponens on odd steps and modus tolens on even steps. When started on a database Δ_1 containing multiple opportunities to use either rule, the procedure first dictates modus ponens, leading to database Δ_2; and then it dictates modus tolens on Δ_2. By contrast, when started on database Δ_2, it dictates modus ponens, since that is an odd step. Thus, the procedure dictates two different successors for the same database; therefore, it cannot be defined as a Markov procedure.

An *incremental inference procedure* is one in which the database on each step of inference is obtained from the previous database by adding zero or more new conclusions. If an inference procedure is incremental, then we can formalize it as a function *new*, which maps a database and a positive integer into the database increment.

$$new : \mathcal{D} \times N \longrightarrow \mathcal{D}$$

Given a value for the function *new*, the value of *step* is just the database obtained by extending the previous database to include the new conclusions.

$$step(\Delta, n) = \begin{cases} \Delta & \text{if } n = 1 \\ append(step(\Delta, n - 1), new(\Delta, n - 1)) & \text{otherwise} \end{cases}$$

The distinguishing characteristic of incremental inference is monotonic growth in the database. We never delete any conclusions. This can cause difficulties when we want to retract previous conclusions for one reason or another. Nevertheless, incremental inference procedures are quite common and useful and, therefore, are worthy of attention.

As an example of incremental inference, consider the following inference procedure. We use just one rule of inference: modus ponens. The inferences are performed in breadth-first fashion; i.e., all inferences involving just the initial premises are done first, then all inferences involving conclusions from the first round of inferences are done, then all inferences involving conclusions from the second round are done, and so on. Our procedure also is *static biased*; i.e., within each round, inferences are performed in the order in which sentences appear in the database.

To visualize this procedure in action, imagine the database written out as an open-ended sequence of sentences. We use two pointers to help us keep our place in the process. On each step, we compare the sentences under the pointers. If we can apply modus ponens to those two sentences to derive a third, we add the new sentence to the end of the list. At the start of the inference process, we initialize both pointers to the head of the list; as inference progresses, we move the pointers down the list. As long as the two pointers point to different positions, we leave the *slow* pointer where it is and advance the *fast* pointer. Whenever both pointers refer to the same position, we move the *fast* pointer to the top of the list, and we move the *slow* pointer one position down the list.

The following sequence of databases illustrates this method. At the start, both pointers are initialized to the head of the list. Since we cannot apply modus ponens to P and itself, no conclusion is added to the database. Since the pointers coincide, the fast pointer is moved to the start of the list (resulting in no change in this case), and the slow pointer is advanced. On the second step, we can apply modus ponens to produce the result Q, which we add to the database for the next step. The slow pointer remains in place and the fast pointer is advanced. On the third step, we cannot perform any inference, and so nothing is added to the database. However, the pointers once again coincide; and so the fast pointer is reinitialized and the slow pointer is advanced. At this point, we can deduce R, which is then added to the database on the next step.

$$
\begin{array}{llll}
\rightarrow\rightarrow\text{P} & \rightarrow\text{P} & \text{P} & \rightarrow\text{P} \\
\text{P} \Rightarrow \text{Q} & \rightarrow \text{P} \Rightarrow \text{Q} & \rightarrow\rightarrow\text{P} \Rightarrow \text{Q} & \text{P} \Rightarrow \text{Q} \\
\text{P} \Rightarrow \text{R} \longrightarrow & \text{P} \Rightarrow \text{R} \longrightarrow & \text{P} \Rightarrow \text{R} \longrightarrow & \rightarrow \text{P} \Rightarrow \text{R} \\
\text{Q} \Rightarrow \text{S} & \text{Q} \Rightarrow \text{S} & \text{Q} \Rightarrow \text{S} & \text{Q} \Rightarrow \text{S} \\
& & \text{Q} & \text{Q}
\end{array}
$$

We can formalize this method as follows. First, we define the function *fast* that maps an initial database and a positive integer into the database fragment pointed to by the fast-moving pointer.

$$
fast(\Delta, n) = \begin{cases}
\Delta & n = 1 \\
append(step(\Delta, n-1), new(\Delta, n)) & \\
\qquad\qquad fast(\Delta, n-1) = slow(\Delta, n-1) \\
append(rest(fast(\Delta, n-1)), new(\Delta, n)) & \text{otherwise}
\end{cases}
$$

The function *slow* maps an initial database and a positive integer into the database fragment pointed to by our slow-moving pointer.

$$slow(\Delta, n) = \begin{cases} \Delta & n = 1 \\ append(rest(slow(\Delta, n - 1)), new(\Delta, n)) \\ \qquad\qquad fast(\Delta, n - 1) = slow(\Delta, n - 1) \\ append(slow(\Delta, n - 1), new(\Delta, n)) & \text{otherwise} \end{cases}$$

Finally, we define *new* as follows. If modus ponens applies to the sentences at the heads of the two database fragments, then the new database fragment is the singleton set containing the conclusion. Otherwise, it is the empty set. The relation *mp* holds of three sentences if and only if the third sentence is the result of applying modus ponens to the first two sentences.

$$new(\Delta, n) = \begin{cases} \Delta & n = 1 \\ [\chi] & mp(first(fast(\Delta, n - 1)), first(slow(\Delta, n - 1)), \chi) \\ [\,] & \text{otherwise} \end{cases}$$

It can be shown that this method systematically explores the entire space of all possible conclusions that can be obtained using modus ponens. Obviously, we can make the method more powerful by including other rules of inference.

3.3 Logical Implication

In the process of inference, we have to be careful about which conclusions we draw. There are good inferences, but there are bad inferences as well. Our example at the start of the chapter illustrates a good inference. From the premise that Art is either at home or at the office and the premise that Art is not at home, we can conclude that he is at the office. On the other hand, given these premises, we do not want to conclude that Art is necessarily working, at least without further information; also, we certainly do not want to conclude that Art is somewhere else; e.g., in his car. In this section, we introduce a very strong notion of inferential correctness, based on the concept of logical implication.

We saw in Chapter 2 that, whenever we formalize information about the world, we have in mind a particular interpretation for the symbols in our language. We also saw that in general we cannot pinpoint this interpretation uniquely for another agent simply by writing down more facts. So, how can the agent know which of a set of possible conclusions are true in our interpretation? One answer to this question is for the agent to derive only those conclusions that are true in *all* interpretations that satisfy the premises. As long as the agent adheres to this constraint it does not have to know exactly which interpretation we had intended. If the premises are true, then the agent's conclusions must be true as well. This is the basis for the notion of logical implication.

A set of sentences Γ *logically implies* (synonymously, *logically entails*) a sentence ϕ (written Γ $\models$ ϕ) if and only if every interpretation and variable assignment that satisfies the sentences in Γ also satisfies ϕ. That is, Γ $\models$ ϕ if and only if $\models_I$ Γ[U] implies $\models_I$ ϕ[U] for all I and U. A set of closed sentences Γ logically entails a closed sentence ϕ if and only if every interpretation that satisfies the sentences in Γ also satisfies ϕ.

Consider the set of closed sentences that follows. These sentences logically imply the sentence Above(A,B). Any interpretation that satisfies these sentences also satisfies Above(A,B).

∀x∀y On(x,y) ⇒ Above(x,y)

On(A,B)

For example, under the intended interpretation for these symbols in our standard Blocks World example (see Figure 2.1), the sentences are clearly satisfied. The first sentence is a general property of the *on* and *above* relations. The second sentence is satisfied in this situation, because block *a* is on block *b*. The interpretation satisfies Above(A,B), because block *a* is also above block *b*.

We could try to construct a counterexample by finding an interpretation that satisfies the premises but does not satisfy the conclusion. For example, we might try an interpretation that maps On into the *under* relation and that maps Above into the *below* relation. Under this interpretation, Above(A,B) clearly is not satisfied, because *a* is not below *b*. The first sentence in the set is satisfied, because *under* implies *below*. Unfortunately, the second sentence in the set is not satisfied, because *a* is in not immediately beneath *b*. Since this interpretation does not satisfy all the sentences in the set, it is not a counterexample.

Given the notion of logical implication, we can define our criteria for evaluating inference procedures. We say that an inference procedure is *sound* if and only if any sentence that can be derived from a database using that procedure is logically implied by that database. We say that an inference procedure is *complete* if and only if any sentence logically implied by a database can be derived using that procedure. Although the procedures presented in the previous section are sound, none are complete. In the next section, we sketch a procedure that is both sound and complete, although somewhat impractical. In the next two chapters, we discuss a more practical procedure that is also sound and complete.

A *theory* is a set of sentences closed under logical implication. Since there are infinitely many conclusions from any set of sentences, a theory is necessarily infinite in extent. A theory $\mathcal{T}$ is *complete* if and only if, for every sentence ϕ, either ϕ or its negation is a member of $\mathcal{T}$.

3.4 Provability

One apparent difficulty with the practical use of logical implication as a criterion for inferential correctness is the infinity lurking in its definition. The definition in the previous section states that a database of sentences Δ logically implies a sentence ϕ if and only if every interpretation that satisfies Δ also satisfies ϕ. The problem is that the number of interpretations of any set of sentences is infinite, so there is no way to check them all in a finite amount of time.

Fortunately, the situation is not hopeless. An important theorem of mathematical logic states that whenever Δ logically implies ϕ, there is a finite "proof" of ϕ from Δ. Therefore, the question of determining logical implication is reduced to the problem of finding such a proof. As it turns out, there is a procedure for enumerating legal proofs; thus, if Δ logically implies ϕ, we can verify it in a finite amount of time.

A *proof* of a sentence ϕ from a database Δ is a finite sequence of sentences in which (1) ϕ is an element of the sequence (usually the last) and (2) every element is a member of Δ, a logical axiom, or the result of applying modus ponens to sentences earlier in the sequence. Note that we allow only one rule of inference in our definition. Thus, a proof is like a derivation, except that we include logical axioms and we use only one rule of inference. As we shall see, if we include enough logical axioms, we can ignore all other rules of inference.

A *logical axiom* is a sentence that is satisfied by all interpretations purely because of its logical form. By adding some basic logical axioms to our set of premises (which latter are called *nonlogical axioms* or *proper axioms*), we can derive conclusions that we cannot derive using modus ponens alone.

Although the number of basic logical axioms is infinite, it is possible to describe the axioms with a finite number of *axiom schemata*. An axiom schema is a sentence pattern with pattern variables (written here as Greek letters) that range over all legal sentences. Each schema denotes the set of all sentences that either match its pattern or are *generalizations* of its pattern, where a generalization of a sentence ϕ is a sentence of the form $\forall \nu \ \phi$.

The *implication introduction* schema (II), together with modus ponens, allows us to infer implications.

$$\phi \Rightarrow (\psi \Rightarrow \phi)$$

The following sentences are all instances of this schema. In the first sentence, ϕ is P(x) and ψ is Q(y). In the second sentence, ϕ is the nonatomic sentence P(x) $\Rightarrow$ R(x). The last three sentences are generalizations of the second sentence.

P(x) $\Rightarrow$ (Q(y) $\Rightarrow$ P(x))

(P(x) $\Rightarrow$ R(x)) $\Rightarrow$ (Q(y) $\Rightarrow$ (P(x) $\Rightarrow$ R(x)))

$$\forall y \ (P(x) \Rightarrow R(x)) \Rightarrow (Q(y) \Rightarrow (P(x) \Rightarrow R(x)))$$

$$\forall z \ (P(x) \Rightarrow R(x)) \Rightarrow (Q(y) \Rightarrow (P(x) \Rightarrow R(x)))$$

$$\forall x \forall y \ (P(x) \Rightarrow R(x)) \Rightarrow (Q(y) \Rightarrow (P(x) \Rightarrow R(x)))$$

The *implication distribution* schema (ID) allows us to distribute one implication over another. If ϕ implies that ψ implies χ, then, if ϕ implies ψ, it also implies χ.

$$(\phi \Rightarrow (\psi \Rightarrow \chi)) \Rightarrow ((\phi \Rightarrow \psi) \Rightarrow (\phi \Rightarrow \chi))$$

The *contradiction realization* schema (CR) permits us to infer the negation of a sentence if that sentence implies both another sentence and the negation of the other sentence.

$$(\psi \Rightarrow \neg \phi) \Rightarrow ((\psi \Rightarrow \phi) \Rightarrow \neg \psi)$$

$$(\neg \psi \Rightarrow \neg \phi) \Rightarrow ((\neg \psi \Rightarrow \phi) \Rightarrow \psi)$$

The *universal distribution* schema (UD) allows us to distribute quantification over implication.

$$(\forall \nu \ \phi \Rightarrow \psi) \Rightarrow ((\forall \nu \ \phi) \Rightarrow (\forall \nu \ \psi))$$

The *universal generalization* schema (UG) allows us to derive universally quantified statements. If a sentence ϕ does not contain ν as a free variable, then it is certainly permissible to conclude that $\forall \nu \ \phi$.

$$\phi \Rightarrow \forall \nu \ \phi \qquad \text{where } \nu \text{ does not occur free in } \phi$$

The *universal instantiation* schema (UI) states that, whenever the database contains a universally quantified sentence $\forall \nu \ \phi$, it is acceptable to add a copy of ϕ in which all occurrences of ν have been replaced by any suitable term.

$$(\forall \nu \ \phi) \Rightarrow \phi_{\nu/\tau} \qquad \text{where } \tau \text{ is free for } \nu \text{ in } \phi$$

Note that the universal instantiation schema is very similar to the universal instantiation rule of inference. In fact, given modus ponens, it allows us to draw all the same conclusions. This is the reason we can drop that rule in our definition of proof. We can drop the other rules of inference for similar reasons.

That our logical axioms are valid can be demonstrated by appeal to the semantics of $\neg$, $\Rightarrow$, and $\forall$. Similarly, we can define the other logical operators in terms of $\neg$, $\Rightarrow$, and $\forall$ by writing additional schemata that capture their semantic definitions.

The $\Leftrightarrow$ operator asserts that its two arguments imply each other. Thus, it can be defined easily in terms of the $\Rightarrow$ operator.

$$(\phi\Leftrightarrow\psi) \;\Rightarrow\; (\phi\Rightarrow\psi)$$

$$(\phi\Leftrightarrow\psi) \;\Rightarrow\; (\psi\Rightarrow\phi)$$

$$(\psi\Rightarrow\phi) \;\Rightarrow\; ((\phi\Rightarrow\psi)\Rightarrow(\phi\Leftrightarrow\psi))$$

The $\Leftarrow$ operator is just the reverse of the $\Rightarrow$ operator. We can state this equivalence using the $\Leftrightarrow$ operator.

$$(\phi\Leftarrow\psi) \;\Leftrightarrow\; (\psi\Rightarrow\phi)$$

The $\wedge$ and $\vee$ operators can be defined in terms of $\neg$ and $\Rightarrow$ operators, as follows:

$$(\phi\vee\psi) \;\Leftrightarrow\; (\neg\phi\Rightarrow\psi)$$

$$(\phi\wedge\psi) \;\Leftrightarrow\; \neg(\neg\phi\vee\neg\psi)$$

$\exists$ can be defined in terms of $\neg$ and $\forall$:

$$(\exists\nu\ \phi) \;\Leftrightarrow\; (\neg\forall\nu\ \neg\phi)$$

As an example of a proof involving logical axioms, consider the problem of proving the sentence $P \Rightarrow R$ from the sentences $P \Rightarrow Q$ and $Q \Rightarrow R$. The proof is as follows:

1.	$P \Rightarrow Q$	Δ
2.	$Q \Rightarrow R$	Δ
3.	$(Q \Rightarrow R) \Rightarrow (P \Rightarrow (Q \Rightarrow R))$	II
4.	$P \Rightarrow (Q \Rightarrow R)$	2, 3, MP
5.	$(P \Rightarrow (Q \Rightarrow R)) \Rightarrow ((P \Rightarrow Q) \Rightarrow (P \Rightarrow R))$	ID
6.	$(P \Rightarrow Q) \Rightarrow (P \Rightarrow R)$	4, 5, MP
7.	$P \Rightarrow R$	1, 6, MP

As with the previous proof, each step of this proof is completely mechanical. Nevertheless, it is somewhat difficult to follow. The difficulty results in large measure from the nonintuitiveness of the logical axioms. We chose these axiom schemata for reasons of minimality, not of perspicuity. In practice, it is often desirable to use a larger and more perspicuous set of axioms, with a resulting improvement in the understandability of proofs.

If there exists a proof of a sentence ϕ from a set Δ of premises and the logical axioms using modus ponens, then ϕ is said to be *provable* from Δ (written as $\Delta \vdash \phi$) and is called a *theorem* of Δ.

Earlier, it was suggested that there is a close connection between provability and logical implication. In fact, they are equivalent.

$$\Delta \vdash \phi \;\equiv\; \Delta \models \phi$$

The concept of provability is important in AI because it suggests how we can automate the determination of logical implication. Starting from a set of premises Δ, we enumerate conclusions from this set. If a sentence ϕ appears, then it is provable from Δ and is, therefore, a logical consequence. If the negation of ϕ appears, then $\neg\phi$ is a logical consequence of Δ and ϕ is not logically implied (unless Δ is inconsistent).

For some sets of sentences, this procedure is guaranteed to find a proof of either a sentence or that sentence's negation. In other words, for these sentences, the question of logical implication is *decidable*. Unfortunately, this is not true for all sentences. It can happen that neither ϕ nor its negation are logically implied by Δ. In cases such as this, the procedure just described will never terminate, so the question of logical implication is only *semidecidable*.

A theory T is *finitely axiomatizable* if and only if there is a finite database Δ that generates all the members of T by logical implication; i.e., if $\phi \in T$, then $\Delta \models \phi$. Obviously, if a theory is finitely axiomatizable, then it is semidecidable. However, a stronger statement can be made if a theory is not only finitely axiomatizable but also complete. (Remember that a theory T is complete if and only either $\phi \in T$ or $\neg\phi \in T$ for every sentence ϕ in the language.) In that case, every sentence or its negation is logically implied by the finite axiomatization. Therefore, if we begin a complete proof procedure and check at each step for either the sentence or its negation, eventually the procedure will halt.

Gödel used this fact to prove an interesting property of arithmetic. As it turns out, there are problems that can be expressed in the language of arithmetic that are not decidable. Therefore, by the preceding argument, no finite (and, more generally, no decidable) axiomatization of arithmetic can be complete. In short, we can never say everything that is true about arithmetic.

3.5 Proving Provability*

In talking about provability, it is often useful to show that a sentence is provable without actually exhibiting the proof. The following theorems show how the provability of one sentence can be reduced to the provability of another sentence. Thus, if the latter sentence is proved, then the former sentence is proved as well.

The deduction theorem is useful in proving sentences of the form $\phi \Rightarrow \psi$. It says that, if we *assume* the antecedent and manage to prove the consequent, then the implication as a whole is provable.

THEOREM 3.1 (Deduction Theorem)   If $\Delta \cup \{\phi\} \vdash \psi$, then $\Delta \vdash (\phi \Rightarrow \psi)$.

Proof Assume that $\Delta \cup \{\phi\} \vdash \psi$ and let n be the length of the proof for ψ. The theorem can be proved by induction on n. The case for $n = 1$ is trivial. If ψ is identical to ϕ, we can prove $\phi \Rightarrow \phi$ from the logical axioms. If ψ is a logical axiom or a member of Δ, then $\phi \Rightarrow \psi$ can be proved using modus ponens and a single instance of implication introduction. For the induction step, assume that the theorem is true for all proofs with fewer than n steps and that the last step in the proof is an application of modus ponens to two previous results χ and $\chi \Rightarrow \psi$. By the induction hypothesis, there must be a proof of $\phi \Rightarrow \chi$ and $\phi \Rightarrow (\chi \Rightarrow \psi)$ from Δ. Using modus ponens and an instance of implication distribution, there is also a proof of $\phi \Rightarrow \psi$. $\square$

Rule T is a statement of the transitivity of provability. If we can prove a set of sentences from a set of premises and we can prove other sentences from those conclusions, then we can prove the latter sentences from the original premises.

THEOREM 3.2 (Rule T) If $\Delta \vdash \phi_1, \ldots, \Delta \vdash \phi_n$ and $\{\phi_1, \ldots, \phi_n\} \vdash \phi$, then $\Delta \vdash \phi$.

Proof If $\{\phi_1, \ldots, \phi_n\} \vdash \phi$, then $\Delta \cup \{\phi_1, \ldots, \phi_n\} \vdash \phi$. By n applications of the deduction theorem, $\Delta \vdash \phi_1 \Rightarrow \ldots \Rightarrow \phi_n \Rightarrow \phi$, and by n applications of modus ponens, $\Delta \vdash \phi$. $\square$

THEOREM 3.3 (Contraposition Theorem) $\Delta \cup \{\phi\} \vdash \neg\psi$ if and only if $\Delta \cup \{\psi\} \vdash \neg\phi$.

Proof If $\Delta \cup \{\phi\} \vdash \neg\psi$, then, by the deduction theorem, $\Delta \vdash (\phi \Rightarrow \neg\psi)$. Using the logical axioms, it can be shown that $\{\phi \Rightarrow \neg\psi\} \vdash (\psi \Rightarrow \neg\phi)$. Therefore, by Rule T, $\Delta \vdash (\psi \Rightarrow \neg\phi)$. Finally, using modus ponens, we arrive at $\Delta \cup \{\psi\} \vdash \neg\phi$. The proof of the theorem in the reverse direction is symmetric. $\square$

The refutation theorem is the basis for the technique of proof by contradiction. It ensures that, if we assume the negation of a sentence and derive a contradiction, there is a direct proof of the original sentence. Remember that a set of sentences Δ is inconsistent if and only if there is some sentence ψ for which $\Delta \vdash \psi$ and $\Delta \vdash \neg\psi$.

THEOREM 3.4 (Refutation Theorem) *If $\Delta \cup \{\phi\}$ is inconsistent, then $\Delta \vdash \neg\phi$.*

Proof If $\Delta \cup \{\phi\}$ is inconsistent, then there is some sentence ψ such that $\Delta \cup \{\phi\} \vdash \psi$ and $\Delta \cup \{\phi\} \vdash \neg\psi$. From the deduction theorem, we have $\Delta \vdash (\phi \Rightarrow \psi)$ and $\Delta \vdash (\phi \Rightarrow \neg\psi)$. Using an instance of contradiction realization, we can show that $\{\phi \Rightarrow \psi, \ \phi \Rightarrow \neg\psi\} \vdash \neg\phi$. But then, by Rule T, $\Delta \vdash \neg\phi$. $\square$

THEOREM 3.5 (Generalization Theorem) *If $\Delta \vdash \phi$ and ν is a variable that does not occur free in Δ, then $\Delta \vdash \forall\nu\ \phi$.*

Proof Suppose that $\Delta \vdash \phi$, that n is the length of the proof for ϕ, and that ν does not occur free in Δ. The theorem is proved by induction on n. The case for $n = 1$ is simple. If ϕ is a member of Δ, then by hypothesis, ν does not occur free in ϕ; therefore, using universal generalization, we can show that $\forall\nu\ \phi$. If ϕ is a logical axiom, then by definition $\forall\nu\ \phi$ also is a logical axiom. For the induction step, assume that the theorem is true for all proofs with fewer than n steps and that the last step of the proof is an application of modus ponens to two previous results, χ and $\chi \Rightarrow \phi$. By the induction hypothesis, $\Delta \vdash \forall\nu\ \chi$ and $\Delta \vdash (\forall\nu\ (\chi \Rightarrow \phi))$. Using universal distribution, we can show $\Delta \vdash ((\forall\nu\ \chi) \Rightarrow (\forall\nu\ \phi))$; therefore, by modus ponens, $\Delta \vdash (\forall\nu\ \phi)$. $\square$

As an example of the use of these theorems in reducing the provability of one sentence to that of another, consider the problem of proving the following sentence.

$$(\exists x \forall y\ P(x,y)) \Rightarrow (\forall y \exists x\ P(x,y))$$

By the deduction theorem, it suffices to show that the consequent can be proved from the antecedent.

$$\exists x \forall y\ P(x,y) \vdash \forall y \exists x\ P(x,y)$$

Since there are no free occurrences of **y** in the set of premises, we know by the generalization theorem that the universally quantified conclusion can be proved if the corresponding unquantified sentence is provable.

$$\exists x \forall y\ P(x,y) \vdash \exists x\ P(x,y)$$

By substituting the definition of ∃, we can reduce this problem to the following.

$$\neg\forall x \neg\forall y\ P(x,y)\ \vdash\ \neg\forall x \neg P(x,y)$$

We can use contraposition to rewrite this problem as follows.

$$\forall x\ \neg P(x,y)\ \vdash\ \neg\neg\forall x \neg\forall y\ P(x,y)$$

Next, we can eliminate the double negative using Rule T and the fact that $\neg\neg\phi$ is provable if and only if ϕ is provable.

$$\forall x\ \neg P(x,y)\ \vdash\ \forall x \neg\forall y\ P(x,y)$$

Again using the generalization theorem, we can drop the universal quantifier.

$$\forall x\ \neg P(x,y)\ \vdash\ \neg\forall y\ P(x,y)$$

By the refutation theorem, it suffices to show that following two sentences are inconsistent.

$$\forall x\ \neg P(x,y)$$

$$\forall y\ P(x,y)$$

Finally, using universal instantiation, we can show that

$$\forall x\ \neg P(x,y)\ \vdash\ \neg P(x,y)$$

and

$$\forall y\ P(x,y)\ \vdash\ P(x,y)$$

In other words, the two sentences are inconsistent; therefore, the original sentence is provable.

In thinking about this example, it is important to keep in mind that the demonstration of the provability of the conclusion is a *metaproof*. It is a proof that a formal proof exists; it is not the formal proof itself. Although it is possible to build a program that can reason about provability at the metalevel, most automated reasoning procedures are oriented toward the generation of formal proofs rather than metaproofs.

3.6 Bibliographical and Historical Remarks

The axiom schemata introduced in this chapter are rather standard and follow the treatment by Enderton [Enderton 1972]. The equivalence of provability and logical implication was first proved by Gödel [Gödel 1930]; proofs appear in textbooks on logic. The incompleteness of any finite axiomatization of arithmetic also was proved by Gödel [Gödel 1931]. Although this result is extremely important in mathematical logic, it does not (as some people have claimed [Lucas 1961]) preclude the possibility that machines will be able to reason as well as people. People cannot prove the consistency of complex systems in this way either!

Exercises

1. *Derivability.* The law says that it is a crime to sell an unregistered gun. Red has several unregistered guns, and all of them were purchased from Lefty. Using the rules of inference given in this text, derive the conclusion that Lefty is a criminal.

2. *Inference procedures.* Define an inference procedure based on modus ponens in which the search is done in depth-first fashion.

3. *Distinctions and confusions.* Distinguish the following three statements.

    a. P $\Rightarrow$ Q

    b. P $\models$ Q

    c. P $\vdash$ Q

4. *Proofs.* Give a formal proof of the sentence $\forall x\ P(x) \Rightarrow R(x)$ from the premises $\forall x\ P(x) \Rightarrow Q(x)$ and $\forall x\ Q(x) \Rightarrow R(x)$. Note that the generalization theorem does not solve this problem. We need to use a generalized axiom schema.

5. *Substitution.* Show that, if it is possible to prove $\phi \Leftrightarrow \psi$, then it is possible to prove $\chi \Leftrightarrow \chi_{\phi/\psi}$, where $\chi_{\phi/\psi}$ is the sentence obtained by substituting ψ for ϕ in χ.

6. *Generalization on constants.* Prove that, if $\Delta \vdash \phi$ and α is an object constant that occurs in ϕ but not in Δ, then $\Delta \vdash \forall \nu\ \phi_{\alpha/\nu}$, where ν is a variable that does not occur in Δ or ϕ and where $\phi_{\alpha/\nu}$ is the expression resulting from the consistent replacement of α by ν in ϕ.

7. *Existential instantiation.* Prove that, if the object constant α does not occur in ψ or Δ and it is possible to prove ψ from Δ and ϕ, then it is possible to prove ψ from Δ and $\exists \nu\ \phi_{\alpha/\nu}$. Hint: Use Exercise 6.

CHAPTER 4

Resolution

IN THIS CHAPTER we describe an inference procedure based on a simple yet extremely powerful rule of inference known as the *resolution principle*. Because it uses just one rule of inference, the procedure is simple to analyze and implement; yet it is known to be both sound and, in a sense, complete. Section 4.1 introduces the variant of predicate calculus used by resolution; Section 4.2 defines the critical concept of unification, and Section 4.3 describes the resolution principle itself. Section 4.4 introduces the resolution procedure. Section 4.5 shows how the procedure can be used in determining satisfiability, Section 4.6 shows how it can be used in answering true-or-false questions, and Section 4.7 shows how it can be used to answer fill-in-the-blank questions. Sections 4.8 and 4.9 offer examples. Section 4.10 discusses the issues of soundness and completeness. The final section shows how resolution can be used in proving results from statements about equality.

4.1 Clausal Form

The resolution procedure takes as argument a set of expressions in a simplified version of predicate calculus, called *clausal form*. The symbols, terms, and atomic sentences of clausal form are the same as those in ordinary predicate calculus. Instead of logical and quantified sentences, however, clausal form has literals and clauses.

```
Procedure Convert (x)
1     Begin x <- Implications_out(x),
2           x <- Negations_in(x),
3           x <- Standardize_variables(x),
4           x <- Existentials_out(x),
5           x <- Universals_out(x),
6           x <- Disjunctions_in(x),
7           x <- Operators_out(x),
8           x <- Rename_variables(x)
      End
```

Figure 4.1   Conversion to clausal form.

A *literal* is an atomic sentence or the negation of an atomic sentence. An atomic sentence is a *positive* literal, and the negation of an atomic sentence is a *negative* literal.

A *clause* is a set of literals representing their disjunction. For example, the sets {On(A,B)} and {¬On(A,B),Above(A,B)} are both clauses. The first states that the block named A is on the block named B. The second clause states that either A is not on B or it is above B. A *Horn clause* is a clause with at most one positive literal.

At first glance, clausal form may appear very restrictive, but this is illusory. For any sentence in predicate calculus, there is a set of clauses that is equivalent to the original sentence in that the sentence is satisfiable if and only if the corresponding set of clauses is satisfiable. The procedure defined in Figure 4.1 sketches a method for converting an arbitrary closed sentence into its clausal form.

In the first step, we eliminate all occurrences of the $\Rightarrow$, $\Leftarrow$, and $\Leftrightarrow$ operators by substituting equivalent sentences involving only the $\neg$, $\wedge$, and $\vee$ operators.

- $\phi \Rightarrow \psi$ is replaced by $\neg\phi \vee \psi$.

- $\phi \Leftarrow \psi$ is replaced by $\phi \vee \neg\psi$.

- $\phi \Leftrightarrow \psi$ is replaced by $(\neg\phi \vee \psi) \wedge (\phi \vee \neg\psi)$.

In the second step, negations are distributed over other logical operators until each such operator applies to a single atomic sentence. The following replacement rules do the job.

- $\neg\neg\phi$ is replaced by ϕ.

- $\neg(\phi \wedge \psi)$ is replaced by $\neg\phi \vee \neg\psi$.

- $\neg(\phi \vee \psi)$ is replaced by $\neg\phi \wedge \neg\psi$.

- ¬∀ν φ is replaced by ∃ν ¬φ.

- ¬∃ν φ is replaced by ∀ν ¬φ.

In the third step, we rename variables so that each quantifier has a unique variable; i.e., the same variable is not quantified more than once within the same sentence. For example, we can replace the formula (∀x P(x,x)) ∧ (∃x Q(x)) by (∀x P(x,x)) ∧ (∃y Q(y)).

In the fourth step, we eliminate all existential quantifiers. The method for doing this is a little complicated, and we describe it in two stages.

If an existential quantifier does not occur within the scope of a universal quantifier, we simply drop the quantifier and replace all occurrences of the quantified variable by a new constant; i.e., one that does not occur anywhere else in our database. Thus, if we have never before used the object constant A, we can replace ∃x P(x) by P(A). The constant used to replace the existential variable in this case is called a *Skolem constant.*

If an existential quantifier is within the scope of any universal quantifiers, there is the possibility that the value of the existential variable depends on the values of the associated universal variables. Consequently, we cannot replace the existential variable with a constant. Instead, the general rule is to drop the existential quantifier and to replace the associated variable by a term formed from a new function symbol applied to the variables associated with the enclosing universal quantifiers. For example, if F is a new function symbol, we can replace ∀x∀y∃z P(x,y,z) with the sentence ∀x∀y P(x,y,F(x,y)). Any function defined in this way is called a *Skolem function.*

In the fifth step, we drop all universal quantifiers. Because the remaining variables at this point are universally quantified, this does not introduce any ambiguities.

In the sixth step, we put the expression into *conjunctive normal form*; i.e., a conjunction of disjunctions of literals. This can be accomplished by repeated use of the following rule.

- φ ∨ (ψ ∧ χ) is replaced by (φ ∨ ψ) ∧ (φ ∨ χ).

In the seventh step, we eliminate operators by writing the conjunction obtained in the sixth step as a set of clauses. For example, we replace the sentence P ∧ (Q ∨ R) with the set consisting of the singleton clause {P} and the binary clause {Q,R}.

In the final step, we rename variables so that no variable appears in more than one clause. This process is called *standardizing the variables apart.*

As an example of this conversion process, consider the problem of transforming the following expression to clausal form. The initial expression appears on the top line, and the expressions on the numbered lines are the results of the corresponding steps of the conversion procedure.

initial: ∀x (∀y P(x,y)) ⇒ ¬(∀y Q(x,y) ⇒ R(x,y))
step 1: ∀x ¬(∀y P(x,y)) ∨ ¬(∀y ¬Q(x,y) ∨ R(x,y))

step 2: $\forall x \ (\exists y \ \neg P(x,y)) \ \lor \ (\exists y \ Q(x,y) \ \land \ \neg R(x,y))$

step 3: $\forall x \ (\exists y \ \neg P(x,y)) \ \lor \ (\exists z \ Q(x,z) \ \land \ \neg R(x,z))$

step 4: $\forall x \ \neg P(x,F1(x)) \ \lor \ (Q(x,F2(x)) \ \land \ \neg R(x,F2(x)))$

step 5: $\neg P(x,F1(x)) \ \lor \ (Q(x,F2(x)) \ \land \ \neg R(x,F2(x)))$

step 6: $(\neg P(x,F1(x)) \ \lor \ Q(x,F2(x))) \ \land$
        $(\neg P(x,F1(x)) \ \lor \ \neg R(x,F2(x)))$

step 7: $\{\neg P(x,F1(x)), \ Q(x,F2(x))\}$
        $\{\neg P(x,F1(x)), \ \neg R(x,F2(x))\}$

step 8: $\{\neg P(x1,F1(x1)), \ Q(x1,F2(x1))\}$
        $\{\neg P(x2,F1(x2)), \ \neg R(x2,F2(x2))\}$

4.2 Unification

Unification is the process of determining whether two expressions can be made identical by appropriate substitutions for their variables. As we shall see, making this determination is an essential part of resolution.

A *substitution* is any finite set of associations between variables and expressions in which (1) each variable is associated with at most one expression, and (2) no variable with an associated expression occurs within any of the associated expressions. For example, the following set of pairs is a substitution in which the variable x is associated with the symbol A, the variable y is associated with the term F(B), and the variable z is associated with the variable w.

$$\{x/A, y/F(B), z/w\}$$

Each variable has at most one associated expression, and no variable with an associated expression occurs within any of the associated expressions.

By contrast, the following set of pairs is not a substitution.

$$\{x/G(y), y/F(x)\}$$

The variable x, which is associated with G(y), occurs in the expression F(x) associated with y; the variable y occurs in the expression G(y) associated with x.

We often speak of the terms associated with the variables in a substitution as *bindings* for those variables; the substitution itself is called a *binding list*; and the variables with bindings are said to be *bound*.

A substitution can be *applied* to a predicate-calculus expression to produce a new expression (called a *substitution instance*) by replacing all bound variables in the expression by their bindings. Variables without bindings are left unchanged. In contrast to the usual functional notation, it is customary to write $\phi\sigma$ to denote the substitution instance obtained by applying the substitution σ to the expression ϕ. For example, applying the preceding legitimate substitution to the expression on the left in the following equation results in the expression shown on the right. Note that both occurrences of the variable x are replaced by A and that variable v, having no associated expression, is simply left alone.

$$P(x, x, y, v)\{x/A, y/F(B), z/w\} = P(A, A, F(B), v)$$

A substitution τ is *distinct* from a substitution σ if and only if no variable bound in σ occurs anywhere in τ (although variables with bindings in τ may occur in σ). Now, consider a substitution σ and a distinct substitution τ. The *composition* of τ with σ (again, written backward as $\sigma\tau$) is the substitution obtained by applying τ to the terms of σ and then adding to σ the bindings from τ. In the following example, the bindings for x and y are plugged into the binding for w in the first substitution, and then the bindings from the second substitution are added to the resulting set of associations.

$$\{w/G(x, y)\}\{x/A, y/B, z/C\} = \{w/G(A, B), x/A, y/B, z/C\}$$

A set of expressions $\{\phi_1, \ldots, \phi_n\}$ is *unifiable* if and only if there is a substitution σ that makes the expressions identical; i.e., $\phi_1\sigma = \cdots = \phi_n\sigma$. In such a case, σ is said to be a *unifier* for the set. For example, the substitution $\{x/A, y/B, z/C\}$ unifies the expression P(A,y,z) and the expression P(x,B,z) to yield P(A,B,C).

$$P(A, y, z)\{x/A, y/B, z/C\} = P(A, B, C) = P(x, B, z)\{x/A, y/B, z/C\}$$

Although this substitution unifies the two expressions, it is not the only unifier. We do not have to substitute C for z to unify the two expressions. We can equally well substitute D or F(C) or F(w). In fact, we can unify the expressions without changing z at all. In looking at these alternatives, it is worth noting that some substitutions are more general than others are; e.g., the substitution $\{z/F(w)\}$ is more general than $\{z/F(C)\}$ is. We say that a substitution σ is as general as or more general than a substitution τ if and only if there is another substitution δ such that $\sigma\delta = \tau$. It is interesting to consider unifiers with maximum generality. A *most general unifier*, or *mgu*, γ of ϕ and ψ has the property that, if σ is any unifier of the two expressions, then there exists a substitution δ with the following property.

$$\phi\gamma\delta = \phi\sigma = \psi\sigma$$

An important property of any most general unifier is that it is unique up to variable renaming. The substitution $\{x/A\}$ is a most general unifier for the expressions P(A,y,z) and P(x,y,z). The less general unifier, $\{x/A, y/B, z/C\}$, can be obtained by composing the most general one with the substitution $\{y/B, z/C\}$. Because of this property, we often speak of *the* most general unifier of two expressions.

```
Recursive Procedure Mgu (x,y)
    Begin x=y ==> Return(),
          Variable(x) ==> Return(Mguvar(x,y)),
          Variable(y) ==> Return(Mguvar(y,x)),
          Constant(x) or Constant(y) ==> Return(False),
          Not(Length(x)=Length(y)) ==> Return(False),
          Begin i <- 0,
                g <- [],
          Tag   i=Length(x) ==> Return(g),
                s <- Mgu(Part(x,i),Part(y,i))
                s=False ==> Return(False),
                g <- Compose(g,s),
                x <- Substitute(x,g),
                y <- Substitute(y,g),
                i <- i + 1,
                Goto Tag
          End
    End

    Procedure Mguvar (x,y)
        Begin Includes(x,y) ==> Return(False),
              Return([x/y])
        End
```

Figure 4.2   Procedure for computing the most general unifier.

Figure 4.2 presents a simple recursive procedure for computing the most general unifier of two expressions. If two expressions are unifiable, the procedure returns the most general unifier. Otherwise, it returns False.

The procedure assumes that an expression is a constant, a variable, or a structured object. The predicate Variable is true of variables, and the predicate Constant is true of constants. A structured object consists of a function constant, relation constant, or operator and some number of arguments. The Length of a structured object is equal to the number of arguments. The top-level function constant, relation constant, or operator in a structured object is its zeroth Part, and the arguments are the other parts. For example, the expression F(A,G(y)) can be represented as a structured object of length 2. The zeroth part is the constant F, the first part is the constant A, and the second part is the term G(y).

The definition uses several subroutines that are undefined in Figure 4.2. Substitute takes as argument an expression and a substitution represented as a set of bindings and returns the expression that results from applying the substitution to the expression. Compose takes as argument two substitutions and returns their composition. The predicate Includes takes as argument a variable and an expression and returns True if and only if the variable is contained in the expression.

The use of Includes in Mguvar is called an *occur check*, since it is used to check whether or not the variable occurs within the term with which it is being unified. Without this check, the algorithm would find that expressions such as P(x) and P(F(x)) are unifiable, even though there is no substitution for x that could ever make them look alike.

4.3 Resolution Principle

The idea of resolution is simple. If we know that P is true or Q is true and we also know that P is false or R is true, then it must be the case that Q is true or R is true. The general definition is a little complicated, and we introduce it in three stages.

Resolution without regard to variables is the simplest case. Given a clause containing a literal ϕ and another clause containing the literal $\neg\phi$, we can infer the clause consisting of all the literals of both clauses without the complementary pair.

$$\frac{\begin{array}{ll}\Phi & \text{with } \phi \in \Phi \\ \Psi & \text{with } \neg\phi \in \Psi\end{array}}{(\Phi - \{\phi\}) \cup (\Psi - \{\neg\phi\})}$$

As an example, consider the following deduction. The first premise asserts that either P or Q is true. The second premise states that either P is false or R is true. From these premises, we can infer by resolution that either Q is true or R is true. The Δ notation on the right indicates that the associated clauses are in the initial database, and the numbers indicate the clauses from which the associated clause is derived.

1. {P,Q} Δ
2. {¬P,R} Δ
3. {Q,R}   1, 2

Since clauses are sets, there cannot be two occurrences of any literal in a clause. Therefore, in drawing a conclusion from two clauses that share a literal, we merge the two occurrences into one, as in the following example.

1. {P,Q} Δ
2. {¬P,Q} Δ
3. {Q}   1, 2

If either of the clauses is a singleton set, we see that the number of literals in the result is less than the number of literals in the other clause. From the clause $\{\neg P, Q\}$ and the singleton clause $\{P\}$, we can derive the singleton clause $\{Q\}$. Note the correspondence between this deduction and that of modus ponens, illustrated on the right.

1.	$\{\neg P, Q\}$	Δ		1.	$P \Rightarrow Q$	Δ
2.	$\{P\}$	Δ		2.	P	Δ
3.	$\{Q\}$	1, 2		3.	Q	1, 2

Resolving two singleton clauses leads to the *empty clause*; i.e., the clause consisting of no literals at all, as shown below. The derivation of the empty clause means that the database contains a contradiction.

1. $\{P\}$ Δ
2. $\{\neg P\}$ Δ
3. $\{\}$ 1, 2

Unfortunately, our simple definition of resolution is too simple. It provides no way to instantiate variables. Fortunately, we can solve this problem by redefining the resolution principle using the notion of unification.

Suppose that Φ and Ψ are two clauses. If there is a literal ϕ in Φ and a literal $\neg\psi$ in Ψ such that ϕ and ψ have a most general unifier γ, then we can infer the clause obtained by applying the substitution γ to the union of Φ and Ψ minus the complementary literals.

$$\begin{array}{ll} \Phi & \text{with } \phi \in \Phi \\ \Psi & \text{with } \neg\psi \in \Psi \\ \hline ((\Phi - \{\phi\}) \cup (\Psi - \{\neg\psi\}))\gamma & \text{where } \phi\gamma = \psi\gamma \end{array}$$

The following deduction illustrates the use of unification in applying the resolution rule. In this case, the first disjunct of the first sentence unifies with the negation of the first disjunct of the second sentence, with mgu $\{x/A\}$.

1. $\{P(x), Q(x,y)\}$ Δ
2. $\{\neg P(A), R(B,z)\}$ Δ
3. $\{Q(A,y), R(B,z)\}$ 1, 2

If two clauses resolve, they may have more than one resolvent because there may be more than one way in which to choose ϕ and ψ. Consider the following deductions. In the first, $\phi = P(x,x)$ and $\psi = P(A,z)$, and the mgu is $\{x/A\}, \{z/A\}$. In the second, $\phi = Q(x)$ and $\psi = Q(B)$, and the mgu is $\{x/B\}$. Fortunately, two sentences can have at most a finite number of resolvents.

1. $\{P(x,x),Q(x),R(x)\}$ Δ
2. $\{\neg P(A,z),\neg Q(B)\}$ Δ
3. $\{Q(A),R(A),\neg Q(B)\}$ 1, 2
4. $\{P(B,B),R(B),\neg P(A,z)\}$ 1, 2

Unfortunately, even this definition is not quite enough. For example, given the clauses $\{P(u),P(v)\}$ and $\{\neg P(x),\neg P(y)\}$, we should be able to infer the empty clause $\{\}$—i.e., a contradiction—and this is impossible with the preceding definition. Fortunately, we can solve this problem with one final modification to our definition.

If a subset of the literals in a clause Φ has a most general unifier γ, then the clause Φ' obtained by applying γ to Φ is called a *factor* of Φ. For example, the literals $P(x)$ and $P(F(y))$ have a most general unifier $\{x/F(y)\}$, so the clause $\{P(F(y)),R(F(y),y)\}$ is a factor of $\{P(x),P(F(y)),R(x,y)\}$. Obviously, any clause is a trivial factor of itself.

Using the notion of factors, we can give our official definition for the *resolution principle*. Suppose that Φ and Ψ are two clauses. If there is a literal ϕ in some factor Φ' of Φ and a literal $\neg\psi$ in some factor Ψ' of Ψ such that ϕ and ψ have a most general unifier γ, then we say that the two clauses Φ and Ψ *resolve* and that the new clause, $((\Phi' - \{\phi\}) \cup (\Psi' - \{\neg\psi\}))\gamma$, is a *resolvent* of the two clauses.

$$
\begin{array}{ll}
\Phi & \text{with } \phi \in \Phi' \\
\underline{\Psi} & \text{with } \neg\psi \in \Psi' \\
((\Phi' - \{\phi\}) \cup (\Psi' - \{\neg\psi\}))\gamma & \text{where } \phi\gamma = \psi\gamma
\end{array}
$$

Standardizing variables apart can be interpreted as a trivial application of factoring. In particular, our definition allows us to rename the variables in one clause so that there are no conflicts with the variables in another clause. Situations in which there are nontrivial factors are extremely rare in practice, and none of the clauses in our subsequent examples contain any nontrivial factors. Consequently, except for variable renaming, we ignore factors in the remainder of our discussion.

4.4 Resolution

A *resolution deduction* of a clause Φ from a database Δ is a sequence of clauses in which (1) Φ is an element of the sequence, and (2) each element is either a member of Δ or the result of applying the resolution principle to clauses earlier in the sequence.

For example, the following sequence of clauses is a resolution deduction of the empty clause from the set of clauses labeled Δ. The clause in line 5 is derived from the clauses in lines 1 and 2; the clause in line 6 is derived from the clauses in lines 3 and 4; and the conclusion (line 7) is derived by resolving these two conclusions (lines 5 and 6) with each other.

1. {P}   Δ
2. {¬P,Q}   Δ
3. {¬Q,R}   Δ
4. {¬R}   Δ
5. {Q}   1, 2
6. {¬Q}   3, 4
7. {}   5, 6

Figure 4.3 outlines a nondeterministic procedure for resolution. There is a termination condition in the first line that varies from use to use. The next few sections describe several uses with different termination conditions. If the termination condition is not satisfied, the procedure selects clauses Phi and Psi, adds their resolvents to the clause set Delta, and repeats. The Resolvents subroutine is assumed to compute all the resolvents of the two clauses and to standardize their variables apart from those in the rest of the database; e.g., by using new variable names.

This procedure could be used to generate the previous resolution deduction. In this case, we made the right choices for Phi and Psi at each point, but we might just as well have chosen other resolutions. Figure 4.4 shows the graph of possible resolutions from the initial database, expanded out to three levels of deduction. A graph of this sort is called a *resolution graph*.

One of the problems with inference graphs such as the one in Figure 4.4 is that they are difficult to lay out in two dimensions. Fortunately, we can encode such graphs in linear form. A *resolution trace* is a sequence of annotated clauses separated into *levels*. The first level contains just the clauses in the initial database. Each subsequent level contains all clauses with at least one parent at the previous level. As with proofs, the annotations specify the clauses from which they are derived. For example, the following resolution trace captures the information from the resolution graph in Figure 4.4.

1. {P}   Δ
2. {¬P,Q}   Δ
3. {¬Q,R}   Δ
4. {¬R}   Δ
_____
5. {Q}   1, 2
6. {¬P,R}   2, 3
7. {¬Q}   3, 4
_____
8. {R}   3, 5
9. {R}   1, 6
10. {¬P}   4, 6

```
Procedure Resolution (Delta)
     Repeat Termination(Delta) ==> Return(Success),
           Phi <- Choose(Delta), Psi <- Choose(Delta),
           Chi <- Choose(Resolvents(Phi,Psi)),
           Delta <- Concatenate(Delta,[Chi])
     End
```

Figure 4.3   The resolution procedure.

11. $\{\neg P\}$ 2, 7
12. $\{\}$ 5, 7

We can generate resolution traces mechanically as follows. We store the database as a list of clauses, with two pointers initialized to the head of the list. We let the first pointer range over the list until it reaches the second pointer, after which the first pointer is reinitialized to the head of the list and the second pointer is advanced to the next element in the list. For each combination of pointers, we compute the resolvents of the corresponding clauses and add them to the end of the list. This procedure in effect searches the inference graph in a breadth-first fashion.

Although it is not part of the definition of resolution, it is common to augment resolution procedures (or indeed any deduction procedure) with

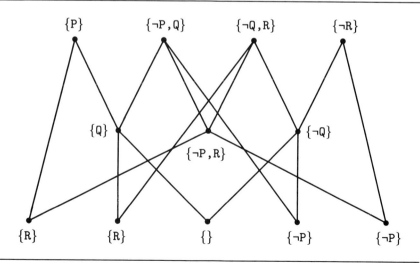

Figure 4.4   Three-level resolution graph.

various instances of *procedural attachment*. This is especially useful when the machine running the procedure has special programs for evaluating the truth of certain literals under their standard interpretations. Typically, evaluations are performed for ground instances. For example, if the predicate symbol > stands for the *greater than* relation between numbers, it is a simple matter to evaluate ground instances such as 7>3 when they occur, whereas we probably would not want to include in the base set a table of numbers that satisfy this relation.

It is instructive to look more closely at what is meant by "evaluating" an expression such as 7>3. Predicate-calculus expressions are linguistic constructs that denote objects, functions, or relations in a domain. Such expressions can be interpreted with reference to a model that associates linguistic entities with appropriate domain entities.

Given a model, we can use any finite processes for interpretation with respect to it as a way of deciding the truth or falsity of sentences. Unfortunately, models and interpretation processes are not, in general, finite—but we often can use partial models. In our inequality example, we can associate with the predicate symbol > a computer program that compares numbers within the finite domain of the program. Let us call this program `Greaterp`. We say that the program `Greaterp` is *attached* to the predicate symbol >. We can associate the linguistic symbols 7 and 3 (i.e., numerals) with the computer data objects 7 and 3, respectively. We say that 7 is attached to 7 and that 3 is attached to 3, and the computer program and arguments represented by `Greaterp(7,3)` are attached to the linguistic expression 7>3. Then we can run the program to determine that 7 is indeed greater than 3.

We also can attach procedures to function symbols. For example, an addition program can be attached to the function symbol +. In this manner, we can establish a connection or procedural attachment between executable computer code and some of the linguistic expressions in our predicate-calculus language. Evaluation of attached procedures can be thought of as a process of interpretation with respect to a partial model. When it can be used, procedural attachment reduces the search effort that would otherwise be required to prove theorems.

A literal is evaluated when it is interpreted by running attached procedures. Typically, not all the literals in a set of clauses can be evaluated, but the clause set can, nevertheless, be simplified by such evaluations. If a literal is determined to be false, then the occurrence of just that literal in the clause can be eliminated. If a literal in a clause is determined to be true, the entire clause can be eliminated without affecting the unsatisfiability of the rest of the set. The clause {P(x),Q(x),7<3} can be replaced by {P(x),Q(x)}, since 7<3 is false. The clause {P(x),Q(x),7>3} can be eliminated, since the literal 7>3 is true. Attachment of linguistic objects to semantic elements is an important idea with general application in AI.

4.5 Unsatisfiability

The simplest use of resolution is in demonstrating unsatisfiability. If a set of clauses is unsatisfiable, then it is always possible by resolution to derive a contradiction from the clauses in the set. In clausal form, a contradiction takes the form of the empty clause, which is equivalent to a disjunction of no literals. Thus, to automate the determination of unsatisfiablity, all we need do is to use resolution to derive consequences from the set to be tested, terminating whenever the empty clause is generated.

The derivation presented in the Section 4.4 is a good example of using resolution to demonstrate unsatisfiability. Since resolution generates the empty clause, the initial set is unsatisfiable.

Demonstrating that a set of clauses is unsatisfiable can also be used to demonstrate that a formula is logically implied by a set of formulas. Suppose we wish to show that the set of formulas Δ logically implies the formula ψ. We can do this by finding a proof of ψ from Δ; i.e., by establishing $\Delta \vdash \psi$. By the refutation theorem (Chapter 3), we can establish $\Delta \vdash \psi$ by showing that $\Delta \cup \{\neg\psi\}$ is inconsistent (unsatisfiable). Thus, if we show that the set of formulas $\Delta \cup \{\neg\psi\}$ is unsatisfiable, we have demonstrated that Δ logically implies ψ.

Let us look at this technique from the standpoint of models. If $\Delta \models \psi$, then all the models of Δ also are models of ψ. Hence, none of these can be models of $\neg\psi$, and thus $\Delta \cup \neg\psi$ is unsatisfiable. Conversely, suppose $\Delta \cup \neg\psi$ is unsatisfiable but that Δ is satisfiable. Let I be an interpretation that satisfies Δ; I does not satisfy $\neg\psi$, because, if it did, $\Delta \cup \neg\psi$ would be satisfiable. Therefore, I satisfies ψ. (An interpretation must satisfy one of either ψ or $\neg\psi$.) Since this holds for arbitrary I satisfying Δ, it holds for all I satisfying Δ. Thus, all models of Δ are also models of ψ, and Δ logically implies ψ.

To apply this technique of establishing logical implication by establishing unsatisfiability using resolution, we first negate ψ and add it to Δ to yield Δ'. We then convert Δ' to clausal form and apply resolution. If the empty clause is produced, the original Δ' was unsatisfiable, and we have demonstrated that Δ logically entails ψ. This process is called a *resolution refutation*; it is illustrated by examples in the following sections.

4.6 True-or-False Questions

One application of proving logical implication through resolution refutation is in answering true-or-false questions. As an example, consider the following resolution trace. The database includes the facts that Art is the father of Jon, that Bob is the father of Kim, and that fathers are parents. To prove that Art is a parent of Jon, we negate the formula representing this fact to get clause 4, which states that Art is not a parent of Jon. The Γ notation indicates that the associated clause is derived from the negated formula to be proved. As in preceding examples, the Δ notation indicates that the associated clause is in the initial database.

1. $\{F(Art,Jon)\}$ Δ
2. $\{F(Bob,Kim)\}$ Δ
3. $\{\neg F(x,y),P(x,y)\}$ Δ
4. $\{\neg P(Art,Jon)\}$ Γ

5. $\{P(Art,Jon)\}$ 1, 3
6. $\{P(Bob,Kim)\}$ 2, 3
7. $\{\neg F(Art,Jon)\}$ 3, 4

8. $\{\}$ 4, 5
9. $\{\}$ 1, 7

We often refer to the formula we are trying to prove as a *goal* and to the clauses that result from its negation as *goal clauses*. In this previous example, there is just one goal clause. The negation and conversion of more complex questions can lead to several goal clauses, all of which must be added to the database. In some cases, several or all of these goal clauses must be used to derive a result.

Suppose, for example, that we knew nothing about Art or John and we wanted to prove the simple tautology that either Art is the father of Jon or he is not. The goal in this case is the disjunction $F(Art,Jon) \vee \neg F(Art,Jon)$. Negating this sentence and converting to clausal form leads to the first two clauses in the following resolution trace. These two clauses can be resolved with each other directly to produce the empty clause and so prove the result.

1. $\{\neg F(Art,Jon)\}$ Γ
2. $\{F(Art,Jon)\}$ Γ

3. $\{\}$ 1, 2

In addition to answering true-or-false questions from databases, resolution is useful in proving mathematical theorems and program correctness. Examples are given in Section 4.9 and in the Exercises.

4.7 Fill-in-the-Blank Questions

In Section 4.6, we saw how to use resolution in answering true-or-false questions (e.g., *Is Art one of Jon's parents?*). In this section, we show how resolution can be used to answer fill-in-the-blank questions as well (e.g., *Who is Jon's parent?*).

A fill-in-the-blank question is a predicate-calculus sentence with free variables specifying the blanks to be filled in. The goal is to find bindings for the free variables such that the database logically implies the sentence obtained by substituting the bindings into the original question. For example, to ask about Jon's parent, we would write the question P(x,Jon). Using the database from the previous section, we see that Art is an answer to this question, since the sentence P(Art,Jon) is logically implied by the database.

An *answer literal* for a fill-in-the-blank question ϕ is a term of the form Ans($\nu_1,\ldots,\nu_n$), where the variables $\nu_1,\ldots,\nu_n$ are the free variables in ϕ. To answer ϕ, we form a disjunction from the negation of ϕ and its answer literal and convert to clausal form. For example, the negation of P(x,Jon) is combined with its answer literal Ans(x) to form the the disjunction ¬P(x,Jon) ∨ Ans(x), which leads to the clause {¬P(x,Jon),Ans(x)}.

We then use resolution as described in Section 4.4, except that we change the termination test. Rather than waiting for the empty clause to be produced, the procedure halts as soon as it derives a clause consisting of only answer literals. The following resolution trace shows how we compute the answer to *Who is Jon's father?*

1. {F(Art,Jon)}   Δ
2. {F(Bob,Kim)}   Δ
3. {¬F(x,y),P(x,y)}   Δ
4. {¬P(z,Jon),Ans(z)}   Γ

5. {P(Art,Jon)}   1, 3
6. {P(Bob,Kim)}   2, 3
7. {¬F(w,Jon),Ans(w)}   3, 4

8. {Ans(Art)}   4, 5
9. {Ans(Art)}   1, 7

If this procedure produces only one answer literal, the terms it contains constitute the only answer to the question. In some cases, the result of a fill-in-the-blank resolution depends on the refutation by which it is produced. In general, several different refutations can result from the same query. In some cases, as in this one, the answers may be the same; in other cases, there may be a difference.

Suppose, for example, that we knew the identities of both the father and mother of Jon and that we asked *Who is one of Jon's parents?* The following resolution trace shows that we can derive two answers to this question.

1. {F(Art,Jon)}   Δ
2. {M(Ann,Jon)}   Δ
3. {¬F(x,y),P(x,y)}   Δ
4. {¬M(u,v),P(u,v)}   Δ
5. {¬P(z,Jon),Ans(z)}   Γ

  6. {P(Art,Jon)}   1, 3
  7. {P(Ann,Jon)}   2, 4
  8. {¬F(s,Jon),Ans(s)}   3, 5
  9. {¬M(t,Jon),Ans(t)}   4, 5
  _____
 10. {Ans(Art)}   5, 6
 11. {Ans(Ann)}   5, 7
 12. {Ans(Art)}   1, 8
 13. {Ans(Ann)}   2, 9

Unfortunately, we have no way of knowing whether or not the answer statement from a given refutation exhausts the possibilities. We can continue to search for answers until we find enough of them. However, due to the undecidabilty of logical implication, we can never know in general whether we have found all the possible answers.

Another interesting aspect of fill-in-the-blank resolution is that in some cases the procedure can result in a clause containing more than one answer literal. The significance of this is that no one answer is guaranteed to work, but one of the answers must be correct.

The following resolution trace illustrates this fact. The database in this case is a disjunction asserting that either Art or Bob is the father of Jon, but we do not know which man is. The goal is to find the father of John. After resolving the goal clause with the database disjunction, we get a clause that can once again be resolved with the goal clause yielding a clause with two answer literals.

  1. {F(Art,Jon),F(Bob,Jon)}   Δ
  2. {¬F(x,Jon),Ans(x)}   Γ
  _____
  3. {F(Bob,Jon),Ans(Art)}   1, 2
  _____
  4. {Ans(Art),Ans(Bob)}   2, 3

In such situations, we can continue searching in hope of finding a more specific answer. However, given the undecidability of logical implication, we can never know in general whether we can stop and say that no more specific answer exists.

4.8 Circuits Example

One advantage of describing a circuit in predicate calculus is that we can use automated deduction procedures, such as resolution, to reason about the circuit in a variety of ways. For example, we can simulate the behavior of the circuit for given values of the inputs, we can diagnose its failures, and we can generate tests to ensure that it is working properly.

The first step in performing any of these tasks is to convert the description to clausal form. Consider the circuit described in Figure 2.3. The structural description of the circuit is easily transformed, since the sentences are all atomic.

1. {Xorg(X1)}
2. {Xorg(X2)}
3. {Andg(A1)}
4. {Andg(A2)}
5. {Org(O1)}

6. {Conn(I(1,F1),I(1,X1))}
7. {Conn(I(2,F1),I(2,X1))}
8. {Conn(I(1,F1),I(1,A1))}
9. {Conn(I(2,F1),I(2,A1))}
10. {Conn(I(3,F1),I(2,X2))}
11. {Conn(I(3,F1),I(1,A2))}
12. {Conn(O(1,X1),I(1,X2))}
13. {Conn(O(1,X1),I(2,A2))}
14. {Conn(O(1,A2),I(1,O1))}
15. {Conn(O(1,A1),I(2,O1))}
16. {Conn(O(1,X2),O(1,F1))}
17. {Conn(O(1,O1),O(2,F1))}

Since the behavior of each of the components is described by a simple implication, there is one clause for each sentence in the behavioral description. Recall that the function (denoted by) I maps an integer and a device into the corresponding input port of the device, the function O maps an integer and a device into the corresponding output port, and the relation V is true of a port and a signal if and only if the specified port is carrying the specified signal.

18. {¬Andg(d),¬V(I(1,d),1),¬V(I(2,d),1),V(O(1,d),1)}
19. {¬Andg(d),¬V(I(n,d),0),V(O(1,d),0)}

20. {¬Org(d),¬V(I(n,d),1),V(O(1,d),1)}
21. {¬Org(d),¬V(I(1,d),0),¬V(I(2,d),0),V(O(1,d),0)}

22. {¬Xorg(d),¬V(I(1,d),y),¬V(I(2,d),z),y=z,V(O(1,d),1)}
23. {¬Xorg(d),¬V(I(1,d),z),¬V(I(2,d),z),V(O(1,d),0)}

24. {¬Conn(x,y),¬V(x,z),V(y,z)}

We also need to express the fact that the two possible digital values are not equal to each other. If there were a large or infinite number of possible values, such inequalities would have to be handled by procedural attachment; since there are only two, however, the following two clauses are sufficient.

25. {1≠0}
26. {0≠1}

Starting with these facts about the circuit, we can use resolution to simulate its behavior, as illustrated by the following resolution proof. The sentences in the first three lines assert that the inputs to the circuit are 1, 0, and 1. The conclusions at the end of the proof state that the outputs of the device are 0 and 1.

A1.	{V(I(1,F1),1)}	Δ
A2.	{V(I(2,F1),0)}	Δ
A3.	{V(I(3,F1),1)}	Δ
A4.	{¬V(I(1,F1),z),V(I(1,X1),z)}	6, 24
A5.	{V(I(1,X1),1)}	A1, A4
A6.	{¬V(I(2,F1),z),V(I(2,X1),z)}	7, 24
A7.	{V(I(2,X1),0)}	A2, A6
A8.	{¬V(I(1,X1),y),¬V(I(2,X1),z),y=z, V(O(1,X1),1)}	1, 22
A9.	{¬V(I(2,X1),z),1=z,V(O(1,X1),1)}	A5, A8
A10.	{1=0,V(O(1,X1),1)}	A7, A9
A11.	{V(O(1,X1),1)}	25, A10
A12.	{¬V(O(1,X1),z),V(I(1,X2),z)}	12, 24
A13.	{V(I(1,X2),1)}	A11, A12
A14.	{¬V(I(3,F1),z),V(I(2,X2),z)}	10, 24
A15.	{V(I(2,X2),1)}	A3, A14
A16.	{¬V(I(1,X2),z),¬V(I(2,X2),z), V(O(1,X2),0)}	2, 23
A17.	{¬V(I(2,X2),1),V(O(1,X2),0)}	A13, A16
A18.	{V(O(1,X2),0)}	A15, A17
A19.	{¬V(I(3,F1),z),V(I(1,A2),z)}	11, 24
A20.	{V(I(1,A2),1)}	A3, A19
A21.	{¬V(O(1,X1),z),V(I(2,A2),z)}	13, 24
A22.	{V(I(2,A2),1)}	A11, A21
A23.	{¬V(I(1,A2),1),¬V(I(2,A2),1), V(O(1,A2),1)}	4, 18
A24.	{¬V(I(2,A2),1),V(O(1,A2),1)}	A20, A23
A25.	{V(O(1,A2),1)}	A22, A24
A26.	{¬V(O(1,A2),z),V(I(1,O1),z)}	14, 24
A27.	{V(I(1,O1),1)}	A25, A26
A28.	{¬V(I(n,O1),1),V(O(1,O1),1)}	5, 20
A29.	{V(O(1,O1),1)}	A27, A28
A30.	{¬V(O(1,X2),z),V(O(1,F1),z)}	16, 24
A31.	{V(O(1,F1),0)}	A18, A30

A32. $\{\neg V(O(1,O1),z),V(O(2,F1),z)\}$ 17, 24
A33. $\{V(O(2,F1),1)\}$ A29, A32

We also can diagnose faults in an instance of the circuit. In this case, let us suppose that the first output of the circuit is 1 instead of 0. Something must be wrong. Either a gate is not working correctly or a connection is bad. For simplicity, assume that all connections are guaranteed to be okay. To avoid contradictions, the type statements about the components must be removed from the knowledge base. By starting with a statement of the symptom (the negation of the expected behavior), we can deduce a set of suspect components, as shown below. B17 asserts that either X1 is not acting as an *xor* gate or X2 is not acting as an *xor* gate; i.e., at least one of the two gates is broken.

B1. $\{\neg V(O(1,F1),0)\}$ Δ
B2. $\{\neg Conn(x,O(1,F1)),\neg V(x,0)\}$ B1, 24
B3. $\{\neg V(O(1,X2),0)\}$ 16, B2
B4. $\{\neg Xorg(X2),\neg V(I(1,X2),z),\neg V(I(2,X2),z)\}$ 23, B3
B5. $\{\neg Xorg(X2),\neg Conn(x,I(1,X2)),$
     $\neg V(x,z),\neg V(I(2,X2),z)\}$ 24, B4
B6. $\{\neg Xorg(X2),\neg V(O(1,X1),z),\neg V(I(2,X2),z)\}$ 12, B5
B7. $\{\neg Xorg(X2),\neg Xorg(X1),\neg V(I(1,X1),u),$
     $\neg V(I(2,X1),v),u=v,\neg V(I(2,X2),1)\}$ 22, B6
B8. $\{\neg Xorg(X2),\neg Xorg(X1),\neg Conn(x,I(1,X1)),$
     $\neg V(x,u),\neg V(I(2,X1),v),u=v,$
     $\neg V(I(2,X2),1)\}$ 24, B7
B9. $\{\neg Xorg(X2),\neg Xorg(X1),\neg V(I(1,F1),u),$
     $\neg V(I(2,X1),v),u=v,\neg V(I(2,X2),1)\}$ 6, B8
B10. $\{\neg Xorg(X2),\neg Xorg(X1),\neg V(I(2,X1),v),$
     $1=v,\neg V(I(2,X2),1)\}$ A1, B9
B11. $\{\neg Xorg(X2),\neg Xorg(X1),\neg Conn(x,I(2,X1)),$
     $\neg V(x,v),1=v,\neg V(I(2,X2),1)\ \}$ 24, B10
B12. $\{\neg Xorg(X2),\neg Xorg(X1),\neg V(I(2,F1),v),1=v,$
     $\neg V(I(2,X2),1)\}$ 7, B11
B13. $\{\neg Xorg(X2),\neg Xorg(X1),1=0,\neg V(I(2,X2),1)\}$ A2, B12
B14. $\{\neg Xorg(X2),\neg Xorg(X1),\neg V(I(2,X2),1)\}$ 25, B13
B15. $\{\neg Xorg(X2),\neg Xorg(X1),\neg Conn(x,I(2,X2)),$
     $\neg V(x,1)\}$ 24, B14
B16. $\{\neg Xorg(X2),\neg Xorg(X1),\neg V(I(3,F1),1)\}$ 10, B15
B17. $\{\neg Xorg(X2),\neg Xorg(X1)\}$ A3, B16

In diagnosing digital hardware, it is common to make the assumption that at any one time a device has at most one malfunctioning component. The following clauses provide a simple but verbose way of encoding this

assumption.   Clauses C1 through C4 together state that either X1 is
a working *xor* gate or the other devices are okay; clauses C1 and C5
through C7 state the same for X2; and so forth. The single-fault assumption
can be stated more succinctly as a single axiom, but the encoding is
somewhat more complex.

C1. {Xorg(X1),Xorg(X2)}
C2. {Xorg(X1),Andg(A1)}
C3. {Xorg(X1),Andg(A2)}
C4. {Xorg(X1),Org(O1)}
C5. {Xorg(X2),Andg(A1)}
C6. {Xorg(X2),Andg(A2)}
C7. {Xorg(X2),Org(O1)}
C8. {Andg(A1),Andg(A2)}
C9. {Andg(A1),Org(O1)}
C10. {Andg(A2),Org(O1)}

Using the single-fault assumption and the fact that a fault is guaranteed
to be in some subset of parts, we can exonerate the parts not in that subset.
For example, knowing that either X1 or X2 is broken, as shown in B17, we
can prove that components A1, A2, and O1 are okay. The following proof
makes the case.

C11. {¬Xorg(X1),¬Xorg(X2)}   Δ
C12. {Andg(A1),¬Xorg(X2)}   C2, C11
C13. {Andg(A1)}   C5, C12
C14. {Andg(A2),¬Xorg(X2)}   C3, C11
C15. {Andg(A2)}   C6, C14
C16. {Org(O1),¬Xorg(X2)}   C4, C11
C17. {Org(O1)}   C7, C16

Finally, we can devise tests to discriminate possible suspects. Starting
with a behavioral rule for one of the suspect components, we can derive a
behavioral expectation for the overall device that implicates a subset of the
suspects. For example, clause D18 states that, if we use the same inputs
as in the previous example and if X1 is an *xor* gate, then the signal on the
second output of the device must be 1. This conclusion can be used as a
test to discriminate the suspects. We set the inputs as before and observe
the output. If it is not 1, as predicted, it must be because of an incorrect
assumption. The only assumption here is that X1 is working correctly.
Therefore, if 1 is not observed, then X1 is broken.

D1. {¬Xorg(X1),¬V(I(1,X1),y),   22
    ¬V(I(2,X1),z),y=z,V(O(1,X1),1)}
D2. {¬Xorg(X1),¬V(I(1,X1),1),   25, D1
    ¬V(I(2,X1),0),V(O(1,X1),1)}

D3. $\{\neg \text{Xorg(X1)}, \neg \text{Conn(x,I(1,X1))},$ 24, D2
     $\neg V(x,1), \neg V(I(2,X1),0), V(O(1,X1),1)\}$

D4. $\{\neg \text{Xorg(X1)}, \neg V(I(1,F1),1),$ 6, D3
     $\neg V(I(2,X1),0), V(O(1,X1),1)\}$

D5. $\{\neg \text{Xorg(X1)}, \neg V(I(1,F1),1),$ 24, D4
     $\neg \text{Conn(x,I(2,X1))}, \neg V(x,0), V(O(1,X1),1)\}$

D6. $\{\neg \text{Xorg(X1)}, \neg V(I(1,F1),1),$ 7, D5
     $\neg V(I(2,F1),0), V(O(1,X1),1)\}$

D7. $\{\neg \text{Xorg(X1)}, \neg V(I(1,F1),1),$ 24, D6
     $\neg V(I(2,F1),0), \neg \text{Conn(O(1,X1),y)}, V(y,1)\}$

D8. $\{\neg \text{Xorg(X1)}, \neg V(I(1,F1),1),$ 13, D7
     $\neg V(I(2,F1),0), V(I(2,A2),1)\}$

D9. $\{\neg \text{Xorg(X1)}, \neg V(I(1,F1),1), \neg V(I(2,F1),0),$ 18, D8
     $\neg \text{Andg(A1)}, \neg V(I(1,A2),1), V(O(1,A2),1)\}$

D10. $\{\neg \text{Xorg(X1)}, \neg V(I(1,F1),1), \neg V(I(2,F1),0),$ 3, D9
     $\neg V(I(1,A2),1), V(O(1,A2),1)\}$

D11. $\{\neg \text{Xorg(X1)}, \neg V(I(1,F1),1), \neg V(I(2,F1),0),$ 24, D10
     $\neg \text{Conn(I(3,F1),I(1,A2))}, \neg V(I(3,F1),1),$
     $V(O(1,A2),1)\}$

D12. $\{\neg \text{Xorg(X1)}, \neg V(I(1,F1),1), \neg V(I(2,F1),0),$ 11, D11
     $\neg V(I(3,F1),1), V(O(1,A2),1)\}$

D13. $\{\neg \text{Xorg(X1)}, \neg V(I(1,F1),1), \neg V(I(2,F1),0),$ 24, D12
     $\neg V(I(3,F1),1), \neg \text{Conn(O(1,A2),y)}, V(y,1)\}$

D14. $\{\neg \text{Xorg(X1)}, \neg V(I(1,F1),1), \neg V(I(2,F1),0),$ 14, D13
     $\neg V(I(3,F1),1), V(I(1,O1),1)\}$

D15. $\{\neg \text{Xorg(X1)}, \neg V(I(1,F1),1),$ 20, D14
     $\neg V(I(2,F1),0), \neg V(I(3,F1),1),$
     $\neg \text{Org(O1)}, V(O(1,O1),1)\}$

D16. $\{\neg \text{Xorg(X1)}, \neg V(I(1,F1),1), \neg V(I(2,F1),0),$ 5, D15
     $\neg V(I(3,F1),1), V(O(1,O1),1)\}$

D17. $\{\neg \text{Xorg(X1)}, \neg V(I(1,F1),1), \neg V(I(2,F1),0),$ 24, D16
     $\neg V(I(3,F1),1), \neg \text{Conn(O(1,O1),y)}, V(y,1)\}$

D18. $\{\neg \text{Xorg(X1)}, \neg V(I(1,F1),1), \neg V(I(2,F1),0),$ 17, D17
     $\neg V(I(3,F1),1), V(O(2,F1),1)\}$

The use of predicate calculus in this application area has several important advantages. The most obvious is that a single design description can be used for multiple purposes. As shown here, we can simulate a circuit, diagnose it, and generate tests of it all from one description. Of course, this is true of any language with descriptive semantics. However, the expressive power of the predicate calculus also allows higher-level design descriptions to be written and used for these purposes. By working with more abstract design descriptions, we can perform these tasks far more efficiently than we could at the gate level. Finally, the flexibility of the language and deductive techniques allows us to perform these tasks even with only incomplete information about the structure or behavior of a design.

4.9 Mathematics Example

Mathematics provides a wealth of problems that can be solved using inference methods such as resolution. As a simple example, consider the problem of demonstrating that the intersection of any two sets is contained in either set.

We start by writing down our definitions. The first of the following axioms is our definition of the intersection function in terms of the membership operator. An object is in the intersection of two sets if and only if it is contained in both sets. The second axiom defines the subset relation. One set is a subset of another if and only if every element of the first is an element of the second.

$$\forall x \forall s \forall t \ x \in s \land x \in t \Leftrightarrow x \in s \cap t$$

$$\forall s \forall t \ (\forall x \ x \in s \Rightarrow x \in t) \Leftrightarrow s \subseteq t$$

Our goal is to prove that the intersection of any two sets is contained in either set. Since the intersection function is commutative, we need to prove only containment in one of the sets.

$$\forall s \forall t \ s \cap t \subseteq s$$

The following trace provides a proof of the theorem. The first three clauses come from the definition of intersection. The next two derive from the definition of the subset relation. Note the use of the Skolem function F. The sixth clause comes from the negation of the goal. In this case, we use the Skolem constants A and B.

1.	$\{x \notin s, x \notin t, x \in s \cap t\}$	Δ
2.	$\{x \notin s \cap t, x \in s\}$	Δ
3.	$\{x \notin s \cap t, x \in t\}$	Δ
4.	$\{F(s,t) \in s, s \subseteq t\}$	Δ
5.	$\{F(s,t) \notin t, s \subseteq t\}$	Δ
6.	$\{A \cap B \not\subseteq A\}$	Γ
7.	$\{F(A \cap B, A) \in A \cap B\}$	4, 6
8.	$\{F(A \cap B, A) \notin A\}$	5, 6
9.	$\{F(A \cap B, A) \in A\}$	2, 7
10.	$\{\}$	8, 9

The proof is quite simple. The clause on lines 7 and 8 are obtained by resolving the goal clause with clauses 4 and 5. Clause 7 then resolves with clause 2 to yield clause 9, which contradicts the conclusion in line 8.

4.10 Soundness and Completeness*

Resolution is sound in that any clause that can be derived from a database using resolution is logically implied by that database. The proof is fairly simple.

THEOREM 4.1 (Soundness Theorem) *If there is a resolution deduction of a clause Φ from a database of clauses Δ, then Δ logically implies Φ.*

Proof The proof is achieved by simple induction on the length of resolution proofs. For the induction, we need to show only that any given resolution step is sound. Suppose, then, that Φ and Ψ are arbitrary clauses that resolve to produce a new clause $((\Phi - \{\phi_1, \ldots, \phi_m\}) \cup (\Psi - \{\neg\psi_1, \ldots, \neg\psi_n\}))\gamma$, where γ is the appropriate unifier, and suppose that ϕ is the literal obtained by applying the unifier to the factors in Φ and Ψ; i.e., $\phi = \phi_i\gamma = \psi_j\gamma$. Let I be an arbitrary interpretation and [V] be an arbitrary variable assignment such that $\models_I \Phi[V]$ and $\models_I \Psi[V]$. If $\models_I \phi[V]$, then $\not\models_I \neg\phi[V]$, and so $\models_I (\Psi\gamma - \{\neg\phi\})[V]$. If $\models_I \neg\phi[V]$, then $\not\models_I \phi[V]$, and so $\models_I (\Phi\gamma - \{\phi\})[V]$. But then $\models_I ((\Phi\gamma - \{\phi\}) \cup (\Psi\gamma - \{\neg\phi\}))[V]$, and so $\models_I ((\Phi - \{\phi_1, \ldots, \phi_m\}) \cup (\Psi - \{\neg\psi_1, \ldots, \neg\psi_n\}))\gamma[V]$. $\square$

As a special case of this theorem, we see that, if there is a deduction of the empty clause from a database Δ, then the database must logically imply the empty clause and, therefore, is unsatisfiable.

Resolution is *not* complete in the sense defined in Chapter 3. By itself, it will not generate every clause that is logically implied by a given database. For example, the tautology {P,¬P} is logically implied by every database, but resolution will not produce this clause from the empty database.

Furthermore, it provides no way of using sentences involving the equality and inequality relations. For example, given a database consisting of only the sentences P(A) and A=B, it cannot prove the sentence P(B). This is because, as far as the database is concerned, the relation constant = is arbitrary. To give it its standard interpretation requires additional axiom schemata.

On the other hand, for databases without sentences involving the equality and inequality relations, the procedure is *refutation complete*; i.e., given an unsatisfiable set of sentences, it is guaranteed to produce the empty clause. Consequently, as described in Section 4.6, we can use it to determine logical implication by negating the clause to be proved, adding it to the given database, and proving its unsatisfiablity.

The proof of refutation completeness is a little complicated and involves the introduction of several new concepts and lemmas. First, we introduce a special class of ground instances for clauses. Then, we show that resolution is complete for ground clauses in general and our special instances in particular. We prove that there is a deduction from a set of clauses whenever there is a deduction from our special instances. Finally, we use these results to prove the completeness theorem in general.

If a set Δ contains object constants, then let $O(\Delta)$ be the set of all object constants appearing in Δ. Otherwise, let $O(\Delta)$ be the singleton set containing an arbitrary constant, say A. Let $F(\Delta)$ be the set of all function constants appearing in Δ. The *Herbrand universe* $H(\Delta)$ is the set of all legal ground terms that can be formed from the elements of $O(\Delta)$ and $F(\Delta)$. The following are examples:

$H(\{\{P(A,B)\},\{Q(B),R(C)\}\}) = \{A,B,C\}$

$H(\{\{P(B)\},\{Q(F(x),G(y))\}\}) =$
$\{B,F(B),G(B),F(F(B)),F(G(B)),G(F(B)),G(G(B)),\ldots\}$

$H(\{\{P(x)\},\{\neg P(y)\}\}) = \{A\}$

The *Herbrand base* for a set Δ of clauses is a set of ground clauses in which all variables have been replaced by all elements of the Herbrand universe for Δ. A *Herbrand interpretation* for a set of clauses is an interpretation that maps ground terms into themselves and ground atoms into either true or false. More specifically, an interpretation I is a Herbrand interpretation for Δ if and only if the following conditions hold.

(1) $|I|$ is just the Herbrand universe for Δ.

(2) I maps each object constant into itself.

(3) If π is an n place function symbol and $\tau_1,\ldots,\tau_n$ are terms, then I maps the term $\pi(\tau_1,\ldots,\tau_n)$ into the term $\pi(\tau_1^I,\ldots,\tau_n^I)$, which turns out to be just $\pi(\tau_1,\ldots,\tau_n)$.

(4) Each ground atom is assigned either true or false.

Note that this definition includes no restriction on the interpretation of relation symbols; so we can choose any interpretation we like. For any satisfiable Herbrand base, we can produce a Herbrand interpretation that satisfies it as follows. Since the Herbrand base is satisfiable, it has a model. We construct our Herbrand interpretation by making true those atomic sentences that are true in the model and making false those atomic sentences that are false in the model. This observation allows us to prove our first theorem.

THEOREM 4.2 (Herbrand Theorem) *If a finite set Δ of clauses is unsatisfiable, then the Herbrand base for Δ is unsatisfiable.*

Proof Let Δ be an unsatisfiable set of clauses. If the Herbrand base for Δ is satisfiable, then we can construct a Herbrand interpretation that satisfies the Herbrand base as described, and we can construct a variable assignment using the substitution defining the Herbrand base. The resulting interpretation and variable assignment satisfy Δ, contradicting the hypothesis; therefore, the Herbrand base must not be satisfiable. $\square$

The *number of literal occurrences* in a database is the sum of the number of literal occurrences in each clause of the database. The *number of excess literals* in a database is the number of literal occurrences minus the number of clauses. Thus, the number of excess literals is an indication of the number of clauses in the database with more than one literal.

THEOREM 4.3 (Ground Completeness Theorem) *If a set Δ of ground clauses is unsatisfiable, then there is a resolution deduction of the empty clause from Δ.*

Proof If the empty clause is in Δ, then there is a trivial resolution deduction of the empty clause from Δ. We prove the case in which Δ does not contain the empty clause by induction on the number n of excess literals in Δ. If $n = 0$, then there are no nonunit clauses in Δ. So, if Δ is unsatisfiable, there must be at least one pair of complementary literals, and this pair can be resolved to yield the empty clause. Suppose now that the theorem is true for all databases with fewer than n excess literals. Since $n > 0$, and Δ does not contain the empty clause, there must be at least one nonunit clause, say Φ. We select a literal ϕ from this clause and form a new clause $\Phi' = \Phi - \{\phi\}$. Φ' is stronger than Φ is, so the set $(\Delta - \{\Phi\}) \cup \{\Phi'\}$ also must be unsatisfiable. This set also contains one fewer excess literals; so, by the induction hypothesis, there is a resolution deduction of the empty clause from this set. Similarly, the set $(\Delta - \{\Phi\}) \cup \{\{\phi\}\}$ is unsatisfiable; so, by the induction hypothesis, there must be a deduction of the empty clause for this set as well. If Φ' is not used in the former refutation, then this refutation also works for Δ. Otherwise, we can construct a refutation for Δ as follows. First, we add ϕ back into Φ' and all its descendants in the refutation, so that the sequence is a refutation from Δ. If the empty clause is still a member of this sequence, then we are done. Otherwise, the addition of ϕ to the empty clause must have created the singleton clause $\{\phi\}$. Now, we can form a deduction of the empty clause from Δ by appending the deduction of the empty clause from $(\Delta - \{\Phi\}) \cup \{\{\phi\}\}$ onto the end of this modified deduction. $\square$

Having dealt with ground clauses, we can now turn to the case of general resolution. Before proving the main result, we show that a ground deduction can be "lifted" to form a deduction from nonground clauses.

LEMMA 4.1 (Lifting Lemma) *If Φ and Ψ are two clauses with no shared variables, if Φ' and Ψ' are ground instances of Φ and Ψ, and if X' is a resolvent of Φ' and Ψ', then there is a resolvent X of Φ and Ψ such that X' is a substitution instance of X.*

Proof If X' is a resolvent of Φ' and Ψ', then there must be a literal ϕ' in Φ' and a literal $\neg\phi'$ in Ψ' such that $X' = (\Phi' - \{\phi'\}) \cup (\Psi' - \{\neg\phi'\})$. Since Φ' and Ψ' are ground instances of Φ and Ψ, there must be a substitution θ such that $\Phi' = \Phi\theta$ and $\Psi' = \Psi\theta$. Let $\{\phi_1, \ldots, \phi_m\}$ be the set of literals in Φ that θ maps to ϕ', and let $\{\neg\psi_1, \ldots, \neg\psi_n\}$ be the set of literals in Ψ that θ maps to $\neg\phi'$. Let σ be the most general unifier of $\{\phi_1, \ldots, \phi_m\}$ yielding the literal ϕ'', and let τ be the most general unifier of $\{\neg\psi_1, \ldots, \neg\psi_n\}$ yielding the literal $\neg\psi''$. Let $\delta = \sigma \cup \tau$ be the joint substitution. By the construction and the definition of most general unifier, ϕ' must be an instance of ϕ'', and ϕ' must be an instance of ψ''. Consequently, there is a unifier of ϕ'' and ψ''. Let γ be the most general unifier of ϕ'' and ψ'', and form the resolvent of Φ and Ψ as follows:

$$X = (\Phi\delta\gamma - \{\phi_1, \ldots, \phi_m\}\delta\gamma) \cup (\Psi\delta\gamma - \{\neg\psi_1, \ldots, \neg\psi_n\}\delta\gamma)$$

Using the definitions we introduced, we can rewrite the expression for X' as follows:

$$X' = (\Phi\theta - \{\phi_1, \ldots, \phi_m\}\theta) \cup (\Psi\theta - \{\neg\psi_1, \ldots, \neg\psi_n\}\theta)$$

Since ϕ' is an instance of ϕ'' and ψ'', θ is less general than $\delta\gamma$, so X' must be an instance of X, thus proving the theorem. $\square$

In the following theorem, we use the lifting lemma to prove that entire ground deductions can be lifted to nonground deductions.

THEOREM 4.4 (Lifting Theorem) *If Δ' is a set of ground instances of clauses in Δ and there is a resolution deduction of a clause X' from Δ', then there is a resolution deduction of a clause X from Δ such that X' is a substitution instance of X.*

Proof We need only a simple induction on the length of resolution deductions. $\square$

Combining all these results, we can prove the refutation completeness of the resolution procedure in general.

THEOREM 4.5 (Completeness Theorem) *If a set Δ of clauses is unsatisfiable, then there is a resolution deduction of the empty clause from Δ.*

Proof If a set Δ of clauses is unsatisfiable, then, by the Herbrand theorem, there is an unsatisfiable set of Herbrand instances of clauses in Δ. By the ground completeness theorem, there is a resolution deduction from the clauses in this set. Finally, by the lifting theorem, this deduction can be converted to a deduction of the empty clause from Δ. $\square$

The completeness of resolution is a satisfying property, since the procedure offers tremendous computational advantages over the techniques introduced in Chapter 3. Furthermore, the procedure can be made even more efficient using the restriction strategies to be introduced in Chapter 5.

4.11 Resolution and Equality

As mentioned in the preceding section, the refutation completeness of resolution does not hold for databases involving the relation constant = intended to be interpreted as the equality relation. There is simply no mechanism for substituting nonvariable terms that are known to be equal, so it is impossible to prove some results even though they are logically implied by the premises.

In many cases, we can circumvent this difficulty by rewriting our sentences so that all potentially equal nonvariable terms occur at the top level of the literals in which they appear; i.e., they are not embedded within other terms.

As an example of this method, consider the following definition of the *factorial* function. The problem with this definition of Fact is that the second sentence involves nested nonvariable terms such as k-1 and Fact(k-1). Even though these terms have deducible values, resolution is too weak to substitute those values.

$$\text{Fact}(0) = 1$$

$$\text{Fact}(k) = k*\text{Fact}(k-1)$$

The alternative is to write our definition as follows. In this case, all nonvariable terms appear at the top level of the literals in which they occur.

When written in this fashion, resolution is powerful enough to derive results that it cannot derive from the preceding formulation.

```
Fact(0) = 1

k-1=j ∧ Fact(j)=m ∧ k*m=n ⇒ Fact(k)=n
```

As an example, consider the following derivation of a value for `Fact(2)`. The first two lines contain the clauses from our definition. The third line is the negated goal. To get line 4, we plug in the definition of `Fact` from line 2. We then use procedural attachment on an instance of line 4 to evaluate the first literal in the definition and produce a clause involving `Fact(1)`. The process repeats, and we get a clause involving `Fact(0)`. We then use the base case of our definition. Finally, after two more steps involving procedural attachments, we get the answer.

1. {Fact(0)=1}   Δ
2. {k-1≠j,Fact(j)≠m,k*m≠n,Fact(k)=n}   Δ
3. {Fact(2)≠n,Ans(n)}   Γ
4. {2-1≠j1,Fact(j1)≠m1,2*m1≠n,Ans(n)}   2, 3
5. {Fact(1)≠m1,2*m1≠n,Ans(n)}   4, PA
6. {1-1≠j2,Fact(j2)≠m2,1*m2≠m1,2*m1≠n,Ans(n)}   2, 5
7. {Fact(0)≠m2,1*m2≠m1,2*m1≠n,Ans(n)}   6, PA
8. {1*1≠m1,2*m1≠n,Ans(n)}   1, 7
9. {2*1≠n,Ans(n)}   8, PA
10. {Ans(2)}   9, PA

Another way of dealing with sentences involving equality is to axiomatize the equality relation and to supply appropriate substitution axioms. The necessary axioms for equality follow. We know that equality is reflexive, symmetric, and transitive.

$$∀x \; x=x$$

$$∀x∀y \; x=y ⇒ y=x$$

$$∀x∀y∀z \; x=y ∧ y=z ⇒ x=z$$

We write substitution axioms that allow us to substitute terms for terms in each of our functions and relations. The following axioms are examples.

$$∀k∀j∀m \; k=j ∧ Fact(j)=m ⇒ Fact(k)=m$$

$$∀k∀j∀m∀n \; j=m ∧ k*m=n ⇒ k*j=n$$

Applying resolution with these axioms allows us to derive conclusions without unnesting terms. The resolution derivation that follows illustrates how this happens in our *factorial* example. The first two lines contain the clauses from our definition of the `Fact` function. Line 3 is the transitivity axiom for equality. Lines 4 and 5 are the clauses for our substitution axioms. Line 6 is the negated goal.

1.	{Fact(0)=1}	Δ
2.	{Fact(k)=k*Fact(k-1)}	Δ
3.	{x≠y,y≠z,x=z}	Δ
4.	{k≠j,Fact(j)≠m,Fact(k)=m}	Δ
5.	{j≠m,k*m≠n,k*j=n}	Δ
6.	{Fact(2)≠n,Ans(n)}	Γ
7.	{Fact(2)≠y,y≠n,Ans(n)}	3, 6
8.	{2*Fact(2-1)≠n,Ans(n)}	2, 7
9.	{Fact(2-1)≠j1,2*j1≠n,Ans(n)}	5, 8
10.	{2-1≠m1,Fact(m1)≠j1,2*j1≠n,Ans(n)}	4, 9
11.	{Fact(1)≠j1,2*j1≠n,Ans(n)}	10, PA
12.	{Fact(1)≠y,y≠j1,2*j1≠n,Ans(n)}	3, 11
13.	{1*Fact(1-1)≠j1,2*j1≠n,Ans(n)}	2, 12
14.	{Fact(1-1)≠j2,1*j2≠j1,2*j1≠n,Ans(n)}	5, 13
15.	{1-1≠m2,Fact(m2)≠j2,1*j2≠j1,2*j1≠n,Ans(n)}	4, 14
16.	{Fact(0)≠j2,1*j2≠j1,2*j1≠n,Ans(n)}	15, PA
17.	{1*1≠j1,2*j1≠n,Ans(n)}	1, 16
18.	{2*1≠n,Ans(n)}	17, PA
19.	{Ans(2)}	18, PA

Of course, for this approach to work, we need to supply substitution axioms for every function and relation within which we want substitutions to occur. This has the advantage that we can implicitly control the process of inference by supplying substitution axioms for some functions and relations and ignoring others. The disadvantage is that it is tedious to write these axioms in situations involving numerous functions and relations.

Although neither of these techniques is perfect, the situation is not hopeless. In fact, there is a rule of inference, called *paramodulation*, that, when added to the resolution principle, guarantees refutation completeness, even in the face of sentences involving equality. There also is a weaker version of paramodulation, called *demodulation*, which is more efficient and easier to understand than paramodulation. Demodulation is the basis for the semantics of functional programming languages such as LISP. Despite their obvious importance to AI, we have chosen not to treat these inference rules here, so that we can concentrate on other topics in the logical foundations of AI. Nevertheless, in many of our examples, we assume the existence of some method for handling equality and, therefore, write axioms with arbitrarily nested terms.

4.12 Bibliographical and Historical Remarks

The resolution principle was introduced by Robinson [Robinson 1965], based on earlier work by Prawitz [Prawitz 1960] and others. Books by Chang and Lee [Chang 1973], Loveland [Loveland 1978], Robinson [Robinson 1979], and Wos et al. [Wos 1984a] describe resolution theorem proving methods and systems. A useful collection of theorem-proving papers can be found in the volumes by Siekmann and Wrightson [Siekmann 1983a, Siekmann 1983b]. See also the reviews by Loveland [Loveland 1983] and by Wos [Wos 1985].

Our procedure for converting sentences into clausal form is based on work by Davis and Putnam [Davis 1960]. Resolution also can be accomplished on formulas not in clausal form (see [Manna 1979, Stickel 1982]).

A unification algorithm and a proof of correctness is presented in Robinson [Robinson 1965]. Several variations have appeared since. Raulefs et al. [Raulefs 1978] survey unification and matching. Paterson and Wegman [Paterson 1968] present a linear-time (and linear-space) unification algorithm. Unification has become increasingly important generally in computer science and in computational linguistics [Shieber 1986]. It is a fundamental operation performed in the computer language PROLOG [Clocksin 1981, Sterling 1986].

The use of an answer literal in resolution was first proposed by Green [Green 1969b], and was investigated in more detail by Luckham and Nilsson [Luckham 1971]. The idea of procedural attachment is extremely important for improving the efficiency of theorem-proving systems. Work by Weyhrauch [Weyhrauch 1980] explains this technique, which he calls *semantic attachment*, in terms of having a *partial model* of the sentences. Semantic attachment is an excellent candidate for the important bridge that is needed between declarative knowledge and procedural knowledge in complex AI systems. Stickel [Stickel 1985] shows how semantic attachment is related to what he calls "theory resolution."

The soundness and completeness of resolution were originally proved in [Robinson 1965]. The concept of excess literals is due to Bledsoe [Bledsoe 1977]. Our proof of the completeness of resolution is based on Herbrand's theorem [Herbrand 1930].

Exercises

1. *Clausal form.* Convert the following sentences to clausal form.

     a. $\forall x \forall y \; P(x,y) \;\Rightarrow\; Q(x,y)$

     b. $\forall x \forall y \; \neg Q(x,y) \;\Rightarrow\; \neg P(x,y)$

c. $\forall x \forall y\ P(x,y) \Rightarrow (Q(x,y) \Rightarrow R(x,y))$

d. $\forall x \forall y\ P(x,y) \wedge Q(x,y) \Rightarrow R(x,y)$

e. $\forall x \forall y\ P(x,y) \Rightarrow Q(x,y) \vee R(x,y)$

f. $\forall x \forall y\ P(x,y) \Rightarrow (Q(x,y) \wedge R(x,y))$

g. $\forall x \forall y\ (P(x,y) \vee Q(x,y)) \Rightarrow R(x,y)$

h. $\forall x \exists y\ P(x,y) \Rightarrow Q(x,y)$

i. $\neg\forall x \exists y\ P(x,y) \Rightarrow Q(x,y)$

j. $(\neg\forall x\ P(x)) \Rightarrow (\exists x\ P(x))$

2. *Unification.* Determine whether the members of each of the following pairs of expressions unify with each other. If so, give the most general unifier; if not, give a brief explanation.

   a. `Color(Tweety,Yellow)`   `Color(x,y)`

   b. `Color(Tweety,Yellow)`   `Color(x,x)`

   c. `Color(Hat(Postman),Blue)`   `Color(Hat(y),x)`

   d. `R(F(x),B)`   `R(y,z)`

   e. `R(F(y),x)`   `R(x,F(B))`

   f. `R(F(y),y,x)`   `R(x,F(A),F(v))`

   g. `Loves(x,y)`   `Loves(y,x)`

3. *Resolution.* Heads I win; tails you lose. Use resolution to show that I win.

4. *Resolution.* If a course is easy, some students are happy. If a course has a final, no students are happy. Use resolution to show that, if a course has a final, the course is not easy.

5. *Resolution.* Victor has been murdered, and Arthur, Bertram, and Carleton are suspects. Arthur says he did not do it. He says that Bertram was the victim's friend but that Carleton hated the victim. Bertram says he was out of town the day of the murder, and besides he didn't even know the guy. Carleton says he is innocent and he saw Arthur and Bertram with the victim just before the murder. Assuming that everyone—except possibly for the murderer—is telling the truth, use resolution to solve the crime.

6. *Logical axioms.* Write down an instance for each of the axiom schemata introduced in Chapter 3, and use resolution to prove the validity of your instances.

CHAPTER 5
Resolution Strategies

ONE OF THE DISADVANTAGES of using the resolution rule in an unconstrained manner is that it leads to many useless inferences. Some inferences are redundant in that their conclusions can be derived in other ways. Some inferences are irrelevant in that they do not lead to derivations of the desired result.

As an example, consider the resolution trace in Figure 5.1. Clauses 9, 11, 14, and 16 are redundant; clauses 10 and 13 are redundant; clauses 12 and 15 are redundant; all these redundancies lead to subsequent redundancies at the next level of deduction. We can remove duplicate clauses and thereby prevent the propagation of redundant conclusions. However, their initial generation is an indication of inefficiency in the unconstrained use of the resolution principle.

This chapter presents a number of strategies for eliminating useless work. In reading the chapter, it is important to bear in mind that we are concerned here not with the order in which inferences are done, but only with the size of a resolution graph and with ways of decreasing that size by eliminating useless deductions.

5.1 Deletion Strategies

A *deletion strategy* is a restriction technique in which clauses with specified properties are eliminated before they are ever used. Since those clauses

95

1.	{P,Q}	Δ
2.	{¬P,R}	Δ
3.	{¬Q,R}	Δ
4.	{¬R}	Γ
5.	{Q,R}	1, 2
6.	{P,R}	1, 3
7.	{¬P}	2, 4
8.	{¬Q}	3, 4
9.	{R}	3, 5
10.	{Q}	4, 5
11.	{R}	3, 6
12.	{P}	4, 6
13.	{Q}	1, 7
14.	{R}	6, 7
15.	{P}	1, 8
16.	{R}	5, 8
17.	{}	4, 9
18.	{R}	3, 10
19.	{}	8, 10
20.	{}	4, 11
21.	{R}	2, 12
22.	{}	7, 12
23.	{R}	3, 13
24.	{}	8, 13
25.	{}	4, 14
26.	{R}	2, 15
27.	{}	7, 15
28.	{}	4, 16
29.	{}	4, 18
30.	{}	4, 21
31.	{}	4, 23
32.	{}	4, 26

Figure 5.1   Example of unconstrained resolution.

are unavailable for subsequent deduction, this can lead to computational savings.

A literal occurring in a database is *pure* if and only if it has no instance that is complementary to an instance of another literal in the database.

A clause that contains a pure literal is useless for the purposes of refutation, since the literal can never be resolved away. Consequently, we can safely remove such a clause. Removing clauses with pure literals defines a deletion strategy known as *pure-literal elimination*.

The database that follows is unsatisfiable. However, in proving this we can ignore the second and third clauses, since they both contain the pure literal S.

$$\{\neg P, \neg Q, R\}$$

$$\{\neg P, S\}$$

$$\{\neg Q, S\}$$

$$\{P\}$$

$$\{Q\}$$

$$\{\neg R\}$$

Note that, if a database contains no pure literals, there is no way we can derive any clauses with pure literals using resolution. The upshot is that we do not need to apply the strategy to a database more than once, and in particular we do not have to check each clause as it is generated.

A *tautology* is a clause containing a pair of complementary literals. For example, the clause $\{P(F(A)), \neg P(F(A))\}$ is a tautology. The clause $\{P(x), Q(y), \neg Q(y), R(z)\}$ also is a tautology, even though it contains additional literals.

As it turns out, the presence or absence of tautologies in a set of clauses has no effect on that set's satisfiability. A satisfiable set of clauses remains satisfiable, no matter what tautologies we add. An unsatisfiable set of clauses remains unsatisfiable, even if we remove all tautologies. Therefore, we can remove tautologies from a database, because we need never use them in subsequent inferences. The corresponding deletion strategy is called *tautology elimination*.

Note that the literals in a clause must be exact complements for tautology elimination to apply. We cannot remove nonidentical literals, just because they are complements under unification. For example, the clauses $\{\neg P(A), P(x)\}$, $\{P(A)\}$, and $\{\neg P(B)\}$ are unsatisfiable. However, if we were to remove the first clause, the remaining set would be satisfiable.

In *subsumption elimination*, the deletion criterion depends on a relationship between two clauses in a database. A clause Φ *subsumes* a clause Ψ if and only if there exists a substitution σ such that $\Phi\sigma \subseteq \Psi$. For example, $\{P(x), Q(y)\}$ subsumes $\{P(A), Q(v), R(w)\}$, since there is a substitution $\{x/A, y/v\}$ that makes the former clause a subset of the latter.

If one member in a set of clauses is subsumed by another member, then the set remaining after eliminating the subsumed clause is satisfiable if and only if the original set is satisfiable. Therefore, subsumed clauses can be eliminated. Since the resolution process itself can produce tautologies and subsuming clauses, we need to check for tautologies and subsumptions as we perform resolutions.

5.2 Unit Resolution

A *unit resolvent* is one in which at least one of the parent clauses is a *unit clause*; i.e., one containing a single literal. A *unit deduction* is one in which all derived clauses are unit resolvents. A *unit refutation* is a unit deduction of the empty clause {}.

As an example of a unit refutation, consider the following proof. In the first two inferences, unit clauses from the initial set are resolved with binary clauses to produce two new unit clauses. These are resolved with the first clause to produce two additional unit clauses. The elements in these two sets of results are then resolved with each other to produce the contradiction.

$$
\begin{array}{lll}
1. & \{P,Q\} & \Delta \\
2. & \{\neg P,R\} & \Delta \\
3. & \{\neg Q,R\} & \Delta \\
4. & \{\neg R\} & \Gamma \\
\hline
5. & \{\neg P\} & 2,\,4 \\
6. & \{\neg Q\} & 3,\,4 \\
\hline
7. & \{Q\} & 1,\,5 \\
8. & \{P\} & 1,\,6 \\
\hline
9. & \{R\} & 3,\,7 \\
10. & \{\} & 6,\,7 \\
11. & \{R\} & 2,\,8 \\
12. & \{\} & 5,\,8 \\
\end{array}
$$

Note that the proof contains only a subset of the possible uses of the resolution rule. For example, clauses 1 and 2 can be resolved to derive the conclusion {Q,R}. However, this conclusion and its descendants are never generated, since neither of its parents is a unit clause.

Inference procedures based on unit resolution are easy to implement and are usually quite efficient. It is worth noting that, whenever a clause is resolved with a unit clause, the conclusion has fewer literals than the parent does. This helps to focus the search toward producing the empty clause and thereby improves efficiency.

Unfortunately, inference procedures based on unit resolution generally are not complete. For example, the clauses {P,Q}, {¬P,Q}, {P,¬Q}, and {¬P,¬Q} are inconsistent. Using general resolution, it is easy to derive the empty clause. However, unit resolution fails in this case, since none of the initial propositions is a single literal.

On the other hand, if we restrict our attention to Horn clauses (i.e., clauses with at most one positive literal), the situation is much better. In fact, it can be shown that there is a unit refutation of a set of Horn clauses if and only if it is unsatisfiable.

5.3 Input Resolution

An *input resolvent* is one in which at least one of the two parent clauses is a member of the initial (i.e., input) database. An *input deduction* is one in which all derived clauses are input resolvents. An *input refutation* is an input deduction of the empty clause {}.

As an example, consider clauses 6 and 7 in Figure 5.1. Using unconstrained resolution, these clauses can be resolved to produce clause 14. However, this is not an input resolution, since neither parent is a member of the initial database.

Note that the resolution of clauses 1 and 2 is an input resolution but not a unit resolution. On the other hand, the resolution of clauses 6 and 7 is a unit resolution but not an input resolution. Despite differences such as this one, it can be shown that unit resolution and input resolution are equivalent in inferential power in that there is a unit refutation from a set of sentences whenever there is an input refutation and vice versa.

One consequence of this fact is that input resolution is complete for Horn clauses but incomplete in general. Again, the unsatisfiable set of propositions {P,Q}, {¬P,Q}, {P,¬Q}, and {¬P,¬Q} provides an example of a deduction on which input resolution fails. An input refutation must (in particular) have one of the parents of {} be a member of the initial database. However, to produce the empty clause in this case, we must resolve either two single literal clauses or two clauses having single-literal factors. None of the members of the base set meet either of these criteria, so there cannot be an input refutation for this set.

5.4 Linear Resolution

Linear resolution (also called *ancestry-filtered resolution*) is a slight generalization of input resolution. A *linear resolvent* is one in which at least one of the parents is either in the initial database or is an ancestor of the other parent. A *linear deduction* is one in which each derived clause is a linear resolvent. A *linear refutation* is a linear deduction of the empty clause {}.

Linear resolution takes its name from the linear shape of the proofs it generates. A linear deduction starts with a clause in the initial database (called the *top clause*) and produces a linear chain of resolutions such as that shown in Figure 5.2. Each resolvent after the first one is obtained from

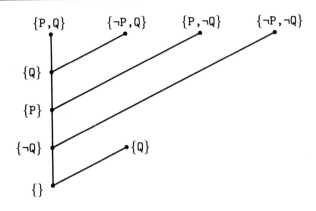

Figure 5.2   Chain of resolutions in a linear deduction.

the last resolvent (called the *near parent*) and some other clause (called the *far parent*). In linear resolution, the far parent must either be in the initial database or be an ancestor of the near parent.

Much of the redundancy in unconstrained resolution derives from the resolution of intermediate conclusions with other intermediate conclusions. The advantage of linear resolution is that it avoids many useless inferences by focusing deduction at each point on the ancestors of each clause and on the elements of the initial database.

Linear resolution is known to be refutation complete. Furthermore, it is not necessary to try every clause in the initial database as top clause. It can be shown that, if a set of clauses Γ is satisfiable and $\Gamma \cup \{\phi\}$ is unsatisfiable, then there is a linear refutation with ϕ as top clause. So, if we knows that a particular set of clauses is consistent, one need not attempt refutations with the elements of that set as top clauses.

A *merge* is a resolvent that inherits a literal from each parent such that this literal is collapsed to a singleton by the most general unifier. The completeness of linear resolution is preserved even if the ancestors that are used are limited to merges. Note that, in this example, the first resolvent (i.e., clause $\{Q\}$) is a merge.

5.5 Set of Support Resolution

If we examine resolution traces such as the one shown in Figure 5.1, we notice that many conclusions come from resolutions between clauses contained in a portion of the database that we know to be satisfiable. For example, in Figure 5.1, the set Δ is satisfiable, yet many of the conclusions in the trace are obtained by resolving elements of Δ with other elements of Δ. As it turns out, we can eliminate these resolutions without affecting the refutation completeness of resolution.

A subset Γ of a set Δ is called a *set of support* for Δ if and only if $\Delta - \Gamma$ is satisfiable. Given a set of clauses Δ with set of support Γ, a *set of support resolvent* is one in which at least one parent is selected from Γ or is a descendant of Γ. A *set of support deduction* is one in which each derived clause is a set of support resolvent. A *set of support refutation* is a set of support deduction of the empty clause {}.

The following trace is a set of support refutation for the example in Figure 5.1, with the singleton set {¬R} as the set of support. The clause {¬R} resolves with {¬P,R} and {¬Q,R} to produce {¬P} and {¬Q}. These then resolve with clause 1 to produce {Q} and {P}, which resolve to produce the empty clause.

1.	{P,Q}	Δ
2.	{¬P,R}	Δ
3.	{¬Q,R}	Δ
4.	{¬R}	Γ
5.	{¬P}	2, 4
6.	{¬Q}	3, 4
7.	{Q}	1, 5
8.	{P}	1, 6
9.	{R}	3, 7
10.	{}	6, 7
11.	{R}	2, 8
12.	{}	5, 8

Obviously, this strategy would be of little use if there were no easy way of selecting the set of support. Fortunately, there are several ways this can be done at negligible expense. For example, in situations where we are trying to prove conclusions from a consistent database, the natural choice is to use the clauses derived from the negated goal as the set of support. This set satisfies the definition as long as the database itself is truly satisfiable. With this choice of set of support, each resolution must have a connection to the overall goal, so the procedure can be viewed as working "backward" from the goal. This is especially useful for databases in which the number of conclusions possible by working "forward" is larger. Furthermore, the goal-oriented character of such refutations often makes them more understandable than refutations using other strategies.

5.6 Ordered Resolution

Ordered resolution is a very restrictive resolution strategy in which each clause is treated as a linearly ordered set. Resolution is permitted only on the first literal of each clause; i.e., the literal that is least in the ordering. The literals in the conclusion preserve the order from their parent clauses with the literals from the positive parent followed by the literals from the negative parent (i.e., the one with the negated atom).

The following trace is an example of an ordered refutation. Clause 5 is the only ordered resolvent of clauses 1 through 4. Clauses 1 and 3 do not resolve, since the complementary literals are not first in each clause. Clauses 2 and 4 do not resolve for the same reason, nor do clauses 3 and 4. Once clause 5 is generated, it resolves with clause 3 to produce clause 6, which resolves with clause 4 to produce the empty clause.

$$
\begin{array}{lll}
1. & \{P,Q\} & \Delta \\
2. & \{\neg P,R\} & \Delta \\
3. & \{\neg Q,R\} & \Delta \\
4. & \{\neg R\} & \Gamma \\
\hline
5. & \{Q,R\} & 1,\ 2 \\
\hline
6. & \{R\} & 3,\ 5 \\
\hline
7. & \{\} & 4,\ 6 \\
\end{array}
$$

Ordered resolution is extremely efficient. In this case, the empty clause is produced at the third level of deduction, and the inference space through that level of deduction includes only three resolvents. By comparison, general resolution through that level results in 24 resolvents.

Unfortunately, ordered resolution is not refutation complete. However, if we restrict our attention to Horn clauses, refutation completeness is guaranteed. Furthermore, we can get refutation completeness in the general case by considering resolvents in which the remaining literals from the positive parent follow the remaining literals from the negative parent, as well as the other way around.

5.7 Directed Resolution

Directed resolution is the use of ordered resolution in an important but restricted set of deductions. In directed resolution, the query takes the form of a conjunction of positive literals, and the database consists entirely of *directed clauses*. A directed clause is a Horn clause in which the positive literal occurs either at the beginning or the end of the clause. The goal is to find bindings for the variables so that the conjunction resulting from the substitution of these bindings is provable from the database.

In looking at directed resolution, we can use a bit of syntactic sugar. Since all the clauses are directional, we can write them in *infix form*. We write clauses with the positive literal at the end using the $\Rightarrow$ operator. We write clauses in which the positive literal is at the beginning using the reverse implication operator $\Leftarrow$. We let the literal in a positive unit clause represent the clause as a whole. We write the negative literals in clauses without positive literals as the antecedents of either implication operator.

$$\{\neg\phi_1,\ldots,\neg\phi_n,\psi\} \leftrightarrow \phi_1,\ldots,\phi_n \Rightarrow \psi$$
$$\{\psi,\neg\phi_1,\ldots,\neg\phi_n\} \leftrightarrow \psi \Leftarrow \phi_1,\ldots,\phi_n$$
$$\{\neg\phi_1,\ldots,\neg\phi_n\} \leftrightarrow \phi_1,\ldots,\phi_n \Rightarrow$$
$$\{\neg\phi_1,\ldots,\neg\phi_n\} \leftrightarrow \Leftarrow \phi_1,\ldots,\phi_n$$

The distinguishing feature of directed resolution is the directionality of the clauses in the database. Some clauses give rise to forward resolution, in which positive conclusions are derived from positive data. Other clauses give rise to backward resolution, in which negative clauses are derived from other negative clauses. As suggested by the preceding equivalences, the directionality of a clause is determined by the position of the positive literal in the clause.

A *forward clause* is one in which the positive literal comes at the end. In directed resolution, forward clauses give rise to forward resolution. To see why this is so, consider the following proof. Using ordered resolution on the first two clauses leads to the conclusion P(A), and then this conclusion is resolved with the negative unit to derive the empty clause. Putting the positive literal at the end makes it possible to work forward to the positive intermediate conclusion (clause 4), but makes it impossible to work backward from the negative clause (clause 3).

1. $\{\neg M(x),P(x)\}$	$M(x) \Rightarrow P(x)$	
2. $\{M(A)\}$	$M(A)$	
3. $\{\neg P(z)\}$	$P(z) \Rightarrow$	
4. $\{P(A)\}$	$P(A)$	
5. $\{\}$	$\{\}$	

Symmetrically, if the positive literal is put at the front of a clause, the clause is *backward*. If we rewrite the previous clauses in this way, we get the opposite behavior. In the following proof, the negative clause is resolved with the first clause to produce the intermediate negative conclusion $\{\neg M(z)\}$, then this result is resolved with the second clause to derive the empty clause.

1. $\{P(x),\neg M(x)\}$	$P(x) \Leftarrow M(x)$	
2. $\{M(A)\}$	$M(A)$	
3. $\{\neg P(z)\}$	$\Leftarrow P(z)$	

4. $\{\neg M(z)\}$ $\Leftarrow M(z)$

5. $\{\}$ $\Leftarrow$

By making some clauses forward and others backward, we can get a mixture of forward and backward resolution. As an example, consider the following proof. The positive data first resolve with forward clause 2 to produce more positive results. These results then resolve with clause 1 to produce some intermediate results. These results resolve with backward clause 3 to produce two subgoals involving N. One of these succeeds, leading to the positive result $\{R(B)\}$. This then resolves with clause 7 to produce the empty clause.

1. $\{\neg P(x), \neg Q(x), R(x)\}$ $P(x), Q(x) \Rightarrow R(x)$
2. $\{\neg M(x), P(x)\}$ $M(x) \Rightarrow P(x)$
3. $\{Q(x), \neg N(x)\}$ $Q(x) \Leftarrow N(x)$
4. $\{M(A)\}$ $M(A)$
5. $\{M(B)\}$ $M(B)$
6. $\{N(B)\}$ $N(B)$
7. $\{\neg R(z)\}$ $R(z) \Rightarrow$

8. $\{P(A)\}$ $P(A)$
9. $\{P(B)\}$ $P(B)$

10. $\{\neg Q(A), R(A)\}$ $Q(A) \Rightarrow R(A)$
11. $\{\neg Q(B), R(B)\}$ $Q(B) \Rightarrow R(B)$

12. $\{\neg N(A), R(A)\}$ $N(A) \Rightarrow R(A)$
13. $\{\neg N(B), R(B)\}$ $N(B) \Rightarrow R(B)$

14. $\{R(B)\}$ $R(B)$

15. $\{\}$ $\Rightarrow$

The possibility of controlling the direction of resolution by positioning the positive literal at one or the other end of a clause raises the question of which direction is more efficient. For the purpose of comparison, consider the following set of sentences.

$$\text{Insect}(x) \Rightarrow \text{Animal}(x)$$

$$\text{Mammal}(x) \Rightarrow \text{Animal}(x)$$

$$\text{Ant}(x) \Rightarrow \text{Insect}(x)$$

$$\text{Bee}(x) \Rightarrow \text{Insect}(x)$$

$$\text{Spider}(x) \Rightarrow \text{Insect}(x)$$

$$\text{Lion}(x) \Rightarrow \text{Mammal}(x)$$

$$\text{Tiger}(x) \Rightarrow \text{Mammal}(x)$$

$$\text{Zebra}(x) \Rightarrow \text{Mammal}(x)$$

Assuming that `Zeke` is a zebra, is `Zeke` an animal? The following proof shows that the search space in this case is quite small.

1. {Zebra(Zeke)}
2. {¬Animal(Zeke)}

---

3. {Mammal(Zeke)}

---

4. {Animal(Zeke)}

---

5. {}

Unfortunately, things are not always so pleasant. As an example, consider the following database of information about zebras. Zebras are mammals, striped, and medium in size. Mammals are animals and warm-blooded. Striped things are nonsolid and nonspotted. Things of medium size are neither small nor large.

$$\text{Zebra}(x) \Rightarrow \text{Mammal}(x)$$

$$\text{Zebra}(x) \Rightarrow \text{Striped}(x)$$

$$\text{Zebra}(x) \Rightarrow \text{Medium}(x)$$

$$\text{Mammal}(x) \Rightarrow \text{Animal}(x)$$

$$\text{Mammal}(x) \Rightarrow \text{Warm}(x)$$

$$\text{Striped}(x) \Rightarrow \text{Nonsolid}(x)$$

$$\text{Striped}(x) \Rightarrow \text{Nonspotted}(x)$$

$$\text{Medium}(x) \Rightarrow \text{Nonsmall}(x)$$

$$\text{Medium}(x) \Rightarrow \text{Nonlarge}(x)$$

The following proof shows that the search space in this case is somewhat larger than in the previous example. The reason is that we can derive more than one conclusion from each clause than we manage to derive.

1. {Zebra(Zeke)}
2. {¬Nonlarge(Zeke)}

---

3. {Mammal(Zeke)}
4. {Striped(Zeke)}

5. {Medium(Zeke)}

---

6. {Animal(Zeke)}
7. {Warm(Zeke)}
8. {Nonsolid(Zeke)}
9. {Nonstriped(Zeke)}
10. {Nonsmall(Zeke)}
12. {Nonlarge(Zeke)}

---

13. {}

Now consider what would happen if we were to reverse the direction of the clauses, as follows.

$$Mammal(x) \Leftarrow Zebra(x)$$

$$Striped(x) \Leftarrow Zebra(x)$$

$$Medium(x) \Leftarrow Zebra(x)$$

$$Animal(x) \Leftarrow Mammal(x)$$

$$Warm(x) \Leftarrow Mammal(x)$$

$$Nonsolid(x) \Leftarrow Striped(x)$$

$$Nonspotted(x) \Leftarrow Striped(x)$$

$$Nonsmall(x) \Leftarrow Medium(x)$$

$$Nonlarge(x) \Leftarrow Medium(x)$$

The following proof shows that the search space of backward resolution in this case is much smaller than that for forward resolution.

1. {Zebra(Zeke)}
2. {¬Nonlarge(Zeke)}

---

3. {¬Medium(Zeke)}

---

4. {¬Zebra(Zeke)}

---

5. {}

Unfortunately, like forward resolution, backward resolution has its drawbacks. As an example, consider the backward version of the clauses in the animal problem.

$$Animal(x) \Leftarrow Insect(x)$$

$$Animal(x) \Leftarrow Mammal(x)$$

$$\text{Insect}(x) \Leftarrow \text{Ant}(x)$$

$$\text{Insect}(x) \Leftarrow \text{Bee}(x)$$

$$\text{Insect}(x) \Leftarrow \text{Spider}(x)$$

$$\text{Mammal}(x) \Leftarrow \text{Lion}(x)$$

$$\text{Mammal}(x) \Leftarrow \text{Tiger}(x)$$

$$\text{Mammal}(x) \Leftarrow \text{Zebra}(x)$$

The following proof shows that the search space for the backward direction is much larger than it is for the forward direction.

1. $\{\text{Zebra}(\text{Zeke})\}$
2. $\{\neg\text{Animal}(\text{Zeke})\}$

---

3. $\{\neg\text{Insect}(\text{Zeke})\}$
4. $\{\neg\text{Mammal}(\text{Zeke})\}$

---

5. $\{\neg\text{Ant}(\text{Zeke})\}$
6. $\{\neg\text{Bee}(\text{Zeke})\}$
7. $\{\neg\text{Spider}(\text{Zeke})\}$
8. $\{\neg\text{Lion}(\text{Zeke})\}$
9. $\{\neg\text{Tiger}(\text{Zeke})\}$
10. $\{\neg\text{Zebra}(\text{Zeke})\}$

---

11. $\{\}$

The fact is that forward resolution is best for some clause sets, and backward resolution is best for others. To determine which is best for which, we need to look at the branching factor of the clauses. In the preceding examples, the search space branches backward in the animal problem and forward in the zebra problem. Consequently, we should use forward resolution in the animal problem and backward resolution in the zebra problem.

Of course, things are not always this simple. Sometimes, it is best to use some clauses in the forward direction and others in the backward direction; deciding which clauses to use in which direction to get optimal performance is a computationally difficult problem. The problem can be solved in polynomial time, if we restrict our attention to *coherent databases*; i.e., those in which all clauses that can be used to prove a literal in the antecedent of a forward clause are themselves forward clauses. In general, however, the problem is NP-complete.

5.8 Sequential Constraint Satisfaction

Sequential constraint satisfaction is the use of ordered resolution in the solution of another restricted but important class of fill-in-the-blank questions. Like directed resolution, the query is posed as a conjunction of positive literals, containing some number of variables. However, unlike directed resolution, the database consists entirely of positive ground literals. The task is to find bindings for the variables such that, after substitution into the query, each of the resulting conjuncts is identical to a literal in the database.

As an example, consider the following database. Art and Ann are the parents of Jon; Bob and Bea are the parents of Kim; and Cap and Coe are the parents of Lem. Ann and Cap are carpenters; Jon and Kim are U.S. senators.

P(Art,Jon)	Carpenter(Ann)	Senator(Jon)
P(Ann,Jon)	Carpenter(Cap)	Senator(Kim)
P(Bob,Kim)		
P(Bea,Kim)		
P(Cap,Lem)		
P(Coe,Lem)		

The following conjunction is a typical query for a database of this sort. We are looking for bindings for the variables x and y such that x is the parent of y, x is a carpenter, and y is a senator.

$$P(x,y) \land Carpenter(x) \land Senator(y)$$

To use resolution on this problem, we need to negate the query, to convert to clausal form, and to add an appropriate answer literal. This results in the following clause:

$$\{\neg P(x,y), \neg Carpenter(x), \neg Senator(y), Ans(x,y)\}$$

We then use ordered resolution to derive an answer. The following sequence of deductions shows a trace of this strategy in solving this query using the preceding data.

1. $\{\neg P(x,y), \neg Carpenter(x), \neg Senator(y), Ans(x,y)\}$

---

2. $\{\neg Carpenter(Art), \neg Senator(Jon), Ans(Art,Jon)\}$
3. $\{\neg Carpenter(Ann), \neg Senator(Jon), Ans(Ann,Jon)\}$
4. $\{\neg Carpenter(Bob), \neg Senator(Kim), Ans(Bob,Kim)\}$

5. $\{\neg\texttt{Carpenter(Bea)},\neg\texttt{Senator(Kim)},\texttt{Ans(Bea,Kim)}\}$
6. $\{\neg\texttt{Carpenter(Cap)},\neg\texttt{Senator(Lem)},\texttt{Ans(Cap,Lem)}\}$
7. $\{\neg\texttt{Carpenter(Coe)},\neg\texttt{Senator(Lem)},\texttt{Ans(Coe,Lem)}\}$

8. $\{\neg\texttt{Senator(Jon)},\texttt{Ans(Ann,Jon)}$
9. $\{\neg\texttt{Senator(Lem)},\texttt{Ans(Cap,Lem)}$

10. $\{\texttt{Ans(Ann,Jon)}\}$

From the standpoint of efficiency, one of the key questions in sequential constraint satisfaction is the order of the literals in the query. Although there is some search involved in the preceding example, it is not great. By comparison, it is interesting to consider what happens with a somewhat larger database and a slightly different ordering of the literals in the query.

To be specific, consider a census database with the following properties. There are 100 U.S. senators; so, if the database is complete and nonredundant, there are 100 solutions to queries of the form $\texttt{Senator}(\nu)$, where ν is a variable. Similarly, there are several hundred thousand carpenters and, therefore, several hundred thousand solutions to queries of the form $\texttt{Carpenter}(\nu)$. There are several hundred million parent–child pairs and, therefore, several hundred million solutions to queries of the form $\texttt{P}(\mu,\nu)$ involving two variables. However, there are only two solutions to queries of the form $\texttt{P}(\nu,\gamma)$, where ν is a variable and γ is a constant, since each person has only two parents. Similarly, there are only a few solutions to queries of the form $\texttt{P}(\gamma,\nu)$, since each person has at most a few children. We indicate the sizes of these solution sets as follows, where the notation $\|\texttt{Q(x)}\|$ is used to denote the number of instances of $\texttt{Q(x)}$ in the database.

$$\|\texttt{Senator}(\nu)\| = 100$$

$$\|\texttt{Carpenter}(\nu)\| \approx 10^5$$

$$\|\texttt{P}(\mu,\nu)\| \approx 10^8$$

$$\|\texttt{P}(\nu,\gamma)\| = 2$$

$$\|\texttt{P}(\gamma,\nu)\| \approx 3$$

Consider the difficulty of answering the preceding query with this expanded database. As before, working on the literals in the order given results in an enumeration of all parent–child pairs, except in this case the search space includes several hundred million possibilities.

A much better way to answer the query is to reorder the literals as shown below. Since there are only 100 senators and only two parents for each senator, this ordering limits the search space to at most 200 possibilities.

$$\texttt{Senator(y)} \wedge \texttt{P(x,y)} \wedge \texttt{Carpenter(x)}$$

This example suggests a useful heuristic for sequential constraint satisfaction, known as the *cheapest first rule*, which states that one should process the literals in a query in order of increasing solution-set size. Unfortunately, the rule does not always produce the optimal ordering. As an example, consider the following problem.

$$P(x) \wedge Q(y) \wedge R(x,y)$$

Assume the database has the characteristics shown below.   The symbols μ and ν here refer to arbitrary variables, and γ is a constant.

$$\|P(\nu)\| = 1000$$

$$\|Q(\nu)\| = 2000$$

$$\|R(\mu,\nu)\| = 100{,}000$$

$$\|R(\gamma,\nu)\| = 100$$

$$\|R(\mu,\gamma)\| = 10$$

In this case, $P(x)$ is the literal with the smallest solution set; therefore, using the cheapest first rule, we enumerate its solutions first, a total of 1000 possibilities. Next we compare the set sizes of the remaining two literals for the case where x is known. There are 2000 solutions to the Q literals but only 100 solutions to the R literal, if x is known. So the R literal is processed next, leading to a total search space of 100,000.

The problem is that there is a better ordering. Working first on $Q(y)$ produces an initial search space of 2000 possibilities. However, given a value for y, there are only 10 solutions for the R literal, leading to a search space of only 20,000, a factor of 5 smaller than the ordering suggested by the cheapest first rule.

One way of guaranteeing the optimal ordering for a set of literals is to search through all possible orderings. For each ordering, we can compute the expected cost. Then, we can compare orderings and select the one that is cheapest.

The following equations show the cost estimates for the six orderings of the literals in the preceding problem. From these estimates, it is easy to see that it is best to process the Q literal first, followed by R, and then P.

$$\|P(x),Q(y),R(x,y)\| = 2{,}000{,}000$$

$$\|P(x),R(x,y),Q(y)\| = 100{,}000$$

$$\|Q(y),P(x),R(x,y)\| = 2{,}000{,}000$$

$$\|Q(y),R(x,y),P(x)\| = 20{,}000$$

$$||R(x,y),P(x),Q(y)|| = 100,000$$

$$||R(x,y),Q(y),P(x)|| = 100,000$$

The problem with enumerating and comparing all possible orderings is inefficiency. For a set of n literals, there are $n!$ possible orderings. Although there are only six possible orderings for three literals, the number jumps to over 40,000 for eight literals.

Fortunately, there are some results that help in cutting down the search necessary to find the optimal ordering. The adjacency theorem (Theorem 5.1) is an example.

Given a set of literals $l_1, \ldots, l_n$, we define the situated literal l_i^j to be the literal obtained by substituting into l_i ground terms for the variables in $l_1, \ldots, l_j$. For example, given the query $P(x) \wedge Q(x,y) \wedge R(x,y)$, the situated literal $P(x)^0$ is just $P(x)$. The situated literal $Q(x,y)^0$ is $Q(x,y)$, but the situated literal $Q(x,y)^1$ is $Q(\gamma,y)$, where γ is a ground term. The situated literal $R(x,y)^0$ is $R(x,y)$; $R(x,y)^1$ is $R(\gamma,y)$; and $R(x,y)^2$ is $R(\gamma_1, \gamma_2)$.

THEOREM 5.1 (Adjacency Theorem) *If $l_1, \ldots, l_n$ is an optimal literal ordering, then $||l_i^{i-1}|| \leq ||l_{i+1}^{i-1}||$ for all i between 1 and $n-1$.*

This theorem supports our intuitions about literal ordering in the simple cases covered by the following corollaries.

COROLLARY 5.1 *The most expensive conjunct should never be done first.*

COROLLARY 5.2 *Given a conjunct sequence of length two, the less expensive conjunct should always be done first.*

The upshot of the adjacency theorem is that we need not search through all the possible orderings to find one guaranteed to be optimal. For example, in the preceding problem, we need look at only two orderings. In this case, we can eliminate two-thirds of the possibilities. As the number of literals grows, the savings becomes more substantial. A short analysis shows that the number of possible orderings that must be considered is

Table 5.1   Reduction of search space by adjacency restriction

n	$G(n,0)$	$n!$
1	1	1
2	1	2
3	2	6
4	5	24
5	16	120
6	61	720
7	272	5040
8	1385	40,320
9	7936	362,880
10	50,521	3,628,800

bounded by $G(n,0)$, where n is the number of literals and G is defined recursively, as shown.

$$G(n,d) = \begin{cases} 0 & \text{if } n = d \\ 1 & \text{if } n = 1, d = 0 \\ \Sigma_{i=0}^{n-d-1} G(n-1,i) & \text{otherwise} \end{cases}$$

Here, d can be thought of as the number of remaining literals that cannot appear as the next literal because of the adjacency restriction. Note that, if the second argument to G is ignored, the formula reduces to $n!$, as expected.

Table 5.1 shows some of the values for this function by comparison to the total number of orderings of n literals. For three literals, the adjacency restriction reduces the search space to only two orderings. For eight literals, the space is reduced from over 40,000 possibilities to fewer than 1400.

The adjacency theorem is an example of a *reduction theorem*. It reduces the space of possible orderings that must be searched to find an optimal ordering, and thereby makes the process of optimization more efficient.

5.9 Bibliographical and Historical Remarks

Many restriction strategies for resolution refutations are discussed in detail by Loveland [Loveland 1978], by Chang and Lee [Chang 1973], and by Wos et al. [Wos 1984a].

Ordered resolution is similar to *lock resolution*, which was originally proposed by Boyer [Boyer 1971], and to *SL-resolution*, which was explored by Kowalski [Kowalski 1971]. Depth-first backward resolution is the strategy used in PROLOG [Clocksin 1981, Sterling 1986], as well as in numerous expert systems. Moore [Moore 1975] was one of the first people to point out the efficiencies to be gained by choosing the appropriate direction for reasoning. Treitel and Genesereth explored the problem of automatically determining optimal directionality [Treitel 1987]. The adjacency theorem for optimal literal ordering was proved by Smith and Genesereth [Smith 1985]. A variety of additional strategies for resolution are discussed in [Kowalski 1970, 1971, 1972, Minker 1973, 1979, Smith 1986].

Although not discussed in this book, it is often helpful to precompute all the possible resolutions that can be performed among a set of clauses and to store the results in a *connection graph*. The actual search for a refutation can then be described in terms of operations on this graph. The use of connection graphs was first proposed by Kowalski [Kowalski 1975]. Other authors who have used various forms of connection graphs are Sickel [Sickel 1976], Chang and Slagle [Chang 1979a, 1979b], and Stickel [Stickel 1982].

Several extremely efficient resolution refutation systems have been written that are able to solve large, nontrivial reasoning problems, including some open problems in mathematics [Winker 1982, Wos 1984b]. A typical challenge problem for testing and illustrating the features of theorem-proving programs is the so-called *Schubert steamroller problem* [Stickel 1986].

Several other nonresolution theorem-proving systems also have been developed. Examples include those of Bledsoe [Bledsoe 1977, Ballantyne 1977], and of Boyer and Moore [Boyer 1979]. Shankar used the Boyer–Moore theorem prover in verifying steps in the proof of Gödel's incompleteness theorem [Shankar 1986].

Exercises

1. *Deletion strategies.* Consider the problem of showing that the clauses {P,Q}, {¬P,Q}, {P,¬Q}, and {¬P,¬Q} are not simultaneously satisfiable.

   a. Show a resolution trace for this problem using tautology elimination.

   b. Show a resolution trace for this problem using subsumption.

2. *Linear resolution.* Use linear resolution to show that the following set of clauses is unsatisfiable.

$$\{P,Q\}$$

$$\{Q,R\}$$

$$\{R,W\}$$

$$\{\neg R, \neg P\}$$
$$\{\neg W, \neg Q\}$$
$$\{\neg Q, \neg R\}$$

3. *Combination strategies.* We know that unit resolution is not complete, but there are some problems for which it is able to derive the empty clause. If we combine unit resolution with ordered resolution, does this make it impossible to prove some things that are provable by unit resolution alone? If so, give an example. If not, prove that there is no difference.

4. *Combination strategies.* Give a counterexample to show that the combination of ordered resolution and set of support resolution is not complete.

5. *Map coloring.* Consider the problem of coloring the following map, using only four colors, such that no two adjacent regions share the same color.

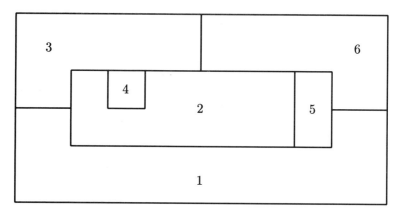

This problem can be set up as a constraint satisfaction problem. Write down the database and the query.

CHAPTER 6
Nonmonotonic Reasoning

WE HAVE ALREADY SEEN some indication of the power of the first-order
predicate calculus as a language for expressing declarative knowledge in AI
systems. We can use the predicate calculus to express any conceptualization
based on objects and their relations in a domain of discourse. Given what
we have presented so far, we might imagine that a typical AI system using
first-order logic would work somewhat as follows. Information that the
system has about its domain is expressed as a finite set Δ of first-order
formulas. We call Δ the database or *base set of beliefs* of the system. To
answer queries or to take appropriate actions, the system typically will
have to decide whether or not some formula ϕ is logically entailed by
its beliefs. We can imagine that the system will make this decision by
performing logical deductions on Δ, perhaps by using resolution on the
clause form of $\Delta \wedge \neg \phi$. (Our notation is simplified by letting Δ also stand
for the conjunction of the formulas in the set Δ.)

Even though this model is quite useful for a variety of tasks requiring
knowledge about a domain, it has major limitations. The three most
important ones are:

(1) Language (probably *any* language) cannot capture all that we want
to say about the world. A finite set of sentences can never be more
than an approximate description of things as they really are. Any
general rule that we might care to frame is subject to an unlimited
number of exceptions and qualifications. If we are going to use
language to describe the world, we will have to use it in a way
that is robust in the face of an ever-expanding set of more highly
articulated statements.

(2) The inference rules of ordinary logic (such as modus ponens and the resolution principle) are *sound*. Thus, deductions from a base set of beliefs never produce *new* knowledge about the world. If ϕ logically follows from Δ, then all the models of Δ, including our intended interpretation, also are models of ϕ. Deriving ϕ in no way eliminates any of the models and thus ϕ tells us nothing about the world that was not already described by Δ. Of course, we want to be able to manipulate our description of the world so that implicit facts about it become represented explicitly, and sound inference rules do just that for us. We also will want, however, to add formulas to Δ that say new (or revised) things about the world, and ordinary logic gives us no hints about how to do that. We need methods for reasoning with tentative statements because they are the only ones we are ever going to have. These reasoning methods will have to anticipate the possibility of later revisions of the knowledge base.

(3) The logical languages that we have used so far are adequate for expressing only those statements that we are willing to take as being either wholly true or wholly false. Often, we have information about a situation that is known to be *uncertain*. For example, we know that it is likely (but not certain) that it will be sunny in Pasadena on New Year's Day.

In the next few chapters, we will be concerned with confronting and overcoming some of these limitations. An important technique involves the use of *nonsound* inferences of various kinds. That is, from a database Δ, we will allow certain inferences that do not logically follow from Δ. Often, these inferences depend globally on *all* of the sentences in Δ rather than on a small subset. In particular, we will be introducing inference techniques the application of which depends on certain sentences *not* being in Δ. With such inference rules, if another sentence is added to Δ, an inference may have to be retracted. For this reason, such inference rules are called *nonmonotonic*. Ordinary logical inference rules, on the other hand, are monotonic because the set of theorems derivable from premises is not reduced by adding to the premises.

There are many situations in which it is appropriate for intelligent systems to augment their beliefs by new ones that do not logically follow from their explicit ones. The press of events sometimes compels *some* action before all the relevant facts are at hand. It would be useful perhaps for systems to be able to assume that the beliefs they have presently about a certain subject are all the beliefs that are important about that subject. Natural-language dialogues among humans, for example, depend on both the speaker and the hearer using several general augmenting conventions of this sort. (Example: "He didn't say John was his brother, so I'll assume he is not.")

Also, as we mentioned earlier, there is a sense in which any attempt to capture *all* the knowledge about the real world by a finite set of sentences is fundamentally impossible. As our own knowledge (and that of science) increases, our conceptualization of a subject area changes. Any conceptualization, put forward for certain purposes, is subject to challenge. Consider, for example, the following sentence about birds: "All birds fly." With the obvious intended interpretation, we might express this as $\forall x \; Bird(x) \Rightarrow Flies(x)$. This sentence might be useful for certain limited purposes, but if we tried to apply it more generally, we might be confronted by the fact that ostriches, which are birds, do not fly. After having this problem pointed out to us, we could correct it by changing our axiom about birds flying to the following:

$$\forall x \; Bird(x) \wedge \neg Ostrich(x) \Rightarrow Flies(x)$$

Even this sentence does not accurately capture the *real* world, however, because we can imagine several other kinds of birds that do not fly: baby birds, dead birds, wingless birds, and so on. The list of such *qualifications* is very long if not endless, leading us, perhaps, to despair of using language for knowledge representation. This problem often is called the *qualification problem*. Most universally quantified sentences will have to include an infinite number of qualifications if they are to be interpreted as accurate statements about the world. Yet, in our everyday reasoning, we humans use sentences that we assume to be true. What we would seem to need for our machines is an inference rule that permits us to make somewhat temporary, or *default*, assumptions that can later be revised when additional qualifications become important.

There are a number of ways to achieve the appropriate nonmonotonic effects. In this chapter, we explore three methods. In one, we adopt a convention that allows us to infer that, if we cannot prove a ground atom, then we can assume its negation. In another, we show how to compute a formula that can be added to Δ that restricts the objects that satisfy a certain predicate to just those that Δ says must satisfy that predicate. In a third, we introduce nonmonotonic rules of inference called *defaults*, and show how they are used to derive default conclusions.

These methods have several potential applications. Through examples in this and the next chapter, we indicate their utility for making reasonable assumptions about what can be inferred from a finite set of sentences. We see these nonmonotonic techniques as promising candidates for extending the reach of logic beyond some of the limitations we have noted.

6.1 The Closed-World Assumption

Recall that a theory $\mathcal{T}$ is *complete* if either every ground atom in the language or its negation is in the theory. Thus, the logical closure of the formula P(A) ∧ (P(A) ⇒ Q(A)) ∧ P(B) is not a complete theory, because neither Q(B) nor ¬Q(B) is in the theory. One convention for augmenting a theory is to complete it.

The most straightforward and simple way to complete a theory is by a convention called the *closed-world assumption (CWA)*. The CWA completes the theory defined by a base set of beliefs, Δ, by including the *negation* of a ground atom in the completed theory whenever that ground atom does not logically follow from Δ. The effect of the CWA is as though we augmented the base belief set with all the negative ground literals the positive versions of which cannot be deduced from Δ. The CWA is nonmonotonic because the set of augmented beliefs would shrink if we added a new positive ground literal to Δ.

We define the effects of the CWA in terms of customary logical notation. We call our belief set, Δ, the *proper axioms* of a theory. The theory, denoted by $\mathcal{T}[\Delta]$, is the closure of Δ under logical entailment. The CWA *augments* $\mathcal{T}[\Delta]$ by adding a set, Δ_{asm}, of *assumed beliefs*. The closure under logical implication of the union of these assumed beliefs with Δ comprises the CWA-augmented set of beliefs CWA[Δ]. The CWA can be stated succinctly as follows:

- The formula ϕ (constructed from elements of a predefined predicate-calculus language) is in $\mathcal{T}[\Delta]$ if and only if $\Delta \models \phi$. (This is the ordinary definition of a theory $\mathcal{T}[\Delta]$ in terms of a base set Δ.)

- $\neg P$ is in Δ_{asm} if and only if the ground atom P is not in $\mathcal{T}[\Delta]$. (Δ_{asm} is a set of added beliefs assumed under the CWA.)

- ϕ is in CWA[Δ] if and only if $\{\Delta \cup \Delta_{asm}\} \models \phi$. (The augmented theory, CWA[Δ], is the closure of all beliefs, explicit and assumed.)

In our example, in which Δ is P(A) ∧ (P(A) ⇒ Q(A)) ∧ P(B), the CWA adds ¬Q(B), since Δ does not logically entail Q(B).

The CWA often is used with database systems. Suppose we have a database listing pairs of countries that are geographic neighbors:

Neighbor(US,Canada)

Neighbor(US,Mexico)

Neighbor(Mexico,Guatemala)

$$\vdots$$

For such a database, it would be useful to adopt the convention that countries that are not listed as neighbors are not neighbors. That convention is an example of the CWA. Without such a convention, we would have to list explictly all the nonneighbor pairs if we wanted to be able to answer queries such as, "Are Brazil and Canada neighbors?"

Note that the CWA depends on a syntactic feature of a set of beliefs; namely, whether a *positive* ground literal can be derived. If we systematically replaced each predicate letter P_i by $\neg Q_i$ (defining $P_i \equiv \neg Q_i$) the theory would be the same, but the CWA would give different results with respect to the original predicates. The convention is most efficient when the "positive facts" are few in number compared to the "negative facts." A database designer who uses the CWA will want to conceptualize the domain in a way that matches this expectation.

We might ask whether the CWA always results in a consistent augmented theory, CWA[Δ]. The following example shows that it does not.

Let Δ contain only the clause P(A) ∨ P(B). Then neither P(A) nor P(B) is in $\mathcal{T}[\Delta]$, so by the CWA their negations are *both* in CWA[Δ]. Together, however, these negations are not consistent with P(A) ∨ P(B).

The source of this difficulty is that Δ contained a disjunction of ground atoms (positive ground literals) but no way to prove any of them. Thus, the conjunction of their negations, which contradicts the original disjunction, is in the augmented theory. The following theorem links this difficulty with the inconsistency of CWA[Δ].

THEOREM 6.1 CWA[Δ] *is consistent if and only if, for every positive-ground-literal clause* $L_1 \vee L_2 \vee \ldots \vee L_n$ *that follows from* Δ, *there is also entailed by* Δ *at least one ground literal* L_i *that subsumes it. (Equivalently, the CWA augmentation* CWA[Δ] *of a consistent* Δ *is inconsistent if and only if there are positive ground literals* $L_1, \ldots, L_n$ *such that* $\Delta \models L_1 \vee L_2 \vee \ldots \vee L_n$ *but, for* $i = 1, \ldots, n$, $\Delta \not\models L_i$.)

Proof CWA[Δ] can be inconsistent only if $\Delta \cup \Delta_{asm}$ is. Then, by the compactness theorem of logic, there is a finite subset of Δ_{asm} that contradicts Δ. Let this subset be $\{\neg L_1, \ldots, \neg L_n\}$. Then Δ implies the negation of the conjunction of these formulas; that is, $\Delta \models L_1 \vee \ldots \vee L_n$. Since each $\neg L_i$ is in Δ_{asm}, by the definition of Δ_{asm}, none of the L_i follow from Δ. The proof in the other direction is obvious. $\square$

The application of Theorem 6.1 depends critically on the terms that we allow as part of the language. For example, if the only object constants in the language are A and B, then the following clauses do not have an inconsistent augmentation (even though one of them is a disjunction of positive literals):

P(x) ∨ Q(x)

P(A)

Q(B)

In this case, the only ground clauses of the form $L_1 \vee L_2 \vee \ldots \vee L_n$ that can be proved from Δ are P(A) $\vee$ Q(A) and P(B) $\vee$ Q(B) (by universal instantiation). Each of these is subsumed by one of the clauses in Δ. On the other hand, if we also admit the object constant C, we also can prove P(C) $\vee$ Q(C), but we can prove neither P(C) nor Q(C) to subsume it, so the CWA produces an inconsistent augmentation in that case.

In the first case of this example, we limited the object constants of the language to those that occurred in Δ. We sometimes also want to make the assumption that the only objects in the domain are the ones that can be named using the object and function constants occurring in the language. This is called the *domain-closure assumption (DCA)*. If there are no function constants in the language, the DCA can be written as the following axiom, the domain-closure axiom:

$$\forall x \; x{=}t_1 \vee x{=}t_2 \vee \ldots$$

where the t_i are the object constants of the language. (If the language contained function constants, there would be an infinite number of terms that could be constructed, and typically the DCA could not be expressed by a first-order formula.) This axiom makes a strong assumption. It allows us, for example, to replace any quantifiers by finite conjunctions and disjunctions; then the belief set would be equivalent to a propositional combination of ground literals.

Another assumption often used in connection with nonmonotonic reasoning is the *unique-names assumption (UNA)*: If ground terms cannot be proved equal, they can be assumed unequal. The UNA is a consequence of the CWA; it is merely an application of the CWA to the equality predicate. The DCA is sometimes used in addition to the CWA to restrict the augmentation further.

Since it may be difficult to test the conditions of Theorem 6.1, the following corollary is important. (Recall that a *Horn clause* is defined to be one that has at most one positive literal.)

COROLLARY 6.1 *If the clause form of Δ is Horn and consistent, then the CWA augmentation* CWA[Δ] *is consistent.*

Proof Suppose the contrary; that is, that Δ is Horn and consistent but that CWA[Δ] is inconsistent. Then, according to Theorem 6.1, we can deduce from Δ a ground clause $L_1 \vee L_2 \vee \ldots \vee L_n$ containing only positive ground literals no one of which is derivable from Δ. Thus, $\Delta \cup \{\neg L_1, \ldots, \neg L_n\}$ is inconsistent. However, because Δ contains only Horn clauses, it must then be the case that for some i, $\Delta \wedge \neg L_i$ is inconsistent (see Exercise 3). Or, for some i, $\Delta \models L_i$. But this contradicts the choice of L_i. $\square$

Thus we see that an important class of theories—the so-called Horn theories—have consistent CWA augmentations. We see from Theorem 6.1, however, that the condition that Δ be Horn is not absolutely necessary for the CWA augmentation of Δ to be consistent.

The CWA is too strong for many applications. We do not always want to assume that *any* ground atom not provable from Δ is false. Weakening this assumption in the natural way leads to the idea of the CWA *with respect to a predicate P*. Under that convention, ground atoms in some particular predicate, P, that are not provable from Δ are assumed to be false. The assumed beliefs, Δ_{asm}, in that case contain only negative ground literals in P.

For example, suppose Δ is:

$$\forall x \ Q(x) \ \Rightarrow \ P(x)$$

$$Q(A)$$

$$R(B) \ \vee \ P(B)$$

Applying the CWA to Δ with respect to P allows us to conclude ¬P(B), because P(B) cannot be concluded from Δ. That, in turn, allows us also to conclude R(B) from Δ. (Unconstrained application of the CWA to Δ would have condoned concluding both ¬R(B) and ¬P(B), which contradict Δ.)

We also can make the CWA with respect to a *set* of predicates. In database applications, this assumption allows us to assume that certain relations in the database are complete and others are not. If the set contains all the predicates in Δ, then we get the same result as we would have got with the ordinary CWA.

It is interesting to note that the CWA with respect to a set of predicates may produce an inconsistent augmentation even when the CWA with respect to each one of the predicates alone produces a consistent augmentation. For example, the CWA with respect to the set {P,Q} is inconsistent with the belief set (PvQ), even though the CWA with respect to either P or Q is consistent with that belief set.

We might be tempted to say that the source of this difficulty is that (P ∨ Q) is not Horn in the set {P,Q}. (We say that a set of clauses is Horn in the predicate P if there is at most one positive occurrence of P in each clause. We say that a set Δ of clauses is Horn in a set of predicates Π if and only if each of the clauses would be Horn in P after substituting the letter P for each occurence of any of the letters in Π in the clauses of Δ.) Even if a belief set were Horn in a set of predicates, however, the CWA with respect to the predicates in this set might produce an inconsistent augmentation. Suppose Δ is {P(A)vQ, P(B)v¬Q}. This set is Horn in the set {P}, and making the CWA with respect to the predicates (just P) in {P} yields both ¬P(A) and ¬P(B). These, together with Δ, are inconsistent.

6.2 Predicate Completion

It happens that we often can express in a single sentence of logic the assumption that the only objects that satisfy a predicate are those that *must* do so—given our beliefs. We will describe several of these methods— all related but of increasing generality and power.

First consider the simple case in which P(A) is the *only* formula in Δ. P(A) is equivalent to the following expression:

$$\forall x \ x{=}A \ \Rightarrow \ P(x)$$

Such a formula could be taken to be the "if" half of a *definition* for P. The assumption that there are no other objects that satisfy P can then be made by writing the "only if" half as

$$\forall x \ P(x) \ \Rightarrow \ x{=}A$$

This half is called the *completion formula* for P. It makes the explicit information about P in Δ *complete*.

The conjunction of Δ with the completion formula is called *the completion of* P *in* Δ, and is denoted by COMP[Δ; P]. In this case, we have

$$\text{COMP}[\Delta; P] \equiv (\forall x \ P(x) \ \Rightarrow \ x{=}A) \wedge \Delta$$
$$\equiv \ \forall x \ P(x) \ \Leftrightarrow \ x{=}A$$

In this example, predicate completion (if augmented by the UNA) produces the same effect as the CWA with respect to P.

If Δ contained only two formulas in P, say P(A) and P(B), the completion formula would be

$$\forall x \ P(x) \ \Rightarrow \ x{=}A \ \vee \ x{=}B$$

Here again, predicate completion of P (together with unique names) has the same effect as the CWA with respect to P.

If Δ contains formulas in which a predicate P occurs disjunctively with other predicates or in which P contains variables, predicate completion is more complex. In fact, we define predicate completion for only certain kinds of clauses.

We say that a set of clauses is *solitary* in P if each clause with a positive occurrence of P has at most *one* occurrence of P. Note that clauses solitary in P are also Horn in P, but not necessarily vice versa. For example Q(A) $\vee$ ¬P(B) $\vee$ P(A) is Horn in P, but not solitary in P.

We define predicate completion of P only for clauses solitary in P. Suppose Δ is a set of clauses solitary in P. We can write each of the clauses in Δ that contains a positive P literal in the following form:

$$\forall y \ Q_1 \wedge \ldots \wedge Q_m \ \Rightarrow \ P(t)$$

where t is a tuple of terms, $[t_1, t_2, \ldots, t_n]$, and the Q_i are literals not containing P. There may be no Q_i, in which case the clause is simply $P(t)$. The Q_i and t may contain variables, say the tuple of variables $\mathbf{y}$.

This expression is equivalent to

$$\forall y \forall \mathbf{x} \ (\mathbf{x}{=}t) \wedge Q_1 \wedge \ldots \wedge Q_m \ \Rightarrow \ P(\mathbf{x})$$

where $\mathbf{x}$ is a tuple of variables not occurring in t and $(\mathbf{x}{=}t)$ is an abbreviation for $(\mathbf{x}_1{=}t_1 \wedge \ldots \wedge \mathbf{x}_n{=}t_n)$. Finally, since the variables $\mathbf{y}$ occur in only the antecedent of the implication, this expression is equivalent to

$$\forall \mathbf{x} \ (\exists y \ (\mathbf{x}{=}t) \wedge Q_1 \wedge \ldots \wedge Q_m) \ \Rightarrow \ P(\mathbf{x})$$

This way of writing the clause is called the *normal form* of the clause. Suppose there are exactly k clauses ($k > 0$) in Δ that have a positive P literal. Let the normal forms of these clauses be

$$\forall \mathbf{x} \ E_1 \ \Rightarrow \ P(\mathbf{x})$$
$$\forall \mathbf{x} \ E_2 \ \Rightarrow \ P(\mathbf{x})$$
$$\vdots$$
$$\forall \mathbf{x} \ E_k \ \Rightarrow \ P(\mathbf{x})$$

Each of the E_i will be an existentially quantified conjunction of literals, as in the preceding generic case. If we group together these clauses as a single implication, we obtain

$$\forall \mathbf{x} \ E_1 \vee E_2 \vee \ldots \vee E_k \ \Rightarrow \ P(\mathbf{x})$$

Here we have an expression that can be taken as the "if" half of a definition for P. It suggests the following, "only if," *completion formula* for P:

$$\forall \mathbf{x} \ P(\mathbf{x}) \ \Rightarrow \ E_1 \vee E_2 \vee \ldots \vee E_k$$

Since the E_i do not contain P, the "if" and "only if" parts together can be thought of as a *definition* for P:

$$\forall \texttt{x} \ P(\texttt{x}) \ \Leftrightarrow \ E_1 \vee E_2 \vee \ldots \vee E_k$$

Since the "if" part already is entailed by Δ, we define the *completion of P in Δ* as

$$\text{COMP}[\Delta; P] \equiv_{def} \Delta \wedge (\forall \texttt{x} \ P(\texttt{x}) \ \Leftrightarrow \ E_1 \vee \ldots \vee E_k)$$

where the E_i are the antecedents of the normal forms of the clauses in Δ, as defined previously.

Let us consider a simple example of predicate completion. Suppose Δ is

$$\forall \texttt{x} \ \texttt{Ostrich(x)} \ \Rightarrow \ \texttt{Bird(x)}$$

$$\texttt{Bird(Tweety)}$$

$$\neg\texttt{Ostrich(Sam)}$$

(All ostriches are birds; Tweety is a bird; Sam is not an ostrich.) We note that Δ is solitary in `Bird`. Let us complete `Bird` in Δ. Writing those clauses containing `Bird` in normal form yields

$$\forall \texttt{x} \ \texttt{Ostrich(x)} \vee \texttt{x=Tweety} \ \Rightarrow \ \texttt{Bird(x)}$$

The completion of `Bird` in Δ is then simply

$$\text{COMP}[\Delta; \texttt{Bird}] \equiv \Delta \wedge (\forall \texttt{x} \ \texttt{Bird(x)} \ \Leftrightarrow \ \texttt{Ostrich(x)} \vee \texttt{x=Tweety})$$

(The only birds are ostriches or Tweety.) With the completion formula added to Δ (and augmented by the UNA) we could prove, for example, $\neg\texttt{Bird(Sam)}$.

What is predicate completion doing for us in this case? Δ tells us that Tweety is a bird, that Sam is not an ostrich, and that all ostriches are birds. Completion of `Bird` in Δ is a way of making the assumption that there are no birds other than those about which Δ tells us. That is, the only birds are Tweety and ostriches. Since Sam is not an ostrich, and since the UNA lets us assume that Sam is not Tweety, we can conclude that Sam is not a bird.

If we did not limit Δ to clauses solitary in P, the completion process might produce circular definitions for P, which would not restrict the objects that satisfy P to those that must do so, given Δ. Sometimes, we can formally apply the completion process to clauses Horn (but not solitary) in P and still get meaningful results. Consider the following Horn clauses that describe the factorial relation (we assume implicit universal quantification):

x=0 ⇒ Factorial(x,1)

x≠0 ∧ Factorial(Minus(x,1),y) ⇒ Factorial(x,Times(x,y))

Writing these expressions in normal form yields

x=0 ∧ z=1 ⇒ Factorial(x,z)

(∃y x≠0 ∧ z=Times(x,y) ∧ Factorial(Minus(x,1),y)) ⇒
Factorial(x,z)

Now we formally perform predicate completion on Factorial (even though the clauses are not solitary in Factorial). The result is

Factorial(x,z) ⇒
(x=0 ∧ z=1) ∨
(∃y x≠0 ∧ z=Times(x,y) ∧ Factorial(x-1,y))

This result is easily interpreted as a recursive definition of factorial. It illustrates that limiting predicate completion to solitary clauses is perhaps unnecessarily restrictive. Not all definitions of a predicate in terms of itself are circular—some are recursive.

There are two special cases of predicate completion that give rise to interesting forms for the completion formulas. Suppose Δ is of the form $(\forall x \ P(x))$. Making use of the atom T, we can write this clause as $(\forall x \ T \Rightarrow P(x))$. Completion of P then gives the completion formula $(\forall x \ P(x) \Rightarrow T)$, which is a valid formula and thus does not further restrict our theory. (Restricting the objects that satisfy P to all objects in the domain is no restriction.)

On the other hand, if there are *no* clauses in Δ that are positive in P, we can assume any valid one; e.g., $(\forall x \ F \Rightarrow P(x))$. Completion of P then gives the completion formula $(\forall x \ P(x) \Rightarrow F)$, which is equivalent to $(\forall x \ \neg P(x))$. In this latter case, Δ says nothing about there being any objects satisfying P; therefore, we assume there are none.

Although in simple cases predicate completion and the CWA have the same effect, in general they are different. For example, suppose that Δ contains the single formula P(A), and that the language also contains the object constant B. Then the CWA extension includes ¬P(B), and the completion formula is $(\forall x \ P(x) \Rightarrow (x=A))$. These two expressions are not equivalent, although ¬P(B) plus the DCA entails $(\forall x \ P(x) \Rightarrow (x=A))$; and $(\forall x \ P(x) \Rightarrow (x=A))$ plus the UNA entails ¬P(B). ([Lifschitz 1985b] derives general conditions relating these two augmenting conventions.)

Predicate completion, like the CWA, is nonmonotonic because, if another clause positive in P were added to Δ, the completion formula for P would be different. In general, it would be weaker; i.e., the augmented theory would allow more objects to satisfy P than the original one did. Thus, some proofs of expressions of the form $\neg P$ could no longer be obtained. In our earlier example about birds, if we were to augment Δ by including Penguin(x)$\Rightarrow$Bird(x), then the new completion formula for Bird would be:

$$\text{Bird(x)} \Rightarrow \text{Ostrich(x)} \vee \text{Penguin(x)} \vee \text{x=Tweety}$$

and we could no longer prove ¬Bird(Sam) as we could earlier. (Sam might be a penguin.)

Extending a set of beliefs by predicate completion preserves their consistency.

THEOREM 6.2 *If Δ is a consistent set of clauses solitary in P, then the completion of P in Δ is consistent.*

This theorem follows from stronger results, Theorem 6.7 or Theorem 6.8, given later in the chapter (also without proof).

We also can perform predicate completion of several predicates in parallel. In *parallel predicate completion* of a set of predicates, each predicate in the set is completed separately (without regard for the others), and the conjunction of these separate completion formulas is added to Δ. The completion process for each uses only the original clauses in Δ and not the formulas added by the completion process for other predicates. Parallel predicate completion allows us to restrict the objects that satisfy any of several predicates to those that are forced to do so by Δ.

For the several completion formulas to avoid circularity, we must impose a condition on the way in which the predicates being completed can occur in Δ. To motivate this condition, consider the following clauses (which are solitary in P, Q, and R):

$$\text{Q(x)} \Rightarrow \text{P(x)}$$
$$\text{R(x)} \Rightarrow \text{Q(x)}$$
$$\text{P(x)} \Rightarrow \text{R(x)}$$

Parallel predicate completion of {P,Q,R} would yield:

$$\text{P(x)} \Leftrightarrow \text{Q(x)} \Leftrightarrow \text{R(x)} \Leftrightarrow \text{P(x)}$$

which is circular.

Recall that writing clauses that are solitary in P in their normal forms allowed us to combine all clauses in Δ containing a positive P literal into a single formula of the form

$$\forall x \ E_1 \lor E_2 \lor \ldots \lor E_k \Rightarrow P(x)$$

Denoting the antecedent of this implication simply by E gives us

$$\forall x \ E \Rightarrow P(x)$$

where E contains *no* occurrences of P.

To perform parallel predicate completion of the set $\Pi = \{P_1, P_2, \ldots, P_n\}$ of predicates in Δ, we first write those clauses in Δ containing members of Π in their normal forms, then combine the clauses containing the same P_is into single formulas.

$$\forall x \ E_1 \Rightarrow P_1(x)$$
$$\forall x \ E_2 \Rightarrow P_2(x)$$
$$\forall x \ E_3 \Rightarrow P_3(x)$$
$$\vdots$$
$$\forall x \ E_n \Rightarrow P_n(x)$$

Parallel predicate completion is then accomplished by adding to Δ the completion formulas $(\forall x \ P_i(x) \Rightarrow E_i)$ for $i = 1, \ldots, n$. To avoid circular definitions of the P_i, we must be able to order the P_i such that each E_i has no occurrences of any of $\{P_i, P_{i+1}, \ldots, P_n\}$ (and has no negative occurrences of any of $\{P_1, \ldots, P_{i-1}\}$). If this ordering can be achieved, we say that the clauses in Δ are *ordered in* Π. In the next section, we illustrate parallel predicate completion with an example.

Note that, if Δ is ordered in Π, it also is solitary in each of the P_i individually (but not necessarily conversely).

Theorem 6.2, about the consistency of predicate completion, can be generalized to the case of parallel predicate completion.

THEOREM 6.3 *If Δ is consistent and ordered in Π, then the parallel completion of Π in Δ is consistent.*

This theorem is a consequence of extended versions of either Theorem 6.7 or Theorem 6.8, given later in the chapter.

6.3 Taxonomic Hierarchies and Default Reasoning

Several AI systems have included simple mechanisms to allow a kind of reasoning called *reasoning by default*. Since typically birds can fly, for example, we assume (by default) that an arbitrary bird can fly unless we know that it cannot. In this section, we describe a technique for stating the *typical* properties of objects and then show how a variant of parallel predicate completion can be used to perform default reasoning.

Often, this style of reasoning is applied to taxonomic hierarchies in which subclasses *inherit* the properties of their superclasses unless these properties are specifically canceled. Suppose, for example, that our beliefs, Δ, include the following formulas that define a taxonomic hierarchy:

$$\text{Thing(Tweety)}$$

$$\text{Bird(x)} \Rightarrow \text{Thing(x)}$$

$$\text{Ostrich(x)} \Rightarrow \text{Bird(x)}$$

$$\text{Flying-Ostrich(x)} \Rightarrow \text{Ostrich(x)}$$

(Tweety is a thing; all birds are things; all ostriches are birds; all flying ostriches are ostriches.)

This subset of Δ that defines the taxonomic hierarchy will be denoted by Δ_H.

Suppose we also want to include in Δ statements that describe some of the properties of the objects in the taxonomic hierarchy. For example, we might want to say that no things except birds can fly, that all birds except ostriches can fly, and that no ostriches except flying ostriches can fly. One way to do this is with the following formulas:

    a. $\text{Thing(x)} \land \neg\text{Bird(x)} \Rightarrow \neg\text{Flies(x)}$
    b. $\text{Bird(x)} \land \neg\text{Ostrich(x)} \Rightarrow \text{Flies(x)}$
    c. $\text{Ostrich(x)} \land \neg\text{Flying-Ostrich(x)} \Rightarrow \neg\text{Flies(x)}$
    d. $\text{Flying-Ostrich(x)} \Rightarrow \text{Flies(x)}$

The subset of Δ that describes properties of objects in the hierarchy will be denoted by Δ_P. Whether we regard a predicate as defining a taxonomic *kind* of object or a nontaxonomic *property* of an object is left to us. In this example, we choose to think of flying simply as a property that certain objects have—not as defining a kind of object.

Here, exceptions to general rules are listed explicitly in the rules. If we had exceptions to birds flying other than ostriches, we would have to list each of these exceptions in rule b. Of course, a general commonsense reasoning system would need to know about other common exceptions, such as penguins and baby birds. As we mentioned earlier in discussing the qualification problem, there would be no particular difficulty in principle with listing all known exceptions in the rule. The problem is that the system designer cannot really think of *all* of the exceptions that the system might later confront—exceptions such as wingless eagles, brain-damaged gulls, and roast ducks. Instead of listing all these exceptions, we would prefer some technique that allows us to say that birds (typically) can fly unless they are abnormal in some respect—an abnormality shared by ostriches, penguins, and such. Exceptions that we think of later can then be simply introduced by conferring this same abnormality on the new exceptions. Similarly, we would want to say that things (typically) cannot fly unless they are abnormal in some other respect—an abnormality shared by birds, airplanes, and mosquitoes. A hierarchy of exceptions would thus have to deal with several different kinds of abnormalities. We make these abnormalities part of the taxonomic hierarchy.

The following rule seems to capture what we want to say about things in general:

$$\text{Thing(x)} \land \neg\text{Ab1(x)} \Rightarrow \neg\text{Flies(x)}$$

where `Ab1` is a predicate that has to do with that particular type of abnormality that must be provably absent if we are to use this general rule to prove that things cannot fly. Thus, our rule states that things do not fly unless they have an abnormality of type 1, say. (We will soon introduce other types of abnormalities.)

Birds are among those objects that have an abnormality of type 1:

$$\text{Bird(x)} \Rightarrow \text{Ab1(x)}$$

We call this rule an *inheritance cancellation rule.* The taxonomic rule `Bird(x)` $\Rightarrow$ `Thing(x)` ordinarily could be used to conclude that birds *inherit* the traits of things generally—including the inability to fly (if they are not abnormal). Cancellation rules, declaring abnormalities, thus block the inheritance of specified traits. We include them in Δ_H, the formulas that define the taxonomic hierarchy.

The designer of a commonsense reasoning system could put in such information as is available about objects that might have abnormalities of type 1; e.g., airplanes, certain insects, and so on. The important feature of this way of dealing with exceptions is that additional axioms about abnormalities can be added at any time. New knowledge about flying objects can be expressed by *adding* axioms to the belief set instead of by having to *change* them!

Continuing with our example, we express the general knowledge that birds (typically) can fly by the rule:

$$\text{Bird(x)} \land \neg\text{Ab2(x)} \Rightarrow \text{Flies(x)}$$

The predicate Ab2 is about a type of abnormality the presence of which in birds prevents us from using this rule to conclude that those birds can fly. Ostriches are among those objects that have this type of abnormality; thus, we have another cancellation rule:

$$\text{Ostrich(x)} \Rightarrow \text{Ab2(x)}$$

Ordinarily, ostriches cannot fly:

$$\text{Ostrich(x)} \land \neg\text{Ab3(x)} \Rightarrow \neg\text{Flies(x)}$$

The predicate Ab3 is about a type of abnormality the presence of which in ostriches prevents us from using this rule to conclude that those ostriches cannot fly. Flying ostriches (if there are such) are among those objects having this type of abnormality:

$$\text{Flying-Ostrich(x)} \Rightarrow \text{Ab3(x)}$$

Using this approach, we now have the following formulas in Δ_H defining the taxonomic hierarchy:

$$\text{Flying-Ostrich(x)} \Rightarrow \text{Ostrich(x)}$$
$$\text{Flying-Ostrich(x)} \Rightarrow \text{Ab3(x)}$$
$$\text{Ostrich(x)} \Rightarrow \text{Bird(x)}$$
$$\text{Ostrich(x)} \Rightarrow \text{Ab2(x)}$$
$$\text{Bird(x)} \Rightarrow \text{Thing(x)}$$
$$\text{Bird(x)} \Rightarrow \text{Ab1(x)}$$
$$\text{Thing(Tweety)}$$

(We include the information that Tweety is a "thing" to illustrate how our approach can be used to reason nonmonotonically about the properties of Tweety.)

This taxonomy is represented graphically by the network of Figure 6.1. Note that our taxonomy does not have to be a tree. (To allow us to use parallel predicate completion, which we will do, our taxonomy does have to be a partial order.)

The properties of objects in the hierarchy are described by the following formulas in Δ_P:

$$\text{Thing(x)} \land \neg\text{Ab1(x)} \Rightarrow \neg\text{Flies(x)}$$
$$\text{Bird(x)} \land \neg\text{Ab2(x)} \Rightarrow \text{Flies(x)}$$

$$\text{Ostrich(x)} \land \neg\text{Ab3(x)} \Rightarrow \neg\text{Flies(x)}$$

$$\text{Flying-Ostrich(x)} \Rightarrow \text{Flies(x)}$$

We now perform parallel predicate completion on the set {Ab1, Ab2, Ab3, Flying-Ostrich, Ostrich, Bird, Thing} in just Δ_H to make the assumption that the only objects that are things, birds, ostriches, flying ostriches, or objects that are abnormal in any respect are those that are forced to be so by Δ_H. The clauses in Δ_H have an ordering in the set {Ab1, Ab2, Ab3, Flying-Ostrich, Ostrich, Bird, Thing}, so parallel predicate completion will not result in circular definitions.

In this simple example, we obtain the following completion clauses (by completing {Ab1, Ab2, Ab3, Flying-Ostrich, Ostrich, Bird, Thing}, in Δ_H):

1. Thing(x) $\Rightarrow$ Bird(x) $\lor$ x=Tweety
2. Bird(x) $\Rightarrow$ Ostrich(x)
3. Ostrich(x) $\Rightarrow$ Flying-Ostrich(x)
4. ¬Flying-Ostrich(x)
5. Ab1(x) $\Rightarrow$ Bird(x)
6. Ab2(x) $\Rightarrow$ Ostrich(x)
7. Ab3(x) $\Rightarrow$ Flying-Ostrich(x)

The only object mentioned is Tweety, and it is a thing, so these clauses appropriately tell us that there are no things other than Tweety, and no birds, ostriches, or flying ostriches at all. Also, there are no objects

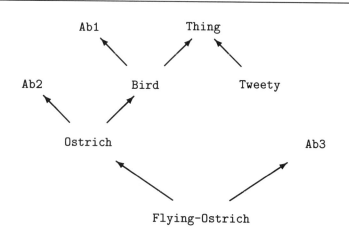

Figure 6.1   A taxonomic hierarchy with abnormalities.

abnormal in any respect. Using the properties mentioned in Δ_P, we can deduce ¬Flies(Tweety) after first proving ¬Flying-Ostrich(Tweety), ¬Ostrich(Tweety), ¬Bird(Tweety), and ¬Ab1(Tweety).

If we were to add Bird(Tweety) to our taxonomic hierarchy, completion formula 2 would change to Bird(x)⇒Ostrich(x)∨(x=Tweety). We would still be able to prove ¬Ab2(Tweety) (but not ¬Ab1(Tweety)), so we would then be able to conclude Flies(Tweety), and so on. As the reasoning system learns about other objects and other ways in which objects might have various types of abnormalities, the taxonomy changes, the predicate completion formulas are recomputed as appropriate, and the conclusions that the system can derive change correspondingly.

We call this process of completing predicates in a subset of Δ *delimited completion*. It is important to note that delimited completion of a set of predicates is not generally the same as completing these same predicates in the full Δ. (The reader should work out full completion in this case as an exercise.) Delimited completion typically produces a stronger augmenting assumption than would be produced by completion of the same predicates in the full Δ, but it is an assumption that is often justified and useful. One must be careful, however, because delimited completion might produce an inconsistent augmentation (see Exercise 6 at the end of the chapter). Later, we shall discuss a more general and robust procedure for augmenting beliefs with default assumptions of this kind.

6.4 Circumscription

Reviewing what we have said about augmentation conventions so far, we have seen that the CWA augments a belief set to include the negations of ground positive literals when these ground atoms cannot be proved true. Predicate completion is defined for belief sets consisting of clauses solitary in a predicate and augments such belief sets by formulas that state that the only objects satisfying the predicate are those that must do so, given the belief set.

Both of these augmenting ideas are based on a kind of *minimization* principle. In the case of predicate completion, the minimality idea is particularly clear. If that part of Δ containing a predicate P to be completed is written as $(\forall x)[E \Rightarrow P(x)]$, then P is *completed* by the formula $(\forall x)[P(x) \Rightarrow E]$. That is, no objects have property P unless Δ says they must.

We might like to use the same minimality assumption (i.e., that the only objects satisfying P are those that must, given Δ) in cases where Δ cannot be written as a set of clauses solitary in a predicate. For example, suppose Δ consists of the single formula $(\exists y\ P(y))$. What can be said about the smallest set of objects satisfying P in this case? This formula is not a clause, so we cannot use predicate completion. We know that there must be at least *one* object satisfying P, but there is nothing in Δ that says that there need be more than one. We can assume there is only one by adding the formula $(\exists y \forall x \ (x=y) \Leftrightarrow P(x))$.

Now, suppose Δ consists of the single clause $(P(A) \lor P(B))$. This clause is not solitary in P, so we cannot use predicate completion here either. Intuitively, however, it would seem that the formula

$$(\forall x \ P(x) \Leftrightarrow x=A) \lor (\forall x \ P(x) \Leftrightarrow x=B)$$

says what we want to say about P being minimized.

To derive augmentations of this sort for arbitrary belief sets, we must delve into the minimization process in more detail. In doing so, we define a process called *circumscription* that, like predicate completion, involves computing a certain formula that, when conjoined to Δ, says that the only objects satisfying a predicate are those that have to do so, given Δ.

Circumscription is based on the idea of *minimal* models. Let $M[\Delta]$ and $M^*[\Delta]$ be two models of Δ. (You may want to refer to Chapter 2 to review the definition of a model in logic.) We say that $M^*[\Delta]$ is no larger than $M[\Delta]$ in predicate P, writing $M^*[\Delta] \preceq_P M[\Delta]$, if (1) M and M^* have the same domain of objects, (2) all other relation and function constants in Δ besides P have the same interpretations in M and M^*, but (3) the extension of (the relation corresponding to) P in M^* is a subset of the extension of P in M. That is, if $M^* \preceq_P M$, then the set of objects satisfying P in M^* is a subset of those satisfying P in M. We write $M^* \prec_P M$ if $M^* \preceq_P M$ and $M \npreceq_P M^*$.

There may be models of Δ that are *minimal in P* according to the ordering $\preceq_P$. M_m is *P-minimal* if, for any $M \preceq_P M_m$, $M = M_m$. (As we shall see later, minimal models do not always exist.) If a model M_m of Δ is P-minimal, then no objects satisfy the extension of P except those that have to do so, given Δ. We would like to find a sentence ϕ_P such that, for any M that is a model of $\Delta \land \phi_P$, there is no M^* that is a model of Δ with $M^* \prec_P M$. That is, the models of $\Delta \land \phi_P$ are P-minimal models of Δ. The sentence ϕ_P when conjoined to Δ asserts that there are no objects that satisfy P except those that have to do so, given Δ. We call this conjunction the *circumscription of P in Δ*.

To find an expression for ϕ_P in terms of P and Δ, we reason as follows. Let P^* be a relation constant of the same arity as P, and let $\Delta(P^*)$ be Δ with each occurrence of the relation constant P in Δ replaced by P^*. We note that any model of

$$(\forall x \ P^*(x) \Rightarrow P(x)) \land \neg(\forall x \ P(x) \Rightarrow P^*(x)) \land \Delta(P^*)$$

is *not* a P-minimal model of Δ because, in such a model, the extension corresponding to P^* would be a strict subset of the extension corresponding to P (and P^* satisfies Δ). (Again, for brevity, we allow x to be possibly a tuple of variables.) Therefore, any model of

$$\neg((\forall x \ P^*(x) \ \Rightarrow \ P(x)) \ \wedge \ \neg(\forall x \ P(x) \ \Rightarrow \ P^*(x)) \ \wedge \ \Delta(P^*))$$

is a P-minimal model of Δ.

Since P^* in the preceding expression can be *any* relation constant of the same arity as P, the ϕ_P that we seek is the second-order logic formula obtained by universally quantifying over the relation variable P*:

$$\forall P* \ \neg((\forall x \ P*(x) \ \Rightarrow P(x)) \ \wedge \ \neg(\forall x \ P(x) \ \Rightarrow P*(x)) \ \wedge \ \Delta(P*))$$

We call this expression the *circumscription formula* for P in Δ. Any model of the circumscription formula is a P-minimal model of Δ. Conjoining the circumscription formula with Δ itself gives us the *circumscription* of P in Δ:

$$\mathrm{CIRC}[\Delta; P] \equiv_{def} \Delta \wedge \forall P* \ \neg((\forall x \ P*(x) \ \Rightarrow \ P(x)) \ \wedge$$
$$\neg(\forall x \ P(x) \ \Rightarrow \ P*(x)) \wedge \Delta(P*))$$

Although the use of a second-order formula is unsettling (since we have not described inference techniques for second-order logics), we shall see that, in many important cases, this formula can be reduced to an equivalent first-order formula.

Before discussing methods for simplifying the second-order formula for circumscription, we shall first rewrite it in some alternative forms.

Distributing the negation over the three conjuncts in the circumscription formula and then rewriting the resulting disjunction as an implication yields the usual form for circumscription:

$$\mathrm{CIRC}[\Delta; P] \equiv \Delta \wedge (\forall P* \ (\Delta(P*) \ \wedge \ (\forall x \ P*(x) \ \Rightarrow \ P(x))) \ \Rightarrow$$
$$(\forall x \ P(x) \ \Rightarrow \ P*(x)))$$

We can get an additional perspective by deriving another form of circumscription. Since the preceding circumscription formula is universally quantified over P*, it holds in particular for $P \wedge P'$ substituted for P* (where P' is a relation constant of the same arity as P):

$$\Delta(P \wedge P') \ \wedge \ (\forall x \ P(x) \ \wedge \ P'(x) \ \Rightarrow \ P(x)) \ \Rightarrow$$
$$(\forall x \ P(x) \ \Rightarrow \ P(x) \ \wedge \ P'(x))$$

This formula reduces to

$$\Delta(P \wedge P') \ \Rightarrow \ (\forall x \ P(x) \ \Rightarrow \ P'(x))$$

Since P' is arbitrary, this formula says that P is circumscribed if and only if any alleged strengthening of P (say to $P \wedge P'$) that still satisfies Δ is no real strengthening because P would then already imply P' anyway.

It is convenient to abbreviate $(\forall \mathbf{x}\ P^*(\mathbf{x}) \Rightarrow P(\mathbf{x}))$ by the expression $P^* \leq P$. We also use the abbreviations $(P^* < P)$ for $((P^* \leq P) \wedge \neg(P \leq P^*))$ and $(P^* = P)$ for $((P^* \leq P) \wedge (P \leq P^*))$. These abbreviations also help us to remember that, when $(\forall \mathbf{x}\ P^*(\mathbf{x}) \Rightarrow P(\mathbf{x}))$, an extension corresponding to P^* is a subset of an extension corresponding to P.

In terms of these abbreviations, we can write the circumscription formula as

$$\forall P* \ (\Delta(P*) \wedge (P* \leq P)) \ \Rightarrow \ (P \leq P*)$$

which is equivalent to

$$\forall P* \ \Delta(P*) \ \Rightarrow \ \neg(P* < P)$$

or

$$\neg(\exists P* \ \Delta(P*) \wedge (P* < P))$$

This last form of the circumscription formula makes the intuitively helpful statement that there can be no P* that, when substituted for P in Δ, still satisfies Δ and that has a corresponding extension that is a strict subset of the extension corresponding to P.

There are several cases in which circumscription can be simplified. The following theorem often is useful:

THEOREM 6.4 *Given a predicate P, an arbitrary belief set $\Delta(P)$ (containing the predicate P), and any P' of the same arity as P but not defined in terms of P, then, if $\Delta(P) \models \Delta(P') \wedge (P' \leq P)$, $\mathrm{CIRC}[\Delta; P] \equiv \Delta(P) \wedge (P = P')$.*

We first discuss the importance of this theorem and then give its proof and an example of its use. The theorem states that, if we have some predicate P' of the same arity as P but not containing P, and if we can prove $\Delta(P') \wedge (P' \leq P)$, given Δ, then $(P = P')$ is equivalent to the circumscription formula for P in Δ. The theorem is most often used to confirm conjectures about circumscription formulas. P' may contain bound predicate variables, so the circumscription formula may still be a second-order formula; in many cases of interest, however, it will be a first-order one.

Proof Assume the conditions of the theorem; namely,

$$\Delta[P] \models \Delta[P'] \wedge (P' \leq P)$$

Left to right: Assume CIRC$[\Delta; P]$; that is, assume

$$\Delta(P) \wedge (\forall \mathrm{P}* \ \Delta[\mathrm{P}*] \wedge (\mathrm{P}* \leq P) \Rightarrow (P \leq \mathrm{P}*))$$

Using the condition of the theorem, we then have

$$\Delta(P') \wedge (P' \leq P)$$

Universal specialization on the circumscription formula yields

$$\Delta(P') \wedge (P' \leq P) \Rightarrow (P \leq P')$$

Modus ponens applied to these last two expressions yields

$$(P \leq P')$$

This result, together with $(P' \leq P)$, yields $(P = P')$.

Right to left: If the circumscription formula did not follow from the conditions of the theorem, we would have some $P*$ such that $\Delta(P*) \wedge (P* < P)$. Assuming $P = P'$ (the right side of the equivalence in the theorem), we then have $\Delta(P*) \wedge (P* < P')$. The conditions of the theorem, however, state that $\Delta(P*)$ logically entails $(P' \leq P*)$—a contradiction. $\square$

As an example of how this theorem is used, let Δ be P(A) $\wedge$ ($\forall$x Q(x)$\Rightarrow$P(x)). If we were going to perform predicate completion on these clauses, we would rewrite Δ as ($\forall$x Q(x) $\vee$ (x=A)$\Rightarrow$P(x)). Predicate completion would yield the completion formula ($\forall$x P(x)$\Rightarrow$Q(x) $\vee$ (x=A)). Since predicate completion was motivated as a technique for minimizing the objects that satisfy a predicate, we might suspect that it gives the same result as does circumscription. We can use Theorem 6.4 to show that it does in this case.

We let the P' of the theorem be the consequent of the completion formula Q(x) $\vee$ (x=A). Strictly speaking, we should write P' as (λx Q(x) $\vee$ (x=A)), a *lambda* expression. Now, to use the theorem, we must prove that Δ logically entails $\Delta(P') \wedge (P' \leq P)$.

Substituting (λx Q(x) $\vee$ (x=A)) for P in Δ yields

$$\Delta(P') \equiv (\forall \mathrm{x} \ \mathrm{Q(x)} \ \Rightarrow \ \mathrm{Q(x)} \ \vee \ \mathrm{x=A}) \wedge (\mathrm{Q(A)} \ \vee \ \mathrm{A=A})$$

We see that $\Delta(P')$ is trivially valid. It remains to show that Δ logically implies $(P' \leq P)$; that is, $(\forall x\; Q(x) \vee (x{=}A){\Rightarrow}P(x))$. The latter formula, however, is just the normal form of Δ. Thus, the conditions of the theorem are satisfied, and the theorem confirms that CIRC$[\Delta; P]$ is $(\forall x\; Q(x) \vee (x{=}A) \Leftrightarrow P(x))$.

This example can be generalized to show that predicate completion gives the same results as circumscription when Δ consists of clauses solitary in P.

In many cases of interest in AI, CIRC$[\Delta; P]$ "collapses" to a first-order formula. (We give some examples later in which it does not.) The simplest case in which circumscription is collapsible is when all occurrences of P in Δ are *positive*. (A formula has a *positive occurrence of P* if P occurs positively in its clause form; it has a *negative occurrence of P* if P occurs negatively in its clause form.)

As an example, consider the case in which Δ is $(\exists y\; P(y))$. P occurs only positively in Δ. By manipulating expressions in second-order logic, it can be shown that the circumscription of P in Δ is $(\exists y \forall x\; (x{=}y) \Leftrightarrow P(x))$. Circumscribing P in this case limits the extension of P to a minimal nonempty set; i.e., a singleton.

An important case in which circumscription is collapsible can best be thought of as a simple generalization of the solitary condition used in defining predicate completion. Earlier, we defined what is meant for clauses to be *solitary* in a predicate P. Recall that a clause is solitary in P if, whenever it contains a positive occurrence of P, it contains only one occurrence of P. Generalizing this definition, we say that a *formula* is *solitary in P* if and only if it can be written in the following *normal form*:

$$N[P] \wedge (E \leq P)$$

where $N[P]$ is a formula that contains no positive occurrences of P, E is a formula that contains no occurrences of P, and $E \leq P$ is our usual abbreviation for $(\forall x\; E(x){\Rightarrow}P(x))$ (where x might be a tuple of variables).

Note that the *normal form* of a conjunction of clauses solitary in P is in the form $E \leq P$. Thus, solitary clauses are a special case of solitary formulas.

For solitary formulas in general, we have the following theorem.

THEOREM 6.5 CIRC$[N[P] \wedge (E \leq P); P] \equiv N[E] \wedge (E = P)$, where $N[E]$ is $N[P]$ with each occurrence of P replaced by E.

Proof This theorem follows directly from Theorem 6.4. First note that, since $N[P]$ has no positive occurrences of P, $N[P] \wedge (E \leq P)$ logically entails $N[E]$. (This entailment can be thought of as a kind of "generalized resolution.") Thus, the conditions of Theorem 6.4 are satisfied. $\square$

Thus, for solitary formulas, circumscription is collapsible to a first-order formula. We see that circumscription gives the same result as predicate completion does in the special case of clauses solitary in P. Using Theorem 6.5, we can compute circumscription for theories not in clause form, as long as they can be written in normal form.

We illustrate with an example. Let Δ be given by

$$\exists x \; \neg On(A,x) \wedge On(A,B)$$

We want to compute the circumscription of On in Δ. We can write Δ in normal form to show that it is solitary in On:

$$(\exists x \; \neg On(A,x)) \wedge (\forall x \forall y \; x=A \wedge y=B \Rightarrow On(x,y))$$

We identify the first conjunct of this expression as $N[On]$ (it has no positive occurrences of On), and the second as $(E \leq On)$ with $E(x,y) \equiv (x=A) \wedge (y=B)$. ($E$ has no occurrences of On.) Thus, by the theorem, $CIRC[\Delta; On]$ is

$$(\forall x \forall y \; On(x,y) \Leftrightarrow x=A \wedge y=B) \wedge (\exists x \; \neg(x=B))$$

(The only thing "on" something is the object denoted by A, and it is on the object denoted by B, and there is at least one object that is not the same as the one denoted by B.)

Some interesting complications arise when attempting circumscription in formulas slightly more general than solitary ones are. Consider an example in which Δ is

$$Ostrich(x) \Rightarrow Bird(x)$$

$$Bird(Tweety) \vee Bird(Sam)$$

We cannot use Theorem 6.5 to compute the circumscription of Bird in Δ, because Δ is not solitary in Bird. Before we attempt circumscription, however, let us see whether we can guess what sort of augmenting statement circumscription might make about Bird. From Δ, we can guess that there might be two alternative minimizations of Bird; namely,

- $\forall x \; Bird(x) \Leftrightarrow Ostrich(x) \vee x=Tweety$

- $\forall x \; Bird(x) \Leftrightarrow Ostrich(x) \vee x=Sam$

The belief set is not sufficiently "definite" to allow us to determine which one of these might be appropriate. This indefiniteness makes it impossible to give a single minimizing Bird. Instead, we can merely say something *about* the minimization of Bird; namely, that it has to be one or the other of these two expressions. That is, all we can apparently say about the minimizing `Bird` is the following:

$$(\forall x \text{ Bird}(x) \Leftrightarrow \text{Ostrich}(x) \lor x=\text{Tweety}) \lor$$
$$(\forall x \text{ Bird}(x) \Leftrightarrow \text{Ostrich}(x) \lor x=\text{Sam})$$

Indeed, we can use circumscription to derive this formula. The general circumscription formula for `Bird` in Δ is

$$\forall \text{Bird*} \ \Delta(\text{Bird*}) \land (\forall x \text{ Bird*}(x) \Rightarrow \text{Bird}(x)) \Rightarrow$$
$$(\forall x \text{ Bird}(x) \Rightarrow \text{Bird*}(x))$$

Let us first substitute `Ostrich(x)`∨`(x=Tweety)` for `Bird*(x)`. This yields (after reduction)

$$(\forall x \text{ Ostrich}(x) \lor x=\text{Tweety} \Rightarrow \text{Bird}(x)) \Rightarrow$$
$$(\forall x \text{ Bird}(x) \Rightarrow \text{Ostrich}(x) \lor x=\text{Tweety})$$

Next, we substitute `Ostrich(x)`∨`(x=Sam)` for `Bird*(x)`. This yields

$$(\forall x \text{ Ostrich}(x) \lor x=\text{Sam} \Rightarrow \text{Bird}(x)) \Rightarrow$$
$$(\forall x \text{ Bird}(x) \Rightarrow \text{Ostrich}(x) \lor x=\text{Sam})$$

Neither of these formulas has an antecedent that follows from Δ, but the disjunction of the antecedents does. That is, from Δ, we can prove

$$(\forall x \text{ Ostrich}(x) \lor x=\text{Sam} \Rightarrow \text{Bird}(x)) \lor$$
$$(\forall x \text{ Ostrich}(x) \lor x=\text{Tweety} \Rightarrow \text{Bird}(x))$$

(In fact, Δ itself can be written in this form. We first rewrite `Bird(Tweety)` and `Bird(Sam)` as $(\forall x \ (x=\text{Tweety}) \Rightarrow \text{Bird}(x))$ and $(\forall x \ (x=\text{Sam}) \Rightarrow \text{Bird}(x))$, respectively. Then, by distributivity, we write the conjunction of these formulas and $(\forall x \text{ Ostrich}(x) \Rightarrow \text{Bird}(x))$ in the form shown previously.)

Since the disjunction of the antecedents of instances of the circumscription formulas follows from Δ, the disjunction of the consequents does also. The disjunction of the consequents, however, is exactly the formula we guessed would be an appropriate statement to make about the minimizing `Bird` in this case.

The interesting point about this example is that we can derive a slightly more restrictive statement about `Bird` from the circumscription formula. In this example, Δ does not force us to accept a formula about `Bird` as general as we have guessed; the perceptive reader may have already noted that the disjunction of definitions can be tighter. The formula we guessed, although true in all `Bird`-minimal models, does allow some non-`Bird`-minimal models as well—in particular when *both* Tweety and Sam are birds. We will return to this example after describing how circumscription collapses for a class of formulas more general than solitary ones are.

Next we consider a more general class of formulas—those we call *separable*. A *formula* is *separable* with respect to a predicate P if any one of the following conditions is satisfied:

(1) It has no *positive* occurrences of P.

(2) It is of the form $(\forall x \; E(x) \; \Rightarrow \; P(x))$, where x is a tuple of variables and $E(x)$ is a formula that does not contain P (we again abbreviate to $E \leq P$).

(3) It is composed of conjunctions and disjunctions of separable formulas.

Note that this definition implies that formulas that are solitary with respect to P also are separable with respect to P. Also, as we shall show, all quantifier-free formulas are separable.

Positive occurrences of P in belief sets of this form are separated into isolated components, and this separation makes possible a collapsed version of circumscription—as we shall see.

First, we point out that a rather wide class of formulas can be put in separable form. In the following pairs of equivalent formulas, the one preceded by a dot is a version in which separability (by the above definition) is obvious. (In the first two cases, the formulas also are solitary in P.)

(1) P(A)

      • ∀x x=A ⇒ P(x)

(2) ∀y P(F(y))

      • ∀x∃y x=F(y) ⇒ P(x)

(3) Bird(Tweety) ∨ Bird(Sam)

      • (∀x x=Tweety ⇒ Bird(x)) ∨ (∀x x=Sam ⇒ Bird(x))

(4) <any unquantified formula>

      • <move negations in and use the method of example 1. to rewrite any positive occurrences of P>

(5) (∀u P(u,A)) ∨ (∀u P(u,B))

      • (∀u∀x x=A ⇒ P(u,x)) ∨ (∀u∀x x=B ⇒ P(u,x))

However, (∀u P(u,A) ∨ P(u,B)) is *not* separable with respect to P because it cannot be written as a propositional combination of separable formulas.

Although our definition of separability can easily be used to check whether or not a formula is separable (taking into account equivalences such as those in the preceding list), it is not obvious what this definition might have to do with circumscription. It happens that there is a *normal form* for separable formulas—somewhat like the normal form used in defining solitary formulas. We describe this normal form next and then show how it is used to compute circumscription.

From the definition of separability, it is straightforward to show that every formula separable with respect to P is equivalent to a formula in the following normal form with respect to P:

$$\bigvee_i [N_i[P] \wedge (E_i \leq P)]$$

where each E_i is a formula that has no occurrences of P, and each $N_i[P]$ is a formula that has no positive occurrences of P.

We obtain this standard form from any conjunction or disjunction of (separable) formulas by distributivity and by applications of the following rules:

$$(\phi \Rightarrow P) \wedge (\psi \Rightarrow P) \equiv (\phi \vee \psi) \Rightarrow P$$
$$(\phi \Rightarrow P) \vee (\psi \Rightarrow P) \equiv (\phi \wedge \psi) \Rightarrow P$$
$$(\phi \Rightarrow P) \equiv \mathsf{T} \wedge (\phi \Rightarrow P)$$
$$\phi \equiv \phi \wedge (\mathsf{F} \Rightarrow P)$$

(The last two rules are sometimes needed to ensure that each disjunct in the normal form has N_i and E_i terms. Use of these rules gives a T for N_i and an F for E_i. In this case, when writing $(E_i \leq P)$ in its expanded form, we write $(\forall \mathbf{x}\ \mathsf{F} \Rightarrow P(\mathbf{x}))$.)

If Δ is in normal form for P, then the circumscription of P in Δ is collapsible to a first-order formula, as defined in the following theorem.

THEOREM 6.6 *Suppose Δ is separable with respect to P and has normal form with respect to P given by*

$$\bigvee_i [N_i[P] \wedge (E_i \leq P)]$$

Then the circumscription of P in Δ is equivalent to

$$\bigvee_i [D_i \wedge (P = E_i)]$$

where D_i is

$$N_i[E_i] \wedge \bigwedge_{j \neq i} \neg[N_j[E_j] \wedge (E_j < E_i)]$$

and each $N[E]$ is $N[P]$ with all occurrences of P replaced by E.

(Recall that the expanded version of $(E_j < E_i)$ is $[(E_j \leq E_i) \land \neg(E_i \leq E_j)]$ which, further expanded, is $(\forall x \ E_j(x) \Rightarrow E_i(x)) \land \neg(\forall x \ E_i(x) \Rightarrow E_j(x)).$)

To demonstrate that circumscription implies a formula of the form $\bigvee_i[N_i[E_i] \land (P = E_i)]$ requires only a simple generalization of the proof of Theorem 6.5. To show that the extra conjuncts can be included in D_i is somewhat more difficult. These extra conjuncts essentially allow us to omit from the disjunction of definitions for P those disjuncts that would be redundant under certain conditions and given the other disjuncts. (The theorem is proved in [Lifschitz 1987b].)

We will illustrate the role of the D_i by some examples later.

In computing circumscription, the result of Theorem 6.6 simplifies in some special cases. If the normal form has only one disjunct, then we have the special case of a formula solitary in P, and D is $N[E]$. Or, if all the N_i are T, then D_i becomes

$$\bigwedge_{j \neq i}(E_i \leq E_j) \lor \neg(E_j \leq E_i)$$

Suppose, for example, that Δ is P(A) ∨ P(B). We rewrite this in normal form for P:

$$(\text{T} \land (\forall x \ x\text{=}A \Rightarrow P(x))) \lor (\text{T} \land (\forall x \ x\text{=}B \Rightarrow P(x)))$$

Here, the normal form has two disjuncts. D_1 and D_2 are, respectively,

$$(\forall x \ x\text{=}A \Rightarrow x\text{=}B) \lor (\exists y \ y\text{=}B \land \neg(y\text{=}A))$$

and

$$(\forall x \ x\text{=}B \Rightarrow x\text{=}A) \lor (\exists y \ y\text{=}A \land \neg(y\text{=}B))$$

which are both true, so the circumscription formula is equivalent to

$$(\forall x \ P(x) \Leftrightarrow x\text{=}A) \lor (\forall x \ P(x) \Leftrightarrow x\text{=}B)$$

(In computing the D_i for this case, it is helpful to use the equivalence $(\forall x \ (x\text{=}A) \Rightarrow P(x)) \Leftrightarrow P(A).$)

In the last example, the D_i "disappeared," and we were left with a simple disjunction of definitions for P. To illustrate how the D_i can act to restrict these disjunctions, consider the following example. Let Δ be given by P(A) ∨ (P(B) ∧ P(C)). In normal form, Δ is

$$(\text{T} \land (\forall x \ x\text{=}A \Rightarrow P(x))) \lor (\text{T} \land (\forall x \ x\text{=}B \lor x\text{=}C \Rightarrow P(x)))$$

Thus,

$$N_1 \equiv N_2 \equiv \text{T}$$
$$E_1 \equiv (\lambda\text{x} \ \text{x=A})$$
$$E_2 \equiv (\lambda\text{x} \ \text{x=B} \ \vee \ \text{x=C})$$
$$D_1 \equiv \text{T}$$
$$D_2 \equiv \text{A=B=C} \ \vee \ (\text{A} \neq \text{B} \ \wedge \ \text{A} \neq \text{C})$$

and Theorem 6.6 gives

$$\text{CIRC}[\Delta; \text{P}] \equiv (\forall\text{x} \ \text{P(x)} \ \Leftrightarrow \ \text{x=A}) \ \vee$$
$$((\forall\text{x} \ \text{P(x)} \ \Leftrightarrow \ \text{x=B} \ \vee \ \text{x=C}) \ \wedge$$
$$(\text{A=B=C} \ \vee \ (\text{A} \neq \text{B} \ \wedge \ \text{A} \neq \text{C})))$$

When (A=B=C), the first disjunct suffices, so this formula simplifies to

$$\text{CIRC}[\Delta; \text{P}] \equiv (\forall\text{x} \ \text{P(x)} \ \Leftrightarrow \ \text{x=A}) \ \vee$$
$$((\forall\text{x} \ \text{P(x)} \ \Leftrightarrow \ \text{x=B} \ \vee \ \text{x=C}) \ \wedge \ (\text{A} \neq \text{B} \ \wedge \ \text{A} \neq \text{C}))$$

This example nicely illustrates the role of the D_i. In this case, they tighten the definitions by taking into consideration the possibility that A may be equal to one of B,C. (If A were equal to one of B,C, then $\Delta \equiv \text{P(A)}$, and circumscription would yield simply $(\forall\text{x} \ \text{P(x)} \ \Leftrightarrow \ (\text{x=A}))$.)

Let us now reconsider the example that we discussed earlier when we attempted to guess the result of circumscription. In that example, Δ was given by

$$(\forall\text{x} \ \text{Ostrich(x)} \ \Rightarrow \ \text{Bird(x)}) \ \wedge \ (\text{Bird(Tweety)} \ \vee \ \text{Bird(Sam)})$$

The normal form is

$$(\text{T} \ \wedge \ (\forall\text{x} \ \text{Ostrich(x)} \ \vee \ \text{x=Tweety} \ \Rightarrow \ \text{Bird(x)})) \ \vee$$
$$(\text{T} \ \wedge \ (\forall\text{x} \ \text{Ostrich(x)} \ \vee \ \text{x=Sam} \ \Rightarrow \ \text{Bird(x)}))$$

Here again, the D_i do not disappear. After some manipulation, we derive

$$D_1 \equiv \text{Sam=Tweety} \ \vee \ \neg\text{Ostrich(Sam)} \ \vee \ \text{Ostrich(Tweety)}$$

Which, after the making the UNA, becomes

$$\neg\text{Ostrich(Sam)} \ \vee \ \text{Ostrich(Tweety)}$$

and

$$D_2 \equiv \text{Tweety=Sam} \ \vee \ \neg\text{Ostrich(Tweety)} \ \vee \ \text{Ostrich(Sam)}$$

which, again after the UNA is

$$\neg \texttt{Ostrich(Tweety)} \lor \texttt{Ostrich(Sam)}$$

Using these values in Theorem 6.6 yields

$$\text{CIRC}[\Delta; \texttt{Bird}] \equiv ((\forall \texttt{x Bird(x)} \Leftrightarrow \texttt{Ostrich(x)} \lor \texttt{x=Tweety}) \land$$
$$(\neg \texttt{Ostrich(Sam)} \lor \texttt{Ostrich(Tweety)})) \lor$$
$$((\forall \texttt{x Bird(x)} \Leftrightarrow \texttt{Ostrich(x)} \lor \texttt{x=Sam}) \land$$
$$(\neg \texttt{Ostrich(Tweety)} \lor \texttt{Ostrich(Sam)}))$$

The circumscription is more restrictive than is the formula we had guessed earlier. Circumscription says that there are two alternative "minimal definitions" of Bird; namely, either something is a bird if it is an ostrich or Tweety (and that definition need be a possibility only if Sam is not an ostrich or if Tweety is an ostrich), or something is a bird if it is an ostrich or Sam (and that definition need be a possibility only if Tweety is not an ostrich or if Sam is an ostrich). In our guess earlier, we did not narrow our definition as much as we might have; e.g., in the case in which Sam was an ostrich and Tweety was not. In that case, a minimal definition of Bird does not really need to include the possibility of conferring "birdhood" on Tweety (in order to satisfy Δ) because Bird(Tweety) $\lor$ Bird(Sam) is satisfied by virtue of Sam being an ostrich.

In all the cases considered so far, we were able to construct a first-order formula the addition of which to Δ achieved the effect of circumscribing a predicate in Δ. There are cases, however, in which circumcription does not collapse to a first-order formula. Here is an example: Suppose Δ contains the single formula

$$(\forall \texttt{u} \forall \texttt{v Q(u,v)} \Rightarrow \texttt{P(u,v)}) \land (\forall \texttt{u} \forall \texttt{v} \forall \texttt{w P(u,v)} \land \texttt{P(v,w)} \Rightarrow \texttt{P(u,w)})$$

In this case, the difficulty in saying that Δ expresses all and the only information about P is that Δ says quite a bit about P. It says that P is (at least) the transitive closure of Q. To circumscribe P in Δ would require saying that P is identically the transitive closure of Q, and this cannot be expressed in a first-order formula. One way of saying this, of course, is by the circumscription formula itself:

$$(\forall \texttt{P*})\ (\forall \texttt{u} \forall \texttt{v Q(u,v)} \Rightarrow \texttt{P*(u,v)})$$
$$\land (\forall \texttt{u} \forall \texttt{v} \forall \texttt{w P*(u,v)} \land \texttt{P*(v,w)} \Rightarrow \texttt{P*(u,w)})$$
$$\land (\forall \texttt{u} \forall \texttt{v P*(u,v)} \Rightarrow \texttt{P(u,v)})$$
$$\Rightarrow (\forall \texttt{u} \forall \texttt{v P(u,v)} \Rightarrow \texttt{P*(u,v)})$$

Besides involving a second-order quantifier, this formula is not in the form of a definition for P. We can use Theorem 6.4 to rewrite the circumscription formula in its equivalent definitional form. We leave it to the reader to verify that the following expression for P' satisfies the conditions of Theorem 6.4:

$$P'(x,y) \Leftrightarrow (\forall P* \ (\forall u \forall v \ Q(u,v) \Rightarrow P*(u,v))$$
$$\wedge(\forall u \forall v \forall w \ (P*(u,v) \wedge P*(v,w) \Rightarrow P*(u,w)) \Rightarrow P*(x,y)))$$

Theorem 6.4 then states that circumscription is equivalent to the following definition for P:

$$\forall u \forall v \ P(u,v) \Leftrightarrow P'(u,v)$$

Another example of the insufficiency of a first-order formula to express circumscription comes from the algebraic axioms for natural numbers. Suppose Δ is

$$NN(0) \wedge (\forall x \ NN(x) \Rightarrow NN(S(x)))$$

That is, 0 is a nonnegative integer and the successor of every nonnegative integer is a nonnegative integer. Circumscribing NN in Δ produces an expression equivalent to the usual second-order formula for induction:

$$\forall NN* \ (NN*(0) \wedge (\forall x \ NN*(x) \Rightarrow NN*(S(x))))$$
$$\wedge \ (\forall x \ NN*(x) \Rightarrow NN(x))$$
$$\Rightarrow (\forall x \ NN(x) \Rightarrow NN*(x))$$

Replacing NN*(x) in this expression by [NN'(x) $\wedge$ NN(x)] allows us to write

$$\forall NN' \ NN'(0) \wedge (\forall x \ NN'(x) \Rightarrow NN'(S(x)))$$
$$\Rightarrow (\forall x \ NN(x) \Rightarrow NN'(x))$$

which is closer to the usual induction formula.

The preceding two examples had belief sets that were neither positive nor separable in the predicates being circumscribed, and therefore it is not surprising that circumscription was not collapsible to first-order formulas in those cases.

It is also possible for Δ to have no minimal models. Consider the following set of formulas:

$$\exists x \ NN(x) \wedge (\forall y \ NN(y) \Rightarrow \neg(x=S(y)))$$

$$\forall x \ NN(x) \Rightarrow NN(S(x))$$

$$\forall x \forall y \ S(x)=S(y) \Rightarrow x=y$$

One interpretation of these formulas involves the claims that there is a number that is not the successor of any number, that every number has a successor that is a number, and that two numbers are equal if their successors are equal. One interpretation for NN is that any integer greater than k satisfies NN. A "smaller" interpretation is that any integer greater than $k + 1$ satisfies NN—and so on. Thus, there is no NN-minimal model for Δ. Since there is no NN-minimal model, we might expect that the circumscription of these formulas in NN is inconsistent, and indeed it is. (If the circumscription formula had a model, that model would be a minimal model of the formulas.)

Various sufficient conditions have been established for the circumscription of a consistent belief set to be consistent. We state some of the results here without proof.

THEOREM 6.7 *If a belief set Δ is consistent and universal, then the circumscription of P in Δ is consistent. (A set of formulas is said to be* universal *if either it is a set of clauses or if the conjunctive normal form of each of its formulas contains no Skolem functions.)*

THEOREM 6.8 *If a belief set Δ is consistent and separable with respect to P, then the circumscription of P in Δ is consistent.*

Since sets of clauses are universal and since circumscription of P reduces to predicate completion of P in clauses solitary (and thus separable) in P, Theorem 6.2 follows from either Theorem 6.7 or Theorem 6.8. (Theorem 6.3 follows from versions of these theorems extended to a more general case of circumscription, discussed in Section 6.7.)

Theorems 6.7 and 6.8 apply to two different kinds of formulas; namely, universal and separable ones. These two classes are instances of a common general class—the *almost universal formulas*. A formula is *almost universal with respect to P* if it has the form $(\forall x)\varphi$, where x is a tuple of object variables, and φ does not contain positive occurrences of P in the scope of quantifiers. Every universal formula is, of course, almost universal with respect to any P. It is not difficult to show that any formula that is separable with respect to P also is almost universal with respect to P.

Theorems 6.7 and 6.8 are thus each a special case of Theorem 6.9.

THEOREM 6.9 *If a belief set Δ is consistent and almost universal with respect to P, then the circumscription of P in Δ is consistent.*

6.5 More General Forms of Circumscription

There are more general versions of circumscription that produce stronger results. First, instead of minimizing only a single predicate, we can minimize a set of predicates. The *parallel circumscription* of $\{P_1, P_2, \ldots, P_N\}$ in Δ is given by the same formula as before, except that we now let P stand for a tuple of predicates:

$$\text{CIRC}[\Delta; P] \equiv \Delta(P) \ \wedge \ \neg(\exists \text{P*} \ \Delta(\text{P*}) \ \wedge \ (\text{P*} < P))$$

where P* is a tuple of predicate variables of the same arities as P, (P* $< P$) is an abbreviation for (P* $\leq P$) $\wedge \neg(P \leq$ P*), and (P* $\leq P$) is (P*$_1 \leq P_1$) $\wedge \ldots \wedge$ (P*$_N \leq P_N$).

Rewriting yields:

$$\text{CIRC}[\Delta; P] \equiv \Delta(P) \ \wedge \ (\forall \text{P*} \ (\Delta(\text{P*}) \ \wedge \ (\text{P*} \leq P)) \ \Rightarrow \ (P \leq \text{P*}))$$

Parallel circumscription is not really any more difficult to compute than is ordinary, single-predicate circumscription. Theorem 6.4, for example, is easily generalized to deal with this case. In fact, when all the predicates in the tuple P occur positively in Δ, we have Theorem 6.10.

THEOREM 6.10 *If all occurrences of $P_1, P_2, \ldots, P_N$ in Δ are positive, then $\text{CIRC}[\Delta; P]$ is equivalent to*

$$\bigwedge_{i=1}^{N} \text{CIRC}[\Delta; P_i]$$

(This theorem is stated without proof in [Lifschitz 1986c], and is proved in [Lifschitz 1987b].)

As an example, we apply Theorem 6.10 to compute the parallel circumscription of $\{$P1,P2$\}$ in ($\forall$x P1(x) $\vee$ P2(x)). Each of P1 and P2 occur positively in Δ, so the parallel circumscription is just the conjunction of the individual circumscriptions of P1 and P2. Since each of $\text{CIRC}[\Delta; \text{P1}]$ and $\text{CIRC}[\Delta; \text{P2}]$ is ($\forall$x P1(x) $\Leftrightarrow$ $\neg$P2(x)), their conjunction is also.

The definitions of formulas solitary or separable in P extend naturally to the case in which P is a tuple of predicates. For example, a formula Δ is *solitary in a tuple of predicates* P if it can be written in the form $N[P] \wedge (E \leq P)$, where $N[P]$ has no positive occurrences of any member of P, and no member of E has any occurrences of any member of P. Theorems 6.5 and 6.6 (interpreting P as a tuple of predicates) can then also be used to compute parallel circumscription.

For parallel circumscription, we can state a stronger result than would be obtained by extending Theorem 6.5 to formulas *solitary* in a tuple of predicates. Generalizing on the definition given in Section 6.2 of *clauses* ordered in P, we say that a *formula is ordered* in $P = \{P_1, P_2, \ldots, P_N\}$ if it can be written in the form:

$$N[P] \wedge (E_1 \leq P_1) \wedge (E_2 \leq P_2) \wedge \ldots \wedge (E_N \leq P_N)$$

where $N[P]$ has no positive occurrences of any of the predicates in P, and each E_i has no occurrences of any of $\{P_i, P_{i+1}, \ldots, P_N\}$ and has no negative occurrences of any of $\{P_1, \ldots, P_{i-1}\}$.

Using this definition, we have the following theorem.

THEOREM 6.11 *Suppose Δ is ordered in P and can be written in the form $N[P] \wedge (E_1 \leq P_1) \wedge (E_2[P_1] \leq P_2) \wedge \ldots \wedge (E_N[P_1, P_2, \ldots, P_{N-1}] \leq P_N)$ (with no positive occurrences of the P_i in N and no occurrences of $P_i, \ldots, P_N$ in E_i).*

Then the parallel circumscription of P in Δ is given by

$$\text{CIRC}[\Delta; P] \equiv N[E_1, \ldots, E_N] \wedge (P_1 = E_1) \wedge (P_2 = E_2[E_1]) \wedge \ldots$$
$$\wedge (P_N = E_N[E_1, \ldots, E_{N-1}])$$

The proof is analogous to that of Theorem 6.5 and, like it, is based on Theorem 6.4.

Note that parallel predicate completion for *clauses* ordered in P is a special case of parallel circumscription.

Another generalization of circumscription allows other predicates to "vary" in addition to those being minimized. That is, we suppose that the extensions of these variable predicates can be changed during the minimization process to allow the predicates being circumscribed to have extensions even smaller than they would have otherwise. This means that an object will be allowed to satisfy one of the variable predicates (to satisfy Δ), so that it does not have to satisfy a predicate being minimized (to satisfy Δ). Which predicates should be allowed to vary depends on the purpose of the circumscription process; the decision is part of what we call the *circumscription policy*. The usual situation is that we are interested in knowing what is the effect of the circumscription of one predicate, P, (or set of predicates) on some other variable predicate, Z, (or set of predicates). We want circumscription to minimize the number of objects satisfying P, even at the expense of allowing more or different objects to satisfy Z, the variable predicate. After defining circumscription with variable predicates, we will give examples of how this process is used.

Suppose P is a tuple of predicates to be minimized and Z (disjoint from P) is a tuple of predicates. The parallel circumscription of P in $\Delta(P; Z)$, with predicates Z also allowed to vary, is

$$\text{CIRC}[\Delta; P; Z] \equiv \Delta(P; Z) \wedge \neg(\exists \text{P*} \exists \text{Z*} \, \Delta(\text{P*}; \text{Z*}) \wedge (\text{P*} < P))$$

where P* and Z* are tuples of predicate variables (of the same arities as P and Z, respectively), and $\Delta(\text{P*}; \text{Z*})$ is the belief set expressed as a single wff with all occurrences of P replaced by P* and all occurrences of Z replaced by Z*.

Rewriting yields

$$\text{CIRC}[\Delta; P; Z]$$
$$\equiv \Delta(P; Z) \wedge (\forall \text{P*} \forall \text{Z*} \, (\Delta(\text{P*}; \text{Z*}) \wedge (\text{P*} \leq P)) \Rightarrow (P \leq \text{P*}))$$
$$\equiv \Delta(P; Z) \wedge (\forall \text{P*} \, (\exists \text{Z*} \, (\Delta(\text{P*}; \text{Z*}) \wedge (\text{P*} \leq P)) \Rightarrow (P \leq \text{P*})))$$
$$\equiv \Delta(P; Z) \wedge \text{CIRC}[(\exists \text{Z*} \, \Delta(P; \text{Z*})); P]$$

From this form, we see that the parallel circumscription of P in $\Delta(P; Z)$ with Z allowed to vary during the minimization is the same as ordinary parallel circumscription of P in $(\exists \text{Z*} \, \Delta[P; \text{Z*}])$. The main difficulty now is how to handle the second-order quantifier in $(\exists \text{Z*} \, \Delta[P; \text{Z*}])$.

This problem can be dealt with if Δ is solitary, separable, or ordered in Z. Recall, for example, that if Δ is solitary in Z, it can be written as $N[Z] \wedge (E \leq Z)$, where $N[Z]$ is a formula that contains no positive occurrences of (any elements of) Z, and E is a formula that contains no occurrences of (any elements of) Z. It is straightforward to show that $(\exists \text{Z*} \, N[\text{Z*}] \wedge (E \leq \text{Z*})) \equiv N[E]$, where $N[E]$ is $N[\text{Z*}]$ with E substituted for Z*.

These results establish the following theorem for the case in which Δ is solitary in Z.

THEOREM 6.12

$$\text{CIRC}[N(Z) \wedge (E \leq Z); P; Z] \equiv N(Z) \wedge (E \leq Z) \wedge \text{CIRC}[N(E); P]$$

where N has no positive occurrences of Z, and E has no occurrences of Z. E, P, and Z can be tuples of predicates.

COROLLARY 6.2

$$\mathrm{CIRC}[E_1 \wedge (E_2 \leq Z); P; Z] \equiv E_1 \wedge (E_2 \leq Z) \wedge \mathrm{CIRC}[E_1; P]$$

where neither E_1 nor E_2 has any occurrences of Z. (That is, in this case varying Z lets us drop the clause $(E_2 \leq Z)$ from Δ when computing the circumscription formula.)

A simple default reasoning example will illustrate the effects on circumscription of letting a predicate vary. Let Δ be

$$\forall x \; \texttt{Bird(x)} \wedge \neg\texttt{Ab(x)} \Rightarrow \texttt{Flies(x)}$$

$$\forall x \; \texttt{Ostrich(x)} \Rightarrow \texttt{Ab(x)}$$

Ordinary circumscription of `Ab` in Δ gives us

$$\mathrm{CIRC}[\Delta; \texttt{Ab}]$$
$$\equiv \Delta \wedge (\forall x \; \texttt{Ab(x)} \Leftrightarrow \texttt{Ostrich(x)} \vee (\texttt{Bird(x)} \wedge \neg\texttt{Flies(x)}))$$

(The only abnormal things are either ostriches or birds that do not fly.)

A tighter characterization of `Ab` can be obtained by letting `Flies` vary. We see that we can use Corollary 6.2 to write

$$\mathrm{CIRC}[\Delta; \texttt{Ab}; \texttt{Flies}] \equiv \Delta \wedge \mathrm{CIRC}[(\forall x \; \texttt{Ostrich(x)} \Rightarrow \texttt{Ab(x)}); \texttt{Ab}]$$
$$\equiv \Delta \wedge (\forall x \; \texttt{Ab(x)} \Leftrightarrow \texttt{Ostrich(x)})$$

(The only abnormal things are ostriches. Allowing `Flies` to vary lets us rule out the possibility that birds might not fly.)

As a more complex example, consider the taxonomic hierarchy we used earlier to illustrate delimited predicate completion. We repeat the formulas used in that example:

$$\texttt{Flying-Ostrich(x)} \Rightarrow \texttt{Ostrich(x)}$$

$$\texttt{Flying-Ostrich(x)} \Rightarrow \texttt{Ab3(x)}$$

$$\texttt{Ostrich(x)} \Rightarrow \texttt{Bird(x)}$$

$$\texttt{Ostrich(x)} \Rightarrow \texttt{Ab2(x)}$$

$$\texttt{Bird(x)} \Rightarrow \texttt{Thing(x)}$$

$$\texttt{Bird(x)} \Rightarrow \texttt{Ab1(x)}$$

$$\texttt{Thing(Tweety)}$$

$$\texttt{Ostrich(x)} \wedge \neg\texttt{Ab3(x)} \Rightarrow \neg\texttt{Flies(x)}$$

$$\text{Thing}(x) \land \neg \text{Ab1}(x) \Rightarrow \neg \text{Flies}(x)$$

$$\text{Bird}(x) \land \neg \text{Ab2}(x) \Rightarrow \text{Flies}(x)$$

Default reasoning can be accomplished by parallel circumscription of all predicates except `Flies`, but letting `Flies` vary. We let `Flies` vary because we are willing to let it take on any value required in the minimization of the other predicates. In being unconcerned about the value of `Flies`, we can use the entire belief set Δ in the minimization process (rather than just the taxonomic part used in delimited completion) to achieve the default assumptions that we want.

Thus, we circumscribe Δ (as before) in the predicates {`Flying-Ostrich, Ostrich, Ab3, Bird, Ab2, Thing, Ab1`}, letting `Flies` vary as well. In applying the procedure for parallel circumscription, we note first that Δ is solitary in `Flies`. To see this, observe that all the preceding clauses except the last one have no positive occurrences of `Flies`, and the antecedent of the last clause has no occurrence of `Flies`. Thus, we can use Theorem 6.12 and substitute `Bird(x) ∧ ¬Ab2(x)` for `Flies(x)` in all but the last clause of the preceding set to yield

$$\text{Flying-Ostrich}(x) \Rightarrow \text{Ostrich}(x)$$

$$\text{Flying-Ostrich}(x) \Rightarrow \text{Ab3}(x)$$

$$\text{Ostrich}(x) \Rightarrow \text{Bird}(x)$$

$$\text{Ostrich}(x) \Rightarrow \text{Ab2}(x)$$

$$\text{Bird}(x) \Rightarrow \text{Thing}(x)$$

$$\text{Bird}(x) \Rightarrow \text{Ab1}(x)$$

$$\text{Thing}(\text{Tweety})$$

$$\text{Ostrich}(x) \land \neg \text{Ab3}(x) \Rightarrow \neg(\text{Bird}(x) \land \neg \text{Ab2}(x))$$

$$\text{Thing}(x) \land \neg \text{Ab1}(x) \Rightarrow \neg(\text{Bird}(x) \land \neg \text{Ab2}(x))$$

The last two clauses are subsumed by the fourth and sixth clauses, so the last two clauses can be eliminated. The circumscription we want can then be obtained by ordinary parallel circumscription of {`Flying-Ostrich, Ostrich, Ab3, Bird, Ab2, Thing, Ab1`} in the conjunction of the first seven clauses (without any predicates variable).

Since these clauses are ordered in {`Flying-Ostrich, Ostrich, Ab3, Bird, Ab2, Thing, Ab1`}, we can circumscribe by parallel predicate completion to obtain the following completion clauses (just as before):

1. $\text{Thing}(x) \Rightarrow \text{Bird}(x) \lor x = \text{Tweety}$
2. $\text{Bird}(x) \Rightarrow \text{Ostrich}(x)$
3. $\text{Ostrich}(x) \Rightarrow \text{Flying-Ostrich}(x)$

4. ¬Flying-Ostrich(x)
5. Ab1(x) ⇒ Bird(x)
6. Ab2(x) ⇒ Ostrich(x)
7. Ab3(x) ⇒ Flying-Ostrich(x)

6.6 Default Theories

We also can deal with the problem of nonmonotonic reasoning by defining a logic that uses nonstandard, nonmonotonic inference rules. Let us call these inference rules *default rules*, and the resulting theories *default theories*.

A default rule is an inference rule used to augment Δ under certain specified conditions, which we will soon describe. If D is a set of such rules, we denote an augmentation of Δ (there may be more than one), with respect to D, by $\mathcal{E}[\Delta, D]$. (As before, augmentations include Δ and are closed under ordinary deduction.) Default rules are written in the form

$$\frac{\alpha(x) : \beta(x)}{\gamma(x)}$$

where x is a tuple of individual constant schema variables, and α, β, and γ are wff schemata. (In running text, we write this rule as $\alpha(x) : \beta(x)/\gamma(x)$.)

The expressions above the line specify conditions on $\mathcal{E}[\Delta, D]$ that, if satisfied, permit (roughly speaking) the inclusion in $\mathcal{E}[\Delta, D]$ of the *consequent* below the line. A default rule is interpreted as follows: If there is an instance, X_0, of x for which the ground instance $\alpha(X_0)$ follows from $\mathcal{E}[\Delta, D]$ and for which $\beta(X_0)$ is consistent with $\mathcal{E}[\Delta, D]$, then $\mathcal{E}[\Delta, D]$ includes $\gamma(X_0)$.

The rules are called *default rules* because they are useful in expressing beliefs about statements that are typically, but not necessarily always, true. For example, we might express the belief that birds typically fly by the default rule Bird(x) : Flies(x) / Flies(x). That is, if x is a bird, and if it is consistent to believe that x can fly, then it can be believed that x can fly (or x can fly "by default.") If Δ contained only the formulas Bird(Tweety) and Ostrich(x)⇒¬Flies(x), then $\mathcal{E}[\Delta, D]$ would contain Flies(Tweety). If we added to Δ the formula Ostrich(Tweety), use of the default rule would be *blocked* because Flies(Tweety) is not consistent with the new Δ. Thus, default theories are nonmonotonic.

Our description of how default rules augment a theory may have been misleadingly simple because default theories may have more than one default rule, and rules may interact. The precise definition of $\mathcal{E}[\Delta, D]$ in terms of Δ and a set of default rules, D, must take into account the contributions of all of the default rules plus the closure of $\mathcal{E}[\Delta, D]$ under ordinary deduction. As we shall see, these interactions operate such as sometimes to warrant the existence of more than one augmentation.

Something like the CWA with respect to a predicate P can be formulated using a default inference rule as follows:

$$\frac{: \neg P(x)}{\neg P(x)}$$

That is, if it is consistent to believe an instance of $\neg P(x)$, then that instance of $\neg P(x)$ may be believed. There is a difference, however, between the effects of the CWA with respect to P and a default theory with this default. The CWA permits inferring an instance of $\neg P(x)$ if that instance is consistent with Δ. The default rule permits it only if the instance is consistent with $\mathcal{E}[\Delta, D]$. Since there may be other default rules contributing to $\mathcal{E}[\Delta, D]$, the two techniques can lead to different augmentations.

Most applications of default rules involve a special case in which default rules take the form $\alpha(x) : \gamma(x)/\gamma(x)$. These are called *normal* default rules, and theories using them are called *normal* default theories. The CWA-type default rule we mentioned is an example of a normal default rule.

(It also is possible to define more general default rules. Consider one of the form $\alpha(x) : \beta_1(x), \beta_2(x), \ldots, \beta_n(x)/\gamma(x)$, the interpretation of which is that, if a ground instance $\alpha(X_0)$ follows from $\mathcal{E}[\Delta, D]$ and if *each* of the $\beta_i(X_0)$ is separately consistent with $\mathcal{E}[\Delta, D]$, then $\gamma(X_0)$ is in $\mathcal{E}[\Delta, D]$. This rule is different from one of the form $\alpha(x) : \beta_1(x) \wedge \beta_2(x) \wedge \ldots \wedge \beta_n(x)/\gamma(x)$, because the conjunction may be inconsistent with $\mathcal{E}[\Delta, D]$, whereas each conjunct may be separately consistent.)

Default theories have a number of interesting properties. (Some of these are particular to normal default theories.) We state, without proof, some of the more important properties here, and illustrate them with some examples.

(1) Just as circumscription sometimes does not produce a unique definition for a predicate, a default theory may have more than one augmentation. Consider, for example, the following (normal) default rules:

$$:\neg A/\neg A$$

$$:\neg B/\neg B$$

Now, if Δ is simply $\{A \vee B\}$, then there are two possible augmentations of Δ; namely, $\{A \vee B, \neg A\}$ and $\{A \vee B, \neg B\}$. Whereas the CWA, with respect to both A and B, would have produced an inconsistent augmentation, our default rules in this example give us two choices. We may select either one as an appropriate augmentation of our beliefs.

(2) The union of the two augmentations of the preceding example is inconsistent. In fact, we have the following result: If a

normal default theory has distinct augmentations, they are mutually inconsistent.

(3) There are default theories with no augmentations. Consider the default :A/¬A. If Δ is empty, so is $\mathcal{E}[\Delta, D]$. However, see (4).

(4) Every normal default theory has an augmentation.

(5) A default theory can have an inconsistent augmentation if and only if Δ itself is inconsistent. Since one can prove anything from an inconsistent augmentation and since augmentations (like theories) are closed under ordinary deduction, if a default theory has an inconsistent augmentation, this is its only augmentation.

(6) If D and D' are sets of normal default rules such that $D' \subseteq D$, then for any $\mathcal{E}[\Delta, D']$ there is an $\mathcal{E}[\Delta, D]$ such that $\mathcal{E}[\Delta, D'] \subseteq \mathcal{E}[\Delta, D]$. Thus, we say that normal default theories are *semimonotonic*. Adding new normal default rules does not require the withdrawal of beliefs, even though adding new beliefs might.

After having specified a set of default rules, how are we to use them to perform the kind of nonmonotonic reasoning inherent in their definitions? Typically, we must decide whether or not the initial beliefs Δ and the default rules D warrant including some arbitrary formula ϕ among the augmented beliefs. That is, we must determine whether or not there is an augmentation $\mathcal{E}[\Delta, D]$ that includes the formula ϕ.

We limit our definition of default proofs to the case of normal default theories. (The computation of augmentations for nonnormal default theories can be extremely complex; in fact, it is not even known yet what might be an appropriate proof theory for nonnormal defaults.) Informally, a default proof of ϕ given Δ and D is just like an ordinary proof of ϕ from Δ, except that the (normal) default rules can be used as rules of inference. The use of a default rule must, in strict accordance with its definition, make the necessary consistency check before inferring its consequent. This test can be performed at the time of rule application in *forward* proofs. *Backward* proofs might best be done in two passes—first ignoring the consistency checks to find potential chains of inferences, and then performing the consistency checks, in forward order, on the default rules in a chain.

Suppose, for example, that D consists of the following two default rules: Bird(x):Flies(x)/Flies(x) (by default, birds can fly), and FC(x):Bird(x)/Bird(x) (by default, feathered creatures are birds). If Δ contains only the statement FC(Tweety), then there is a default proof of Flies(Tweety). If, however, Δ contains instead the statements Ostrich(Tweety), Ostrich(x) $\Rightarrow$ ¬Flies(x), and Ostrich(x) $\Rightarrow$ FC(x), then there is no default proof of Flies(Tweety), because the rule instance Bird(Tweety):Flies(Tweety)/Flies(Tweety) cannot be used consistently.

Because default rules interact in complex ways, one must be careful about how knowledge is expressed. An illustrative instance of the sort of knowledge-representation difficulty that might arise is provided by the fact that default rules can be transitive. Suppose, for example, we have $D = \{\texttt{D}(x)\texttt{:A}(x)/\texttt{A}(x), \texttt{A}(x)\texttt{:E}(x)/\texttt{E}(x)\}$. We might interpret these expressions as saying: Typically, high-school dropouts are adults; and, typically, adults are employed. One of the consequences of these two rules also could be obtained by the combined rule $\texttt{D}(x)\texttt{:E}(x)/\texttt{E}(x)$, the corresponding interpretation of which would be: Typically, high-school dropouts are employed. Although we might assent to the first two rules, we would not necessarily want to use the combination.

This unwelcome transitivity can be blocked in one of two ways. We could change the second default rule to the nonnormal rule $\texttt{A}(x)$: $[\neg\texttt{D}(x) \wedge \texttt{E}(x)]/\texttt{E}(x)$. Nonnormal defaults do not enjoy the simple and desirable properties of normal defaults, however. We often can block transitivity by a more careful formulation using only normal defaults. In our example, because, typically, adults are not high-school dropouts, we could use the following normal defaults: $\{\texttt{D}(x)\texttt{:A}(x)/\texttt{A}(x), [\texttt{A}(x)$ $\wedge \neg\texttt{D}(x)]\texttt{:E}(x)/\texttt{E}(x), \texttt{A}(x)\texttt{:}\neg\texttt{D}(x)/\neg\texttt{D}(x)\}$. Now we would not conclude that some particular high-school dropout was employed.

6.7 Bibliographical and Historical Remarks

Almost all interesting applications of AI require some form of nonmonotonic reasoning because the knowledge that AI systems contain about their domains is always subject to change and elaboration, yet it is still necessary for AI systems to reason as best they can with the knowledge they currently have. Reiter gave an excellent summary of nonmonotonic reasoning and its applications in AI [Reiter 1987b]. An important, typical application is to the problem of equipment diagnosis [Reiter 1987a]. McCarthy discussed several applications of one type of nonmonotonic reasoning [McCarthy 1986].

The closed-world assumption (CWA) is an important convention of database design. Reiter [Reiter 1978] was the first to describe and prove several of its properties. Theorem 6.1 is taken from [Shepherdson 1984]. The domain-closure assumption (DCA) and unique-names assumption (UNA) were discussed by Reiter [Reiter 1980b].

The *qualification problem* was discussed by McCarthy [McCarthy 1980]. It often is cited as one of the reasons that a strictly logical approach to AI will not work, and it has motivated much of the work in nonmonotonic reasoning.

Predicate completion of a set of clauses was first described by Clark [Clark 1978]. Parallel predicate completion suggests itself by analogy with parallel circumscription. Taxonomic hierarchies are ubiquitous in AI applications. Several frame-based systems have facilities for property inheritance and default reasoning in these hierarchies [Stefik 1986]. Our use of the **Ab** predicate in this connection is based on a suggestion by McCarthy [McCarthy 1986].

Circumscription as a method of nonmonotonic reasoning was first proposed by McCarthy [McCarthy 1980]. Our notation follows that of Lifschitz [Lifschitz 1985a]. (The alternative form of circumscription—which says that any alleged strengthening of P by P' is no real strengthening because the circumscription of P already implies P'—was attributed by Minker and Perlis [Minker 1984] to Reiter.) The circumscription formula is a formula in second-order logic. Although our treatment of circumscription in this book is essentially limited to those cases that collapse to first order, the reader may want to look at Enderton's chapter on second-order logic [Enderton 1972].

Theorems 6.4 through 6.6 all were developed by Lifschitz; their proofs are given in [Lifschitz 1987b]; Theorems 6.5 and 6.6 are stated without proof in [Lifschitz 1985a]. That CIRC$[\Delta; P]$ is collapsible to a first-order formula if all occurrences of P are positive in Δ follows immediately from results in Lifschitz [Lifschitz 1986c], and also was proved in [Lifschitz 1987b].

Etherington, Mercer, and Reiter showed that the circumscription of a formula having no minimal model is inconsistent, and they also proved a sufficient condition on the consistency of circumscription (Theorem 6.7) [Etherington 1985]. Theorem 6.8 was developed by Lifschitz [Lifschitz 1986b]. Theorems 6.7 and 6.8 are each special cases of Theorem 6.9, also developed by Lifschitz [Lifschitz 1986b]. Perlis and Minker [Perlis 1986] also have done work relating properties of circumscription to minimal models.

Parallel circumscription is a natural extension of ordinary circumscription. Theorem 6.10, developed by Lifschitz [Lifschitz 1986c, Lifschitz 1987b], often is useful in computing parallel circumscription. Otherwise, for *ordered* formulas, parallel circumscription can be computed using Theorem 6.11. (Ordered formulas and Theorem 6.11 are original here.) Theorem 6.12, developed by Lifschitz [Lifschitz 1987b], is useful for computing circumscription with variable predicates.

Etherington [Etherington 1986] and Lifschitz [Lifschitz 1986b] independently extended Theorem 6.7 to the case of parallel circumscription with variable predicates. That is, the parallel circumscription of universal theories (even with variable predicates) is consistent if the theory itself is consistent.

Several authors have been concerned with the relationship between circumscription and other nonmonotonic reasoning methods. For example, there are conditions under which parallel circumscription and the CWA augment a belief set identically. Lifschitz [Lifschitz 1985b] showed that the CWA applied to the belief set produces the same effect as does the parallel circumscription of all predicates in the belief set if (1) the CWA can be applied to a belief set consistently, (2) constant terms in the belief set name all possible objects in the domain (the DCA), and (3) different constant terms in the belief set denote different objects in the domain (the UNA). Gelfond, Przymusinska, and Przymusinski studied the relationships among various generalizations of the CWA and circumscription [Gelfond 1986]. Reiter was the first person to show that predicate completion is a special case of circumscription (using an argument similar to that used in the proof of Theorem 6.4) [Reiter 1982].

Przymusinski [Przymusinski 1986] proposed a method for deciding whether or not there is a minimal model of a theory T that also satisfies a formula ϕ; it can be used to answer queries in circumscriptive theories.

Imielinski and Grosof each investigated relationships between default logics and circumscription [Imielinski 1985, Grosof 1984].

Default logic was originally proposed and analyzed in a paper by Reiter [Reiter 1980a]. Our discussion of default theories is based on that paper. He shows that default logic is not even semidecidable, but describes a resolution theorem prover that can be used for top-down or backward searches for default proofs. Reiter and Criscoulo [Reiter 1983] gave examples of default-rule formulations of typical commonsense reasoning problems and showed how to avoid various pitfalls without using nonnormal defaults.

Other methods of nonmonotonic reasoning also have been proposed. McDermott and Doyle [McDermott 1980, McDermott 1982a] defined a logic having a *modal operator* **M**. (Modal operators are discussed in Chapter 9.) In the semantics for such a logic, the formula **M**P has value true just in case P is consistent (with the theory based on Δ). Any derivations of **M**P or its consequences are nonmonotonic because the meaning of **M** depends globally on the theory. If we add another formula to Δ, **M**P may no longer be consistent. With a somewhat different application in mind, Moore [Moore 1985b] proposed a variant, which he called *autoepistemic logic*, and compared it with McDermott and Doyle's nonmonotonic logic. Konolige [Konolige 1987] analyzed the connections between default theories and autoepistemic logic.

Several additional papers appear in the proceedings of a workshop on nonmonotonic reasoning [Nonmonotonic 1984].

Exercises

1. *Idempotence.* We denote the CWA augmentation of Δ by CWA[Δ]. Prove that

$$\text{CWA}[\text{CWA}[\Delta]] = \text{CWA}[\Delta]$$

(Assume CWA[Δ] is consistent.)

2. *Insensitivity to negative clauses.* Suppose Δ is Horn and consistent. Show that deleting a negative clause (i.e., one without any positive literals) from Δ does not change the CWA augmentation of Δ.

3. *Inconsistencies.* Prove that, if a consistent Δ contains only Horn clauses and is inconsistent with $\neg L_1 \wedge \neg L_2$ (where L_1 and L_2 are positive literals), then either $\Delta \wedge \neg L_1$ or $\Delta \wedge \neg L_2$ is inconsistent also.

4. *Even and odd.* Compute the completion of EVEN in the conjunction of the following formulas:

$$\forall x \; \text{ODD}(x) \wedge x{>}0 \Rightarrow \text{EVEN}(\text{Succ}(x))$$

$$\forall x \; \text{ODD}(x) \wedge x{>}0 \Rightarrow \text{EVEN}(\text{Pred}(x))$$

5. *Integers.* Compute the completion of INT in $\text{INT}(0) \wedge (\text{INT}(x) \Rightarrow \text{INT}(\text{Succ}(x)))$.

6. *Delimited predicate completion.* Discuss how *delimited* predicate completion might produce an inconsistent augmentation.

7. *Completion.* Compute the completion of P in the following clauses:

$$\text{Q1}(x) \wedge \text{Q2}(x) \Rightarrow \text{P}(\text{F}(x))$$

$$\text{Q3}(x) \Rightarrow \text{P}(\text{G}(x))$$

8. *Is there a* Q *that is not a* P*?* Express in words what the effect would be of circumscribing Q in P < Q.

9. *Parallel.* Compute $\text{CIRC}[(\forall x \; \text{Q}(x) \Rightarrow \text{P1}(x) \vee \text{P2}(x)); \text{P1}, \text{P2}]$.

10. *Knights and Knaves.* Let Δ be the conjunction of the following formulas:

$$\forall x \; \text{KNIGHT}(x) \Rightarrow \text{PERSON}(x)$$

$$\forall x \; \text{KNAVE}(x) \Rightarrow \text{PERSON}(x)$$

$$\forall x \; \text{KNAVE}(x) \Rightarrow \text{LIAR}(x)$$

$$\exists x \; \neg\text{LIAR}(x) \wedge \neg\text{KNAVE}(x)$$

$$\text{LIAR}(\text{MORK})$$

$$\text{KNAVE}(\text{BORK})$$

     a. Compute $\text{CIRC}[\Delta; \text{LIAR}]$.

     b. Compute $\text{CIRC}[\Delta; \text{LIAR}, \text{KNAVE}]$.

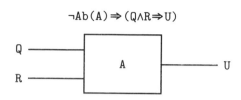

Figure 6.2   An AND gate.

11. *AND gate.*   The AND gate, A, shown in Figure 6.2, is described by the following formula:

$$\neg Ab(A) \Rightarrow (Q \wedge R \Rightarrow U)$$

(Unless A is abnormal, Q and R imply U. Q denotes the proposition "input 1 is on;" R denotes the proposition "input 2 is on;" U denotes the proposition "the output is on.")

a. Suppose, in fact, that Q, R, and U are true. Use the circumscription of Ab in this theory to prove that nothing is abnormal. The "theory" in this case is

$$Q \wedge R \wedge U \wedge (\neg Ab(A) \Rightarrow (Q \wedge R \Rightarrow U))$$

b. Suppose now, instead, that Q and R are true, but U is false. Use the circumscription of Ab in *this* theory to show that the *only* abnormal thing is A.

12. *Both* P *and* Q.   Let Δ consist of these two formulas:

$$\forall x \ R(x) \Rightarrow P(x)$$

$$\forall x \ R(x) \Rightarrow Q(x)$$

Show how to use circumscription to assert that the only objects that satisfy both P and Q also satisfy R. Hint: Use $(\forall x \ (P(x) \wedge Q(x)) \Rightarrow Ab(x))$ and minimize Ab with P and Q variable.

CHAPTER 7

Induction

THE ABILITY TO GENERALIZE from examples is one of the hallmarks of intelligence. Our experience of the world is specific, yet we are able to formulate general theories that account for the past and predict the future. Such reasoning is commonly known as *induction*.

As an example of induction, consider the following problem. We are asked to select a card of our choice from a deck of cards. If we select a "good" card, we are given a reward; otherwise, we get nothing. We know that in the past people have been given rewards for the four of clubs, for the seven of clubs, and for the two of spades, but not for the five of hearts or for the jack of spades. Assuming we are not allowed to repeat a card that has already been selected, which card should we choose?

Many people in this situation would choose a numbered black card. There is no way we can deduce with certainty that this is the right choice. However, we can argue that all the rewards we know of were given for numbered black cards, whereas for no card that is not both numbered and black has a reward been given. Thus, we formulate a theory about which cards are rewarded and which cards are not, and we use this theory to make our choice.

7.1 Induction

In induction, we start with a consistent set of sentences representing our beliefs about the world. We separate out a subset of these beliefs as *data* to be generalized and treat the rest as a *background theory*. In making this division, we require that the background theory Γ not logically imply the data Δ.

$$\Gamma \not\models \Delta$$

Given a background theory Γ and a data set Δ, we define a sentence ϕ to be an *inductive conclusion* (written $\Gamma \cup \Delta \bumpeq \phi$) if and only if the following conditions hold.

(1) The hypothesis is consistent with the background theory and data.

$$\Gamma \cup \Delta \not\models \neg\phi$$

(2) The hypothesis explains the data.

$$\Gamma \cup \{\phi\} \models \Delta$$

As an example of this definition, consider the card problem we introduced previously. Let us denote each card in the deck by a term of the form $[\rho, \sigma]$, where ρ denotes the rank of the card and σ denotes the suit. In specifying rank, we use digits for numbered cards and the symbols J, Q, and K for face cards. In specifying suit, we use the constant S for spades, D for diamonds, C for clubs, and H for hearts. In describing cards, we use the unary relations Num, Face, Red, and Black.

Our background theory contains the definitions of these four relations. Also, although we do not show them here, there are axioms defining the $\leq$ and $>$ operators and inequality axioms for ranks and suits.

$$\forall n \forall z \ n{\leq}10 \Leftrightarrow \text{Num}([n,z])$$

$$\forall n \forall z \ n{>}10 \Leftrightarrow \text{Face}([n,z])$$

$$\forall n \forall z \ (z{=}S \vee z{=}C) \Leftrightarrow \text{Black}([n,z])$$

$$\forall n \forall z \ (z{=}D \vee z{=}H) \Leftrightarrow \text{Red}([n,z])$$

Our data set includes sentences saying which cards are rewarded and which are not. None of the sentences in this list are logically implied by the background theory.

$$\text{Reward}([4,C])$$

$$\text{Reward}([7,C])$$

$$\text{Reward}([2,S])$$

$$\neg\text{Reward}([5,H])$$

$$\neg\text{Reward}([J,S])$$

From this information, it is reasonable to propose the inductive conclusion that all numbered, black cards are rewarded and that only numbered, black cards are rewarded.

$$\forall x \; \text{Num}(x) \; \land \; \text{Black}(x) \; \Leftrightarrow \; \text{Reward}(x)$$

This conclusion is clearly consistent with the background theory. Furthermore, it explains the data insofar as it allows us to infer the known rewards and to account for the known nonrewards.

In thinking about induction, it is important to bear in mind that this approach is not necessarily sound. Although an inductive conclusion must be consistent with the sentences in its background theory and data, it need not be a logical conclusion of those sentences. In other words, there can be models of the premises in an inductive problem that are not models of the conclusion. For example, the conclusion that numbered black cards are rewarded, while plausible, is not a logical consequence of the background theory and data listed previously.

On the other hand, not every induction is unsound. For example, once we have seen all the cards in the deck, any inductive conclusion also is a logical conclusion. This is an example of what Aristotle called a *summative induction*; i.e., the inference of a universal statement from information about the properties of a set of individuals and the knowledge that those individuals exhaust the set of possibilities.

Another important point to note about our definition is that, for any background theory and data set, there are numerous inductive conclusions. To cope with this multiplicity of possibilities, researchers have appealed to *model-maximization* techniques and the use of various types of *theoretical bias* in excluding or ordering potential conclusions.

The basis for model maximization is the observation that some inductive conclusions are less conservative than are others, with the result that they have fewer models. For example, in our card problem, we concluded that numbered, black cards are rewarded. We might equally well have decided that numbered black cards are rewarded *and* it is raining outside. Adding the extra condition does not hurt in any way; the conclusion still satisfies the conditions in the definition of induction. On the other hand, it is completely superfluous.

The idea behind model maximization is to order inductive conclusions on the basis of their models. According to this ordering, one conclusion is better than another if and only if its models are a proper superset of the models of the other conclusion. In our example, both conclusions are consistent and explain the data; but the *numbered and black* conclusion is better than the *numbered and black and raining* conclusion, because every model of the latter is a model of the former.

Note that model maximization does *not* help us to choose among competing conclusions that are incompatible. For example, it does not help us to discriminate between our *black and numbered* conclusion and the conclusion that rewards are restricted to the four of clubs, the seven of clubs, and the two of spades. These two theories are incompatible in that there are models of each that are not models of the other.

Theoretical bias is another way of dealing with the multiplicity of inductive conclusions. Instead of considering all predicate-calculus sentences as potential conclusions, we can restrict our candidates to formulas with a particular vocabulary (conceptual bias) or a particular logical form (logical bias).

Conceptual bias is an example of an acceptability condition for inductive conclusions. The idea is to lessen the number of acceptable conclusions by considering only those sentences that can be written in terms of a fixed vocabulary (called the *basis set*).

As an example, consider the card problem with a basis set consisting of the relation symbols `Num`, `Face`, `Black`, `Red` and the name of the target concept `Reward`. Note that we are *not* including the names of the individual cards in this basis set. With this bias, our theory about numbered, black cards is acceptable, since it is expressed entirely in terms of this vocabulary. By contrast, the concept of a card that is either the four of clubs, the seven of clubs, or the two of spades is not acceptable. Although it can be described by the following formula, this formula uses symbols that are not in the basis set; viz., the names of the individual cards. Consequently, it is not acceptable.

$$\forall x \ (x=[4,C] \lor x=[7,C] \lor x=[2,S]) \Leftrightarrow Reward(x)$$

Although the application of conceptual bias is clear, our discussion here leaves open the question of how to select a suitable basis set. This is a difficult question to answer. Although it seems safe to restrict the basis set to those symbols occurring in the background theory, even this can cause problems in situations where we need to hypothesize the existence of new objects in order to provide satisfactory explanations of the data.

Logical bias is another way of limiting the range of possible conclusions. For example, we can restrict our attention to *conjunctive definitions*; i.e., bidirectional implications in which one side mentions the concept being defined and the other side is a conjunction of atoms.

$$\forall x \ \phi_1(x) \land \ldots \land \phi_n(x) \Leftrightarrow \rho(x)$$

This restriction does not exclude our theory about numbered, black cards, since that theory is written in this form. However, we cannot state the theory that rewards are given to cards that are either numbered *or* red, since the corresponding formula (which follows) is not conjunctive and there is no equivalent conjunctive formula (without mentioning individual cards).

$$\forall x\ \mathtt{Num(x)}\ \lor\ \mathtt{Red(x)}\ \Leftrightarrow\ \mathtt{Reward(x)}$$

The restriction to conjunctive definitions is quite strong and makes it impossible to define some common concepts, such as that of a pair in poker. However, we can eliminate this problem by generalizing the language slightly to include *existential conjunctive definitions*; i.e., those that can be written as existentially quantified conjunctions of atoms with equality and inequality. The following formula defines the notion of a pair in this language. The Part relation here holds of a card and the hand to which it belongs.

$$\forall x\ (\exists n\exists s\exists t\ \mathtt{Part([n,s],x)}\ \land\ \mathtt{Part([n,t],x)}\ \land\ \mathtt{s{\neq}t})\ \Leftrightarrow\ \mathtt{Pair(x)}$$

The restriction to existential conjunctive definitions is fairly common in research on automated induction, even in the face of a need for more flexibility. As a partial remedy, Michalski [Michalski 1983c] has proposed some extensions to the definition of an atom in predicate calculus to capture limited disjunction.

The primary argument for logical bias is that formulas with restricted logical structure often are more understandable and allow greater efficiency in subsequent deduction than do more complex formulas. Unfortunately, to date there has been little formal analysis to support this argument.

7.2 Concept Formation

Our card problem is an instance of a common type of inductive inference called *concept formation*. The data assert a common property of some objects and deny that property to others, and the inductive hypothesis is a universally quantified sentence that summarizes the conditions under which an object has that property. In such cases, the problem of induction reduces to that of forming the *concept* of all objects that have that property.

Our treatment of the card problem in the preceding section shows we can formalize concept formation in terms of premises and conclusions. However, in presenting the issues involved in concept formation, it is simpler to think about the latter in terms of objects, functions, and relations.

Formally, we define a *concept-formation problem* as a tuple $\langle P, N, C, \Lambda \rangle$, where P is a set of *positive instances* of a concept, where N is a set of *negative instances*, where C is a set of concepts to be used in defining the concept, and where Λ is a language to use in phrasing the definition. The set C here captures our conceptual bias, and the language Λ captures our logical bias.

Note that there are learning situations in which erroneous assumptions or observations lead to situations in which an agent believes that an object is both a positive instance and a negative instance of a concept. In such situations, P may share some elements with N. However, we ignore such situations in our treatment here and assume that P and N are disjoint.

Given a concept-formation problem $\langle P, N, C, \Lambda \rangle$, we define a relation to be *acceptable* if and only if it is definable in terms of the concepts from C in language Λ. (See Chapter 2 for the definition of definability.)

The criterion of acceptability restricts the relations that can be considered as solutions to a concept-formation problem. Consider, for example, a version of the cards problem in which the conceptual basis includes the relations *numbered*, *face*, *black*, and *red*, and in which the language of definition is restricted to conjunctive definitions. For this problem, the concept of numbered *and* black cards is acceptable, but the concept of numbered *or* black cards is not.

Given a concept formation problem $\langle P, N, C, \Lambda \rangle$, we say that an acceptable relation r is *characteristic* if and only if it is satisfied by all the positive instances. An acceptable relation r is *discriminant* if and only if it is not satisfied by any of the negatives instances. An acceptable relation is *admissible* if and only if it is both characteristic and discriminant.

In the cards example, the *numbered* relation is characteristic but not discriminant, since it covers all the positive instances but also some of the negative instances. The relation *club* is discriminant but not characteristic, since it excludes all the negative instances but also some of the positive instances. The relation formed from the intersection of the *numbered* relation and the *black* relation is both characteristic and discriminant and, therefore, is admissible.

A *version space* for a concept-formation problem is the set of all admissible relations for the problem. A *version graph* is a directed acyclic graph in which the nodes are the elements of a version space and in which there is an arc from a node p to a node q if and only if (1) p is less general than q (i.e., the relation p, viewed as a set of elements, is a proper subset of q) and (2) there is no node r that is more general than p and less general than q. If relations p and q satisfy both of these properties, we say that p is *below* q (written *below*(p, q)).

As an example, let us look once again at the card problem. Our basis set contains the specific relations for each rank and suit and the general relations *numbered*, *face*, *black*, and *red*. Our language restricts the space of possible definitions to conjunctions of atoms. Figure 7.1 illustrates the version graph for the case in which the four of clubs is the sole positive instance and there are no negative instances. In labeling the nodes, we have abbreviated relations by two-letter formulas. The first letter designates the rank of the card; the second letter designates that card's suit. In both cases, the letter a stands for "any;" i.e., no constraint. Thus, the notation ab stands for the relation satisfied by any black card.

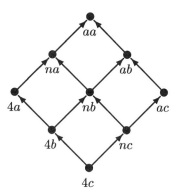

Figure 7.1   Version graph for the card problem in which the four of clubs is the sole positive instance.

The minimal node in this version graph is the singleton relation satisfied by the four of clubs. Notice that the graph does not contain a similar relation for any other specific card. Any such relation would not cover the four of clubs and so would not be characteristic. The maximal node corresponds to the most general relation; i.e., the relation true of all cards.

In this case, we can see that there are still many admissible relations. Additional instances can help to prune this space. For example, if at this point we discover that the seven of clubs is a positive instance, we can eliminate the three concepts that mention the rank of 4, leading to the updated version graph in Figure 7.2. A negative instance such as the five of hearts allows us to prune aa and na, since both concepts cover that instance. This leads to the graph in Figure 7.3. A succeeding positive

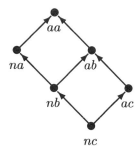

Figure 7.2   Version graph updated with the seven of clubs as a positive instance.

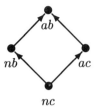

Figure 7.3   **Version graph updated with the five of hearts as a negative instance.**

instance of the two of spades allows us to prune out the relations restricted to clubs, leading to the graph in Figure 7.4. Finally, the fact that the jack of spades is a negative instance reduces the space to the single concept nb in Figure 7.5; i.e., a numbered black card.

Although a version graph with more than one node is ambiguous with respect to the concept being learned, it can still be of use in classifying instances that we have not seen before, on the assumption that the correct solution is a member of the version space.

For example, given the version graph in Figure 7.3, we see that the eight of clubs must be an instance, since it is satisfies every relation in the version space. We also see that the six of diamonds must be a negative instance, since it does not satisfy any relation in the graph.

The chief problem in representing and using a version space in concept formation is the graph's size. Even in a conjunctive-theory language, the number of elements in the space can be exponential in the cardinality of the basis set. Fortunately, we can achieve a substantial economy by restricting our attention to the *boundary sets* of the space and by updating these boundary sets during concept formation using a process known as *candidate elimination*.

A relation is a *minimal* (i.e., *maximally specific*) element of a version space if and only if there is no other relation in the version space that is less general. A relation is a *maximal* element of a version space if and

Figure 7.4   **Version graph updated with the two of spades as a positive instance.**

nb

Figure 7.5   Version graph updated with the jack of spades as a negative instance.

only if there is no other relation that is more general. For example, the 4c relation is the minimal element of the version space in Figure 7.1, and *aa* is the maximal element.

A version space is *well structured* if and only if every chain of relations has a maximal and a minimal element. Obviously, any version space over a finite universe must be well structured.

Given a well-structured version space V, we define the *specific boundary set S* of V to be the set of minimal elements of V and the *general boundary set G* to be the set of maximal elements.

The specific boundary set for the version space in Figure 7.1 consists of the single relation 4c, and the general boundary set consists of the single relation *aa*. Although in this case the boundary sets are singletons, this need not be true in general.

One interesting property of boundary sets is that they do indeed bound the version spaces with which they are associated.

THEOREM 7.1 (Boundary Set Theorem) *If $\langle P, N, C, \Lambda \rangle$ is a concept-formation problem with a well-structured version space V and boundary sets S and G, then a relation r is in V if and only if it is bounded from below by an element of S and bounded from above by an element of G.*

In other words, it is possible to get to any element of the version space by following a finite number of arcs from an element of the specific boundary set or by following a finite number of arcs from an element of the general boundary set. Therefore, from the boundary sets we can determine whether or not a given relation is in the version space.

Another important property of the boundary-set representation of a version graph is that it is a simple matter to define the boundary sets after the addition of a new positive or a negative instance.

After receiving a new positive instance, we obtain the new general boundary set $pg(x, S, G)$ by pruning the old general boundary set to exclude any elements that do not cover the new instance.

$$pg(x, S, G) = \{g \in G | g(x)\}$$

The update to the specific boundary set $ps(x, S, G)$ is a little more complicated. In particular, we include a relation in the new boundary set if and only if (1) it is an element of the old specific boundary set or a generalization thereof, (2) it is a specialization of some element in the new general boundary set, (3) it covers the new instance, and (4) there is no more specific relation with these three properties. If a relation has all these properties, we say that it is a *positive update* (written $pup(x, S, G, r)$).

$$ps(x, S, G) = \{r \mid pup(x, S, G, r)\}$$

The handling of a negative instance is symmetric. After receiving a new negative instance, we obtain the new specific boundary set $ns(x, S, G)$ by pruning the old specific boundary set to exclude any elements that cover the negative instance.

$$ns(x, S, G) = \{s \in S \mid \neg s(x)\}$$

In the update to the general boundary set $ng(x, S, G)$, we include a relation if and only if (1) it is an element of the old general boundary set or a specialization thereof, (2) it is a generalization of some element in the new specific boundary set, (3) it does not cover the new instance, and (4) there is no more general relation with these three properties. If a relation has all these properties, we say that it is a *negative update* (written $nup(x, S, G, r)$).

$$ng(x, S, G) = \{r \mid nup(x, S, G, r\}$$

The following theorem guarantees that these updates are correct for any well-structured concept-formation problem. Furthermore, given the boundary set theorem, we know that we can compute these updates in finite time.

THEOREM 7.2 (Candidate Elimination Theorem) *If $\langle P, N, C, \Lambda \rangle$ is a concept-formation problem with a well-structured version space V and boundary sets S and G, then $ps(x, S, G)$ and $pg(x, S, G)$ are the boundary sets of the version space for $\langle P \cup \{x\}, N, C, \Lambda \rangle$, and $ns(x, S, G)$ and $ng(x, S, G)$ are the boundary sets of the version space for $\langle P, N \cup \{x\}, C, \Lambda \rangle$.*

At this point, it is probably wise for the reader to consider the boundary sets for our card problem and to compute the updates for each instance in the sequence. Note that, after the fifth instance, the general boundary set equals the specific boundary set. In other words, there is just a single node in the version space, and no further instances are necessary.

7.3 Experiment Generation

In some concept-formation situations, we have no control over the instances with which we have to work. They are provided by others—sometimes by a teacher, sometimes by nature. In many cases, however, it is possible for us to select instances and to acquire information about their classification. In other words, we can design and execute experiments. This raises the question of what instances we should use so as to maximize our concept-formation performance.

A common strategy in such situations is to select an instance that *halves* the number of candidate formulas; i.e., one that satisfies one-half of the candidates and does not satisfy the other half. The advantage of this is that, by getting the classification of such an instance, we can eliminate one-half of the remaining candidates, whether the instance turns out to be positive or negative.

Suppose, for example, that we had already seen that the four of clubs and the seven of clubs were positive instances of a concept and that we had no negative instances. This would lead to the version space in Figure 7.2. At this point, which card should we ask about next? Obviously, the nine of clubs would be a bad choice, since it satisfies all the concepts in the version space. Assuming that the concept to be learned is one of the candidates in the version space, then we already know the instance must be a positive. The jack of hearts is a little better, in that it satisfies one of the six candidates. This is very good if the instance turns out to be positive, because then we can shrink the version space to a single candidate in one step. On the other hand, if it turns out to be a negative instance, the net result is to prune only one candidate, leaving us with five candidates to discriminate. It would be much better to select an instance such as the jack of clubs, because this card satisfies three of the candidates and fails to satisfy the other three. Thus, getting its classification is guaranteed to prune at least one-half of the candidates, no matter what the classification turns out to be.

On the average, the halving strategy will diminish the set of candidates more rapidly than any other technique will. Furthermore, if the candidate concepts are equally likely, then on the average the halving strategy will lead to the shortest sequence of experiments necessary to identify the correct candidate. Under these conditions, we can isolate a single candidate from among n alternatives in $O(\log n)$ steps.

For situations in which we cannot find an instance that divides the alternatives into two groups of exactly equal size, we should choose the instance that comes closest. We can formalize this strategy by computing the information value of each instance with respect to a candidate set and by choosing the instance that yields the most information.

The main problem with the halving strategy by itself is computational expense. In the worst case, we need to compare each instance with each concept to determine whether or not the instance satisfies the concept. If there are m instances and n candidates, then in the worst case we need mn steps to select the best instance. This is infeasible when either m or n is very large.

Fortunately, we can improve this situation in cases where the concept to be learned can be "factored" into multiple independent concepts. For example, the rank of a card is independent of its suit in that the set of all cards contains an instance of every combination of rank and suit. Consequently, many solutions to the card problem can be factored into independent concepts, one having to do with rank and the other concerned with suit. The factoring of the alternatives in a concept-formation problem leads to a factoring of the associated version space into separate, smaller version spaces. The advantage is that the experiment-generation procedure we described can be much more efficient if applied to these smaller version spaces than it is when used with the unfactored space.

A version space U and a version space V are *independent* if and only if, for every u in U and every v in V, there is an object that satisfies both u and v; in other words, every intersection of an element of U with an element of V is nonempty.

As an example, consider one version space consisting of the relations 4 (i.e., rank 4), *numbered*, and *anyrank*; and consider a second version space consisting of the relations *club*, *black*, and *anysuit*. These two version spaces are independent, since membership in any of the relations from the first version space does not imply or deny membership in any of the relations in the second version space.

The *product W* of a version space U and an independent version space V is the set of relations formed from the intersections of elements from U and V. In this case, we say that U and V are *factors* of W.

For example, the product space for the two version spaces in the last example consists of nine elements, one for each pair of relations from the two spaces.

A version graph $\langle W, C \rangle$ is the *product* of version graphs $\langle U, A \rangle$ and $\langle V, B \rangle$ if and only if (1) W is the product of U and V and (2) there is an arc in C from a node $w_m = u_i \cap v_k$ to a node $w_n = u_j \cap v_l$ if and only if there is an arc in A from u_i to u_j and an arc in B from v_k to v_l. A version graph is *prime* if and only if it has no nontrivial version graph factors.

For example, the graph shown in Figure 7.1 can be factored into the two graphs shown in Figure 7.6. Every node in Figure 7.1 corresponds to a node in each of the graphs in Figure 7.6, and vice versa. Furthermore, the ordering is correct.

As it turns out, there are several nice results from graph theory that apply to the problem of factoring version graphs. Given a unique factorization for the nodes of a directed acyclic graph, there is a unique factorization of the graph into prime subgraphs. Furthermore, there is an algorithm for computing these factors in polynomial time.

One way we can use the factors of a version graph is to generate experiments within each factor and to combine the resulting "subinstances" into a single instance to be tested. The value of an instance derived in

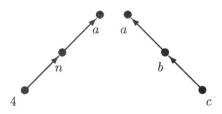

Figure 7.6   Factors of the version graph in Figure 7.1.

this way depends on the nature of information available from the learning environment.

We say that an experimentation environment offers *independent credit assignment* (ICA) if and only if, when presented with an instance from a factorable version space, it assigns positive or negative status to each factor independently. For example, when we ask about the five of hearts, we get the information that its rank is okay but its suit is bad.

An environment that provides ICA has several pleasant properties. First, it can be shown that the initial version graph (the one given by a single positive instance) for a factorable concept is factorable. Under ICA, all updates to a version graph preserve its factorability, and the best instance to use in candidate elimination is the one formed from the best instances for each of the factors.

The computational advantages of factoring are striking. Suppose that we can factor a version graph into k factors, with p nodes each. Whenever this is the case, the size of the unfactored graph must be p^k. If we can factor the graph, then we can "factor" each instance into k parts, one for each factor of the graph. If there are q possibilities for each part, then there must be q^k instances. As we discussed, the total cost of experiment generation without factoring is $p^k q^k$, whereas the total cost with factoring is just kpq, a substantial saving whenever p or q is large.

Without ICA, things are not so pleasant. The boundary-set updates for the unfactored graph do not necessarily preserve factorability, and the instance formed from the best instances of the factors is not necessarily the best instance for the unfactored graph. For example, under ICA the jack of hearts is a good test case for the graph in Figure 7.1, whereas it is a terrible one without ICA.

Fortunately, even without ICA, we can fix this problem if we are willing to perform extra experiments. Suppose that we select an instance that is best for each of the factors. If the instance is positive, then we update the graphs accordingly and continue. However, if the instance is negative, we need to figure out which factor or factors are responsible; i.e., we need to assign *credit* for the failure. We can do this by generating a series of *near misses*, or controlled experiments. We take a positive instance and, for each factor, find an instance that (1) differs from it in only that factor, and (2) for that factor has the value in the failed test case. By trying out each of these k instances, we simulate ICA and restore factorability to the version graph.

7.4 Bibliographical and Historical Remarks

Within the AI commmunity, substantial results on automated induction first began to emerge in the mid-sixties. The earliest efforts were concerned primarily with psychological modeling, and the tasks were relatively simple. For example, the CLS system [Hunt 1966] was restricted to classifying instances on the basis of unary predicates only. Later in the decade, researchers began the study of more complicated problems.

The concept-formation program described by Winston in his thesis [Winston 1975] was a landmark development in this direction. It accepted as input a sequence of descriptions of complicated Blocks World configurations, each classified as a positive or negative instance of the concept to be learned. The output was a definition of an admissible relation for the concept. One weakness in the program was that it maintained a single nondisjunctive hypothesis at all times, and as a result it was forced to make arbitrary choices in updating that hypothesis each time it was presented with a negative instance that differed from its hypothesis in more than one way. For this reason, the program was most successful when presented with a near miss, which disagreed with its current hypothesis in at most one way.

Mitchell addressed the shortcoming in Winston's program by suggesting in his thesis [Mitchell 1978] that multiple hypotheses be retained. This led to the notion of a version space, the idea of boundary sets, and the candidate-elimination algorithm, all of which are described in this chapter.

At about the same time, a number of other researchers reported methods for solving special cases of the concept-formation problem. Hayes-Roth used the technique of *interference matching* in a system called SPROUTER[Hayes-Roth 1978], which was capable of learning existential conjunctive concepts from positive instances. Vere described a similar method for finding *maximal unifying generalizations* in his program, called THOTH [Vere 1975, 1978]. Quinlan used a variation of CLS in building ID3 [Quinlan 1983], a program capable of learning concept definitions involving disjunctions as well as conjunctions. In his paper on generalization as search [Mitchell 1982], Mitchell explained how these methods are special cases of his own method.

The work by Michalski et al. on the INDUCE systems[Larson 1977, Michalski 1980] is especially noteworthy. In their approach, the set of candidate theories was represented in the form of a description called a *star*, essentially a disjunction of existential conjunctive theories similar to the specific boundary of a version space. Their inductive inference method was distinctive in that it used an extensive set of inductive rules of inference; e.g., generalizing variables and dropping conditions.

In addition to this work on domain-independent concept formation, there have been several interesting investigations of more or less domain-dependent inductive inference. The META-DENDRAL program [Buchanan 1976] is a prime example. It took as input a set of mass spectra and descriptions of the corresponding molecules, and generated classification rules for use in the DENDRAL program [Lindsay 1980]. In generating its candidate rules, it used a set of heuristics based on extensive knowledge of chemistry. The goal of the BACON systems [Langley 1983] was the formation of hypotheses to explain scientific data. Its rules of inductive inference were specialized to the task of forming mathematical theories of certain specific forms. In other ways, however, the systems were domain independent.

An important issue in comparing these inductive systems is the nature of the learning situation. Some of the systems assume that all the data are available at the start of induction; e.g., META-DENDRAL, BACON, INDUCE, and, to some extent, ID3. For obscure reasons, such systems often are said to be *model-driven*. The other systems are *incremental*, or *data-driven*, in that they assume a stream of data, they create intermediate hypotheses, and they are capable of updating these hypotheses to account for each new instance. Although all the incremental systems mentioned here are passive learners, there has recently been much talk about experiment generation. The results in this chapter on factorization and experiment generation were developed by Subramanian and Feigenbaum [Subramanian 1986].

Although we do not discuss it here, *conceptual clustering* is another important type of induction. The inputs for a conceptual-clustering problem include a set of objects with known attributes. The goal is to produce a small taxonomy for the objects; i.e., a subset hierarchy of classes of similar objects in which the subclasses of each class are mutually exclusive and jointly exhaustive. Although there has been considerable work on this problem in statistics, those results are inadequate in general because the methods do not always produce results that are meaningful in terms of known concepts. The CLUSTER program [Michalski 1983b] deals with this problem by taking as input a basis set of concepts and restricting its attention to taxonomies that can be defined conjunctively in terms of this basis set.

Finally, there is *constructive induction*, in which new terms are introduced in the formation of inductive conclusions. Winston's program, the INDUCE system, and the BACON systems are all capable of constructive induction, but only of a limited sort.

Lenat's AM [Lenat 1976] program is perhaps the most interesting constructive-induction program to date. His method for inventing new terms depended on a theory of *interestingness* that allowed the program to concentrate its efforts in rewarding directions. Starting from an initial database of information about sets and set operations, AM managed to invent various simple arithmetic operations as well as complicated notions, such as the prime numbers.

For further reading on machine learning, the reader is referred to [Michalski 1983a, Michalski 1986, Mitchell 1986, and Angluin 1983].

Exercises

1. *Concept formation.* Consider the concept-formation problem with the four of clubs, the seven of clubs, and the two of spades as positive instances and with the five of hearts and the jack of spades as negative instances. Assuming that the relations with the following extensions are all acceptable, classify each as admissible, characteristic, or discriminant.

   a. All cards except the five of hearts and jack of spades

   b. All black cards

   c. All clubs

   d. All cards

   e. No cards

2. *Boundary sets.* What goes wrong with the boundary-set representation if we relax the assumption that the candidate set is well structured?

3. *Independence.* Consider the following two sets of relations. The first consists of the 13 rank relations (i.e., the relations satisfied by those cards of a specific rank), *numbered*, *face*, and *anyrank*. The second consists of the 13 rank relations, *odd*, *even*, and *anyrank*. Are these two sets of relations independent?

4. *Experiment generation.* Consider the version graph in Figure 7.3.

   a. Find a useful test instance that is good with ICA but bad without ICA.

   b. Find a test instance that is good whether or not the environment offers ICA.

CHAPTER 8
Reasoning with Uncertain Beliefs

WE HAVE ALREADY MENTIONED that the information about the world possessed by intelligent agents is better described as *beliefs* than as *knowledge*. Typically, an agent can never be sure that its beliefs are *true*. Notwithstanding this basic epistemological uncertainty, we have been assuming so far that agents nevertheless assent to their beliefs with the same total commitment that they would assent to knowledge. That is, if an agent believes P and also believes $P \Rightarrow Q$, then it is justified in believing Q. The fact that P and $P \Rightarrow Q$ have the status of beliefs (instead of knowledge) in no way weakens the strength of belief in the conclusion, Q.

There are circumstances, however, in which it would not be appropriate for an agent to invest its beliefs with such total commitment. An agent may realize that not only does it merely *believe P* instead of *knowing P*, but that it does not believe P very strongly. There are many situations in which humans possess and reason with *uncertain* beliefs. We may *believe* that we will meet an old friend for lunch at an agreed-upon time, but our commitment to this belief is not total because we also somehow take into account the possibility that he (or we) might be late. A physician may *believe* that penicillin will be effective in treating a certain bacterial infection but would be likely to describe this belief as *partial* in some way. Clearly, the notion of *strength* of a belief seems to make intuitive sense; can we give a precise technical meaning to this intuition?

It is important to realize that the subject of partial or uncertain beliefs, in the sense we are talking about them here, has no necessary connection with nonmonotonic reasoning. In nonmonotonic reasoning, as long as an agent believes something, it believes that something totally, even though it might retract the belief later upon absorbing new beliefs. Also, as we shall see, it is possible to describe systems for reasoning with uncertain beliefs that are monotonic in the sense that new beliefs do not contradict previously derived ones. Thus, the two notions—nonmonotonic reasoning and reasoning with uncertain beliefs—are quite independent.

8.1 Probabilities of Sentences

In searching for ways to formalize the idea of beliefs having strengths, we are tempted to consider a generalization of logic in which truth values can take on values intermediate between true and false. To believe P with total commitment is to assign it the value true. To disbelieve P totally (or, equivalently, to believe $\neg P$ totally) is to assign P the value false. Inventing truth values *between* true and false allows for various degrees of partial belief. Indeed, *multivalued logics* have been studied—sometimes with this application in mind.

Of course, any mention of degrees of certainty or uncertainty of a proposition also brings to mind the idea of probability. For some events, such as penicillin being effective against pneumonococci, probability measures grounded in large-sample statistics might be available. For other, less frequently occuring events, such as the volcano Anak Krakatoa erupting catastrophically during the next year, *subjective probability* measures (still based on axiomatic probability theory) can be used. Our treatment in this chapter of uncertain beliefs is based on combining logic with probability theory in various ways.

To extend the apparatus of first-order logic to permit the use of probability theory in reasoning about uncertain statements, we must connect the idea of a *sentence* in logic with the idea of a *random variable* in probability theory. The ordinary truth-theoretic semantics of first-order logic associates a value true or false with each sentence. To use probability theory, we modify the semantics such that each sentence is associated with a *probability distribution* on a binary-valued random variable. This distribution is the *interpretation* of the sentence. For example, with the sentence P, we might associate the distribution $\{(1 - p), p\}$. By this interpretation, we mean that the probability of P being true is p. (We often use the phrase *the probability of P* as an abbreviation for *the probability of P being true*.) Of course, as in ordinary logic, one cannot consistently give *arbitrary* interpretations to sentences. For example, the distribution $\{(1 - p), p\}$ assigned to P implies that the probability of $\neg P$ must be $(1-p)$. Later, we will be more precise about the notion of consistent probability values for sentences. It is helpful to begin our discussion, however, on more intuitive grounds.

Consider two ground atoms P and Q. If the probabilities of P and Q are given, what can be said about the probability of $P \wedge Q$? It all depends on the *joint distribution* of P and Q. It will turn out that what might be called a *probabilistic interpretation* for a set of sentences will involve something like an assignment of a joint probability distribution to the ground instances of the atoms in those sentences. An interpretation for the set of sentences $\{P, Q\}$ consists of a joint probability distribution for P and Q. That is, we must specify probabilities for the four combinations of each of P and Q being true and false.

For purposes of discussion, let the four joint probabilities in this example be given by

$$p(P \wedge Q) = p_1$$
$$p(P \wedge \neg Q) = p_2$$
$$p(\neg P \wedge Q) = p_3$$
$$p(\neg P \wedge \neg Q) = p_4$$

where $p(\phi)$ denotes the probability of the formula ϕ being true.

The probabilities of P and Q alone are called *marginal probabilities* and are given as sums of the joint probabilities as follows:

$$p(P) = p_1 + p_2$$
$$p(Q) = p_1 + p_3$$

We see that merely specifying probabilities (generalized truth values) for P and Q individually does not fully determine the four joint probabilities, and therefore (unlike ordinary logic) it does not allow us to calculate probabilities (generalized truth values) for composite formulas such as $P \wedge Q$.

In ordinary logic, modus ponens allows us to conclude Q, given P and $P \Rightarrow Q$. In probabilistic logic, however, we cannot analogously calculate a probability for Q given probabilities for P and $P \Rightarrow Q$, because these probabilities do not fully determine the four joint probabilities. This lack of analogous inference rules makes reasoning with uncertain beliefs more complex than reasoning with certain beliefs is. Joint probability distributions over n atoms have 2^n component terms—an impractically large number, even for small numbers of atoms. Nevertheless, there are some reasoning procedures for uncertain beliefs that under restricted circumstances produce intuitively satisfactory results, and we shall be discussing some of these in this chapter.

8.2 Using Bayes' Rule in Uncertain Reasoning

In some situations involving uncertain beliefs, we can perform a reasoning step somewhat similar to modus ponens while using probability information that is available. Suppose we want to calculate the probability of Q when we know that P is true and we also know some information about the relationship between P and Q. The probability of Q given that P is true, written $p(Q|P)$ and called the *conditional probability* of Q given P, is just that fraction of the cases in which P is true for which Q also is true. In terms of the joint probabilities defined previously, this fraction is $p_1/(p_1 + p_2)$. Or, $p(Q|P) = p(P,Q)/p(P)$, where $p(P,Q)$ stands for the probability of both P and Q being true (which is the same as $p(P \wedge Q)$.)

Similarly, we could calculate $p(P|Q) = p(P,Q)/p(Q)$. Combining these two expressions allows us to write

$$p(Q|P) = \frac{p(P|Q)p(Q)}{p(P)}$$

which is known as *Bayes' rule*. $p(Q|P)$ is called the *conditional* or *posterior* probability of Q given P, and (in this context) $p(Q)$ and $p(P)$ are called the *prior* or *marginal* probabilities of Q and P, respectively. The importance of Bayes' rule for uncertain reasoning lies in the facts that (1) one often has (or can reasonably assume) prior probabilities for P and Q, and (2) in situations in which some evidence P bears on a hypothesis Q, one's knowledge of the relationship between P and Q often is available in terms of $p(P|Q)$. From these given quantities, the essential *reasoning* step involves using Bayes' rule to calculate $p(Q|P)$.

An example will help to clarify the use of Bayes' rule in uncertain reasoning. Suppose P stands for the sentence, "The automobile's wheels make a squeaking noise," and Q stands for the sentence, "The automobile's brakes need adjustment." We would ordinarily think of P as a symptom and of Q as a hypothesis about the cause of the symptom. The relationship between cause and symptom usually can be expressed in terms of the probability that the symptom occurs given the cause, or $p(P|Q)$. Let us suppose that poorly adjusted brakes often (but not always) produce wheel squeaks, say $p(P|Q) = 0.7$. Suppose, to further specify our example, that $p(P) = 0.05$ and $p(Q) = 0.02$. If we are in a situation in which we observe squeaking wheels and want to determine the probability that the brakes need adjustment, then we calculate $p(Q|P) = 0.28$ using Bayes' rule. Many instances of reasoning with uncertain information are analogous to this example, in which we have information about "symptoms" and want to infer "causes."

To use Bayes' rule, we must have a value for $p(P)$. In practice, prior probabilities of "symptoms" are often much more difficult to estimate than are prior probabilities of "causes," so it is worth inquiring whether or not Bayes' rule can be expressed in terms of quantities that are easier to obtain. Fortunately, there is another version of Bayes' rule in which $p(P)$ does not occur. To derive this version, we first observe that, although $p(\neg Q|P) = 1 - p(Q|P)$, the expression also can be written using Bayes' rule as follows:

$$p(\neg Q|P) = \frac{p(P|\neg Q)p(\neg Q)}{p(P)}$$

Dividing the Bayes' rule expression for $p(Q|P)$ by that of $p(\neg Q|P)$ yields

$$\frac{p(Q|P)}{p(\neg Q|P)} = \frac{p(P|Q)p(Q)}{p(P|\neg Q)p(\neg Q)}$$

The probability of an event divided by the probability that the event does not occur usually is called the *odds* of that event. If we denote the odds of E by $O(E)$, we have $O(E) =_{\text{def}} p(E)/p(\neg E) = p(E)/(1 - p(E))$. Using this notation, we rewrite the quotient of the two Bayes' rule expressions as

$$O(Q|P) = \frac{p(P|Q)}{p(P|\neg Q)}O(Q)$$

The remaining fraction in this expression is an important statistical quantity, usually called the *likelihood ratio* of P with respect to Q. We will denote it here by λ. Thus,

$$\lambda =_{\text{def}} \frac{p(P|Q)}{p(P|\neg Q)}$$

The *odds-likelihood* formulation of Bayes' rule is now written as

$$O(Q|P) = \lambda O(Q)$$

This formula has a satisfying intuitive explanation. It tells us how to compute posterior odds on Q (given P) from the prior odds on Q (the odds that applied before we observed that P was true). Upon learning that P is true, to update the strength of our belief in Q (measured in terms of its odds), we simply multiply the previous odds by λ. The ratio λ can be thought of as information about how influential P is in helping to convert indifferent odds on Q to high odds on Q. When λ is equal to one, then knowing that P is true has absolutely no effect on the odds of Q. In that case, Q is independent of P being true. Values of λ less than one depress the odds of Q; values of λ greater than one increase the odds of Q. Note that, even though we have expressed Bayes' rule in terms of odds, we can easily recover the underlying probability by the formula:

$$p(Q) = O(Q)/(O(Q) + 1)$$

Knowledge about how causes and symptoms are related often can be expressed conveniently by estimating values for the appropriate λs. Even when people knowledgeable about these relations might not be able to estimate conditional probabilities, they often can express their knowledge in terms of how the odds of a probable cause are affected upon learning about a symptom. Probabilities based on subjective estimates or probabilities calculated from estimated values of λ usually are called *subjective probabilities.* Although they are not necessarily based on large-sample statistics, they nevertheless are useful for approximate reasoning.

Just as we can calculate the posterior odds of Q given that P is true, we also can calculate odds given that P is false. The odds version of Bayes' rule for that case is

$$O(Q|\neg P) = \frac{p(\neg P|Q)}{p(\neg P|\neg Q)}O(Q)$$

If we denote the likelihood ratio of $\neg P$ with respect to Q by $\bar{\lambda}$, we have

$$O(Q|\neg P) = \bar{\lambda}O(Q)$$

The ratio $\bar{\lambda}$ is a measure of the effect that learning $\neg P$ has on the odds of Q.

The ratios λ and $\bar{\lambda}$ are numbers that would ordinarily be obtained from someone who has expert knowledge about how P and $\neg P$ affect the odds on Q. When estimating effects of this sort, people usually give numbers that are more a measure of the logarithm of likelihood ratios than of likelihood ratios themselves. Let us define ℓ to be the (natural) logarithm of λ and $\bar{\ell}$ to be the logarithm of $\bar{\lambda}$. We might call ℓ a *sufficiency index;* it measures the degree to which learning that P is true is sufficient for believing that Q is true. Similarly, we could call $\bar{\ell}$ a *necessity index;* negative values of $\bar{\ell}$ indicate the extent to which learning that P is true is necessary for believing Q, because, if P were assumed false, a large negative value of $\bar{\ell}$ would heavily depress the odds of Q.

We illustrate the use of these versions of Bayes' rule with our example about automobile brakes. Suppose the prior odds of Q (the brakes need adjustment) are 0.020. An automobile expert tells us that $\lambda = 19.1$ and $\bar{\lambda} = 0.312$. (These numbers are calculated to be consistent with those of the earlier example; we would not ordinarily expect that an expert would be so precise.) Then we calculate

$$O(Q|P) = 0.39$$

(the odds that the brakes need adjustment given that the wheels squeak), and

$$O(Q|\neg P) = 0.00635$$

(the odds that the brakes need adjustment given that the wheels do not squeak).

Even though λ and $\overline{\lambda}$ must be provided separately, they cannot be specified independently. From their definitions, we can derive the relationship

$$\overline{\lambda} = \frac{1 - \lambda p(P|\neg Q)}{1 - p(P|\neg Q)}$$

For $0 < p(P|\neg Q) < 1$, we see that $\lambda > 1$ implies $\overline{\lambda} < 1$, and $\lambda < 1$ implies $\overline{\lambda} > 1$. Also, $\lambda = 1$ if and only if $\overline{\lambda} = 1$. Since the people who provide estimates of λ and $\overline{\lambda}$ might not be aware of these constraints, the constraints must be enforced by the designer of the reasoning system.

Let us review what we have developed so far. If two events P and Q (which we take to be expressed as logical sentences) are related by statistical measures λ and $\overline{\lambda}$, then when either P or $\neg P$ is observed, we can calculate the posterior probability of Q using Bayes' rule. This probability serves as a measure of our strength of belief in Q under these conditions. We must next ask, suppose we are *uncertain* about P itself? How then do we proceed to calculate a "posterior" probability for Q? One approach is to pretend that our system observes some event, let us call it P', that causes it to believe P with probability $p(P|P')$. Now we can calculate a posterior probability for Q given P' (of which we are certain) to learn how it depends on the intermediate and *uncertain* P. For present purposes, we shall not analyze how $p(P|P')$ itself is calculated, but rather will assume that it is what is meant when we say that the system comes to believe P with a certain probability. (In our automobile example, P' might be taken as the event of someone saying something like, "I thought I heard the wheels squeak." $p(\text{P}|\text{P}')$ is the probability that they did squeak given that assertion.)

Formally, what we must calculate is

$$p(Q|P') = p(Q, P|P') + p(Q, \neg P|P')$$
$$= p(Q|P, P')p(P|P') + p(Q|\neg P, P')p(\neg P|P')$$

The expressions $p(Q|P, P')$ and $p(Q|\neg P, P')$ give the probability of Q conditioned on knowing both the observed event P' *and* knowledge of whether or not P is true. It seems reasonable to presume that, if we knew whether or not P was true, knowledge about the observed event P' would provide no additional information. After all, P' is an event that was invented to tell us about P; loosely speaking, if we already have *certain* knowledge about P (or $\neg P$), we do not need P'.

Assuming then that $p(Q|P, P') = p(Q|P)$ and also that $p(Q|\neg P, P') = p(Q|\neg P)$, the expression for the posterior probability for Q (given P') becomes

$$p(Q|P') = p(Q|P)p(P|P') + p(Q|\neg P)p(\neg P|P')$$

To use this expression, we first calculate $p(Q|P)$ and $p(Q|\neg P)$ using the odds-likelihood version of Bayes' rule and converting these odds to probabilities. $p(Q|P')$ is a linear interpolation between these two extreme cases of P known true and P known false using the probability of P as a weighting factor. It is interesting to note that, in the special case in which $p(P|P') = p(P)$, $p(Q|P') = p(Q)$. That is, when there is no more information about P than that it has its prior probability, then we have no more information about Q than that it, too, has its prior probability.

In our example about automobile brakes, suppose that $p(\mathsf{P}|\mathsf{P}') = 0.8$, in addition to the assumptions made previously. (The person reporting wheel-squeaking has a slight hearing problem.) Then, assuming the conditional independence of Q on P' given P or given $\neg\mathsf{P}$, we have

$$p(\mathsf{Q}|\mathsf{P}') = 0.28 \times 0.8 + 0.00639 \times 0.2$$
$$= 0.225$$

and

$$O(\mathsf{Q}|\mathsf{P}') = 0.29$$

When we have just one "symptom" or other piece of "evidence" that bears on a "hypothesis," the interpolation formula provides the basis for computing the probability of the hypothesis and thus for taking the evidence into account. The whole process of reasoning with uncertain beliefs is more robust, however, when several beliefs together contribute to the inference of some implied belief. Suppose we have a set of sentences $\{P_1, P_2, \ldots, P_n\}$ that are related to Q. If a system believes these sentences with certain probabilities, what probability might it then attach to Q? We seek a technique that allows us to compute the probability of Q incrementally as new information about the P_i's becomes available. Under rather special assumptions about conditional independence (which cannot be justified in general but may often be approximately satisfied), we can show that the probability of Q given several P_i can be computed incrementally on the P_i. Again, we use the ploy of assuming that the probability of the $\{P_1, P_2, \ldots, P_n\}$ is conditioned on corresponding invented observations, $\{P'_1, P'_2, \ldots, P'_n\}$.

We look at the special case of calculating the probability of a sentence Q given the observations P'_1 and P'_2. We want to express this conditional probability in terms of the probability of Q conditioned on P'_1 alone. That is, we assume that we have already calculated $p(Q|P'_1)$ and want to *update* it by taking into account the additional observation P'_2. (Extending this incremental calculation to the case in which there are more than two observations is straightforward.) We make the special assumption that $p(P_2|P'_1, P'_2) = p(P_2|P'_2)$; that is, P_2 depends only on P'_2 and not on P'_1. Also, $p(\neg P_2|P'_1, P'_2) = p(\neg P_2|P'_2)$. Our belief about P_2 is thus represented by the probability $p(P_2|P'_2)$.

The conditional probability for Q given both observations is

$$p(Q|P'_1, P'_2) = p(Q, P_2|P'_1, P'_2) + p(Q, \neg P_2|P'_1, P'_2)$$

$$= p(Q|P_2, P_1', P_2')p(P_2|P_1', P_2')$$
$$+ p(Q|\neg P_2, P_1', P_2')p(\neg P_2|P_1', P_2')$$

Making use of our assumption that P_2 is independent of P_1' and also assuming again that Q is independent of P_2' if P_2 is already known, we can write this as

$$p(Q|P_1', P_2') = p(Q|P_2, P_1')p(P_2|P_2') + p(Q|\neg P_2, P_1')p(\neg P_2|P_2')$$

This expression is seen to be an interpolation between $p(Q|P_2, P_1')$ and $p(Q|\neg P_2, P_1')$ weighted by the probability of P_2. An odds-likelihood version of Bayes' rule gives us the two extreme values used in the interpolation:

$$O(Q|P_2, P_1') = \frac{p(P_2|Q, P_1')}{p(P_2|\neg Q, P_1')} O(Q|P_1')$$

Using our assumption that P_2 is independent of P_1', the ratio of probabilities in this expression is seen to be $p(P_2|Q)/p(P_2|\neg Q)$, which we define as λ_2. Similarly,

$$O(Q|\neg P_2, P_1') = \overline{\lambda_2} O(Q|P_1')$$

We interpret and summarize these results as follows. Assume that there are two sentences that bear on Q and that we obtain new information about the probability of one of them, P_2. This information is in the form of a conditional probability $p(P_2|P_2')$. The posterior odds of Q, given this new information (and taking into account the previous information about the other sentence) are then computed by

$$p(Q|P_2', P_1') = p(Q|P_2, P_1')p(P_2|P_2') + p(Q|\neg P_2, P_1')p(\neg P_2|P_2')$$

where the probabilities of Q conditioned on P_2 and $\neg P_2$ are computed from their odds, which are given by

$$O(Q|P_2, P_1') = \lambda_2 O(Q|P_1')$$

and

$$O(Q|\neg P_2, P_1') = \overline{\lambda_2} O(Q|P_1')$$

The expression $O(Q|P_1')$ takes the place of the prior odds used in the case in which we had only one sentence, P. We can perform the computation incrementally, taking into account only P_2' and using the just-computed value of $O(Q|P_1')$ in place of the prior odds of Q. Of course, this method is justified only in the case in which each of the P_is does not depend on any of the observations, P_i', except the one corresponding to it, and in which, given a P_i, Q does not depend additionally on P_i'.

In our example about automobile brakes, suppose P2 corresponds to the sentence, "the brake pedal goes down too far," and P2' corresponds to the sentence, "I think the brake pedal goes down too far." To use this incremental approach to take into account information about brake pedals after already taking into account information about wheel-squeaking, we would have to assume that the brake pedal's going down too far is conditionally independent of a report about wheel-squeaking, given a report about the brake pedal's going down too far. Although this assumption sounds reasonable in this example, an exact analysis would reveal that the assumption can be inconsistent with all the probabilities involved.

In the next section, we show how collections of the various conditional probabilities just described might be used in expert systems.

8.3 Uncertain Reasoning in Expert Systems

Human judgments in many specialized subject areas seem to involve reasoning methods similar to the probabilistic one developed in the previous section. Pieces of evidence, in the form of sentences to which one commits less than total belief, are used to arrive at conclusions. Sometimes, the evidence strongly suggests the conclusion; sometimes, the influence is weaker. Often, human experts are able to provide subjective information (which we can interpret as logarithms of likelihood ratios) about the relationship between evidence and conclusion. After this expert information is coded into a computer system that can perform the kinds of calculations we have just outlined, a *user*, who may not be an expert, can interact with the system by providing probabilities for pieces of evidence in cases of special interest. The system's computations can then provide the user with estimates about probabilities of conclusions of interest. Such systems often are called *rule-based expert systems*.

In these systems, expert knowledge usually is captured in the form of *rules*. Each rule is a sentence of the form $P \longrightarrow Q$. The symbol $\longrightarrow$ has different meanings in different systems, but it is usually intended to mean something like *suggests*. In the version of probabilistic reasoning that we have just outlined, $\longrightarrow$ involves values for λ and $\overline{\lambda}$, so a posterior probability for Q can be computed given a prior probability for Q.

As in systems using ordinary logical expressions, the many statements of the form $P \longrightarrow Q$ will link together. The consequent of one statement will be the antecedent of another. In a simple version of such a system, the network of statements will form a tree with a final conclusion, say Q_f, as the root at the top, and with primitive pieces of evidence at the tips. Intermediate nodes will be labeled by sentences that are the consequents of some of the rules and are the antecedents of others. Forward reasoning in such a tree starts by taking into account all the evidence at the tips, *propagating* this evidence (using λ and $\overline{\lambda}$ calculations) to establish new probabilities for the antecedents of rules higher in the tree, and continuing until a probability for Q_f has been calculated. We illustrate such a tree in Figure 8.1. This tree has six rules: P1 $\longrightarrow$ A, P2 $\longrightarrow$ A, P3 $\longrightarrow$ B, P4 $\longrightarrow$ B,

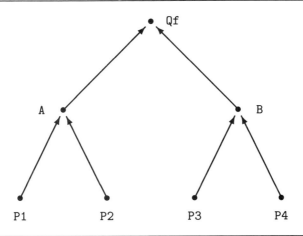

Figure 8.1   An inference net.

A $\longrightarrow$ Qf, and B $\longrightarrow$ Qf. Six λ, $\overline{\lambda}$ pairs also must be specified. If P1, P2, P3 and P4 are conditionally independent, if A depends only on P1 and P2, and if B depends on only P3 and P4, then A and B will be independent also, and the methods we described in Section 8.2 can be used to calculate the posterior probability of Qf.

Networks such as that of Figure 8.1 have been called *inference nets.* The reasoning involved in using probabilities for statements at the tips of the tree to calculate probabilities for statements higher in the tree is analogous to ordinary forward logical inference. A form of backward reasoning also is used with these networks. The system examines the tree to determine which of the tip nodes is likely to provide information that leads to the greatest change in the probability of Q_f. The system then asks the user for the probability of this tip node. The user's information is then propagated up the tree, and the process repeats until the user is satisfied that additional interaction will not materially affect the probability of Q_f. This *interactive* mode is appropriate when information about the tip nodes can be obtained only from a user and when it is important to save the user's time by not asking for information about all the tip nodes when that might not be necessary.

This general style of reasoning about uncertainty is used in many expert systems, although the systems differ in how they propagate *uncertainty* (probability) values through the network. Some use ad hoc procedures, with the major justification that, with tuning, the approach seems to work well on practical problems. When the network is not a tree, the evidence that bears on some of the propositions is not independent, and nonindependence (whatever its cause) creates anomalies in systems based on independence assumptions. Such anomalies usually are dealt with by additional ad hoc mechanisms and tuning.

One important question in expert systems of this type is how one deals with nonatomic rule antecedents. Given a rule of the form $P \longrightarrow Q$ (and the associated λs), we can calculate the posterior probability of Q when we have information about the probability of the sentence P. If P is nonatomic, we may not easily be able to obtain a probability for it; rather, we may have information about only its constituents. Suppose, for example, that $P \equiv P_1 \wedge P_2 \wedge \ldots \wedge P_k$, and that we can state a probability value for each of the P_i. What is the probability of P? In general, we cannot answer this question without more information. Recall that we began our discussion of uncertain reasoning by noting the general difficulty in calculating the probability of Q given probabilities for P and $P \Rightarrow Q$. Similar difficulties surround calculating the probability of any formula in terms of formulas from which the first can be inferred. We shall describe a general solution to this problem in the next section.

Short of a general solution to probabilistic inference, various ad hoc methods have been proposed for calculating the probability of a sentence from either its conjunctive or its disjunctive components. Specifically, expert systems often use the assumptions

$$p(P_1 \wedge P_2 \wedge \ldots \wedge P_k) = \min_i\{p(P_i)\}$$

and

$$p(P_1 \vee P_2 \vee \ldots \vee P_k) = \max_i\{p(P_i)\}$$

Note that, if the individual P_i were statistically independent, the joint probability would be given by the product of their individual probabilities—a value that in general would be less than that given by the formula we gave for the conjunction. These combination formulas arise naturally in *fuzzy set* theory [Zadeh 1975] and also reduce to the standard Boolean truth-table results for conjunction and disjunction when probabilities must be either zero or one.

Used with the rule $p(\neg P) = 1 - p(P)$, the rules given here for conjunction and disjunction allow us to compute the probability of any formula in terms of its atomic constituents. Inference networks can then be constructed from atomic sentences, and the user need only provide information about atomic sentences.

The reasoning methods that we have outlined for inference nets depend on strong assumptions about conditional independence and about the consistency of subjective probabilities. We intuitively feel that separate pieces of independent evidence warrant stronger belief in a conclusion than would be justified by any one piece alone. Yet, if the evidence is not really independent, assuming independence is like counting some of it twice. Taking full account of dependencies requires proper use of the underlying joint probabilities, and, as we shall see, doing so can involve us rapidly in calculations that grow exponentially with the number of propositions. About the most that can be done to preserve the theoretical justification for the simple methods we have just outlined is to attempt to pose the overall reasoning problem in terms of groups of sentences that are "as independent as possible."

Another problem arises from the fact that even experts in a field of knowledge cannot be expected to provide consistent subjective probabilities. For example, the required relationship between λ and $\overline{\lambda}$ is unlikely to be maintained in the estimates for these quantities given to us by experts. Another example of subjective inconsistency occurs in inference nets in which the consequent of one rule is the antecedent of another. Consider, for example, a rule of the form $P \longrightarrow Q$. The expert provides us with a prior probability for the antecedent, P. Assuming that this rule is embedded in an inference net in which Q is the antecedent of another rule, the expert may be asked to provide a prior probability for Q. These two prior probabilities are related by the requirement that, when the posterior probability of P is the same as the prior probability, the posterior probability of Q calculated using our interpolation formula must turn out to be identical with the expert-supplied prior probability for Q. Of course, it would be mere coincidence if the subjective values of the λs and the prior probabilities gave this result. Yet, if this relationship is not maintained over the entire inference net, the calculations performed in the net become meaningless.

We show in Figure 8.2 one way of enforcing the required relationship between the two prior probabilities. Instead of using the standard linear interpolation between $p(Q|\neg P)$ and $p(Q|P)$, we use a "kinked curve" that forces the posterior probability of Q to be equal to the prior probability when the probability of P is equal to its prior value. We then use linear interpolation between the prior probability value and the extreme values.

8.4 Probabilistic Logic

So far, we have relied mainly on intuitive ideas about what might be meant by the *probability* of a sentence. One can be more formal about these notions and develop a *probabilistic logic* that combines the ideas of probability theory and of ordinary first-order logic. Probabilistic logic provides a solid theoretical foundation for developing systems that are able to reason with uncertain information. To define what we mean by the probability of a sentence, we must start with a sample space over which to define probabilities.

A sentence ϕ can be either true or false. If we were concerned about just the one sentence ϕ, we could imagine two sets of *possible worlds*—one,

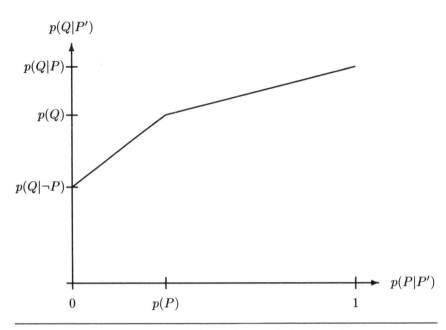

Figure 8.2   A consistent interpolation function.

say $\mathcal{W}_1$, containing worlds in which ϕ was *true* and one, say $\mathcal{W}_2$, containing worlds in which ϕ was false. The *actual* world, the world which we are actually in, must be in one of these two sets, but we might not know which one. We can model our uncertainty about the actual world by imagining that it is in $\mathcal{W}_1$ with probability p_1, and is in $\mathcal{W}_2$ with some probability $p_2 = 1 - p_1$. In this sense, we can say that the probability of ϕ (being true) is p_1.

If we have more sentences, we have more sets of possible worlds. Sentences may be true in some worlds and false in others—in different combinations. Each set of worlds contains all those worlds in which a particular combination of truth values of the sentences is consistent. If we have L sentences, we might have as many as 2^L sets of possible worlds. Typically, however, we will have fewer than this maximum number because some combinations of true and false values for our L sentences will be logically inconsistent. We cannot, for example, imagine a world in which ϕ_1 is false, ϕ_2 is true, and $\phi_1 \land \phi_2$ is true.

As an example, consider the following sentences:

$$\{\mathsf{P}, \mathsf{P} \Rightarrow \mathsf{Q}, \mathsf{Q}\}$$

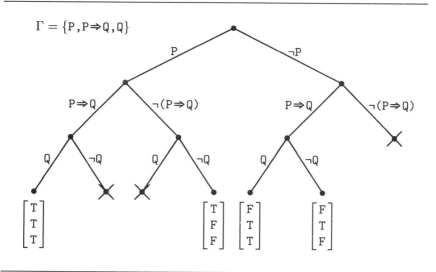

$\Gamma = \{P, P \Rightarrow Q, Q\}$

Figure 8.3   A semantic tree.

The consistent sets of truth values for these three sentences are given by the columns in the following table:

P	true	true	false	false
P⇒Q	true	false	true	true
Q	true	false	true	false

In this case, there are four sets of possible worlds, each corresponding to one of these four sets of truth values.

One method for determining the sets of consistent truth values, given a set Γ of sentences, is based on developing a binary *semantic tree*. At each node, we branch left or right, depending on whether or not we assign one of the sentences in Γ a value of true or of false, respectively. Just below the root, we branch on the truth value of one of the sentences in Γ, next on another sentence in Γ, and so on. Each path in the tree corresponds to a unique assignment of truth values to the sentences of Γ. We check the consistency of the truth-value assignments as we go, and we close off those paths corresponding to inconsistent valuations. A semantic tree for this example is shown in Figure 8.3. Closed-off paths are indicated by an ×; consistent sets of valuations are indicated in columns at the tips of their corresponding paths.

The sets of possible worlds corresponding to the different sets of consistent truth values for the sentences in Γ comprise a sample space over which we can define a probability distribution. This probability distribution specifies for each set, $\mathcal{W}_i$, of possible worlds, what is the probability, p_i, that the real world is in $\mathcal{W}_i$. (We sometimes say, loosely, that p_i is the probability of the set of worlds, $\mathcal{W}_i$.) The individual p_i sum to one because the sets of possible worlds are mutually exclusive and exhaustive. The probability of any sentence ϕ in Γ is then reasonably taken to be just the sum of the probabilities of all the sets of worlds in which ϕ is true. Since we typically do not know the ordinary (true–false) truth value of ϕ in the actual world, we define a probabilistic logic that has truth values intermediate between true and false and define the truth value of ϕ in this logic to be the probability of ϕ. In the context of discussing uncertain beliefs, we use the phrases the *probability of ϕ* and the *(probabilistic logic) truth value of ϕ* interchangeably.

Because the sets of possible worlds are identified with sets of truth values for sentences, the former also correspond to equivalence classes of interpretations for these sentences. Each interpretation in the equivalence class associated with a set of possible worlds leads to the same set of truth values for the sentences in Γ. We sometimes refer to the possible worlds as interpretations.

It is convenient to introduce some vector notation to rephrase mathematically what we have just said. Suppose there are K nonempty sets of possible worlds for our L sentences in Γ. These sets can be ordered in an arbitrary manner. Let the K-dimensional column vector $\mathbf{P}$ represent the probabilities of the sets of possible worlds. The i-th component, p_i, is the probability of the i-th set of possible worlds, $\mathcal{W}_i$.

The sets of possible worlds themselves are characterized by the different consistent truth valuations that can be given to the sentences of Γ. Let us arrange the sentences ϕ_j of Γ in arbitrary order and let the L-dimensional column vectors $\mathbf{V}_1, \mathbf{V}_2, \ldots, \mathbf{V}_K$ correspond to all the consistent truth valuations of the sentences in Γ. That is, in the i-th set of worlds, $\mathcal{W}_i$, the sentences in Γ have truth valuations characterized by $\mathbf{V}_i$. We take each $\mathbf{V}_i$ to have components equal to either zero or one. The j-th component of $\mathbf{V}_i$, $v_{ji} = 1$ if ϕ_j has value true in the worlds in $\mathcal{W}_i$; $v_{ji} = 0$ if ϕ_j has value false in the worlds in $\mathcal{W}_i$.

The K column vectors $\mathbf{V}_1, \ldots, \mathbf{V}_K$ can be grouped together, in the same order given to the sets of possible worlds, into an $L \times K$ matrix $\mathbf{V}$. Let us denote the probability of each sentence ϕ_i in Γ by π_i. We can arrange the π_i in an L-dimensional column vector $\mathbf{\Pi}$. The probabilities of the sentences can then be related to the probabilities of the possible worlds by the following simple matrix equation:

$$\mathbf{\Pi} = \mathbf{VP}$$

This equation concisely expresses what we said in words earlier; namely, that the probability of a sentence is the sum of the probabilities of the sets of possible worlds in which that sentence is true.

In using these ideas for reasoning with uncertain beliefs, we typically are not given the probabilities, p_i, for the different sets of possible worlds, but must instead induce them from what we are given. We consider two related types of reasoning problems. In the first, which we call *probabilistic entailment*, we have a base set of sentences (called *beliefs*) Δ with associated probabilities. From these, we deduce a new belief, ϕ, and its associated probability. Using the notation we have just introduced, in this problem our set Γ of sentences consists of $\Delta \cup \{\phi\}$. We are given probabilities for the sentences in Δ, we must solve the matrix equation for $\mathbf{P}$, and then use it again to compute the probability of ϕ. There are several difficulties in carrying out these steps, and we shall discuss them in detail momentarily.

In the second type of problem, which is more closely related to the kind of reasoning we discussed earlier in connection with expert systems, we are given a set of beliefs Δ and their associated probabilities. (We might presume that this information has been provided by an expert in the subject matter under consideration.) In this problem, we might learn new information about the actual world. For example, we might learn that in the actual world, some sentence ϕ_0 in Δ is true (or false). Or, more typically, we might learn information that gives us a new (posterior) probability for ϕ_0. Given this information, we want to compute a posterior probability for some sentence of interest, ϕ. The reasoning process in this case is somewhat different from that in probabilistic entailment.

8.5 Probabilistic Entailment

In ordinary logic, modus ponens allows us to infer Q from P and $P \Rightarrow Q$. Also, Q is *logically entailed* by the set $\{P, P \Rightarrow Q\}$. (Modus ponens is a sound rule of inference.) In this section, we investigate the analogue of logical entailment for probabilistic logic. We shall be concerned with the question of determining the probability of an arbitrary sentence ϕ given a set Δ of sentences and their probabilities. That is, we consider the *probabilistic entailment* of ϕ from Δ.

We begin our discussion by considering the three sentences P, P $\Rightarrow$ Q, and Q. Just as we cannot consistently assign arbitrary truth values to these three sentences, neither can we consistently assign arbitrary probability values to them. The consistent truth-value assignments are given by the columns in the matrix $\mathbf{V}$, where true is represented by one and false is represented by zero.

$$\mathbf{V} = \begin{bmatrix} 1 & 1 & 0 & 0 \\ 1 & 0 & 1 & 1 \\ 1 & 0 & 1 & 0 \end{bmatrix}$$

The first row of the matrix gives truth values for P in the four sets of possible worlds. The second row gives truth values for P $\Rightarrow$ Q, and the third row gives truth values for Q. Probability values for these sentences are constrained by the matrix equation

$$\Pi = \mathbf{VP}$$

and by the rules of probability, $\sum_i p_i = 1$ and $0 \le p_i \le 1$ for all i.

These constraints can be given a simple geometric interpretation. The matrix equation maps a space of probability values over possible worlds into a space of probability values over sentences. The mapping is linear, and therefore extreme values of $\mathbf{P}$ are mapped into extreme values of Π. The extreme values of $\mathbf{P}$ are those for which individual values of p_i are equal to one. But only one p_i in $\mathbf{P}$ can be equal to one; the rest must be zero. Thus, there are four extreme $\mathbf{P}$ vectors; namely, [1,0,0,0], [0,1,0,0], [0,0,1,0], and [0,0,0,1]. (These are all column vectors; we write them in row format in running text.) The extreme Π vectors corresponding to these extreme $\mathbf{P}$ vectors are simply the columns of the $\mathbf{V}$ matrix. This result is not surprising; when the sentences are given an interpretation corresponding to one of the sets of possible worlds, then the truth values of the sentences are the truth values assigned in that possible world. The principal benefit of this analysis comes from observing that, for arbitrary values of $\mathbf{P}$, Π must lie within the convex hull of the extreme values of Π.

A picture of this mapping is shown in Figure 8.4. The extreme values of Π are indicated by solid dots. Consistent values for the probabilities of the three sentences must lie in the convex hull of these points which is the solid region shown in the figure.

(One interesting point about these convex hulls is that the closest vertex of the unit cube to a point inside the convex hull is not necessarily a vertex of the convex hull. Consider, for example, the interior point $\pi_1 = 0.6$, $\pi_2 = 0.6$, $\pi_3 = 0.3$ of the convex hull in Figure 8.4. Its closest vertex of the cube is $(1,1,0)$, which is not a vertex of Π.)

Now suppose we are given the probability values for the sentences P and P $\Rightarrow$ Q. In terms of our notation, the probability of P, denoted by $p(\text{P})$, is π_1; the probability of P $\Rightarrow$ Q, denoted by $p(\text{P} \Rightarrow \text{Q})$, is π_2. We can see that π_3 or $p(\text{Q})$ must then lie between the two extreme points shown in Figure 8.4. Calculating these bounds analytically results in the following inequality:

$$p(\text{P} \Rightarrow \text{Q}) + p(\text{P}) - 1 \le p(\text{Q}) \le p(\text{P} \Rightarrow \text{Q})$$

(Setting $p(\text{Q})$ equal to its lower and upper bounds gives equations for the lower and upper bounding planes of Figure 8.4.)

This example reveals some interesting points about probabilistic logic. First, just as it is possible to assign inconsistent *true–false* truth values to sentences, it is also possible to assign to them inconsistent probabilities (i.e., *probabilistic* truth values). For the sentences {P, P$\Rightarrow$Q, Q}, any assignment

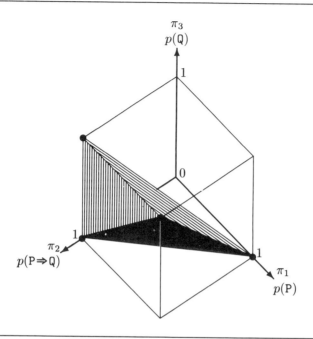

Figure 8.4   The convex region of consistent probability values for P, P ⇒ Q, and Q.

outside the convex region shown in Figure 8.4 is inconsistent. (Assignment of consistent subjective probabilities to sentences is a well-known problem in designing expert systems. A solution suggested by our geometric view would be to move an inconsistent Π vector to a "nearby" point in the consistent region, perhaps preferring larger adjustments to the probabilities of some sentences than to the probabilities of others.) Second, even if consistent probabilities are assigned to P and to P ⇒ Q, the probability of Q is not, in general, determined uniquely, but is bounded by the expressions we have given. Thus, we can expect that probabilistic entailment will, as a rule, merely bound (rather than precisely specify) the probability of the entailed sentence.

Solving probabilistic-entailment problems can be done by adding the entailed sentence, ϕ, to the base set of beliefs, Δ, computing the consistent sets of truth values for this expanded set (the columns of $\mathbf{V}$), computing the convex hull of these points, and then entering this convex hull along coordinates given by the probabilities of the sentences in Δ to find the probability bounds on ϕ. The three sentences of our example produced a simple, three-dimensional probabilistic-entailment problem. In general, when we have L sentences and K sets of possible worlds, we will have to find the bounding hyperplanes of a K-vertex solid in L dimensions.

Before continuing with our discussion about solution methods for probabilistic-entailment problems, let us consider one more example small enough to permit three-dimensional geometric insight. This time, we consider a simple problem in first-order logic.

Let Δ be the set $\{(\exists y\ P(y)), (\forall x\ P(x) \Rightarrow Q(x))\}$, and let ϕ be the sentence $(\exists z\ Q(z))$. We are given probabilities for the sentences in Δ and want to compute bounds on the probability of $(\exists z\ Q(z))$.

We first create Γ by adding ϕ to Δ, and then compute the consistent sets of truth values for the sentences in Γ by the semantic-tree method illustrated in Figure 8.5. In that figure, we have represented sentences and their negations in Skolem form; A, B, and C are Skolem constants. Paths corresponding to inconsistent sets of truth values are closed off by ×s. The consistent sets of truth values (in 0,1 notation) are indicated in columns at the tips of their corresponding paths. These column vectors are shown as points in Figure 8.6, and their convex hull is indicated. This region contains all consistent probabilities for the three sentences in Γ. In terms of consistent probability values for $(\exists y\ P(y))$ and $(\forall x\ P(x) \Rightarrow Q(x))$, the bounds on $p((\exists z\ Q(z)))$ are given by

$$p((\exists y\ P(y))) + p((\forall x\ P(x) \Rightarrow Q(x))) - 1 \leq p((\exists z\ Q(z))) \leq 1$$

As is apparent from Figure 8.6, these bounds loosen markedly as we move away from $p((\exists y\ P(y))) = 1$ and $p((\forall x\ P(x) \Rightarrow Q(x))) = 1$.

In principle, the probabilistic-entailment problem can be solved by linear-programming methods, but the size of problems encountered in probabilistic reasoning usually is much too large to permit a direct solution. Our focus will be to look for solution methods—sometimes approximate ones—that reduce the full problem to smaller problems of practical size. We first outline a canonical form for setting up probabilistic-entailment problems. We have already mentioned that we arbitrarily order the sentences in Γ to permit specifying the consistent truth values as column vectors, $\mathbf{V}_i$. We include the constraint that $\sum_i p_i = 1$ by adding a row vector of all ones as the top row of the matrix $\mathbf{V}$. This row can be made to appear in $\mathbf{V}$ merely by including the sentence T as the first element of Γ. (T has value true in all possible worlds.) By convention, we include the entailed sentence, ϕ, as the last sentence in Γ; thus, the last row of $\mathbf{V}$ represents the consistent truth values of ϕ in the various sets of possible worlds. The other rows of $\mathbf{V}$ (except the first and last) then represent the consistent truth values for the sentences in the base set of beliefs, Δ.

We assume that we are given consistent probability values for all but the last sentence in Γ. (The probability of the first sentence—namely, T—is

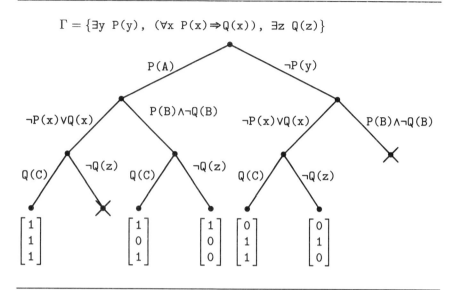

Figure 8.5   A semantic tree for a problem in first-order logic.

one.) We compute the $L \times K$ matrix $\mathbf{V}$ (perhaps using the semantic tree method). Next, we consider the matrix equation

$$\mathbf{\Pi} = \mathbf{VP}$$

The K-dimensional column vector, $\mathbf{P}$, is unknown—as is the last element of $\mathbf{\Pi}$. To solve for $\mathbf{P}$ formally, we first construct the $(L-1) \times K$ matrix $\mathbf{V}'$ from $\mathbf{V}$ by eliminating the last row, call it the vector ϕ, of $\mathbf{V}$. We construct the $(L-1)$-dimensional column vector $\mathbf{\Pi}'$ by eliminating the last element of $\mathbf{\Pi}$. Now we attempt to solve $\mathbf{\Pi}' = \mathbf{V}'\mathbf{P}$ for $\mathbf{P}$. Having done so, we can compute $\pi_L = p(\phi) = \phi\mathbf{P}$.

Usually, the equation $\mathbf{\Pi}' = \mathbf{V}'\mathbf{P}$ is underdetermined and permits many solutions for $\mathbf{P}$. In these cases, assuming $\mathbf{V}$ is small enough to permit computations on it, we will be interested in those solutions that give bounds for $p(\phi)$. We will postpone until later a discussion of approaches to solving problems with impractically large $\mathbf{V}$ matrices.

8.6 Computations Appropriate for Small Matrices

Using the notation of Section 8.5, we denote the last row of $\mathbf{V}$ by the row vector ϕ. This vector gives the truth values for the entailed sentence ϕ that are consistent with the truth values for the other sentences in Γ. Then the probability, $p(\phi)$, of ϕ is given by $\phi\mathbf{P}$, where $\mathbf{P}$ is a solution to $\mathbf{\Pi}' = \mathbf{V}'\mathbf{P}$.

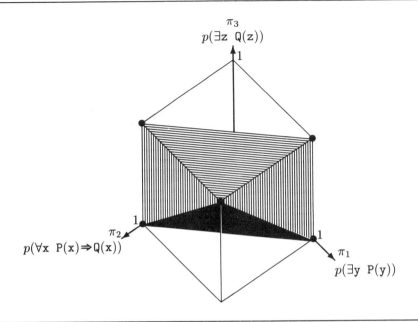

Figure 8.6   The region of consistent probability values.

Analogously, we might denote the other rows in $\mathbf{V}$ by the row vectors $\boldsymbol{\phi}_i$. Recall that $\boldsymbol{\phi}_1 = [1, 1, \ldots, 1]$, and $\boldsymbol{\phi}_L = \boldsymbol{\phi}$. (This notation is suggestive; the rows of $\mathbf{V}$ represent the sentences in Γ in terms of all possible truth values that are consistent with the truth values for the other sentences.)

In certain degenerate cases, we can compute a unique $\boldsymbol{\phi}\mathbf{P}$ given $\mathbf{V}'$ and $\boldsymbol{\Pi}'$. For example, if $\boldsymbol{\phi}$ happens to be identical to the i-th row of $\mathbf{V}'$, then $\boldsymbol{\phi}\mathbf{P} = \pi_i$. More generally, if $\boldsymbol{\phi}$ can be written as a linear combination of rows of $\mathbf{V}'$, then $\boldsymbol{\phi}\mathbf{P}$ can be written simply as the same linear combination of the π_i. For example, this method can be used to establish the following identities:

$$p(Q) = p(P) + p(P \Rightarrow Q) - p(Q \Rightarrow P)$$
$$p(Q) = p(P \Rightarrow Q) + p(\neg P \Rightarrow Q) - 1$$

(To illustrate, we observe that, in the first of these identities, after setting up the matrix $\mathbf{V}$, P is represented by the row vector $[1, 1, 0, 0]$, $P \Rightarrow Q$ by $[1, 0, 1, 1]$, $Q \Rightarrow P$ by $[1, 1, 0, 1]$, and Q by $[1, 0, 1, 0]$. The last vector is the sum of the first two minus the third.)

We also might imagine that, if $\boldsymbol{\phi}$ can be approximated (in some sense) by a linear combination of the rows of $\mathbf{V}'$, then $\boldsymbol{\phi}\mathbf{P}$ can be approximated by the same linear combination of the π_i. Such approximations may well be useful and worth looking for. An approximation that we might consider is ϕ^*, the projection of ϕ onto the subspace defined by the row vectors of $\mathbf{V}'$. The projection of ϕ onto the subspace defined by the row vectors of $\mathbf{V}'$ is a vector $\phi^* = \sum_{i=1}^{L-1} c_i \phi_i$ such that $\phi = \phi^* + \phi_N$, where the c_i are such that ϕ_N is orthogonal to each of the row vectors in $\mathbf{V}'$.

Suppose we use this method to approximate the probability of Q given the sentences P, with probability $\pi_2 = p(\text{P})$, and P $\Rightarrow$ Q, with probability $\pi_3 = p(\text{P} \Rightarrow \text{Q})$. (Recall that we include the sentence T, with probability $\pi_1 = 1$, in Γ.) $\mathbf{V}'$ and $\mathbf{\Pi}'$ are then given by:

$$\mathbf{V}' = \begin{bmatrix} 1 & 1 & 1 & 1 \\ 1 & 1 & 0 & 0 \\ 1 & 0 & 1 & 1 \end{bmatrix} \quad \mathbf{\Pi}' = \begin{bmatrix} 1 \\ \pi_2 \\ \pi_3 \end{bmatrix}$$

The row vector representation for Q (that is, the last row of $\mathbf{V}$) is $\mathbf{Q} = [1, 0, 1, 0]$, and its projection onto the subspace defined by the row vectors of $\mathbf{V}'$ is $\mathbf{Q}^* = [1, 0, 1/2, 1/2]$. The coefficients, c_i, are given by $c_1 = -1/2$, $c_2 = 1/2$, and $c_3 = 1$. Using these, the approximate value for $p(\text{Q})$ is:

$$-1/2 \times \pi_1 + 1/2 \times \pi_2 + 1 \times \pi_3 = -1/2 + \frac{p(\text{P})}{2} + p(\text{P} \Rightarrow \text{Q})$$

It is interesting to note that this value happens to be midway between the two bounds on $p(\text{Q})$ established in our earlier example.

Another technique that can be used when we are given underdetermined (but consistent) $\mathbf{V}'$ and $\mathbf{\Pi}'$ is to select from among the possible solutions for $\mathbf{P}$ that solution with maximum entropy. This distribution assumes the minimum additional information about $\mathbf{P}$ given the sentences in Δ and their probabilities.

The *entropy* of a probability distribution, $\mathbf{P}$, is defined to be

$$H = -\sum_i p_i \log p_i = -\mathbf{P}^t \log \mathbf{P}$$

where $\mathbf{P}^t$ is the *transpose* (i.e., the row-vector form) of the column vector $\mathbf{P}$, and $\log \mathbf{P}$ is a (column) vector the components of which are the logarithms of the corresponding components of $\mathbf{P}$.

To maximize H, by varying $\mathbf{P}$, subject to the constraint that $\mathbf{\Pi}' = \mathbf{V}'\mathbf{P}$, we use the method of Lagrange multipliers from the calculus of variations. First, we write H as follows:

$$H = -\mathbf{P}^t \log \mathbf{P} + l_1(\pi_1 - \phi_1\mathbf{P}) + l_2(\pi_2 - \phi_2\mathbf{P}) + \cdots + l_{(L-1)}(\pi_{(L-1)} - \phi_{(L-1)}\mathbf{P})$$

where $l_1, \ldots, l_{(L-1)}$ are Lagrange muliptiers; $\pi_1, \ldots, \pi_{(L-1)}$ are the components of $\mathbf{\Pi}'$; and $\phi_1, \ldots, \phi_{(L-1)}$ are the row vectors of $\mathbf{V}'$.

Differentiating this expression with respect to p_i and setting the result to zero yields

$$- \log p_i - 1 - l_1 v_{1i} - \cdots - l_{(L-1)} v_{(L-1)i} = 0$$

where v_{ji} is the i-th component of the j-th row vector in $\mathbf{V'}$.

Thus, the distribution that maximizes the entropy has components

$$p_i = e^{-1}e^{-(l_1 v_{1i})}\ldots e^{-(l_{(L-1)} v_{(L-1)i})}$$

The following definitions simplify this expression:

$$a_1 = e^{-1}e^{-(l_1)}$$
$$a_j = e^{-(l_j)}, \quad j = 2,\ldots,(L-1)$$

We then see that each p_i can be written as a product of some of the a_j, where a_j is included in p_i if v_{ji} is one, and is not included otherwise. We note that a_1 is included in each of the p_i because $v_{1i} = 1$ for all i.

Now we can solve directly for the a_j by substituting these expressions for p_i as components of $\mathbf{P}$, and solving the equation $\mathbf{\Pi'} = \mathbf{V'P}$ for the a_j.

Let us calculate the maximum-entropy distribution given the sentences P with probability π_2 and P $\Rightarrow$ Q with probability π_3. As before, $\mathbf{V'}$ and $\mathbf{\Pi'}$ are given by

$$\mathbf{V'} = \begin{bmatrix} 1 & 1 & 1 & 1 \\ 1 & 1 & 0 & 0 \\ 1 & 0 & 1 & 1 \end{bmatrix} \qquad \mathbf{\Pi'} = \begin{bmatrix} 1 \\ \pi_2 \\ \pi_3 \end{bmatrix}$$

We can read down the columns of $\mathbf{V'}$ to express each (entropy-maximizing) p_i in terms of products of the a_j:

$$p_1 = a_1 a_2 a_3$$
$$p_2 = a_1 a_2$$
$$p_3 = a_1 a_3$$
$$p_4 = a_1 a_3$$

Using these values in $\mathbf{\Pi'} = \mathbf{V'P}$ yields these equations:

$$a_1 a_2 a_3 + a_1 a_2 + 2a_1 a_3 = 1$$
$$a_1 a_2 a_3 + a_1 a_2 = \pi_2$$
$$a_1 a_2 a_3 + 2a_1 a_3 = \pi_3$$

Solving yields

$$a_1 = (1 - \pi_2)(1 - \pi_3)/2(\pi_2 + \pi_3 - 1)$$
$$a_2 = 2(\pi_2 + \pi_3 - 1)/(1 - \pi_2)$$
$$a_3 = (\pi_2 + \pi_3 - 1)/(1 - \pi_3)$$

Thus, the entropy-maximizing $\mathbf{P}$ is given by

$$\mathbf{P} = \begin{bmatrix} \pi_2 + \pi_3 - 1 \\ 1 - \pi_3 \\ (1 - \pi_2)/2 \\ (1 - \pi_2)/2 \end{bmatrix}$$

Using this probability distribution, we see that the probability of Q is $[1, 0, 1, 0]\mathbf{P} = \pi_2/2 + \pi_3 - 1/2 = p(\mathsf{P})/2 + p(\mathsf{P} \Rightarrow \mathsf{Q}) - 1/2$. (This happens to be the same value calculated by the "projection-approximation" method!)

8.7 Dealing with Large Matrices

The techniques described in Section 8.6 all involved computing a possible-worlds probability vector, $\mathbf{P}$, from $\mathbf{V}'$ and $\mathbf{\Pi}'$. When $\mathbf{V}'$ is as large as it might be with even, say, a dozen sentences, these methods become impractical. Perhaps there are much simpler techniques for computing the approximate probability of a sentence ϕ probabilistically entailed by Δ.

Some approximation methods are based on subdividing Δ into smaller sets. Suppose, for example, that Δ could be partitioned into two parts—namely, Δ_1 and Δ_2—with no atom that occurs in Δ_1 occurring in Δ_2 or in ϕ. Clearly, Δ_1 could be eliminated from Δ without any effect on probabilistic-entailment calculations for ϕ. In this case, we say that the subset, Δ_2, is a *sufficient subset* for ϕ.

Or, suppose two sentences, ϕ_1 and ϕ_2, could be found such that a subset of Δ, say Δ_1, was sufficient for ϕ_1, and another subset, say Δ_2, was sufficient for ϕ_2. Then we could split the probabilistic entailment of ϕ from Δ into two smaller problems, as follows. First compute the probabilistic entailments of ϕ_1 from Δ_1 and of ϕ_2 from Δ_2. Next, compute the probabilistic entailment of ϕ from $\{\phi_1, \phi_2\}$. The idea here is to find sentences, ϕ_1 and ϕ_2, such that, together, they "give as much information" about ϕ as does Δ. In this case, Δ_1 and Δ_2 are similar to what have been called *local event groups*. This method, of course, is only approximate; its accuracy depends on how well the probabilities of ϕ_1 and ϕ_2 determine the probability of ϕ.

We next describe a process for finding an approximate (and smaller) matrix $\mathbf{V}'$ given Δ, $\mathbf{\Pi}'$, and ϕ. This approximate matrix, which we denote by $\mathbf{V}'^*$, can be made sufficiently small to permit practical computation of approximate probabilistic entailment. The approximation is exact in the nonprobabilistic case when $\mathbf{\Pi}'$ consists of only ones and zeros. It can be made as precise as desired by making $\mathbf{V}'^*$ larger.

We follow the usual process for computing the matrix $\mathbf{V}'$—except that in computing $\mathbf{V}'^*$ we do not include *all* the consistent sets of truth values. Instead, we construct a smaller set that includes only vectors "close to" the given $\mathbf{\Pi}'$.

We first compute an approximate matrix, $\mathbf{V}^*$, as follows:

(1) Construct a *true–false* vector, $\mathbf{\Pi}'_b$, from $\mathbf{\Pi}'$ by changing to one the values of those components π_i that have values greater than or equal to one-half. Change the values of the other components to zero.

(2) If ϕ can have the value true consistent with the truth values for the sentences in Δ given by $\mathbf{\Pi}'_b$, then include in $\mathbf{V}^*$ the vector formed

from $\mathbf{\Pi}'_b$ by appending to it a final component equal to one. If ϕ can have the value false consistent with the valuations for the sentences in Δ given by $\mathbf{\Pi}'_b$, then include in $\mathbf{V}^*$ the vector formed from $\mathbf{\Pi}'_b$ by appending to it a final component equal to zero. If $\mathbf{\Pi}'_b$ itself corresponds to an inconsistent valuation of the sentences in Δ (which is possible), go to step (3).

(3) Reverse the values of the components of $\mathbf{\Pi}'_b$, one at a time, two at a time, and so on, starting with those components the corresponding components of which in $\mathbf{\Pi}'$ have values closest to one-half. For each of the altered true–false vectors thus obtained that represent consistent true–false truth values over Δ, add new vector(s) to $\mathbf{V}^*$ according to the procedure described in step (2).

We use as many of these consistent, altered vectors as computational resources permit. The more vectors used, the better the approximation. (The ordering of the column vectors in $\mathbf{V}^*$ is arbitrary.)

We next construct the matrix, $\mathbf{V}'^*$, by deleting the last row of $\mathbf{V}^*$. (We take this last row to be an approximate vector representation, ϕ^*, for the sentence ϕ.)

It should be clear that, as we include more and more vectors in $\mathbf{V}^*$, $\mathbf{V}^*$ approaches $\mathbf{V}$, and $\mathbf{V}'^*$ approaches $\mathbf{V}'$. Also, if $\mathbf{\Pi}'$ is the vector with components all equal to one, then $\mathbf{\Pi}' = \mathbf{\Pi}'_b$. In that case, if ϕ logically follows from Δ, $\mathbf{V}'^*$ need have only a single column (of ones), $\mathbf{P} = [1]$, $\phi^* = [1]$, and $p(\phi) = 1$. If $\neg\phi$ logically follows from Δ, $\mathbf{V}'^*$ still need have only a single column (of ones), $\mathbf{P} = [1]$, $\phi^* = [0]$, and $p(\phi) = 0$. If both ϕ and $\neg\phi$ are consistent with Δ, then $\mathbf{V}'^*$ would have two identical columns (of ones), $\mathbf{P}$ could have permissible solutions

$$\begin{bmatrix} 1 \\ 0 \end{bmatrix} \text{ and } \begin{bmatrix} 0 \\ 1 \end{bmatrix}$$

and $\phi^* = [1, 0]$, and $p(\phi)$ could range consistently between zero and one.

Thus, our approximation behaves well at the limits of large $\mathbf{V}'^*$ and at the nonprobabilistic extreme. Continuity arguments suggest that performance ought to degrade only gradually as we depart from these limits, although to our knowledge the method has not yet been tested on large examples. Recalling that the region of consistent probability vectors, $\mathbf{\Pi}$, occupies the convex hull of the region defined by the extreme (0,1) probability vectors, we note that our approximation method constructs an approximate region—namely, the convex hull of just those extreme vectors that are close to the given probability vector, $\mathbf{\Pi}'$. We suspect that the more uncertain are the sentences in Δ, the more vectors will have to be included in $\mathbf{V}^*$ to get accurate entailment.

8.8 Probabilities Conditioned on Specific Information

In typical applications of these ideas, experts in the subject matter of the application would provide us with a base set Δ of beliefs and their probabilities, Π. We would then like to use these uncertain beliefs to calculate the probability of some sentence, ϕ, given information about some sentence, ϕ_0. The information about ϕ_0 might be that ϕ_0 is true, or that it is false, or that it has some probability, $p(\phi_0)$. In general, neither ϕ nor ϕ_0 need be in Δ—although either or both could be.

Suppose we are given that ϕ_0 is true. Then we want to calculate the *conditional probability* $p(\phi|\phi_0)$. In deriving Bayes' Rule, we defined conditional probability as follows:

$$p(\phi|\phi_0) = \frac{p(\phi, \phi_0)}{p(\phi_0)} = \frac{p(\phi \wedge \phi_0)}{p(\phi_0)}$$

The probabilities $p(\phi \wedge \phi_0)$ and $p(\phi_0)$ can be calculated using any of the methods described in this chapter. If the method gives unique values for these probabilities, then the conditional probability also will have a unique value. If the method gives bounds on the probabilities, then the conditional probability also will be bounded.

We can derive a similar expression if we are given that ϕ_0 is false:

$$p(\phi|\neg\phi_0) = \frac{p(\phi, \neg\phi_0)}{p(\neg\phi_0)} = \frac{p(\phi \wedge \neg\phi_0)}{p(\neg\phi_0)}$$

As we observed earlier in discussing these conditional probabilities, we often do not know whether ϕ_0 is true or false, but might instead have only a *posterior* probability for ϕ_0, say $p(\phi_0|\phi_0')$. As before, we associate the sentence ϕ_0' with the event of having received some information about ϕ_0 that permits us to assign the probability $p(\phi_0|\phi_0')$ to ϕ_0. (We must not confuse $p(\phi_0|\phi_0')$ with $p(\phi_0)$. The former is a new or posterior probability, calculated after having learned specific information about a particular case; the latter is the prior probability based on general expert knowledge.)

Now we can compute an expression for $p(\phi|\phi_0')$ as a weighted average of $p(\phi|\phi_0)$ and $p(\phi|\neg\phi_0)$. Assuming that $p(\phi|\phi_0, \phi_0') = p(\phi|\phi_0)$ and that $p(\phi|\neg\phi_0, \phi_0') = p(\phi|\neg\phi_0)$, the expression for the posterior probability for ϕ (given ϕ_0') becomes

$$p(\phi|\phi_0') = p(\phi|\phi_0)p(\phi_0|\phi_0') + p(\phi|\neg\phi_0)p(\neg\phi_0|\phi_0')$$

Substituting the expressions we had derived earlier for $p(\phi|\phi_0)$ and $p(\phi|\neg\phi_0)$, we obtain

$$p(\phi|\phi_0') = \frac{p(\phi \wedge \phi_0)}{p(\phi_0)}p(\phi_0|\phi_0') + \frac{p(\phi \wedge \neg\phi_0)}{p(\neg\phi_0)}p(\neg\phi_0|\phi_0')$$

If we want to compute the probability of ϕ given additional, specific information about more than one sentence, we can use an incremental updating method similar to that described near the end of Section 8.2.

Our methods usually justify only the calculation of bounds on probabilities. Indeed, we may know only bounds on the probabilities of the sentences in Δ. If the probability of a sentence ϕ is known only to lie between a lower bound, π_l, and an upper bound, π_u, then the difference $\pi_u - \pi_l$ expresses our *ignorance* about ϕ. Using *upper* and *lower* probabilities gives us a method to distinguish between situations in which our beliefs can be described by a single probability value and those in which we have even less information. To have good reason to believe, for example, that a particular treatment method for a certain disease is effective in one-half of the cases is to have arguably more information than to have no justifiable beliefs at all about its effects. In the latter case, the appropriate lower and upper probabilities would be zero and one, respectively.

All the methods described in this chapter can be modified to deal with sentences with upper and lower probabilities. In calculating bounds on the probability of some sentence ϕ, one uses first those extreme values of probabilities that give one of the bounds and then the extremes that give the other.

8.9 Bibliographical and Historical Remarks

There is extensive mathematical literature on probabilistic and plausible inference. The interested reader may wish to see (for example) [Lukasiewicz 1970, Carnap 1950, Hempel 1965, Suppes 1966, Adams 1975] as background. Also see [Hoel 1971, DeFinetti 1974] for textbooks on probability theory.

One of the early systems designed to handle uncertain knowledge was MYCIN [Shortliffe 1976]. Our discussion of the use of Bayes' rule in reasoning about uncertain information is based on the techniques described in [Duda 1976] and used in the PROSPECTOR system [Duda 1984]. Several authors have written about coherent propagation of probabilities in Bayesian inference networks. A thorough account with many references can be found in [Pearl 1986a].

Many of the techniques for handling uncertain information have been used in expert systems. We have already mentioned MYCIN, a system for aiding physicians in medical diagnosis and treatment tasks (see also [Buchanan 1984, Clancey 1984]), and PROSPECTOR, a system for aiding economic geologists in mineral exploration (see also [Campbell 1982]). Such systems have been developed in several other specialized subject areas including business [Reitman 1984, Reboh 1986, Winston 1984], equipment diagnosis [Genesereth 1984], and agriculture [Roach 1985, Lemmon 1986].

Our treatment of probabilistic logic is taken from a paper by Nilsson [Nilsson 1986]. (Dr. Gernot Kleiter of Salzburg subsequently pointed out to us that several of the ideas in that paper—such as probability spaces, linear dependence, and convex hulls—had been studied previously by DeFinetti [DeFinetti 1974, pp. 89–116, Vol. I].) Constraining the joint probability distribution of several propositional variables so that it has maximum entropy is a familiar technique that has been investigated by several authors [Lemmer 1982a, Lemmer 1982b, Konolige 1982, Cheeseman 1983]. Our computational technique for maximizing entropy is taken from [Cheeseman 1983]. (See, for example, [Margenau 1956] for a brief discussion of the use of Lagrange multipliers.)

Other (nonprobabilistic) approaches also have been suggested for dealing with uncertain beliefs. Although we have not described these here, see [Halpern 1983] for a treatment based on modal operators; [Zadeh 1975, Zadeh 1983] for fuzzy logic; [Dempster 1968, Shafer 1979, Lowrance 1982, Lowrance 1983, Garvey 1981], for what some have called *evidential reasoning*; and [Shortliffe 1976] for methods based on *certainty factors*. (Lee [Lee 1972] has shown how to adapt resolution to deal with fuzzy logic.)

Heckerman [Heckerman 1986] discussed how the certainty factors used in MYCIN can be given a probabilistic interpretation. Horvitz and Heckerman [Horvitz 1986] presented a framework for comparing several of the nonprobabilistic techniques with probabilistic ones. Grosof [Grosof 1986a, Grosof 1986b] generalized probabilistic logic to encompass Dempster–Shafer theory, Bayesian updating in inference networks, and certainty factor methods. Pearl [Pearl 1986b] also compared Bayesian networks with Dempster–Shafer methods.

Several additional papers appear in the proceedings of workshops on reasoning with uncertain information [Uncertain 1985, Uncertain 1986].

Exercises

1. *Inequality.*   Prove that $p(P) \geq p(Q)$ if $p(P|Q) = 1$.

2. *Poker.*   Nine times out of 10, Sam closes one eye just before dropping out of a poker hand. Sam drops out of one-half of the hands and is in the habit of closing one eye during 60 percent of the hands. What is the probability that he will drop out given that he closes one eye?

3. *Biology 15.*   Recent statistics for the Bio 15 course are as follows:

   • Twenty-five percent of the people in Bio 15 get an A.

   • Eighty percent of the people who get an A do all the homework.

   • Sixty percent of the people who do *not* get an A do all the homework.

   • Seventy-five percent of the people who get an A are biology majors.

- Fifty percent of the people who do *not* get an A are biology majors.

Given only that John does all his Bio 15 homework, what are his odds of getting an A? Given only that Mary is a biology major, what are her odds of getting an A? What are her odds if we also are given that she does all her Bio 15 homework? (Assume that being a biology major is conditionally independent of doing homework for people getting As and for people not getting As.)

4. *Manipulating probabilities.* Given $p(\mathrm{P}|\mathrm{Q}) = 0.2$, $p(\mathrm{P}|\neg\mathrm{Q}) = 0.4$, and $p(\mathrm{P})$, what is $p(\mathrm{P} \Rightarrow \mathrm{Q})$?

5. *Another inequality.* Use the matrix equation $\mathbf{\Pi} = \mathbf{VP}$ to prove the following inequality: $p(\neg(P \Leftrightarrow Q)) \leq p(P) + p(Q)$.

6. *Entailment.* Let the probability of $(\exists\mathrm{x})\,[\mathrm{P(x)} \wedge \mathrm{Q(x)}]$ be 0.25, and let the probability of $\mathrm{P(A)}$ be 0.75. What are the bounds on the probability of $\mathrm{Q(A)}$?

7. *Independence.* Given the sentences P, with probability π_2, and Q, with probability π_3, find the maximum-entropy probability of $\mathrm{P} \wedge \mathrm{Q}$. Also calculate the probability of $\mathrm{P} \wedge \mathrm{Q}$ that would be given by the projection-approximation method. Do these two methods give the same answer in this case?

8. *Not necessarily the same.* Under what conditions is $p(P \Rightarrow Q) = p(Q|P)$?

CHAPTER 9
Knowledge and Belief

AN AGENT'S REPRESENTATION of the world begins with a conceptualization that involves objects in the world and relations among these objects. As long as these objects and relations are relatively "concrete," we have not had undue difficulty either in conceptualizing them or in expressing these conceptualizations in the language of first-order logic. Thus, we can express propositions about many objects that exist in the world—objects such as blocks, minerals, bacteria, and so on. We can even be somewhat loose about the sorts of things we think of as "objects." Objects are not necessarily limited to "physical" objects—they can be numbers, diseases, corporations, or other abstractions.

As we become even more tolerant about objects and relations, we find some that present serious difficulties. Units and intervals of time; actions, events and processes; provability and truth; knowledge, beliefs, goals, and intentions; sentences and propositions—all these require "special handling." In the rest of the book, we will be concerned with problems of representing propositions concerning some of these subjects. In this chapter, we deal with the topic of representing and reasoning about propositions about the knowledge and beliefs of agents.

People find it useful to attribute *beliefs* to others; beliefs help us to make predictions about what other people will do. It is important to note that it is not too relevant whether or not beliefs have any kind of real existence somewhere in our minds (whatever that might mean). We observe merely that our reasoning processes seem to make use of these abstractions.

We imagine that the concept of beliefs will be useful in designing intelligent agents. In fact, in this book, we have already committed ourselves to the idea that what an intelligent agent knows about its world is represented in its database by a set of first-order sentences that we have sometimes called *beliefs*. Since our agents have beliefs, and since other agents are a part of the world about which we want our agents to know, we also must enable agents to have beliefs about the beliefs of other agents and of themselves. For example, a robot cooperating with other robots will have to know something about what those other robots believe. An expert system, interacting smoothly with a human user, will need to know something about what the user already knows about the subject matter under consideration.

The concepts of *knowledge* and *belief* are related but different. We would not want to say, for example, that an agent could *know* something that is false; it might, however, *believe* something that is false. We typically will be dealing with the *beliefs* (rather than with the *knowledge*) of an agent because we want to allow for the possibility that these beliefs are false. Sometimes, in English usage, the word *knows* really means something more like "has appropriate beliefs" (as in, "An agent knows about its world"). We will sometimes use "knows" in this sense. We will alternate between discussions of knowledge and discussions of belief in this chapter, in order to emphasize their similarities while highlighting their differences. When we intend to distinguish the two concepts, that intention will be made clear.

9.1 Preliminaries

To represent our ideas about the beliefs of agents, we must first describe what we think these beliefs are. This conceptualization will then form the foundation for the semantics of logical sentences about knowledge and belief. We will describe two alternative conceptualizations. In the *sentential* conceptualization, we associate with each agent a set of formulas called the agent's *base beliefs*. We say that an agent believes a proposition just in case the agent can prove the proposition from these base beliefs. In the *possible-worlds* conceptualization, we associate with each agent sets of possible worlds. We say that an agent believes a proposition in a given world just in case that proposition holds in all worlds accessible for the agent from the given world. We will present a full semantic account for each of these conceptualizations. Although both are important, the first is more literally consistent with the approach taken in this book.

After settling on a conceptualization, we define a language and then base the semantics of that language on the conceptualization. We find it convenient to extend our ordinary language of first-order predicate calculus to express statements about beliefs. The extension that we need involves what is called a *modal operator*. It will be used with both conceptualizations.

We are familiar with the use of the connectives ∧ and ∨ in first-order logic. When a connective such as ∨ links two formulas, we could say that it constructs a new formula the truth value of which depends on the truth values of the constituents and on the special properties of ∨.

We want to represent statements about the beliefs of agents by logical formulas; however, these formulas would seem to have to involve other formulas (that represent for us or for the agent the proposition that is believed). We introduce the modal operator **B** into our first-order language to represent statements about beliefs. **B** takes two arguments: The first is a term denoting the individual who has the belief, and the second is a formula representing the statement that is believed. For example, to say that John believes that the father of Zeus is Cronus, we would write

$$\textbf{B}(\texttt{John},\texttt{Father-Of}(\texttt{Zeus},\texttt{Cronus}))$$

Note that `Father-Of(Zeus,Cronus)` is a formula. The sentence formed by combining **B** with the term `John` and the formula `Father-Of(Zeus,Cronus)` yields a new formula the intended meaning of which is, "John believes that the father of Zeus is Cronus."

We also will introduce a modal operator **K** used to represent statements about knowledge. To say that John knows that the father of Zeus is Cronus, we would write

$$\textbf{K}(\texttt{John},\texttt{Father-Of}(\texttt{Zeus},\texttt{Cronus}))$$

(Occasionally, throughout the text, we will use the abbreviations $\textbf{K}_\alpha(\phi)$ for $\textbf{K}(\alpha,\phi)$ and $\textbf{B}_\alpha(\phi)$ for $\textbf{B}(\alpha,\phi)$, where α denotes an agent and ϕ is a formula.)

Since one cannot know something that is not true, we might attempt to define **K** in terms of **B** by the schema $\textbf{K}_\alpha(\phi) \equiv \textbf{B}_\alpha(\phi) \wedge \phi$. Philosophers have argued about how knowledge might be defined in terms of belief. These arguments need not concern us here, and we will use both concepts— sometimes treating them both as primitive.

We must now give a more formal definition of the syntax of this new language and of its semantics. Our first treatment will be based on a sentential conceptualization.

9.2 Sentential Logics of Belief

We begin by defining a limited syntax for a language in which to express a class of sentences about beliefs. We will expand this syntax gradually, after treating some of the fundamental ideas. We begin with the first-order predicate-calculus language that we have been using so far in this book. Let us call any wff in that language an *ordinary* wff (to distinguish it from the wffs we are about to introduce). Our new language will admit only the following wffs:

(1) All ordinary wffs are wffs.

(2) If ϕ is an ordinary, closed wff (one with no free variables), and if α is a ground term, then $\mathbf{B}(\alpha,\phi)$ is a wff. Such wffs are called *belief atoms*.

(3) If ϕ and ψ are wffs, then so are any expressions that can be constructed from ϕ and ψ by the usual propositional connectives.

Note that the following are not wffs:

(a) $\exists$x $\mathbf{B}$(R,P(x)) (because P(x) is not a closed wff).

(b) $\mathbf{B}$(R1,$\mathbf{B}$(R2,P(A))) (because $\mathbf{B}$(R2,P(A)) is not an ordinary wff).

(c) $\mathbf{B}$(($\exists$x G(x)),P(A)) (because ($\exists$x G(x)) is not a ground term).

The following, however, are wffs:

(d) $\mathbf{B}$(R,($\exists$x P(x))).

(e) P(A)$\Rightarrow$$\mathbf{B}$(R,P(A)).

Later, we will extend the syntax to include examples (a) and (b) as wffs, but first we discuss the semantics of this more restricted language.

The semantics for this language is based on a conceptualization that involves the sentences believed by agents. We begin with the usual semantics for a first-order language; namely, we define a mapping between elements of the ordinary language and associated objects, relations, and functions in a domain. With that, we can define the truth values of ordinary wffs. It remains to define the truth values of belief atoms; namely, expressions of the form $\mathbf{B}(\alpha,\phi)$. From those, using the usual semantics for the propositional connectives, we can define the truth values of all other wffs.

It is worth digressing to note that the semantics of belief atoms must have quite different properties than those of classical logic. In ordinary first-order (and higher-order) logics, the truth value of any expression depends on only the *denotations* of its subexpressions. (The denotation of a term is the object to which it refers, the denotation of a relation constant is the relation to which it refers, and the denotation of a formula is its truth value.) Thus, if we followed the rules of classical logic, the truth value of $\mathbf{B}(\alpha,\phi)$ would depend on the truth value of ϕ such that any other expression ψ, with the same truth value as that of ϕ, could be substituted for ϕ without changing the truth value of $\mathbf{B}(\alpha,\phi)$. Clearly, this property of classical logic is not appropriate when dealing with modal operators such as $\mathbf{K}$ and $\mathbf{B}$. Whether or not an agent knows or believes a proposition certainly depends on the proposition as well as on the truth value of the expression the intended meaning of which is that proposition.

Neither do we want the truth value of a belief or knowledge statement necessarily preserved when substituting a *term* for one with the same denotation. For example, Zeus and Jupiter denote the same individual (the supreme classical deity), and Cronus and Saturn denote the same individual (his father). If we substituted either Jupiter for Zeus or Saturn for Cronus, however, we would expect the truth value of B(A,Father-Of(Zeus,Cronus)) to change if A knew Greek but not Roman mythology.

Thus, we cannot generally substitute equivalent expressions into formulas *inside* of **B** (or **K**) operators. We say that these operators set up *opaque* contexts, and that knowledge and belief are *referentially opaque*. (The ordinary logical operators, such as ∧ and ∨, are said to be *referentially transparent*. One can substitute equivalent expressions within these contexts.) The referential opacity of **B** and **K** must be respected in logics containing these operators.

To define the semantics of **B**, we extend our notion of a domain as follows. We identify a denumerable set of *agents* in the domain. With each agent, a, we associate a base set of beliefs Δ_a, composed of ordinary closed wffs, and a set of inference rules ρ_a. We denote by T_a the theory formed by the closure of Δ_a under the inference rules in ρ_a. We express provability in agent a's theory, using a's inference rules, by the symbol $\vdash_a$. Thus, $P \in T_a$ if and only if $\Delta_a \vdash_a P$. (If our language uses the symbol A to denote agent a, then we will sometimes abuse notation by using the symbols $\vdash_A$, Δ_A, T_A, and ρ_A in place of $\vdash_a$, Δ_a, T_a, and ρ_a, respectively.)

This semantic groundwork is based on the supposition that each reasoning agent in the world has a theory (about the world, say) composed of ordinary, closed wffs and closed under that reasoning agent's deductive apparatus. Note that we do not assume that an agent's theory is closed under logical implication; it is closed only under the inference rules of that agent. An agent may have an incomplete set of inference rules, and therefore its theory might not be logically closed. This distinction is important if we want to reason about agents that themselves may have limited reasoning power. Limitations in an agent's reasoning abilities often can be captured by limiting the power of the inference rules. For example, if an agent can generate proofs consisting of no more than a bounded number of steps, we arrange that its inference rules refer to and generate a counter index that keeps track of how many times rules have been applied. When we want to assume that an agent is *logically omniscient*, we merely have to give that agent a complete set of inference rules.

Now, to define the truth value of any belief atom, we constrain our semantics so that the object associated with the first term of a belief atom is an agent. $\mathbf{B}(\alpha,\phi)$ has the value true just in case ϕ is in the theory associated with the agent denoted by α. That is, an agent denoted by α believes the proposition denoted by ϕ only when the sentence ϕ is in the theory of the agent denoted by α. This *sentential semantics* is in keeping with the ideas of this book. All along, we have been calling the formulas expressing information about the world a *belief set*. Now we exploit that point of view by saying that, for us to say that an agent believes something, the corresponding formula must be in its belief set.

Note also that this semantics for **B** is referentially opaque, as desired. Substituting an equivalent expression within the context of a **B** operator does not necessarily preserve truth value, because the equivalent expression might not be in the agent's theory. (It might be equivalent in only *our* theory.)

9.3 Proof Methods

Since we seldom will be able to construct explicit theories as parts of the model for our belief language, we turn to proof methods for manipulating belief expressions. The language we have just defined has a particularly simple and complete proof technique. It is based on the idea of *semantic attachment* to a *partial model* of an agent's beliefs. In its simplest form, the proof method capitalizes on the idea that, if we want to prove that an agent a that believes the proposition denoted by ϕ also believes the proposition denoted by ψ, we start a deduction process (using the agent's inference rules) to establish $\phi \vdash_a \psi$. This deduction process is, of course, a computation (as is the application of any inference rule) and permits concluding an expression of the form $\mathbf{B}(\alpha, \psi)$ from one of the form $\mathbf{B}(\alpha, \phi)$. Our proof technique does assume that we have (as part of our model) models of the deduction processes of each of the agents.

We can capture this idea in a special inference rule. The rule is like resolution and is defined for formulas in clausal form. In converting to clausal form, we assume that belief atoms are atoms. We do not convert the formulas inside of **B** operators.

We call the following inference-rule schema *attachment*. (α is a schema variable that can be replaced by any symbol denoting an agent.)
From

$$\mathbf{B}(\alpha, \phi_1) \vee \psi_1$$
$$\mathbf{B}(\alpha, \phi_2) \vee \psi_2$$
$$\vdots$$
$$\mathbf{B}(\alpha, \phi_n) \vee \psi_n$$
$$\neg\mathbf{B}(\alpha, \phi_{n+1}) \vee \psi_{n+1}$$

and

$$\phi_1 \wedge \ldots \wedge \phi_n \vdash_\alpha \phi_{n+1}$$

conclude

$$\psi_1 \vee \ldots \vee \psi_{n+1}$$

To understand this rule, it is helpful first to imagine the special case in which there are no ψs. In that case, the rule says that, if we can prove ϕ_{n+1} from $\phi_1 \wedge \ldots \wedge \phi_n$ (using the inference rules that we attribute to the agent denoted by α), then it is inconsistent for that agent to believe the propositions denoted by ϕ_i, for $i = 1, \ldots, n$ and not to believe the proposition denoted by ϕ_{n+1}. Konolige [Konolige 1984] has proved the soundness and completeness of this and related rules for belief logics of this kind. We call the rule *attachment* because, to apply it, we must use our (attached) model of an agent's inference process.

Let us look at an example of reasoning about beliefs using this inference rule. We consider first an example in which there are no ψs. Suppose Nora believes P⇒Q but does not believe Q. We want to prove that Nora does not believe P. The clauses that result from the given statements and from the negation of what we want to prove are

1. **B**(Nora,P⇒Q)
2. ¬**B**(Nora,Q)
3. **B**(Nora,P)

To show that these clauses are contradictory by the attachment rule, we set up the deduction:

$$(P{\Rightarrow}Q) \wedge P \vdash_{\text{Nora}} Q$$

We assume that Nora can make that deduction—completing the proof.

As another example, note that we cannot deduce **B**(A,P(C)) from **B**(A,P(B)) $\wedge$ (B=C). There are simply no deductions that can be made from the given clauses. If we also have **B**(A,(B=C)), however, then attachment can be used to show that the given clauses contradict ¬**B**(A,P(C)) using attachment in our theory and equality reasoning in $\vdash_A$.

Finally, suppose we have the following axioms:

$$(\forall x\ R(x) \Rightarrow B(x)) \Rightarrow \mathbf{B}(J,(\forall x\ R(x){\Rightarrow}B(x)))$$

(If all ravens were black, John would believe all ravens were black.)

$$R(\text{Fred}) \Rightarrow \mathbf{B}(J,R(\text{Fred}))$$

(If Fred were a raven, John would believe that Fred was a raven.)

$$\neg\mathbf{B}(J,B(\text{Fred}))$$

(John does not believe that Fred is black.)

Putting these in clausal form yields:

1. R(Sk) ∨ **B**(J,(∀x R(x)⇒B(x)))
2. ¬B(Sk) ∨ **B**(J,(∀x R(x)⇒B(x)))
3. ¬R(Fred) ∨ **B**(J,R(Fred))
4. ¬**B**(J,B(Fred))

where Sk is a Skolem constant.

We can use attachment either on the last three clauses or on the first clause and last two. Either process involves demonstrating ((∀x R(x) ⇒ B(x)) ∧ R(Fred)) ⊢_J B(Fred). Assuming that John's inference mechanism permits this simple deduction, attachment then justifies our concluding both of the following formulas:

5. ¬B(Sk) ∨ ¬R(Fred)

(Either there is a special nonblack thing or Fred is not a raven) and

6. R(Sk) ∨ ¬R(Fred)

(Either there is a special raven or Fred is not a raven.)

Each of these is a valid conclusion. They can be combined to yield:

7. (¬B(Sk) ∧ R(Sk)) ∨ ¬R(Fred)

(Either there is a nonblack raven or Fred is not a raven.)

9.4 Nested Beliefs

A simple extension of the syntax of this language allows us to make statements about nested beliefs. The following definition differs from the earlier, more restricted one only in that (2) permits ϕ to be any closed wff (rather than just an ordinary closed wff):

(1) All ordinary wffs are wffs.

(2) If ϕ is a closed wff (one with no free variables), and if α is a ground term, then **B**(α,ϕ) is a wff. Such wffs are called *belief atoms*.

(3) If ϕ and ψ are wffs, then so are any expressions that can be constructed from ϕ and ψ by the usual propositional connectives.

With this change, an expression such as **B**(R1,**B**(R2,P(A))) is now a wff.

The semantics of this language is the same as before, except that with each attached theory $\mathcal{T}$ we now can associate a set of any closed wffs (rather than just ordinary closed wffs).

Regarding proof methods for this extended language, we might assume that each of the agents has the attachment rule among its inference rules.

This assumption allows us to include attachment to the deduction system of an agent a_j among the inference rules of agent a_i when attaching to the deduction system of agent a_i (that is, when performing a computation such as $\phi_1 \wedge \ldots \wedge \phi_n \vdash_{a_i} \phi_{n+1}$). Just as we use *our* model of a_i's inference procedure in reasoning about a_i's beliefs, we must use our model of a_i's model of a_j's inference procedure in performing a *nested attachment* associated with a_i's reasoning about a_j's beliefs. We associate the symbol $\vdash_{a_i,a_j}$ with the inference procedure used in this nested attachment. Proofs in such an attachment use those inference rules that we believe a_i believes a_j uses. We can carry attachment to arbitrary levels of nesting provided we have (or can assume) information about the inference rules to be used at that level. The symbol $\vdash_{a_i,a_j,a_k}$ is used to indicate proofs using our model of a_i's model of a_j's model of a_k's inference rules (and so on).

There are several interesting puzzles involving agents reasoning about one anothers' beliefs. One of these is the so-called wise-man puzzle. Suppose there are three wise men who are told by their king that at least one of them has a white spot on his forehead; actually, all three have white spots on their foreheads. We assume that each wise man can see the others' foreheads but not his own, and thus each knows whether the others have white spots. There are various versions of this puzzle, but suppose we are told that the first wise man says, "I do not know whether I have a white spot," and that the second wise man then says, "I also do not know whether I have a white spot." We can formulate this puzzle in our logic of belief to show that the third wise man then knows that he has a white spot.

We illustrate the formulation and show how the reasoning goes by considering the simpler, two-wise-man version of this puzzle. We give the wise men names A and B. The information that we will need is contained in the following assumptions derived from the statement of the puzzle:

(1) A and B know that each can see the other's forehead. Thus, for example,

(1a) If A does not have a white spot, B will know that A does not have a white spot,

(1b) A knows (1a).

(2) A and B each know that at least one of them has a white spot, and they each know that the other knows that. In particular,

(2a) A knows that B knows that either A or B has a white spot.

(3) B says that he does not know whether he has a white spot, and A thereby knows that B does not know.

We use our language of belief to express statements (1b), (2a), and (3). (Even though we used the word "knows" in these statements, we formalize them using **B**.)

1b. $\mathbf{B_A}(\neg\text{White(A)} \Rightarrow \mathbf{B_B}(\neg\text{White(A)})))$

2a. $\mathbf{B_A}(\mathbf{B_B}(\text{White(A)} \vee \text{White(B)}))$

3. $\mathbf{B_A}(\neg\mathbf{B_B}(\text{White(B)})))$

The formulas are in clause form. We want to prove $\mathbf{B_A}(\text{White(A)})$. Using resolution refutation, we must show that the negation of $\mathbf{B_A}(\text{White(A)})$ is inconsistent with these formulas. Attachment to wise man **A**'s inference system allows us to make that inference. Attachment sets up the following proof problem:

$$((\neg\text{White(A)} \Rightarrow \mathbf{B_B}(\neg\text{White(A)})))$$
$$\wedge \mathbf{B_B}(\text{White(A)} \vee \text{White(B)}) \wedge \neg\mathbf{B_B}(\text{White(B)})) \vdash_A \text{White(A)}$$

Assuming reasonable rules for $\vdash_A$, we next attempt this proof (after converting the antecedents to clause form):

1. $\mathbf{B_B}(\neg\text{White(A)}) \vee \text{White(A)}$
2. $\mathbf{B_B}(\text{White(A)} \vee \text{White(B)})$
3. $\neg\mathbf{B_B}(\text{White(B)})$

The desired result follows from attachment if we can prove

$$(\neg\text{White(A)} \wedge (\text{White(A)} \vee \text{White(B)})) \vdash_{A,B} \text{White(B)}$$

But this proof is trivial by resolution (assuming reasonable rules for $\vdash_{A,B}$). Thus, our entire proof goes through.

In the three-wise-man version, there is another level of nested reasoning, but the basic strategy is the same. In fact, one can solve the k-wise-man puzzle (for arbitrary k) assuming that the first $(k-1)$ wise men each claims that he does not know whether or not he has a white spot.

9.5 Quantifying-In

In our examples so far, **K** and **B** have operated on only closed formulas. Operating on formulas containing free variables quantified *outside* the context of the operator presents special problems. In that case, we say that we have *quantified-in* to the context of the modal operator. We now extend our language to allow formulas such as $(Q\mathbf{x})\mathbf{B}(\alpha,\phi(\mathbf{x}))$, where Q is the quantifier $\exists$ or $\forall$ and $\phi(\mathbf{x})$ is a wff schema over wffs having a free variable $\mathbf{x}$.

The semantics of these new formulas is rather complicated and needs some motivating discussion. Consider an expression such as

$$(\exists\mathbf{x} \ \ \mathbf{B}(\text{A,Father-Of(Zeus,x)}))$$

Suppose we attempt to apply the usual semantics for existentially quantified sentences in first-order predicate calculus combined with our sentential semantics for the **B** operator. The formula (∃x **B**(A,Father-Of(Zeus,x))) would then have the value true whenever there is some element, k, of our domain of objects, such that **B**(A,Father-Of(Zeus,x)) had the value true when x denoted k. Now, in order for **B**(A,Father-Of(Zeus,x)) to have the value true when x denotes k (according to our sentential semantics for **B**), there would have to be in A's theory a closed formula of the form Father-Of(Zeus,C), where C is a term that denotes k for agent A.

In this account, each agent a_i may have its own map between terms and objects in the domain. In fact, there may be objects in the domain for which an agent has no object constants. (The agent may not "know about" some objects.)

Even if the denotations of terms were the same for all agents (and for us), we would need to have a way of referring to the constants used by agents for denoting objects (because the constants used by these agents might not appear in our theory). Consider the formula (∃x **B**(A,P(x))). Suppose we were to Skolemize this formula by replacing the existential variable by a Skolem constant, say Sk. Sk denotes an object—*we* do not know which one, but A does know! (We know that A knows which object Sk denotes because the semantics of **B** tells us that there is an expression of the form P(C) in A's theory such that C denotes whatever Sk is supposed to denote.) Therefore, we need a constant to denote whatever it is that Sk denotes. We introduce an operator •, called the *bullet operator*, that transforms any term inside the context of the **B** operator to a constant denoting, for the believer, whatever that term is supposed to denote for us. The Skolemized form of (∃x **B**(A,P(x))) is then **B**(A,P(•Sk)). Assuming that A has an object constant for each of the objects in our domain, the Skolemized form of (∃x Q(x) ∧ **B**(A,P(x))) can then be written as Q(Sk) ∧ **B**(A,P(•Sk)). (An English version of the intended meaning of this latter sentence is something like this: There is some object, which we denote by the Skolem constant Sk because we do not know what object it is, that satisfies the property Q, and A believes of that object—having an object constant for it—that it satisfies the property P.)

It is useful to identify a class of constants, called *standard names*, that denote for all agents, and for us, the same objects in the domain. If a constant C is a standard name, then •C=C. Since Skolem constants are not standard names, the bullet operator applied to a Skolem constant produces *the* standard name for whatever that Skolem constant is supposed to denote.

Now we can give a more formal account of the semantics of (∃x **B**(α,ϕ(x))). An expression of this form has value true just when there is an object in the domain, call it k, such that an expression of the form $\phi(C)$ occurs in agent α's theory and C denotes k for α.

Note that, using this account of the semantics of quantifying-in (and assuming that α can do existential generalization), the following formula schema is valid:

$$(\exists x\ \mathbf{B}(\alpha, \phi(x)))\ \Rightarrow\ \mathbf{B}(\alpha, (\exists x\ \phi(x)))$$

(If α believes there is some particular object satisfying ϕ, then it certainly believes there is *some* object satisfying ϕ.) However, the converse is not valid.

If our agents do not have object constants for all the objects in the domain, then we have to have a way of saying for which objects they do have names. We use the formula $\mathtt{I}(\alpha, x)$ to stand for the fact that agent α has a name for the object that we denote by x. With this notation, the Skolemized form of $(\exists x\ \mathbf{B}(\mathtt{A}, \mathtt{P}(x)))$ is $\mathbf{B}(\mathtt{A}, \mathtt{P}(\bullet\mathtt{Sk}))\ \wedge\ \mathtt{I}(\mathtt{A},\ \mathtt{Sk})$. (When we make the simplifying assumption that agent $\mathtt{A}$ has names for everything we do, then $\mathtt{I}(\mathtt{A},x)$ is identically true for all x.)

What about expressions of the form $(\forall x\ \mathbf{B}(\alpha, \phi(x)))$? According to the semantics of $\forall$ and $\mathbf{B}$, such an expression is true if and only if for each object, k_i, in the domain, there is an expression of the form $\phi(C_i)$ in α's theory, with each C_i denoting k_i for α. If the agent denoted by α has object constants for all the objects in our domain (and if α's inference rules include universal instantiation), then we have the *converse Barcan formula*:

$$\mathbf{B}(\alpha, (\forall x\ \phi(x)))\ \Rightarrow\ (\forall x\ \mathbf{B}(\alpha, \phi(x)))$$

If the agent denoted by α has object constants for all the objects in our domain, and for no more than these, then we have the *Barcan formula* itself:

$$(\forall x\ \mathbf{B}(\alpha, \phi(x)))\ \Rightarrow\ \mathbf{B}(\alpha, (\forall x\ \phi(x)))$$

These schemata can be used to make these assertions about the vocabulary of object constants for agents.

9.6 Proof Methods for Quantified Beliefs

We would like to extend the attachment rule given earlier, so that it can be applied to belief sentences having free variables that are quantified outside the belief operator. A formal extension is a subtle matter, but we can give a relatively straightforward informal account here. (See [Konolige 1984] for further details.)

To motivate our discussion, consider the problem of proving

$$(\exists x \ \mathbf{B_A}(P(x))) \ \Rightarrow \ \mathbf{B_A}(\exists x \ P(x))$$

Let us negate this expression and convert it to clause form preliminary to attempting a refutation. We obtain first:

$$(\exists x \ \mathbf{B_A}(P(x))) \ \wedge \ \neg\mathbf{B_A}(\exists x \ P(x))$$

Skolemizing yields the following clauses:

    I(A,Sk)
    $\mathbf{B_A}$(P(•Sk))
    $\neg\mathbf{B_A}$(∃x P(x))

Next, we would like to use attachment to yield a contradiction. The problem is to decide how to deal with the bullet term when setting up the attached deduction. The bullet operator is a construct of *our* language that lets *us* refer to objects that are referred to in the agent's language. Now we want to use a language and inference procedures that correspond to our model of the agent's reasoning process; to do so, we need to have terms in that language to take the place of "bulleted" terms in our language. We have to be careful that such terms are not confused with any other terms in (our model of) the agent's language, so we invent a special function constant, $\mathbf{G_A}$, that is used only when performing a deduction in an attached model of A's reasoning process. When attaching to a belief atom $\mathbf{B_A}(\phi(\bullet t))$, where t is any term, we create the expression $\phi(\mathbf{G_A}(t))$ in the attached theory. Thus, in the attached theory, $\mathbf{G_A}$ takes the place of the bullet operator. Loosely speaking, we let $\mathbf{G_A}(t)$, denote in the attached theory whatever we denote by t. When we make the simplifying asssumption that agent A uses the same object constants that we do, then $\mathbf{G_A}(t) = t$ for all t.

Continuing our example, we can use attachment on the last two clauses to produce the desired contradiction if we can establish that

$$P(\mathbf{G_A}(Sk)) \ \vdash_A \ \exists x P(x)$$

Assuming that agent A can make this deduction, we have our contradiction and thus have established what we were trying to prove.

The same technique can be used for belief atoms having a free variable that is universally quantified outside of the belief operator. In that case, when converting to clause form, we replace the free variable by a "bullet-operated" free variable. When performing attachment, these bullet variables become schema variables inside a G-functional expression, and we attempt to find instances of the schema variables for which we can establish the attached deduction. These substitution instances are then applied to the clause inferred by the attachment inference.

We illustrate this approach with an example: We want to prove $\mathbf{B_A}(\exists x\ Q(x))$ from $(\exists x\ \neg\mathbf{B_A}(P(x)))$ and $(\forall x\ (\mathbf{B_A}(P(x)) \lor \mathbf{B_A}(Q(x))))$. We convert the premises to clause form:

$$\neg\mathbf{B_A}(P(\bullet Sk)) \land I_A(Sk)$$

$$(\mathbf{B_A}(P(\bullet x)) \lor \mathbf{B_A}(Q(\bullet x))) \land I_A(x)$$

where $I_A(\phi)$ is an abbreviation for $I(A,\phi)$. Rearranging the clauses and adding the negated goal clause, we have:

1. $I_A(x)$
2. $I_A(Sk)$
3. $\mathbf{B_A}(P(\bullet x)) \lor \mathbf{B_A}(Q(\bullet x))$
4. $\neg\mathbf{B_A}(P(\bullet Sk))$
5. $\neg\mathbf{B_A}(\exists x\ Q(x))$

We use attachment on clauses 3 and 4. The attached deduction is:

$$P(G_A(x)) \vdash_A P(G_A(Sk))$$

where x is a schema variable. Let us assume that A's rules are strong enough to permit this deduction with the substitution $\{x/Sk\}$. Applying this substitution to the remaining literals in clause 3 yields the inference permitted by this attachment; namely,

$$\mathbf{B_A}(Q(\bullet Sk))$$

This clause, in turn, can be used in an attachment with clause 5 to set up the following deduction:

$$Q(G_A(Sk)) \vdash_A \exists x Q(x)$$

Completing this deduction (which we assume we can do) completes our refutation and establishes what we were trying to prove.

Without special assumptions, we cannot prove the Barcan formula $\forall x\ \mathbf{B_A}(P(x)) \Rightarrow \mathbf{B_A}(\forall x\ P(x))$. The clause form of the negation of this formula is

$$I_A(x)$$
$$\mathbf{B_A}(P(\bullet x))$$
$$\neg\mathbf{B_A}(\forall x\ P(x))$$

We might try attachment on the last two clauses to attempt a contradiction. Such attachment would set up the deduction:

$$P(G_A(x)) \vdash_A (\forall x\ P(x))$$

This deduction cannot go through unless we assume the equivalent of $G_A(x)$ = x for all x that might name objects in the domain. Such an assumption is just what is needed to establish the validity of the Barcan formula.

Neither can we prove the invalid formula

$$\mathbf{B_A}(\exists x\ P(x)) \Rightarrow (\exists x\ \mathbf{B_A}(P(x)))$$

Converting the negation of this formula into clause form yields

$\mathbf{B_A}(\exists x\ P(x))$
$I_A(x)$
$\neg\mathbf{B_A}(P(\bullet x))$

Attempting to produce a contradiction from the first and last clauses sets up the deduction:

$$(\exists x\ P(x)) \vdash_A P(G_A(x))$$

which cannot be established because there is no instance of the conclusion that can be established from the premise.

9.7 Knowing What Something Is

Suppose we say that John knows that Mike has a telephone number. We might express this as $\mathbf{B_J}(\exists x\ PN(Mike,x))$. We would not want to conclude from this statement that John knows *what* Mike's telephone number is. Alternatively, we could say that John knows that whatever Mike's number is, Lennie's number is the same as Mike's: $\mathbf{B_J}(\forall x\ PN(Mike,x) \Rightarrow PN(Lennie,x))$. Still, we would not want to conclude that John knows Lennie's telephone number (or Mike's). To say that John knows the number, we would have to say (or deduce) something like, "There is a number, and John knows *of that number* that it is Mike's telephone number." Quantifying-in allows us to say this about John without our having to know the number: $(\exists x\ \mathbf{B_J}(PN(Mike,x)))$.

If we add to this last statement the one about John knowing that whatever Mike's number is, Lennie's number is the same as Mike's, we also can deduce that John knows Lennie's number. We perform this deduction as a final example. We want to prove $(\exists x\ \mathbf{B_J}(PN(Lennie,x)))$ from $(\exists x\ \mathbf{B_J}(PN(Mike,x)))$ and $\mathbf{B_J}((\forall x\ PN(Mike,x) \Rightarrow PN(Lennie,x)))$. The clauses arising from the negated conclusion and premises are

1. $I_J(x)$
2. $\neg B_J(PN(Lennie,\bullet x))$
3. $I_J(Sk)$
4. $B_J(PN(Mike,\bullet Sk))$
5. $B_J(\forall x\ PN(Mike,x) \Rightarrow PN(Lennie,x))$

Using attachment on clauses 4, 5, and 2, we set up the deduction:

$$PN(Mike,G_J(Sk))\ \wedge\ (\forall x\ PN(Mike,x)\ \Rightarrow\ PN(Lennie,x))$$
$$\vdash_J PN(Lennie,G_J(x))$$

where x is a schema variable. Assuming that this deduction goes through, we have our proof.

9.8 Possible-Worlds Logics

In this section, we present another important conceptualization of knowledge. In this conceptualization, we include objects, $w_0, w_1, w_2, \ldots, w_i, \ldots$ called *possible worlds*. (Remember that conceptualizations need not be limited to objects that we might think *actually exist*; they can also include objects that we find useful to imagine—such as numbers, for example. Do not be troubled yet by the lack of a concrete picture about what possible worlds actually are; imagine them as alternatives to the actual world.)

Possible worlds will play a key role in specifying a semantics for sentences containing the modal operator **K**. We assume that the language is the same as the one we used earlier; namely, an ordinary first-order language augmented by **K** operators—allowing nested operators and also allowing quantifying-in to the operators. Again, an *ordinary* wff is one in which there are no modal operators.

We first define the semantics for ordinary wffs. We no longer say that a wff is true or false absolutely, but instead introduce the notion of it being true or false *with respect to a possible world*. Instead of an interpretation consisting of single sets of objects, functions, and relations, we now have such sets for each possible world. An ordinary wff ϕ has the value true with respect to the world w_i only when it evaluates to true using the interpretation associated with w_i. (Of course, we can have something like our previous idea of nonrelative truth by evaluating a wff with respect to the actual world.) Loosely speaking, this device allows us to say that the expression White(Snow), say, has the value true in w_0 and the value false in some other imaginable world, w_{16} (where snow is black).

So far, it is not apparent why we need these other worlds and their associated interpretations. We will use them in evaluating the truth values of wffs containing the modal operators. First, we introduce one other important idea—the notion of *accessibility*. We define an *accessibility relation*, $k(a, w_i, w_j)$, among agents and worlds. When $k(a, w_i, w_j)$ is satisfied, we say that world w_j is accessible from world w_i for agent a. A knowledge atom $\mathbf{K}(\alpha, \phi)$ has the value true with respect to world w_i if and only if ϕ has the value true in *all* the worlds accessible from w_i for the agent denoted by α. This semantic rule can be applied recursively to any wff ϕ—even to those containing nested modal operators. The semantics for arbitrary formulas (ones made up of complex combinations of knowledge atoms using the usual propositional connectives) is determined by the ordinary truth-recursion rules for the connectives.

We might imagine that we could similarly define an accessibility relation b for belief. As we shall see in the next section, however, possible-worlds semantics implies that agents are logically omniscient; that is, they know all the logical consequences of their knowledge. Although such a property is a convenient idealization, and therefore might be appropriate for knowledge, it seems obviously inappropriate for belief. Therefore, we will restrict our discussion of possible-worlds semantics to knowledge only.

The intended meaning of $\mathbf{K}(\alpha, \phi)$ is, of course, that the agent denoted by α knows the proposition denoted by ϕ. Let us see how this intended meaning is supported by our possible-worlds semantics. Consider a knower (denoted by) A. Suppose (in world w_0) A does not know the truth of a proposition denoted by the formula P. The possible-worlds conceptualization captures this state of affairs by associating with A (in world w_0, say) some worlds in which P has the value true and some in which P has the value false. We could say that *for all* A *knows* (in w_0), there may be worlds in which P is true and there may be worlds in which it is false. A cannot rule out that these different worlds might actually exist, because (after all) it does not actually know whether P is true or false. On the other hand, if A knows P to be true (in w_0), then in *all* the worlds associated with A in w_0, P must have the value true. The worlds *associated* with A in a world are just those that are accessible for it from that world. When we do not refer explicitly to the world in which an agent knows a proposition, we assume that we mean that the agent knows the proposition in the actual world, w_0.

These concepts can be made more concrete with a specific example. Suppose the accessibility relation for knower A is as depicted by the arcs in Figure 9.1. Worlds w_0, w_1, w_2, and w_3 are all accessible for A from w_0. P is true and R is false in worlds w_0, w_1, w_2, and w_3; Q is true in worlds w_0, w_1, and w_3 and false in w_2. From this information, we conclude that A knows P and ¬R in w_0 but does not know Q or R in w_0. (Note that, since A knows ¬R in w_0, it does not know R in w_0.)

Characterizing knowledge in terms of an accessibility relation also gives an intuitively satisfying account of nested knowledge statements. Thus, to say that (in the real world w_0) the agent (denoted by) A knows that agent B knows P is to say that, in all worlds, $\{w_i\}$ accessible for A from w_0, $\mathbf{K}(\mathtt{B,P})$ has value true. In addition, of course, for $\mathbf{K}(\mathtt{B,P})$ to have the

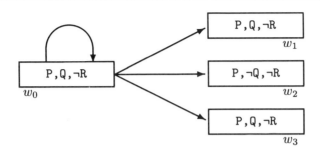

Figure 9.1   The worlds accessible to A in w_0 (after [Moore 1985a]).

value true in any of the worlds $\{w_i\}$, means that in all worlds accessible for B in each w_i, P has the value true. We can illustrate the role played by accessibility relations in nested knowledge statements by the diagram in Figure 9.2. (The accessibility relation for knower A is indicated by arcs labeled by k_a; that for B is indicated by arcs labeled by k_b.) Note that P is

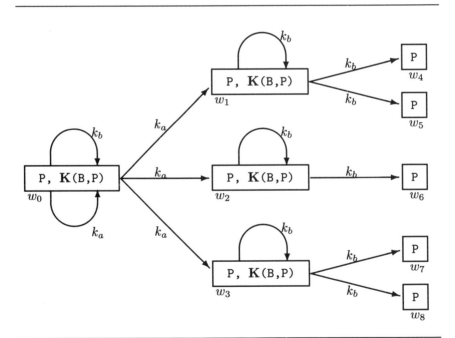

Figure 9.2   The worlds accessible to A and to B (after [Moore 1985a]).

true in all the worlds that are accessible to B from all the worlds that are accessible to A from w_0.

9.9 Properties of Knowledge

If the **K** and **B** operators are to capture our intuitive ideas about knowledge and belief, they must satisfy several properties. Many of these properties can be achieved by imposing special constraints on the accessibility relation. Since physically realizable agents can be said more accurately to have beliefs than to have knowledge, knowledge properties must be regarded as idealizations that will not necessarily transfer to belief. We will first deal with properties of knowledge, and then discuss belief.

First, we want to say that an agent ought to be able to reason with its knowledge. That is, if an agent α knows the proposition denoted by ϕ and also knows the proposition denoted by $\phi \Rightarrow \psi$, then it also knows the proposition denoted by ψ. This property is expressed by the following axiom schema:

$$(\mathbf{K}_\alpha(\phi) \wedge \mathbf{K}_\alpha(\phi \Rightarrow \psi)) \Rightarrow \mathbf{K}_\alpha(\psi) \qquad \text{(Axiom 9.1)}$$

Note that this axiom schema is sometimes written in the equivalent form:

$$\mathbf{K}_\alpha((\phi \Rightarrow \psi)) \Rightarrow (\mathbf{K}_\alpha(\phi) \Rightarrow \mathbf{K}_\alpha(\psi))$$

This axiom is called the *distribution axiom* because it sanctions distributing the **K** operator over implications.

Possible-worlds semantics for knowledge implies that, if agent a knows ϕ in w_1, then ϕ must be true in every world w_2 that satisfies $k(a, w_1, w_2)$. The distribution axiom is a consequence of assuming the converse also; namely, that, if ϕ is true in every world w_2 that satisfies $k(a, w_1, w_2)$, then a knows ϕ in w_1. Thus, this axiom comes with the possible-worlds approach itself—regardless of any constraints we might place on k.

Another axiom schema that seems appropriate, called the *knowledge axiom*, states that an agent cannot possibly *know* something that is false. Someone might have false *beliefs*, but false *knowledge* would seem to violate any reasonable definition of knowledge.

$$\mathbf{K}_\alpha(\phi) \Rightarrow \phi \qquad \text{(Axiom 9.2)}$$

The knowledge axiom is satisfied if the accessibility relation (considered as a binary relation for a fixed knower) is *reflexive*; i.e., if $k(a, w_1, w_1)$ for any knower a and all worlds w_1. (If a knows ϕ in w_1, ϕ must be true in w_1.)

(Axiom 9.2 implies that an agent does not know contradictions: $\neg \mathbf{K}(\alpha, \mathbf{F})$. This latter fact also would follow by forcing k to be *serial*. For a fixed knower a, k is serial if for all w_1 there is some w_2 that satisfies

$k(a, w_1, w_2)$. That is, there are no "trap states" w_1 in which no world is accessible. *Some* world is compatible with a's knowledge in w_1.)

As a third property of knowledge, it seems reasonable to assume that, if an agent knows something, it knows that it knows it. This property is expressed by the *positive-introspection axiom*:

$$\mathbf{K}_\alpha(\phi) \;\Rightarrow\; \mathbf{K}_\alpha(\mathbf{K}_\alpha(\phi)) \qquad\qquad \text{(Axiom 9.3)}$$

The positive-introspection axiom follows if the accessibility relation is *transitive*; i.e., $k(a, w_1, w_2)$ and $k(a, w_2, w_3)$ imply $k(a, w_1, w_3)$ for any a and all w_1, w_2, and w_3. (You are asked to prove this result, as well as others, in Exercise 7 at the end of the chapter.)

In some axiomatizations of knowledge, we also state that, if an agent does not know something, it knows that it does not know it—the *negative-introspection axiom*:

$$\neg\mathbf{K}_\alpha(\phi) \;\Rightarrow\; \mathbf{K}_\alpha(\neg\mathbf{K}_\alpha(\phi)) \qquad\qquad \text{(Axiom 9.4)}$$

The negative-introspection axiom follows if the accessibility relation is *Euclidean*. (k is Euclidean if $k(a, w_1, w_2)$ and $k(a, w_1, w_3)$ imply $k(a, w_2, w_3)$ for any a and all w_1, w_2, and w_3.)

(Another common property of binary relations is symmetry. k is symmetric if $k(a, w_1, w_2)$ is equivalent to $k(a, w_2, w_1)$. It can be shown that a symmetric accessibility relation implies $\neg\mathbf{K}(\alpha, \neg\mathbf{K}(\alpha, \phi)) \Rightarrow \phi$. This is called the Brouwer axiom, and can be shown to follow from some of our other axioms. See Exercise 4 at the end of the chapter.)

The next property we might want is that any agent knows all these axioms (as well as all of the logical axioms). We can express this property by adding to our logic another rule of inference. This rule, called *epistemic necessitation*, allows us to infer $\mathbf{K}_\alpha(\phi)$ if ϕ is provable. We can write this rule of inference as

$$\text{from } \vdash \phi \text{ infer } \mathbf{K}_\alpha(\phi) \qquad\qquad \text{(Rule 9.5)}$$

Necessitation also follows from possible-worlds semantics. (If ϕ is a theorem of the logic, it is true in *all* possible worlds. Thus, in particular, it is true in those possible worlds accessible to an agent, and thus the agent knows ϕ.)

Rule 9.5 must be applied with care; the rule says that $\mathbf{K}_\alpha(\phi)$ can be inferred if ϕ is provable (i.e., if ϕ is a theorem). The rule must not be misunderstood to justify an inference of $\mathbf{K}_\alpha(\phi)$ from some *proper* axiom ϕ or from some logical consequence ϕ of a proper axiom. (A *proper* axiom is distinguished from a *logical* axiom. The latter is valid under all interpretations, whereas the former occurs in a theory about the world to express some fact or general rule about the world.) We do not mean to say that an agent knows the consequences of the proper axioms of our theory.

If we could conclude $\mathbf{K}(\alpha, \phi)$ from a proper axiom ϕ, then (from the deduction theorem) we could conclude $\phi \Rightarrow \mathbf{K}(\alpha, \phi)$, which is sometimes called an *observation axiom*. It says that an agent knows ϕ whenever ϕ happens to be true of the world (which is different than saying that an agent knows ϕ whenever ϕ is a logical theorem). Rule 9.5 says only that agents know the consequences of the *logical* axioms.

Sometimes, we will indeed want to say of certain agents that they will know whether certain facts are true because they have special mechanisms for perceiving the truth of those facts. Suppose, for example, that agent **A** has a perceptual mechanism that allows it to know whether it is raining. Then we would be justified in having the observation formula `Raining` $\Rightarrow$ `K(A,Raining)`.

Since modus ponens is the only inference rule needed in propositional logic, Axiom 9.1 and Rule 9.5 enable us to conclude that an agent knows *all* the propositional consequences of its knowledge; that is, it is *logically omniscient*. We can express this fact as an inference rule as follows:

$$\text{from } \phi \vdash \psi \text{ and from } \mathbf{K}_\alpha(\phi) \text{ infer } \mathbf{K}_\alpha(\psi) \qquad \text{(Rule 9.6)}$$

An equivalent formulation of this rule is:

$$\text{from } \vdash \phi \Rightarrow \psi \text{ infer } \mathbf{K}_\alpha(\phi) \Rightarrow \mathbf{K}_\alpha(\psi) \qquad \text{(Rule 9.7)}$$

Logical omniscience seems unrealistic for finite agents, who, after all, cannot derive *all* the consequences of whatever they might know explicitly. If an agent cannot derive a proposition (even though it follows from other propositions it knows), can it really be said that it *knows* that proposition? Does someone who knows the axioms of number theory *know all* of the theorems? It depends on what we take *know* to mean. We might have, for example, a *Platonic* view of knowledge in which, by definition, an agent *knows* all the consequences of its knowledge—even though it might not necessarily explicitly *believe* them. Even though logical omniscience does seem too strong, it is useful as an approximation since intelligent agents will do *some* reasoning. In any case, these concerns are not very important for us because we will put our major emphasis on belief rather than on knowledge, and we need not have logical omniscience for belief.

From logical omniscience (Rule 9.6), we can derive:

$$\mathbf{K}(\alpha,\phi) \land \mathbf{K}(\alpha,\psi) \Leftrightarrow \mathbf{K}(\alpha,(\phi\land\psi))$$

That is, the **K** operator *distributes* over conjunctions. However, it is not the case that $\mathbf{K}(\alpha,(\phi\lor\psi))$ implies $\mathbf{K}(\alpha,\phi) \lor \mathbf{K}(\alpha,\psi)$. Thus, we can distinguish between knowing a disjunction and a disjunction of knowings. Also, $\mathbf{K}(\alpha,\neg\phi)$ implies $\neg\mathbf{K}(\alpha,\phi)$, but not vice versa.

We can represent that an agent knows whether or not ϕ, without *our* knowing whether or not ϕ, by the expression $\mathbf{K}(\alpha,\phi) \lor \mathbf{K}(\alpha,\neg\phi)$. (This is not a tautology.)

We can carry out proofs of some statements about the knowledge of agents using only the axioms of knowledge and epistemic necessitation (with modus ponens). Let us consider the simple example about Nora again. Nora knows P⇒Q but does not know Q. We can use our axioms to show that Nora does not know P.

1. $K_{Nora}(P \Rightarrow Q)$ given
2. $K_{Nora}(P) \Rightarrow K_{Nora}(Q)$ Axiom 9.1
3. $\neg K_{Nora}(Q) \Rightarrow \neg K_{Nora}(P)$ contrapositive of 2
4. $\neg K_{Nora}(Q)$ given
5. $\neg K_{Nora}(P)$ 3, 4, MP

Various combinations of Axioms 9.1 through 9.4, with the axioms of ordinary propositional logic, the ordinary inference rules, and Rule 9.5, constitute what we will call the *modal logics of knowledge*. For a fixed agent A, Axioms 9.1 through 9.4 are the axioms of a system of modal logic called *S5*. Logicians have given special names to various modal-logic systems—each having somewhat different axiom schemes. If we left out Axiom 9.4, we would have the system *S4*. If we left out Axioms 9.3 and 9.4, we would have *system T*. If we left out Axioms 9.2, 9.3, and 9.4, we would have *system K*.

We cannot arbitrarily pick and choose which of the axioms to include in a logic of knowledge. The five properties that we have defined for accessibility relations (namely, reflexive, transitive, Euclidean, symmetric, and serial) are not themselves independent. The following constraints hold among these properties:

P1: symmetric and transitive together imply Euclidean.

P2: symmetric, transitive, and serial together are equivalent to reflexive and Euclidean together.

P3: reflexive implies serial.

P4: symmetric implies serial.

Using (*P2*) we can show that Axioms 9.2 (reflexive) and 9.4 (Euclidean) together imply Axiom 9.3 (transitive). Thus, Axiom 9.3 does not need to be stated explicitly in *S5* if Axiom 9.2 and Axiom 9.4 are already stated. This also means, of course, that we cannot have a system that includes Axioms 9.2 and 9.4 and leaves out Axiom 9.3. Fortunately, our study of the properties of knowledge can build on what logicians have already learned about these systems.

As a final example to illustrate how these axioms can be used to reason about the knowledge of agents, let us consider the two-man version of the wise-man puzzle again. We repeat the information that we need from the statement of the puzzle:

(1b) A knows that if A does not have a white spot, B will know that A does not have a white spot.

(2a) A knows that B knows that either A or B has a white spot.

(3) A knows that B does not know whether or not B has a white spot.

Statements (1b), (2a), and (3) are written as the first three lines, respectively, of the following proof of $\mathbf{K}(\mathtt{A},\mathtt{White(A)})$:

1. $\mathbf{K}_A(\neg\mathtt{White(A)} \Rightarrow \mathbf{K}_B(\neg\mathtt{White(A)}))$
2. $\mathbf{K}_A(\mathbf{K}_B(\neg\mathtt{White(A)} \Rightarrow \mathtt{White(B)}))$
3. $\mathbf{K}_A(\neg\mathbf{K}_B(\mathtt{White(B)}))$
4. $\neg\mathtt{White(A)} \Rightarrow \mathbf{K}_B(\neg\mathtt{White(A)})$ 1, Axiom 9.2
5. $\mathbf{K}_B(\neg\mathtt{White(A)}) \Rightarrow \mathtt{White(B)}$ 2, Axiom 9.2
6. $\mathbf{K}_B(\neg\mathtt{White(A)}) \Rightarrow \mathbf{K}_B(\mathtt{White(B)})$ 5, Axiom 9.1
7. $\neg\mathtt{White(A)} \Rightarrow \mathbf{K}_B(\mathtt{White(B)})$ 4, 6
8. $\neg\mathbf{K}_B(\mathtt{White(B)}) \Rightarrow \mathtt{White(A)}$ contrapositive of 7
9. $\mathbf{K}_A(\neg\mathbf{K}_B(\mathtt{White(B)}) \Rightarrow \mathtt{White(A)})$ 1–5, 8, Rule 9.6
10. $\mathbf{K}_A(\neg\mathbf{K}_B(\mathtt{White(B)})) \Rightarrow \mathbf{K}_A(\mathtt{White(A)})$ Axiom 9.1
11. $\mathbf{K}_A(\mathtt{White(A)})$ 3, 10, MP

To derive line 9 in the proof we use Rule 9.6 to justify stating that A believes a consequence of a proof (line 8) from premises (lines 4 and 5) when it believes those premises (lines 1 and 2).

9.10 Properties of Belief

Even though we do not find possible-worlds semantics appropriate for belief, we can state some desired properties of belief as axiom schemata that can be compared with those for knowledge. Since an agent might have false beliefs, a logic of belief would not contain the knowledge axiom (Axiom 9.2). In fact, some people have maintained that the essential difference between belief and knowledge is the presence of the knowledge axiom for knowledge; that is, knowledge is *true* belief. This criterion gives an overly generous definition of knowledge, because an agent might happen to have some true beliefs that we would not want to characterize as knowledge. Someone might, for example, *believe* that it is always noon; we would not want to say that he actually *knew* that it was noon once a day. A more restrictive characterization of knowledge in terms of belief is that knowledge is *justified* true belief. It has proved difficult, however, to be sufficiently precise about when a belief is justified.

Since we do not have the knowledge axiom, we include the axiom that states that agents do not believe contradictions:

$$\neg\mathbf{B}(\alpha,\mathbf{F}) \hspace{4cm} \text{(Axiom 9.8)}$$

It would be inappropriate for a logic of belief to have the distribution axiom (Axiom 9.1) or the necessitation rule (Rule 9.5) because finite agents cannot realistically be said to believe all of the logical consequences of their beliefs, even if their beliefs are closed under their own (incomplete) inference rules.

It seems reasonable to have something like the positive-introspection axiom for belief. Thus,

$$\mathbf{B}(\alpha,\phi) \;\Rightarrow\; \mathbf{B}(\alpha,\mathbf{B}(\alpha,\phi)) \qquad\qquad \text{(Axiom 9.9)}$$

It even seems safe to assume that, if an agent believes something, it knows that it believes it:

$$\mathbf{B}(\alpha,\phi) \;\Rightarrow\; \mathbf{K}(\alpha,\mathbf{B}(\alpha,\phi)) \qquad\qquad (9.10)$$

Negative-introspection axioms seem much more problematic for beliefs, however. They might require more reasoning resources than an agent has for it to determine that it does not believe something.

If we had an axiom like the knowledge axiom, then we could derive $\mathbf{B}(\alpha,\phi)$ from $\mathbf{B}(\alpha,\mathbf{B}(\alpha,\phi))$. It seems reasonable to allow this derivation (even without the knowledge axiom) by including the converse of Axiom 9.9; namely,

$$\mathbf{B}(\alpha,\mathbf{B}(\alpha,\phi)) \;\Rightarrow\; \mathbf{B}(\alpha,\phi) \qquad\qquad (9.11)$$

If agents have confidence in the beliefs of other agents, we also might want to say that an agent believes ϕ if it believes that some other agent believes ϕ:

$$\mathbf{B}(\alpha_1,\mathbf{B}(\alpha_2,\phi)) \;\Rightarrow\; \mathbf{B}(\alpha_1,\phi) \qquad\qquad (9.12)$$

9.11 Group Knowledge

Reasoning about knowledge often involves nested knowledge assertions. In the wise-man puzzle, for example, all the wise men, as a group, knew certain facts, and knew that the others knew that, and so on. There are several ways in which a finite group, G, of agents might be said to know a fact. We can introduce new modal operators for each of these ways: $\mathbf{IK}(G,\phi)$ is intended to mean that the group, G, has *implicit knowledge* of ϕ. $\mathbf{IK}(G,\phi)$ is *true* if and only if there is a set of formulas $\{\phi_i\}$ such that $\{\phi_i\} \vdash \phi$ and, for each ϕ_i in $\{\phi_i\}$, there is an agent A_k in G such that $\mathbf{K}(A_k,\phi_i)$. Intuitively, the group implicitly knows ϕ if and only if its agents could pool what they know individually to derive ϕ.

$\mathbf{SK}(G,\phi)$ is intended to mean that *some* agent in G knows ϕ. That is,

$$\mathbf{SK}(G,\phi) \equiv \bigvee_{A_i \in G} \mathbf{K}(A_i,\phi)$$

EK(G, ϕ) is intended to mean that *every* agent in G knows ϕ. That is,

$$\mathbf{EK}(G, \phi) \equiv \bigwedge_{A_i \in G} \mathbf{K}(A_i, \phi)$$

We also can say that every agent in G knows **EK**(G, ϕ). We denote this by **EK**$^2(G, \phi)$. That is,

$$\mathbf{EK}^2(G, \phi) \equiv \mathbf{EK}(G, \mathbf{EK}(G, \phi))$$

This process of saying that every member knows that every member knows, and so on, can be carried on indefinitely. For $k \geq 1$ we have,

$$\mathbf{EK}^{k+1}(G, \phi) \equiv \mathbf{EK}(G, \mathbf{EK}^k(G, \phi))$$

where **EK**$^1(G, \phi) \equiv$ **EK**(G, ϕ). When **EK**$^k(G, \phi)$ is true, we say that every member of G knows ϕ to degree k.

CK(G, ϕ) is intended to mean that ϕ is *common knowledge* in G. A group has common knowledge of ϕ if ϕ is true and if every member of G knows ϕ to degree k for *all* $k \geq 1$. That is,

$$\mathbf{CK}(G, \phi) \equiv \phi \wedge \mathbf{EK}(G, \phi) \wedge \mathbf{EK}^2(G, \phi) \wedge \ldots \wedge \mathbf{EK}^k(G, \phi) \wedge \ldots$$

These notions of group knowledge form a hierarchy with

$$\mathbf{CK}(G, \phi) \Rightarrow \cdots \Rightarrow \mathbf{EK}^k(G, \phi) \Rightarrow \cdots \Rightarrow \mathbf{EK}(G, \phi) \Rightarrow$$
$$\mathbf{SK}(G, \phi) \Rightarrow \mathbf{IK}(G, \phi) \Rightarrow \phi$$

Depending on how the agents share memory, some of these notions might be equivalent. For example, if all the agents in the group shared the same memory, it would seem that

$$\mathbf{CK}(G, \phi) \Leftrightarrow \cdots \Leftrightarrow \mathbf{EK}^k(G, \phi) \Leftrightarrow \cdots \Leftrightarrow \mathbf{EK}(G, \phi) \Leftrightarrow$$
$$\mathbf{SK}(G, \phi) \Leftrightarrow \mathbf{IK}(G, \phi)$$

Even though **CK** is an "infinitary" operator, we can treat it (and **EK**) as a primitive concept with an axiomatization similar to that given for **K**. (For simplicity, we suppress the argument G in the following axioms.)

$$\mathbf{CK}(\phi) \wedge \mathbf{CK}(\phi \Rightarrow \psi) \Rightarrow \mathbf{CK}(\psi)$$

$$\mathbf{CK}(\phi) \Rightarrow \phi$$

$$\mathbf{CK}(\phi) \Rightarrow \mathbf{EK}(\mathbf{CK}(\phi))$$

$$\mathbf{CK}(\phi \Rightarrow \mathbf{EK}(\phi)) \Rightarrow (\phi \Rightarrow \mathbf{CK}(\phi))$$

(The last axiom is sometimes called the *induction axiom* for common knowledge.)

We also have the following rule of inference, similar to ordinary epistemic necessitation:

$$\text{from } \vdash \phi \text{ infer } \mathbf{CK}(\phi) \tag{9.13}$$

We can give a possible-worlds semantics for a version of common knowledge. We define a common-knowledge accessibility relation $c(g, w_1, w_2)$, which is satisfied when world w_2 is accessible to the group g in world w_1. The possible-worlds semantics for $\mathbf{CK}$ is that $\mathbf{CK}(G, \phi)$ is true in world w_i just in case ϕ is true in all worlds accessible to (the group denoted by) G (using c) from w_i. It is helpful to imagine a fictitious knower (sometimes called *any fool*) whose accessibility relation is the same as that of the group. That which "any fool" knows can then be taken as (a slightly weaker version of) common knowledge. (It is slightly weaker because the induction axiom for common knowledge does not follow from this definition.)

In the wise-man puzzle, one might ask why was it necessary for the king to tell the wise men that there was at least one white spot? After all, in the puzzle all three wise men had white spots, and each could see the others. It was perfectly obvious to each of them that there was at least one white spot! This is a subtle but important question, and its answer will help us to understand the role of common knowledge.

Line 2 of the wise-man proof is derived from the fact that the king said, in the presence of all, that there was at least one white spot. Although agent A knows (from his own observation) that there is at least one white spot, without the king having said it, A would not know that agent B knows that there is at least one white spot. Using the definition of $\mathbf{EK}$, line 2 could be derived from $\mathbf{EK}^2[\text{White(A)} \lor \text{White(B)}]$. We can show similarly that in the k-wise-men version of this puzzle, we need $\mathbf{EK}^k$. If we assume that the king's statement gives the wise men *common knowledge* that there is at least one white spot, then we can be assured that the degree of $\mathbf{EK}$ is high enough.

The concept of group knowledge plays an important role in reasoning about the effects of communication among agents. In fact, most communication among agents of a group has as its goal "climbing up the hierarchy" of group knowledge. These ideas have seen application in the analysis of distributed computer systems and in understanding communication among humans in natural language. In the latter case, it often is assumed that a statement uttered in the presence of other agents will result in those agents having common knowledge of the statement.

9.12 Equality, Quantification, and Knowledge

We next examine how the possible-worlds model handles some of the subtle problems that we described earlier during our discussion of the sentential model. One of these problems concerned substituting into knowledge statements. That is, we do not want (Cronus=Saturn),

(Jupiter=Zeus) and K(A,Father-Of(Zeus,Cronus)) to entail logically
K(A,Father-Of(Jupiter,Saturn)). Let us see how possible-worlds
semantics blocks this entailment. Our given statements have the value
true in the actual world, w_0. From the knowledge axiom (Axiom 9.2)
and K(A, Father-Of(Zeus,Cronus)), we observe that Father-Of(Zeus,
Cronus) has the value true in w_0, and therefore so does Father-Of(Jupiter,Saturn). Now, for K(A, Father-Of(Jupiter,Saturn)) to have
the value true in the actual world w_0, Father-Of(Jupiter,Saturn) must
have the value true in all worlds accessible to A from w_0. That cannot
be the case unless (Cronus=Saturn) and (Jupiter=Zeus) each have the
value true in all worlds accessible to A from w_0. For these statements to
have the value true in those worlds, however, A would have to know the
statements. Therefore, only if A does know these equalities would we be able
to conclude K(A,Father-Of(Jupiter,Saturn)); otherwise, we would not.
(In carrying out this analysis, we have assumed that the relation constant
"=" denotes the identity relation in all possible worlds.)

A possible-worlds analysis also allows us to make sense of quantified
knowledge formulas. There is no difficulty with a formula such as
K(A,(∃x Father-Of(Zeus,x))). For it to have the value true (in w_0),
(∃x Father-Of(Zeus,x)) must have the value true in all worlds accessible
to A from w_0. That is, in each of these worlds, there must be *someone*
who is the father of Zeus. It certainly does not have to be the same
individual in each world—a mild condition. Since the father of Zeus might
be different in each of A's worlds, it would not make sense to say that A
knows who is the father of Zeus. He merely knows that there is some
individual who is the father of Zeus, and that is all that is asserted by
K(A,(∃x Father-Of(Zeus,x))).

How would we represent that A knows who is the father of Zeus? It would
seem that in each of the worlds accessible to A from w_0, the father of Zeus
would have to be the same individual. That is exactly the meaning of the
formula (∃x K(A,Father-Of(Zeus,x))) under possible-worlds semantics
(assuming the obvious denotations for Father-Of and Zeus). A semantical
account of that formula is as follows. There is some object in the domain,
call the object k, such that in each world, w, accessible to A from w_0, the
formula Father-Of(Zeus,C_w) has the value true, where C_w is the object
constant associated with k in world w. Although k may have different
names in each of the worlds (one such name might be Saturn, another
Cronus), these names denote the same individual in all worlds. Therefore,
it seems reasonable to say that A knows *who* is the father of Zeus.

Although it might not yet have been obvious, the same object constant,
function constant, or relation constant might have different denotations in
different possible worlds. Thus, for K(A,White(Snow)) to represent that A
knows that snow is white in w_0, we would have to ensure that Snow and
White have the same denotations in all the worlds accessible to A from w_0.
The possibility of having different denotations for terms in different worlds

allows us to model agents with different vocabularies and concepts, but this flexibility greatly complicates the notation, and it is convenient sometimes to assume that the denotations of terms are the same in all worlds.

If the interpretation of a term is the same in all possible worlds, then that term is called a *rigid designator*. Constant symbols that are rigid designators are candidates for *standard names* for objects—names that are universally used and understood by all knowers. In possible-worlds semantics, one assumes that an agent knows who or what is denoted by a rigid designator. Usually, we think of numerals such as 3 and π as being rigid designators for the numbers they denote. However, `Plus(1,2)` might not be a rigid designator unless `Plus` had the same interpretation in all possible worlds. For example, from `K(A,(PN(Mike) = 854-0449))`, we could conclude that `A` knows Mike's telephone number if `854-0449` is a rigid designator. However, if `A` merely knows that Mike's telephone number is the same as Lennie's (i.e., `K(A,(PN(Mike) = PN(Lennie)))`), we would not necessarily want to conclude that `A` knows Mike's telephone number. (The interpretations of `PN(Mike)` might be different in different possible worlds.)

9.13 Bibliographical and Historical Remarks

Reasoning about knowledge and belief has a long tradition in philosophical logic and in AI. In logic, much of the work is based on Kripke's possible-world semantics, which he developed for the modal logic of necessity and possibility [Kripke 1963, Kripke 1971]. It was Kripke who showed that the different axiom systems for modal logics correspond to certain restrictions on the accessibility relation for the possible-world models of those systems. Sets of possible worlds and accessibility relations among them are often called *Kripke structures*. Modal logics have a variety of applications: There are modal epistemic (knowledge) and doxastic (belief) logics, modal temporal logics, modal deontic logics (having to do with obligation), modal dynamic logics (used in the study of program semantics), and others. [Hughes 1968] is the classic text on modal logics.

(There has been much discussion about the ontological status of possible worlds—that is, do they really exist? Since we take the position that what "exists" are exactly those *invented* objects that we find useful to include in our conceptualizations, we find much of the philosophical arguments about possible worlds rather meaningless. For a sample of the issues raised in these arguments see [Stalnaker 1985].)

Hintikka [Hintikka 1962, 1971] used notions similar to Kripke's possible-world semantics in his modal logics of knowledge and belief, which are the basis for our Section 9.8. Moore [Moore 1979, 1985a] then showed how this semantics could be captured in ordinary (nonmodal) first-order logic. Moore's major result was to show how to combine methods for reasoning about knowledge with similar techniques for reasoning about action.

Appelt [Appelt 1985a, 1985b] used Moore's method in a planning system for generating natural-language expressions calculated by a "speaker" to have specified effects on the "cognitive structure" of a "hearer."

Focusing on possible-world semantics, Halpern [Halpern 1985, 1987] presented thorough surveys of the modal logics of knowledge and belief; Halpern and Moses discussed the application of these logics in distributed systems [Halpern 1984]. Our treatment of common knowledge is based on that of Moses [Moses 1986].

We find sentential semantics for a logic of belief somewhat more appealing than possible-world semantics. It is consistent with our view that an agent's knowledge actually consists of declarative sentences, and it also is well adapted to modeling resource-limited reasoning. Our treatment of sentential semantics and proof methods is based on the work of Konolige [Konolige 1984, 1985] (who also describes conditions under which his sentential logics correspond to the modal systems K, T, $S4$, and $S5$.)

Haas [Haas 1986] gave an alternative (and nonmodal) sentential logic for knowledge and belief based on a quoting convention. An agent A believes P just when A has a string denoting P among its sentences. Haas's convention is to let 'P' denote P; BEL(A, 'P') then has intended meaning, "The agent denoted by A believes the proposition denoted by 'P'." We use this convention ourselves in Chapter 10. See also [Perlis 1987].

Reasoning about one's own beliefs can involve us also in a study of self-referring formulas and attempts to describe the truth and consistency of formulas in the very language of the formulas. Perlis has done some interesting work in this area [Perlis 1985].

Levesque [Levesque 1984] and Fagin [Fagin 1985] separately proposed modifications to possible-world semantics that attempt to take into account resource-limited reasoning.

"Quantifying-in" to modal contexts has been a controversial topic in logic. Quine [Quine 1971] argued that quantifying-in is meaningless, although we think that (suitably interpreted) it can be used to say that someone knows or believes *that* something is the case without saying *what* is the case. Moore [Moore 1979, 1985a] and Konolige [Konolige 1984, 1985] gave good accounts of the notion for possible-world and sentential semantics, respectively. Kripke [Kripke 1972] called those terms having the same denotation in all possible worlds *rigid designators*. Moore linked standard names with rigid designators, saying: "The conclusion that standard identifiers are rigid designators seems inescapable. If a particular expression can always be used by an agent to identify its referent for any other agent, then there must not be any possible circumstances under which it could refer to something else. Otherwise, the first agent could not be sure that the second was in a position to rule out those other possibilities" [Moore 1985a, p. 332].

The bullet operator was suggested by Konolige [Konolige 1984]. Geissler and Konolige [Geissler 1986, Konolige 1986] adapted a resolution theorem prover to prove theorems in the sentential modal logic of belief (with bullet operators).

Other approaches to representing statements about knowledge and belief have been proposed. McCarthy [McCarthy 1979a] showed how several problems of knowledge and belief could be dealt with by including in one's conceptualization of the world the *concept* of ordinary objects as well as the objects themselves.

Rosenschein and Kaelbling[Rosenschein 1986] proposed using a modal language (based on possible-world semantics) for expressing what a designer would have an agent know (or believe). Then, instead of using these statements directly to populate the declarative knowledge base of the agent, they showed how to compile this description into a finite-state-machine realization of the agent. Even though one then would not say that the agent had any *sentences* in its implementation, one could still say that it *believed* this or that. McCarthy [McCarthy 1979b] also discussed circumstances under which one might say that a machine (even a very simple one) *believed* things.

A volume edited by Halpern [Halpern 1986] contains several papers on representing and reasoning about knowledge and belief.

Exercises

1. *One cannot both know ϕ and know $\neg\phi$.* Prove

$$\mathbf{K}_\alpha(\phi) \;\Rightarrow\; \neg\mathbf{K}_\alpha(\neg\phi)$$

2. *Resolution.* Show that a logic of knowledge that includes Axiom 9.1 and Rule 9.5 also permits the following rule:

$$(\mathbf{K}_\alpha(L_1 \vee L_2) \;\wedge\; \mathbf{K}_\alpha(\neg L_1)) \;\Rightarrow\; \mathbf{K}_\alpha(L_2)$$

where L_1 and L_2 are positive atoms. That is, agents can use *resolution* as well as modus ponens.

3. *Conjunction.* Prove

$$\mathbf{K}(\alpha,\phi) \;\wedge\; \mathbf{K}(\alpha,\psi) \;\Leftrightarrow\; \mathbf{K}(\alpha,(\phi \wedge \psi))$$

4. *Brouwer Axiom.* Prove the Brouwer Axiom in the system $S5$:

$$\neg\mathbf{K}_\alpha(\neg\mathbf{K}_\alpha(\phi)) \;\Rightarrow\; \phi$$

Which axioms are needed to prove it?

5. *Rule 9.7.* Prove the metatheorem in Rule 9.7.

6. *Sam and John.* Suppose we are given the following sentences:

$$\mathbf{B_J}(\mathbf{B_S}(P) \lor \mathbf{B_S}(Q))$$

(John believes that Sam believes P or that Sam believes Q.)

$$\mathbf{B_J}(\mathbf{B_S}(P \Rightarrow R))$$

(John believes that Sam believes P⇒R.)

$$\mathbf{B_J}(\mathbf{B_S}(\neg R))$$

(John believes that Sam believes ¬R.)

  a. Prove $\mathbf{B_J}(\mathbf{B_S}(Q))$ using attachment. What assumptions did you make about the agents' reasoning abilities?

  b. Replace $\mathbf{B}$ by $\mathbf{K}$ in the given formulas and prove $\mathbf{K_J}(\mathbf{K_S}(Q))$. What axioms of knowledge and inference rules did you use?

7. *Properties of accessibility.*

  a. Prove that a reflexive accessibility relation among possible worlds implies the knowledge axiom, $\mathbf{K}_\alpha(P) \Rightarrow P$.

  b. Prove that a transitive relation implies the positive-introspection axiom.

  c. Prove that a Euclidean relation implies the negative-introspection axiom.

  d. Prove that a symmetric relation implies the Brouwer axiom.

  e. Show that Axiom 9.1 follows from this statement about possible-worlds semantics: If ϕ is true in every world accessible for α from world w, then $\mathbf{K}(\alpha, \phi)$ is true in w.

8. *Brouwer and belief.* Is it reasonable for the Brouwer axiom to hold for belief? Discuss.

9. *A visiting Swede.* Consider the sentence, "John believes that a Swede will visit him." There are two possible interpretations of this sentence. In one, John has a belief that a particular individual will visit him (perhaps not even realizing that the individual is a Swede), and the speaker of the sentence uses the phrase "a Swede" to describe that individual. This interpretation is called the *de re* reading of the sentence.

   In the other interpretation, called the *de dicto* reading, John believes that some Swede will visit him (perhaps not knowing who that person will turn out to be). In this case, "a Swede" is John's description of the person who will visit him.

Express both the *de re* and the *de dicto* readings of the sentence in a logical language using the **B** operator.

CHAPTER 10

Metaknowledge and Metareasoning

ALTHOUGH THE CONCEPTS DISCUSSED in Chapter 9 allow us to talk about the logical properties of knowledge and belief, they are inadequate for formalizing the *process* of inference. For this purpose, we need to treat expressions, subexpressions, and sets of expressions as objects in our universe of discourse, so that we can describe how those objects are manipulated in the course of inference. In this chapter, we introduce a suitable conceptualization and predicate-calculus vocabulary. We show how to use our vocabulary in describing the process of inference, and we discuss a number of ways in which such descriptions can be used.

The existence of a formal description for the process of inference is important because it allows us to refine our characterization of belief. As mentioned in Chapter 9, it is inappropriate to assume that an intelligent agent believes the logical closure of the sentences in its database. It is more appropriate to define an agent's beliefs as those sentences that it can derive in a given amount of time using a given inference procedure. Our conceptualization of the inference process allows us to define this notion of belief formally; as a result, we can create agents capable of reasoning in detail about the inferential abilities and beliefs of other agents.

Another important use of our conceptualization and vocabulary is in introspection. An intelligent agent should be able to observe and describe its own problem-solving processes, and it should be able to understand problem-solving hints provided by others. It should be able to reason about its problem-solving performance; e.g., to assess the merits of a particular problem-solving method or to compare it to alternatives. An intelligent agent also should be able to use the results of this deliberation in controlling subsequent inference. All these abilities require an adequate formalism for representing information about reasoning.

A warning about reading this chapter: Throughout the discussion, we talk about expressions using a particular syntax, and it is easy to get the impression that we are implying that such expressions must exist explicitly in an agent's "mind." This is not our intention. Rather, we are dealing with an abstraction of an agent's beliefs, and their physical representation may be different from the expressions we describe. It is convenient, however, to describe an agent's inference processes *as if* the agent were manipulating sentences of this form.

10.1 Metalanguage

In formalizing the process of inference, we use a conceptualization in which expressions, subexpressions, and sequences of expressions are objects in the universe of discourse and in which there are functions and relations appropriate to these objects. In this respect, our treatment of language here is similar to that in Chapter 2. The key difference is that in Chapter 2 we used English to describe our conceptualization, whereas in this chapter we use predicate calculus. This is interesting in that we are using a formal language to describe a formal language; in this case, the latter is a formal language with essentially the same syntax as the language of description.

In our conceptualization of expressions, we treat symbols and operators as primitive objects. There are two types of symbols: variables and constants. Constants are further classified as object constants, function constants, and relation constants.

We conceptualize complex expressions as sequences of subexpressions. In particular, every complex expression is viewed as a sequence of its immediate subexpressions. For example, we conceptualize the literal ¬P(A+B+C,D) as a sequence consisting of the operator ¬ and the atomic sentence P(A+B+C,D). The atomic sentence is the sequence consisting of the relation constant P and the terms A+B+C and D. The first of these terms consists of the function constant + and the object constants A, B, and C.

It is important to note that we are *not* conceptualizing expressions as sequences of characters. This has the disadvantage that we cannot describe certain details of syntax such as parenthesization and spacing. However, in this chapter we are concerned with the process of inference, and for that purpose such details are nonessential.

The key issue in describing expressions is naming. Suppose that we have some sentences about a person named John; e.g., the sentence Large(John), asserting that John is a large person. Suppose also that we want to say something about the symbol John; e.g., that it is a small symbol. How can we refer to this symbol in order to express this property?

Clearly we cannot simply use the symbol itself, or we would end up with the contradictory sentence `Small(John)`.

Fortunately, it is easy to avoid contradictions of this sort in describing expressions by using terms to refer to symbols that are distinct from the terms we use to refer to the objects those symbols represent. Although we could do this without extending our language at all, an easy language extension dramatically simplifies the task of naming expressions. In particular, we add infinitely many new object constants, each of which is a legal expression in quotation marks. The intention is to have each such symbol designate the expression enclosed by those quotation marks. Thus, the symbol `"John"` designates the symbol `John`, and the symbol `"Father(John)"` designates the expression `Father(John)`.

With this extension, we can deal with the difficulty mentioned above. When we want to say something about the person named `John`, we use the symbol `John`. When we want to say something about the symbol `John`, we use the symbol `"John"`.

```
Large(John)

Small("John")
```

Note that, by nesting quoted expressions within quotes, we can talk about quoted symbols and expressions involving quoted symbols. In fact, we can define a tower of languages in which the sentences at each level describe the sentences at lower levels. In this chapter, we concentrate on just two levels.

Unfortunately, this quoting extension alone is inadequate for our purposes. In particular, we often need to write metalevel sentences that quantify over parts of expressions, and we cannot do this with this extension alone. Suppose, for example, we wanted to say that John and Mary agree about what Bill's telephone number is. We could try to write this as shown below. The symbol `Bel` here is intended to denote the relation holding between each individual and the sentences that individual believes.

```
∃n Bel(John,"Phone(Bill)=n") ∧ Bel(Mary,"Phone(Bill)=n")
```

The problem with this is that the variable n appearing in the quoted expressions is taken literally. As written, this sentence says that John believes the sentence `Phone(Bill)=n` (literally n), and so does Mary. What we want to say is that there is some specific number that both John and Mary ascribe to Bill. That is the purpose of the surrounding quantifier, but quantifiers have no effect on the constituents of quoted expressions. We could equally well have used a different quantifier or a different variable, or we could have dropped the quantifier altogether.

To solve this problem, we use an alternative technique for naming expressions. Since an expression in our conceptualization is a sequence of subexpressions, it is appropriate to use sequence notation in denoting an expression, instead of using the quoted symbol for that expression. Thus, we can denote the expression ¬P(A+B+C,D) with either the quoted symbol "¬P(A+B+C,D)" or the list ["¬","P(A+B+C,D)"]. We can denote the expression P(A+B+C,D) with either the quoted symbol "P(A+B+C,D)" or the list ["P","A+B+C","D"]. We can denote the expression A+B+C with either the quoted symbol "A+B+C" or the list ["+","A","B","C"].

This alternative approach to naming allows us to solve the telephone-number problem. We simply say that there is a numerical symbol n and both John and Mary believe that the corresponding number is Bill's telephone number.

$$\exists n \; \text{Bel}(\text{John},["=","\text{Phone(Bill)}",n]) \land$$
$$\text{Bel}(\text{Mary},["=","\text{Phone(Bill)}",n])$$

While the use of list notation allows us to describe the structure of complex expressions in arbitrary detail, it is somewhat awkward. For example, the list ["=","Phone(Bill)",n] does not look much like a sentence. Fortunately, we can eliminate this difficulty by employing a suitable "unquoting" convention. Rather than using list notation in designating an expression, we write the expression in quotes and add unquoting marks < and > around any subexpression that is not to be taken literally. For example, we would write the expression "Phone(Bill)=<n>" instead of the preceding version. With this convention, our assertion about John's and Mary's belief would be stated as follows.

$$\exists n \; \text{Bel}(\text{John},"\text{Phone(Bill)}=<n>") \land \text{Bel}(\text{Mary},"\text{Phone(Bill)}=<n>")$$

In addition to our vocabulary for denoting expressions, we assume that our metalevel language contains the relation constants Objconst, Funconst, Relconst, and Variable to denote the corresponding properties. The following sentences are examples of the use of these constants.

$$\text{Variable}("x")$$

$$\text{Objconst}("John")$$

$$\text{Funconst}("Father")$$

$$\text{Relconst}("Large")$$

With this vocabulary and semantics, we can write arbitrary sentences about expressions, just as in our baselevel language we write sentences about apples and oranges, children's blocks, and digital circuits. The next few sections provide examples.

10.2 Clausal Form

One thing we can do with our metalevel language is to define other languages; e.g., in this section we define the syntax of clausal form. The axiomatization proceeds as in Chapters 2 and 4, working from symbols to more complex expressions.

A *constant* is either an object constant, a function constant, or a relation constant.

$$\forall x \ \text{Constant}(x) \Leftrightarrow \text{Objconst}(x) \lor \text{Funconst}(x) \lor \text{Relconst}(x)$$

A *term* is either an object constant, a variable, or a functional expression.

$$\forall x \ \text{Term}(x) \Leftrightarrow \text{Objconst}(x) \lor \text{Variable}(x) \lor \text{Funexpr}(x)$$

A *term list* is an ordered list of terms.

$$\forall l \ \text{Termlist}(l) \Leftrightarrow (\forall x \ \text{Member}(x,l) \Rightarrow \text{Term}(x))$$

A *functional expression* is an expression made up of a function constant and a list of terms. In our definition here, we ignore the arity of the function constant.

$$\forall f \forall l \ \text{Funexpr}(f.l) \Leftrightarrow (\text{Funconst}(f) \land \text{Termlist}(l))$$

An *atomic sentence* is an expression made up of a relation constant and a suitable list of terms. Again, we ignore arity.

$$\forall r \forall l \ \text{Atom}(r.l) \Leftrightarrow (\text{Relconst}(r) \land \text{Termlist}(l))$$

A *literal* is either an atomic sentence or the negation of an atomic sentence.

$$\forall x \ \text{Literal}(x) \Leftrightarrow (\text{Atom}(x) \lor (\exists z \ x = "\neg <z>" \land \text{Atom}(z)))$$

A *clause* usually is defined as a set of literals, in which ordering is unimportant. However, to facilitate the definition of ordered resolution, we here define a clause as an ordered list of literals.

$$\forall c \ \text{Clause}(c) \Leftrightarrow (\forall x \ \text{Member}(x,c) \Rightarrow \text{Literal}(x))$$

A *database* often is defined as an unordered set of clauses. For ease in subsequent exposition, however, we here define a database as an ordered list of clauses.

$$\forall d \; \text{Database}(d) \Leftrightarrow (\forall x \; \text{Member}(x,d) \Rightarrow \text{Clause}(x))$$

Having defined clausal form, we now turn to the definition of the resolution principle.

10.3 Resolution Principle

Recall from Chapter 4 that the resolution principle is a rule of inference that allows us to derive a conclusion from a pair of premises. In this section, we formalize the resolution principle as a ternary relation that holds of three clauses whenever the third clause is a resolvent of the first two clauses.

The basic element in resolution is unification, and the basic element in unification is the notion of substitution. In our formalization, we represent a substitution as a list of pairs, each associating a variable with its replacement. Thus, the following term designates the substitution associating the variable x with the expression F(z) and the variable y with the term B.

$$["x"/"F(z)","y"/"B"]$$

We use the binary function constant Subst to designate the function that maps an expression and a substitution into the expression that results from applying the substitution to the expression. The sentences shown below describe this function. The result of applying the empty substitution to an expression is just the expression itself. If the expression is a constant, then the substitution has no effect. If the expression is a variable and the variable has a binding in the substitution, the result is the expression associated with that variable in the substitution. If the expression is a composite expression, the result is the expression formed by applying the substitution to the parts of the expression.

$\forall x \; \text{Subst}(x,[])=x$

$\forall x \forall s \; \text{Constant}(x) \Rightarrow \text{Subst}(x,s)=x$

$\forall x \forall z \forall s \; \text{Variable}(x) \Rightarrow \text{Subst}(x,(x/z).s)=z$

$\forall x \forall y \forall z \forall s \; \text{Variable}(x) \wedge y \neq x \Rightarrow \text{Subst}(x,(y/z).s)=\text{Subst}(x,s)$

$\forall x \forall l \forall s \; \text{Subst}(x.l,s)=\text{Subst}(x,s).\text{Subst}(l,s)$

We can extend a substitution to include a binding for a new variable by substituting the value into the bindings for the variables in the initial substitution and then adding the new association to the old substitution.

```
∀x∀z Extend([],x,z)=[x/z]

∀u∀v∀x∀z∀s
    Extend((u/v).s,x,z)=(u/Subst(v,[x/z])).Extend(s,x,z)
```

Two substitutions can be combined by incrementally extending one with each of the elements of the other, as described by the following axioms.

```
∀s Combine(s,[])=s

∀s∀t∀x∀z Combine(s,(x/z).t)=Combine(Extend(s,x,z),t)
```

We use the ternary relation constant Mgu to designate the relation that holds between two expressions and their most general unifier, if one exists. The mgu of two identical expressions is just the empty list. If one of the expressions is a variable and is not contained in the other expression, then the mgu is the singleton substitution in which the variable is bound to the other expression. The mgu of two composite expressions is the mgu of the parts of the expresssicns.

```
∀x Mgu(x,x,[])

∀x∀y Variable(x) ∧ ¬Among(x,y) ⇒ Mgu(x,y,[x/y])

∀x∀y ¬Variable(x) ∧ Variable(y) ∧ ¬Among(y,x)
        ⇒ Mgu(x,y,[y/x])

∀x∀y∀l∀m∀s∀t Mgu(x,y,s) ∧ Mgu(Subst(l,s),Subst(m,s),t)
                ⇒ Mgu(x.l,y.m,Combine(s,t))
```

Finally, we use the Mgu relation to define the resolution principle. Ordered resolution is simpler than general resolution, so we present that definition first. If a clause begins with a literal x and another clause begins with a negative literal the argument of which unifies with x, then one resolvent of the two clauses is obtained by substituting the unifier into the clause formed of the remaining elements of the two clauses.

```
∀x∀y∀s Mgu(x,y,s)) ⇔
        Resolvent(x.l,"¬<y>".m,Subst(Append(l,m),s))
```

In the general case, we allow resolution on any literals in the two clauses. If a literal x is an element of one clause, ¬y is an element of another clause, and there is a most general unifier for x and y, then the resolvent of the two clauses is formed by deleting the complementary literals, appending the remaining literals, and applying the unifier. To be rigidly accurate, we also should change the names of the remaining variables, but we have omitted that detail here for simplicity.

```
∀c∀d∀x∀y∀s  Member(x,c) ∧ Member("¬<y>",d) ∧ Mgu(x,y,s)) ⟺
    Resolvent(c,d,Subst(Append(Delete(x,c),Delete("¬<y>",d)),s))
```

In the following sections, we use this definition of the resolution principle in formalizing various resolution strategies.

10.4 Inference Procedures

In Chapter 3, we defined an inference procedure to be a function that maps an initial database Δ and a positive integer n into the database for the n-th step of inference on Δ. In what follows, we use the function constant `Step` to denote an arbitrary inference procedure.

A Markov inference procedure is a function that maps a database into a successor database; in other words, the choice of database on each step is determined entirely by the database for the last step, and all other information about history is ignored. Given a Markov inference procedure named `Next`, it is easy to define the corresponding inference procedure. The value on the first step is just the initial database. Thereafter, the value is the result of applying `Next` to the preceding database.

```
∀d Step(d,1)=d
```

```
∀d∀n  n>1 ⟹ Step(d,n)=Next(Step(d,n-1))
```

Although there is no explicit dependence on history in a Markov inference procedure, it is possible to define some history-based procedures in this way by exploiting the information about history implicit in the form and order of sentences in each database.

As an example, consider the case of depth-first, statically biased, ordered resolution. If we restrict our attention to backward–Horn-clause databases with queries restricted to conjunctions of positive literals, we can define this procedure very simply.

First, we define the function `concs`, which maps a clause and a database into a list of all resolvents in which the specified clause is a parent and in which the other parent is a member of the specified database.

```
∀c Concs(c,[])=[]
```

```
∀c∀d∀e∀l Resolvent(c,d,e) ⟹ Concs(c,d.l)=e.Concs(c,l)
```

```
∀c∀d∀e∀l ¬Resolvent(c,d,e) ⟹ Concs(c,d.l)=Concs(c,l)
```

The initial database is obtained by adding the clause (with answer literal, if desired) obtained from the negation of the query to the front of the database of backward Horn clauses. On each step, the procedure removes the first element of the database and adds all one-step conclusions to the remainder of the database.

$$\texttt{Next(d)=Append(Concs(Car(d),d),Cdr(d))}$$

The following sequence of databases illustrates this procedure in operation. The goal is to show that there is a z such that R(z) is true. On the first step, the goal clause is removed and is replaced by two subgoals. The first of these is then reduced to a further subgoal on the second step. This subgoal then resolves with the unit clause to produce the the empty clause.

	[¬P(z)]	[¬M(z)]	[]
[¬R(z)]	[¬Q(z)]	[¬Q(z)]	[¬Q(z)]
[M(A)]	[M(A)]	[M(A)]	[M(A)]
[P(x),¬M(x)]	[P(x),¬M(x)]	[P(x),¬M(x)]	[P(x),¬M(x)]
[Q(x),¬N(x)]	[Q(x),¬N(x)]	[Q(x),¬N(x)]	[Q(x),¬N(x)]
[R(x),¬P(x)]	[R(x),¬P(x)]	[R(x),¬P(x)]	[R(x),¬P(x)]
[R(x),¬Q(x)]	[R(x),¬Q(x)]	[R(x),¬Q(x)]	[R(x),¬Q(x)]

This procedure is interesting because we normally think of depth-first search as requiring information about history; in fact, the procedure works only because the necessary historical information is captured implicitly in the database ordering.

10.5 Derivability and Belief

In this section, we use the formalization presented in the previous few sections in defining the concept of resolution derivability. We present two nonequivalent definitions. In both cases, derivability is conceptualized as a binary relation between a database and an individual sentence.

According to our first definition, a sentence is derivable from a database if and only if it is in the database or is a consequence of applying a rule of inference to sentences that are derivable from that database. Using the Resolvent relation defined earlier, we can formalize this definition as follows.

```
∀d∀r Derivable(d,r) ⇔
  Member(r,d) ∨
  (∃p∃q Derivable(d,p) ∧ Derivable(d,q) ∧ Resolvent(p,q,r))
```

This is equivalent to saying that there is a proof of the sentence from the database using the resolution principle. There is no mention of restrictions on the application of the resolution rule and there is no mention of any ordering on applications of the rule. This means that there are sentences that are derivable according to this definition yet cannot be derived by resolution procedures with specific applicability or ordering restrictions.

To eliminate this peculiarity, we introduce the notion of *restricted derivability*. We say that a sentence is derivable by a resolution procedure Step from an initial database if and only if on some step the procedure produces a database containing that sentence.

$$\forall d \forall p \ \text{Derivable(d,p)} \Leftrightarrow (\exists n \ \text{Member(p,Step(d,n))})$$

As mentioned in Chapter 4, resolution is not *generatively* complete, but it is *refutation* complete. Derivability concerns the generation of sentences, not their refutation; and so we need another concept. We say that a sentence is provable by a resolution procedure if and only if the empty clause can be derived by that procedure from the clauses in the database and those in the clausal form of the negated sentence.

$$\forall d \forall p \ \text{Provable(d,p)} \Leftrightarrow \text{Derivable(Append(Clauses("}\neg\text{<p>"),d),[])}$$

The function Clauses maps a sentence into a list of the clauses in its clausal form. The definition is straightforward, and we leave it for the reader to work out.

Finally, we can use the the notion of provability in defining what it means for an agent to believe a sentence. We assume that there is a function named Data that maps an agent into a list of sentences explicitly stored in that agent's database. Then, we define belief as a binary relation that holds between an agent and a sentence if and only if the sentence is provable from the agent's database.

$$\forall a \forall p \ \text{Bel(a,p)} \Leftrightarrow \text{Provable(Data(a),p)}$$

Like the sentential notion of belief defined in Chapter 9, this version of belief depends on the inference procedure of the agent being described. In Chapter 9, this dependence takes the form of a belief operator defined via procedural attachment. The treatment in this chapter has the advantage that it allows the inference procedures of agents to be described declaratively, an approach more in keeping with the general theme of this book.

10.6 Metalevel Reasoning

One of the advantages of encoding metalevel knowledge as sentences in predicate calculus is that we can use automated reasoning procedures in answering questions about any reasoning process so described. Insofar as this involves reasoning about reasoning, we often speak of the process as *metalevel reasoning*, or *metareasoning*.

Unfortunately, the automated reasoning procedures presented earlier in this book are not wholly adequate for metareasoning. In our formalization of knowledge about reasoning procedures, we assume definitions for the fundamental type relations `Variable`, `Objconst`, `Funconst`, and `Relconst`, and we exploit the relationship between quoted symbols and lists of quoted symbols. For example, we assume that `Variable("x")` is true and that the symbol `"P(A,B)"` designates the same expression as the term `["P","A","B"]`. Although we can encode such information in our metalanguage, there is a problem. Since there are infinitely many symbols and we cannot quantify over parts of symbols, we need infinitely many axioms to define such relationships completely. Fortunately, we can get the same effect as having this infinity of axioms by making several simple modifications to our automated reasoning procedures.

As an example, consider a metareasoning procedure based on resolution. In this procedure, we implicitly encode information about the fundamental type relations by adding appropriate procedural attachments, and we deal with the equivalence of quoted symbols and lists of quoted symbols by modifying the unifier.

The procedural attachments for the four relations are similar to one another. As an example, consider a clause containing a literal of the form `Variable("$\nu$")`. (The Greek letter ν here stands for any expression in our language; we do not mean the symbol ν literally, which is not an expression of the language.) If ν is a variable, the literal is true, and the clause can be dropped from the database (since it cannot be used in deriving the empty clause). If ν is anything other than a variable, the literal is false, and it can be dropped from the clause. For clauses containing a literal of the form `¬Variable("$\nu$")`, the results are reversed.

The equivalence of quoted symbols and lists of quoted symbols is handled through the use of an appropriately modified unifier (see Figure 10.1). The procedure is the same as the one defined in Chapter 4, except for the handling of quoted expressions. When the modified procedure encounters a quoted expression, it calls the auxiliary procedure `Match` on its other argument and the expression within the quotes to determine whether the latter expression is properly described by the former. The `Match` procedure makes this determination by recursively examining the the two expressions (using the `Explode` procedure which expands quoted symbols into their subparts) and returns an appropriate binding list unless a mismatch occurs. For example, when called with the expressions `"P(A,B)"` and `["P",x,"B"]`, this procedure would return the binding list `[x/"A"]`.

As an illustration of the entire reasoning procedure in operation, recall the first definition of derivability given in Section 10.5, and consider the problem of showing that the empty clause is derivable from a database

```
Recursive Procedure Mgu (x,y)
    Begin x=y ==> Return(),
          Variable(x) ==> Return(Mguvar(x,y)),
          Variable(y) ==> Return(Mguvar(y,x)),
          Quoted(x) ==> Return(Match(y,Part(x,2))),
          Quoted(y) ==> Return(Match(x,Part(y,2))),
          Constant(x) or Constant(y) ==> Return(False),
          Not(Length(x)=Length(y)) ==> Return(False),
          Begin i <- 0,
                g <- [],
          Tag   i=Length(x) ==> Return(g),
                s <- Mgu(Part(x,i),Part(y,i))
                s=False ==> Return(False),
                g <- Compose(g,s),
                x <- Substitute(x,g),
                y <- Substitute(y,g),
                i <- i+1,
                Goto Tag
          End
    End

Recursive Procedure Match (x,y)
    Begin Variable(x) ==> Return([x/"y"]),
          Quoted(x) ==> (Explode(x)=y ==> Return()),
          Constant(x) or Constant(y) ==> Return(False),
          Not(Length(x)=Length(y)) ==> Return(False),
          Begin i <- 0,
                g <- [],
          Tag   i=Length(x) ==> Return(g),
                s <- Match(Part(x,i),Part(y,i))
                s=False ==> Return(False),
                g <- Compose(g,s),
                x <- Substitute(x,g),
                i <- i+1,
                Goto Tag
          End
    End
```

Figure 10.1   Procedure for computing the most general unifier.

consisting of the two clauses [Q] and [¬Q]. The following sequence of clauses is an abbreviated set of support derivation of this result.

1. [¬Derivable("[[Q],[¬Q]]",[])]
2. [¬Derivable("[[Q],[¬Q]]",p),¬Derivable("[[Q],[¬Q]]",q),
   ¬Resolvent(p,q,[])]
3. [¬Member(p,"[[Q],[¬Q]]"),¬Derivable("[[Q],[¬Q]]",q),
   ¬Resolvent(p,q,[])]
4. [¬Derivable("[[Q],[¬Q]]",q),¬Resolvent("[Q]",q,[])]
5. [¬Member(q,"[[Q],[¬Q]]"),¬Resolvent("[Q]",q,[])]
6. [¬Member(q,"[[¬Q]]"),¬Resolvent("[Q]",q,[])]
7. [¬Resolvent("[Q]","[¬Q]",[])]
8. [¬Mgu("Q","Q",s)]
9. []

According to the definition in Section 10.5, a clause is derivable if it is the resolvent of two other derivable clauses. We use this fact at the start of our derivation to reduce the goal in the first clause to the subgoals in the second clause. The definition also tells us that a clause is derivable from a database if it is a member of that database. This allows us to reduce the second clause to the third. At this point, we use the Mgu procedure described previously to unify the literal Member(p,"[[Q],[¬Q]]") from clause 3 and the literal Member(x,x.1) from the definition of the Member relation. We then substitute the first element of the quoted list for p and drop the first literal of this clause to get clause 4. The handling of the other derivability goal is similar and ultimately leads to clause 7. Finally, using the definitions of ordered resolvent and mgu, we produce the empty clause.

Working through an example of this sort makes clear the problem with metalevel reasoning: It can be extremely expensive. Reasoning about one step of a baselevel deduction can require numerous steps of metalevel deduction.

10.7 Bilevel Reasoning

Baselevel reasoning and metalevel reasoning are both *monolevel* in that the databases they manipulate consist entirely of sentences of one type (either baselevel or metalevel). In this section, we discuss *bilevel-reasoning* techniques that apply to databases consisting of both baselevel and metalevel sentences.

A *bilevel database* is a database that consists of baselevel and/or metalevel sentences. Either set can be empty, but then the situation is much less interesting. Note that each sentence in a bilevel database must be either a baselevel or a metalevel sentence. No mixed-level sentences are allowed. Note also that no metametalevel sentences are allowed.

For the purposes of our discussion here, we assume that it is possible to tell whether each sentence in a bilevel database is baselevel or metalevel; therefore, we can partition any bilevel database into two disjoint lists, one containing only baselevel sentences and one containing only metalevel sentences. We use the function *data* in referring to these subsets. If Ω is a bilevel database, then $data(\Omega, 1)$ is the set of baselevel sentences in Ω, and $data(\Omega, 2)$ is the set of metalevel sentences.

The simplest sort of bilevel reasoning procedure is one in which the baselevel and metalevel databases are treated independently. Suppose, for example, that we are given a Markov inference procedure *next* defined for monolevel databases. We can extend this procedure to bilevel databases by applying it to its two subsets and adjoining the results. (We revert here to our informal mathematical language to avoid confusion between our informal description of this bilevel procedure and the formal description of the baselevel procedure in the metalevel database.)

$$next(\Omega) = append(next(data(\Omega, 2)), next(data(\Omega, 1))$$

The situation becomes much more interesting when there is a connection between the two databases. In writing a bilevel database, we often use metalevel sentences to describe the baselevel database and to prescribe or constrain baselevel inference actions.

As an example, consider the following bilevel database. We assume that P, Q, and R are baselevel relation constants, and we use the Next function as a prescription for manipulations of the baselevel sentences in this database.

```
[Next("[[P],[¬P,Q],[¬P,R]]")="[[P],[¬P,Q],[¬P,R],[Q]]"]

[P]

[¬P,Q]

[¬P,R]
```

Since Next is interpreted prescriptively here, we probably would want our inference procedure to produce the following database. The baselevel portion corresponds exactly to the database prescribed in the metalevel sentence.

```
[Next("[[P],[¬P,Q],[¬P,R]]")="[[P],[¬P,Q],[¬P,R],[Q]]"]

[P]

[¬P,Q]

[¬P,R]

[Q]
```

On the other hand, we probably would be less happy with a procedure that produced the following database. Although R is a logical consequence of the preceding baselevel sentences, its inclusion in the baselevel database contradicts the metalevel prescription.

[Next("[[P],[¬P,Q],[¬P,R]]")="[[P],[¬P,Q],[¬P,R],[Q]]"]

[P]

[¬P,Q]

[¬P,R]

[R]

We can formalize this intuition for Markov inference procedures as follows. We say that a bilevel Markov procedure *next* is *introspectively faithful* on a database Ω if and only if on every step the procedure produces the database prescribed by $data(\Omega, 2)$ (if there is one) and never produces a baselevel database that is forbidden by $data(\Omega, 2)$ (important on steps for which no database is prescribed).

$$(data(\Omega, 2) \models (next("data(\Omega, 1)")="\Delta")) \text{ implies } data(next(\Omega), 1) = \Delta$$

$$(data(\Omega, 2) \models (next("data(\Omega, 1)")\neq"\Delta")) \text{ implies } data(next(\Omega), 1) \neq \Delta$$

The informal mathematical expressions within quotes here denote databases; they should not be taken literally. Thus, "$data(\Omega, 1)$" means the symbol composed of the database $data(\Omega, 1)$ enclosed by quotes.

In the bilevel database in the example we just considered, there is just one metalevel sentence, and that sentence prescribes a baselevel database for just one step. Consequently, it is easy to define an inference procedure that works in this case. In fact, there are infinitely many of them, all agreeing on the first step. However, as illustrated by our example, not every procedure is introspectively faithful.

The existence of introspectively faithful inference procedures for specific databases raises the question of whether there are inference procedures that are introspectively faithful on all databases. Unfortunately, the answer is no.

THEOREM 10.1 *No inference procedure is introspectively faithful on all databases.*

Proof Any inconsistent metalevel database logically implies that every baselevel database is both prescribed and forbidden on every step. Obviously, no procedure can satisfy the definition of introspective fidelity on such a database. □

On the other hand, if we restrict our attention to a particular subset of databases, things are much nicer. We say that a metalevel database is *introspectively complete* if and only if it prescribes a baselevel database for every initial baselevel database and every step.

Now consider an inference procedure defined as follows. The bilevel database on each step is the union of the initial metalevel database and a baselevel update. The baselevel update is computed by applying resolution to the initial metalevel database to determine the baselevel database for the current step.

$$data(\Omega, 2) \vdash (next("data(\Omega, 1)")="\Delta")$$

$$\text{implies}$$

$$next(\Omega) = append(data(\Omega, 2), \Delta)$$

We can define more efficient versions of this inference procedure, but this one is particularly simple to analyze. In recognition of its propensity to reason about reasoning on every step, the method is called *compulsive introspection*.

THEOREM 10.2 *Compulsive introspection is introspectively faithful on every consistent and introspectively complete database.*

Proof Consider an initial database Ω. If Ω is introspectively complete, then $data(\Omega, 2)$ logically implies some new baselevel database Δ. Since resolution is complete, compulsive introspection requires that Δ be the next baselevel database. Since resolution is sound and the database is consistent, Δ cannot be forbidden and no other database can be prescribed. Consequently, both parts of the definition of introspective fidelity are satisfied. □

Unfortunately, this guarantee breaks down on databases that are not introspectively complete. On a step without a prescribed baselevel database, the resolution process may not terminate. In other words, compulsive introspection is not computable for such databases; therefore, it is not a well-defined inference procedure.

Introspective fidelity places constraints on the transformations that an inference procedure is allowed to perform on a bilevel database. These constraints are the basis for a notion of derivability known as introspective implication.

A bilevel database Ω *introspectively implies* a baselevel sentence ϕ if and only if there is a procedure *next* that is introspectively faithful on Ω and we can derive ϕ from Ω using *next*.

Obviously, the initial database in our bilevel example introspectively implies Q, since there is an inference procedure that is introspectively faithful on this database and that allows us to derive Q. In fact, Q is derivable using any of the procedures.

Although it may be less obvious, the initial database also introspectively implies R. Although there is no introspectively faithful inference procedure that allows us to derive R on the first step, there is nothing preventing us from deriving it on some subsequent step.

On the other hand, R would not be introspectively implied if we were to include in our metalevel database the following sentence and the axioms defining Member, since this would eliminate any procedure that dictated a baselevel database containing R.

$$\forall d \; \neg \texttt{Member}(\texttt{"R"}, \texttt{Next}(d))$$

As this example points up, logical implication does not necessarily entail introspective implication. The metalevel sentences in a database can rule out the derivation of a sentence, even if it is logically implied by the database.

At the same time, introspective implication does not entail logical implication. For example, the metalevel sentences may prescribe an unsound inference procedure. Although this may appear undesirable, it is useful when one wants to describe various extensions of logical implication, such as analogical reasoning or nonmonotonic reasoning. Besides, when unsound inference is not prescribed, we can always force this entailment by adding to our metalevel database the sentences defining logical implication.

10.8 Reflection*

Often in the course of trying to solve a problem, we find it desirable to suspend work on the problem itself and to think instead about the problem of solving that problem. In so doing, we might, for example, decide that our problem-solving method is doomed to failure or that some other method is more likely to succeed. This process of suspending the process of reasoning, reasoning about that process, and using the results to control subsequent reasoning is called *reflection*.

Consider a multilevel inference procedure *next* and a multilevel database Ω. We say that *next* produces a *change* at level k for database Ω if and only if the level k data in $next(\Omega)$ is different from the level k data in Ω.

$$data(next(\Omega), k) \neq data(\Omega, k)$$

On each step of its operation, *step* may cause changes at any level of the metalevel tower or at any combination of levels. We define the *level* of a given step to be the lowest level at which a change occurs.

Finally, we say that a multilevel inference procedure is *reflective* if and only if it dictates inference at different levels on different databases. For example, a procedure might dictate a few steps of baselevel inference, followed by some steps of metalevel inference, followed once again by baselevel inference.

For this reflection to be interesting, we assume that there is some type of *causal connection* between the database and inference at one level and the database and inference at the next higher level. For example, the higher-level inference may depend on the contents of the lower-level database, and the subsequent inference at the lower level may depend on the conclusions reached at the higher level.

Universal subgoaling is an especially interesting type of reflective behavior. Although the idea was originally introduced in the context of general problem solving, we can apply it to deduction, as shown here.

Consider a reasoning procedure that is undefined for certain steps on certain databases because of difficulties in supplying a satisfactory definition. For example, the procedure may not dictate any further inferences, or there may be too many possibilities. Universal subgoaling is the process of dealing with these undefined cases by reflection.

As an example, consider a variant of the Markov inference procedure introduced in Section 10.4. Our variant agrees with the procedure whenever there are five or fewer successors to the top clause in the database; otherwise, it is undefined.

$$length(concs(car(\Omega), \Omega)) \leq 5$$
$$implies$$
$$next(\Omega) = append(concs(car(\Omega), \Omega), cdr(\Omega))$$

We can use universal subgoaling to complete this definition by dictating reflection for the other cases.

$$length(concs(car(\Omega), \Omega)) > 5 \quad implies \quad next(\Omega) = reflect(\Omega)$$

The reflective inference in this case consists of reasoning at the metalevel about the next baselevel database to produce. The reflection step seeds this inference by changing the database to include the appropriate negated metalevel query and a suitable set of metalevel sentences (here called Θ). Again, remember that "Ω" means the symbol formed by enclosing the sentences of Ω within quotes.

$$reflect(\Omega) = [\texttt{Next}("\Omega") \neq \texttt{d}, \texttt{Ans}(\texttt{d})].\Theta$$

Given this metalevel database, our reflective procedure applies its deductive powers in deriving an answer to this metalevel query. When the answer is obtained, the procedure dictates a reversion to baselevel inference by making the database correspond to the answer to the query.

$$[\texttt{Ans("}\Delta\texttt{")}] \in \Omega \quad \text{implies} \quad next(\Omega) = \Delta$$

To complete our definition, we need to specify the metalevel database Θ used in deriving this answer. A subset of these sentences follows. The procedure these sentences describe is identical to our baselevel procedure, when there are five or fewer successors. When there are more than five successors, the procedure described by these sentences differs from the baselevel procedure in that it orders the successors by length before adding them to the database.

```
Length(Concs(Car(d),d))≤5 ⇒
   Next(d)=Append(Concs(Car(d),d),d)

Length(Concs(Car(d),d))>5 ⇒
   Next(d)=Append(Order(Concs(Car(d),d)),d)

Order([])=[]

Order(x.l)=Add(x,Order(l))

Add(x,[])=[x]

Length(x)<Length(y) ⇒ Add(x,y.l)=x.y.l

Length(x)≥Length(y) ⇒ Add(x,y.l)=y.Add(x,l)
```

Suppose, for example, that our reflective inference procedure were applied to the following database. Note that the first clause resolves with all six nonunit clauses.

```
[¬S(z),Ans(z)]

[S(x),¬P1(x),¬Q1(x)]

[S(x),¬P2(x),¬Q2(x),¬R2(x)]

[S(x),¬P3(x)]

[S(x),¬P4(x,y),¬Q4(y)]

[S(x),¬P5(x,y),¬Q5(x,z)]

[S(x),¬P6(x),¬Q6(x),¬R6(x)]

[P3(A)]
```

Since there are six successors, the condition for reflection is met. This leads to the database consisting of the following clause, together with the clauses from Θ.

```
[Next("[[¬S(z),Ans(z)],
        [S(x),¬P1(x),¬Q1(x)],
        [S(x),¬P2(x),¬Q2(x),¬R2(x)],
        [S(x),¬P3(x)],
        [S(x),¬P4(x,y),¬Q4(y)],
        [S(x),¬P5(x,y),¬Q5(x,z)],
        [S(x),¬P6(x),¬Q6(x),¬R6(x)],
        [P3(A)]]")≠d,
 Ans(d)]
```

Since this clause resolves with only two clauses from Θ, the procedure dictates nonreflective inference. This inference continues for a number of cycles, as a result of which the agent derives its answer for the query.

```
[Ans("[[¬P3(z),Ans(z)]
        [¬P1(z),¬Q1(z),Ans(z)],
        [¬P4(z,y),¬Q4(y),Ans(z)],
        [¬P5(z,y),¬Q5(z,z),Ans(z)],
        [¬P2(z),¬Q2(z),¬R2(z),Ans(z)],
        [¬P6(z),¬Q6(z),¬R6(z),Ans(z)],
        [S(x),¬P1(x),¬Q1(x)]
        [S(x),¬P2(x),¬Q2(x),¬R2(x)],
        [S(x),¬P3(x)],
        [S(x),¬P4(x,y),¬Q4(y)],
        [S(x),¬P5(x,y),¬Q5(x,z)],
        [S(x),¬P6(x),¬Q6(x),¬R6(x)],
        [P3(A)]]")]
```

The presence of this answer literal in the database satisfies the condition for reversion to the baselevel, so the procedure at this point installs the following derived database.

```
[¬P3(z),Ans(z)]

[¬P1(z),¬Q1(z),Ans(z)]

[¬P4(z,y),¬Q4(y),Ans(z)]

[¬P5(z,y),¬Q5(z,z),Ans(z)]

[¬P2(z),¬Q2(z),¬R2(z),Ans(z)]
```

```
[¬P6(z),¬Q6(z),¬R6(z),Ans(z)]

[S(x),¬P1(x),¬Q1(x)]

[S(x),¬P2(x),¬Q2(x),¬R2(x)]

[S(x),¬P3(x)]

[S(x),¬P4(x,y),¬Q4(y)]

[S(x),¬P5(x,y),¬Q5(x,z)]

[S(x),¬P6(x),¬Q6(x),¬R6(x)]

[P3(A)]
```

One thing to note about this procedure is that its metalevel inference is the same as its baselevel inference. In fact, if at some point in its metalevel reasoning it were to encounter a literal with more than five successors, it would reflect to the metametalevel. Although this never occurs with the metalevel axioms in Θ, it can happen with other axiom sets; and it is important in designing a reflective procedure to be sure that such reflection does not continue in an unbounded fashion.

Another point to note is that the set of metalevel axioms is fixed in the definition of *next*. Given a fixed set of metalevel axioms, it is easy to implement a nonreflective procedure that behaves identically on the baselevel axioms in a database. So why design a procedure that does any metalevel reasoning at all? It is bound to be less efficient and is certainly more complicated.

In this case, there is little advantage to be gained with this approach. However, consider a slightly more complicated situation in which the database supplied to the procedure contains not only baselevel sentences but also metalevel sentences that constrain the baselevel inference procedure. In this situation, we would like a procedure that uses these metalevel sentences in deciding what baselevel inferences to perform.

For example, we might want to supply axioms describing a procedure in which clauses are ordered on the basis of their literals rather than of their lengths. To do this, we would include in our initial database all of the clauses in Θ except for the ones that define Add. We would then redefine Add in terms of an ordering relation Better. Finally, we would include appropriate statements about Better.

```
Add(x,[])=[x]

Better(x,y)  ⇒  Add(x,y.1)=x.y.1

¬Better(x,y)  ⇒  Add(x,y.1)=y.Add(x,1)

Among("P1",c) ∧ Among("P2",d)  ⇒  Better(c,d)
```

We can easily devise a procedure that uses metalevel sentences of this sort. As before, *next* is defined nonreflectively when there are five or fewer literals.

$$length(concs(car(\Omega), \Omega)) \leq 5 \quad \text{implies}$$
$$next(\Omega) = append(concs(car(\Omega), \Omega), cdr(\Omega))$$

When there are more than five literals, *next* dictates reflection.

$$length(concs(car(\Omega), \Omega)) > 5 \quad \text{implies} \quad next(\Omega) = reflect(\Omega)$$

Given a bilevel database, *reflect* produces a new database consisting of the metalevel axioms from the original database together with the goal of finding the successor for the baselevel sentences in that database. Notice that we do not add the axioms from Θ, on the assumption that they are in the initial database.

$$reflect(\Omega) = [\text{Next}("data(\Omega, 1)") \neq \text{d}, \text{Ans}(\text{d})] . data(\Omega, 2)$$

Once an answer is obtained, *next* dictates reversion to the baselevel. First, the pure metalevel database is stripped of all clauses with answer literals; then, the derived baselevel database is appended.

$$[\text{Ans}("\Delta")] \in \Omega \quad \text{implies} \quad next(\Omega) = append(delete(answers(\Omega), \Omega), \Delta)$$

One nice feature of this procedure is that its baselevel behavior agrees with the description in its metalevel database, at least when there are more than five successors. Unfortunately, when there are five or fewer successors, the procedure dictates its usual inference steps, no matter what the metalevel database says to do.

Compulsive reflection is one way of ensuring that the higher-level axioms in a multilevel database are used in determining the course of lower-level inference. Although compulsive reflection is more expensive than universal subgoaling is, it is more reliable.

Our definition of compulsive reflection assumes that, in addition to the metalevel axioms defining the desired baselevel behavior, the initial database contains an appropriate clause to seed its metalevel reasoning. The clause is obtained by applying the function *newmeta* to the initial baselevel database.

$$newmeta(\Delta) = [\text{Next}("\Delta") \neq \text{d}, \text{Ans}(\text{d})]$$

So long as no answer to the Next question has been derived, the procedure dictates inference on the metalevel clauses in the database. There is no change to the baselevel database.

$$[\text{Ans}("\Delta")] \notin \Omega \quad \text{implies}$$
$$next(\Omega) = append(concs(car(data(\Omega, 2)), data(\Omega, 2)), data(\Omega, 1))$$

Once an answer is obtained, the baselevel portion of the database is updated accordingly. At the same time, the metalevel database is pruned of answer literals and is seeded for the new database.

$$[\texttt{Ans}("\Delta")] \in \Omega \quad \text{implies}$$
$$next(\Omega) = append(data(\Omega, 2) - answers(data(\Omega, 2)), newmeta(\Delta), \Delta)$$

Compulsive reflection is almost identical to compulsive introspection. The only difference is that every step of compulsive introspection is a baselevel inference step (i.e., all metalevel inference happens between steps) whereas in compulsive reflection individual steps of metalevel inference are also steps of the overall inference procedure. This distinction is important for procedures capable of reflecting through many different levels.

Although our definition of compulsive reflection is restricted to bilevel databases, we can equally well define a version for databases with three levels, four levels, and so on. In fact, we can define an n-level version that works on databases with sentences that span any number of levels. The procedure performs inference at the level of the highest-level sentence in the database and thereby controls inference at the next lower level. This inference controls the inference at the level below that, and so forth. An n-level version of compulsive reflection also allows one to write sentences at level n that control the reflection at levels lower than n.

In this section, we have shown how to define a procedure capable of reflection. At this time, little is known about when a procedure should reflect. Much more work is needed in this area.

10.9 Bibliographical and Historical Remarks

The idea of describing the process of reasoning with sentences in a formally defined metalanguage began to be discussed extensively in the early 1970s. In an early paper [Hayes 1973b], Hayes introduced a language for writing rules of inference and for expressing constraints on the application of those rules. He showed that, by slightly varying the constraints, it was possible to describe markedly different reasoning methods. He proposed a system called GOLUX based on his language, but the system was never built.

In a compelling but informal paper published a few years later [Davis 1977], Davis and Buchanan argued for the utility of metalanguage in writing expert systems. In his thesis [Davis 1976], Davis described the implementation of various metalevel capabilities in the MYCIN system [Shortliffe 1976], including explanation, debugging, and the analysis of new rules. In designing a program to teach medical diagnosis in the MYCIN domain, Clancey [Clancey 1983] analyzed the system's rules and found it useful to separate out the baselevel medical knowledge from the metalevel knowledge about diagnostic strategy.

Weyhrauch's work on FOL [Weyhrauch 1980] was the first thorough treatment of reflection. FOL was the first program to use semantic attachment and reflection principles in a substantial way.

In the early 1980s, a number of other researchers published designs for programs capable of using metalevel constraints in controlling their reasoning. Doyle described a system called SEAN [Doyle 1980]; deKleer and others described a system called AMORD [deKleer 1977]; and Genesereth described a system called MRS [Genesereth 1983]. Kowalski [Kowalski 1974] showed how metalevel and baselevel inference could be amalgamated in PROLOG [Clocksin 1981]. Brian Smith described a LISP interpreter capable of reflecting an arbitrary number of levels [Smith 1982]. Laird, Rosenbloom, and Newell described a reflective problem-solving architecture called SOAR [Laird 1986]. The idea of universal subgoaling is taken from their work. [Maes 1987] is a survey of work on metalevel architecture and reflection.

The most recent development in this area is the formal analysis of multilevel-reasoning architectures. The notions of introspective fidelity and introspective implication are outgrowths of this research [Genesereth 1987a].

Exercises

1. *Syntax.* Give formal definitions for the syntax of logical sentences and quantified sentences in predicate calculus.

2. *Rules of inference.* Define modus ponens.

3. *Restriction strategies.* Formalize the following resolution strategies.

   a. Subsumption.

   b. Set of support resolution. Note: Assume that the set of support consists of expressions taken from the negation of the goal, and remember that answer literals are added only to goal clauses.

   c. Linear resolution.

4. *Ordering strategies.* Formalize the cheapest first rule introduced in Chapter 5.

5. *Reflection.* A *trilevel* database is one consisting entirely of baselevel, metalevel, and metametalevel sentences. Assume that the metametalevel function constant **Next** denotes the function that maps every bilevel database into its bilevel successor. Extend the definition of introspective fidelity for databases of this sort, and define a reflective procedure that satisfies the definition for databases that are consistent and introspectively complete at the metametalevel. Note: In general, it is not possible for a trilevel procedure to be introspectively faithful at all levels simultaneously.

CHAPTER 11
State and Change

IN OUR DISCUSSION SO FAR, we have assumed that the world is unchanging. Facts have been treated as though true or false for all time, and no attention has been paid to possible changes in the state of the world whereby new facts become true and others become false. In this chapter, we show how to express information about the state of the world, and we talk about actions that change world states.

11.1 States

The notion of state is central in most conceptualizations of the physical world. A *state*, or *situation*, is a snapshot of the world at a given point in time. At different points in time, the world can be in different states.

This idea is nicely illustrated in the context of a microcosm such as the Blocks World. Consider a variation of this world in which there are just three blocks. Each block can be somewhere on the table or on top of exactly one other block. Each block can have at most one other block immediately on top of it. Different states of this world correspond to different configurations of blocks.

One state of this Blocks World is shown in Figure 11.1. Block c is on block a, block a is on the table, and block b is also on the table. Figure 11.2 illustrates a different state of the same world. In this case, the blocks are all stacked on top of one another. Block a is on block b, b is on c, and c is on the table.

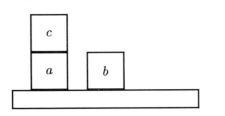

Figure 11.1   A scene from the Blocks World.

For a Blocks World with three blocks, there are 13 possible states. Figure 11.3 shows all of the possibilities. There is one state in which all of the blocks are on the table. There are six states containing a stack of two blocks—three choices for the top block and two choices for its support. There are also six states containing a stack of three blocks; again three choices for the top block, two choices for the middle block, and only one choice for the bottom.

Note that a conceptualization of states need not be unique. For example, the state space in Figure 11.3 takes into account the vertical relationship of blocks and ignores their lateral position altogether. If the scene in Figure 11.1 were drawn with block b to the left of c and a, it would picture the same state in our conceptualization.

The value of the notion of state is that it allows us to describe changing worlds. In conceptualizing a changing world, we include states as objects in the universe of discourse, and we invent functions and relations that depend on them. Given this conceptualization, we then write sentences about which objects satisfy which relations in which states.

Naming states is easy. Since they are objects in the universe of discourse, we simply invent appropriate object constants; e.g., S1 and S2. Later, we

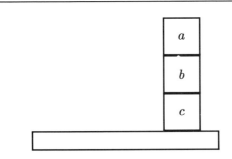

Figure 11.2   Another scene from the Blocks World.

use more complex terms to designate states. We call a term that denotes a specific state a *state designator*.

We express the fact that an object is a state using a unary relation constant. For example, the sentence State(S1) asserts that the object designated by S1 is a state.

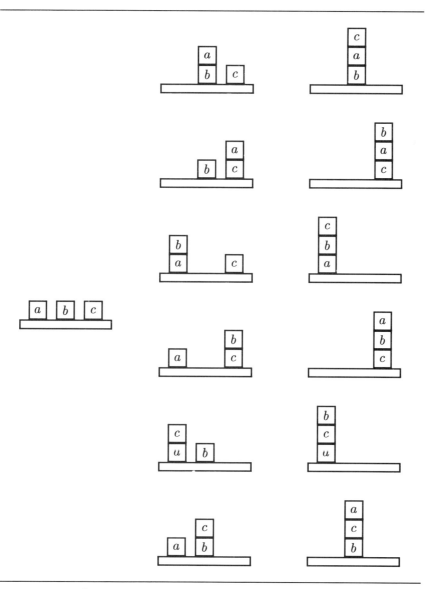

Figure 11.3 State space for the Blocks World.

The simplest way of describing a state is to use a single function or relation for each piece of information about the state. In describing a scene in the Blocks World, we can use the ternary relation symbol On to assert that one block is directly on top of another block in a given state. We can use the binary relation symbol Clear to assert that a block has no blocks on top of it in a given state. We can use the binary relation symbol Table to assert that a block is on the table in a given state. For example, the following sentences describe the states pictured in Figures 11.1 and 11.2.

On(C,A,S1)	On(A,B,S2)
Clear(C,S1)	On(B,C,S2)
Clear(B,S1)	Clear(A,S2)
Table(A,S1)	Table(C,S2)
Table(B,S1)	

In what follows, we use an alternative to this approach in which we conceptualize state-dependent properties as state-independent functions that map objects into the sets of states in which those objects have the associated state-dependent properties. For example, we use On as a binary function constant, and we write the term On(A,B) to designate the set of states in which block A is on block B. We call a term of this form a *state descriptor*, and we call the state set it designates a *fluent*.

To write state-dependent sentences, we use the binary relation constant T to assert that a property is true of a particular state. For example, we write T(On(A,B),S2) to mean that block A is on block B in state S2. In effect, we are saying that the state named S2 is a member of the set of states designated by the term On(A,B). Using this approach, we can describe the states pictured in Figures 11.1 and 11.2 as follows.

T(On(C,A),S1)	T(On(A,B),S2)
T(Clear(C),S1)	T(On(B,C),S2)
T(Clear(B),S1)	T(Clear(A),S2)
T(Table(A),S1)	T(Table(C),S2)
T(Table(B),S1)	

Since state descriptors designate sets of states, it makes sense to talk about compositions of state descriptors, which designate the complements, unions, and intersections of those sets. We could write such compositions with the usual set operators, but instead we use symbols identical to the logical operators to emphasize the intuition that the descriptors represent properties of states. In particular, we use the negation operator to designate the complement of a state descriptor, we use the conjunction and disjunction operators to designate intersection and union, and we use the implication operator to assert that the antecedent is a subset of the consequent. With these conventions, we find that T is transparent to logical operators and vice versa. The following axioms formalize this property.

$$\forall p \forall s \ T(\neg p, s) \Leftrightarrow \neg T(p, s)$$

$$\forall p \forall q \forall s \ T(p \land q, s) \Leftrightarrow (T(p, s) \land T(q, s))$$

$$\forall p \forall q \forall s \ T(p \lor q, s) \Leftrightarrow (T(p, s) \lor T(q, s))$$

$$\forall p \forall q \forall s \ T(p \Rightarrow q, s) \Leftrightarrow (T(p, s) \Rightarrow T(q, s))$$

Note that not every function and relation need be dependent on state. For example, in our version of the Blocks World, the property of being a block is unchanging; if an object is a block in one state, it is a block in every state. We could express this information by conceptualizing such properties as state-dependent functions and relations and by writing appropriate universally quantified sentences. However, it is simpler to conceptualize such properties as state-independent functions and relations and to write sentences that do not mention state at all. For example, we can conceptualize the property of being a block as a simple unary relation that is true of the blocks in our universe of discourse.

Similarly, some facts are true in all states even though they involve state-dependent functions or relations. We call such facts *state constraints*. The following are examples of state constraints for the Blocks World:

$$\forall x \forall s \ T(Table(x), s) \Leftrightarrow \neg \exists y \ T(On(x, y), s)$$

$$\forall y \forall s \ T(Clear(y), s) \Leftrightarrow \neg \exists x \ T(On(x, y), s)$$

$$\forall x \forall y \forall z \forall s \ T(On(x, y), s) \Rightarrow T(On(x, z) \Leftrightarrow y{=}z, s)$$

The first sentence asserts that an object is on the table if and only if it is not on some other object. The second sentence asserts that an object is clear if and only if then there is nothing on top of it. The last sentence states that an object can be on at most one other object.

11.2 Actions

Whereas the intuition behind the notion of state is persistence, the intuition behind the notion of action is change. The world persists in one state until an *action* is performed that changes it to a new state.

As with states, we conceptualize actions as objects in our universe of discourse. The action of moving block c from block a to block b can be considered as an object, albeit an object of a very special sort. The action of unstacking c from a and placing it on the table is another object altogether. The action of picking up b and stacking it on block c is another possibility. Finally, there is the action of doing nothing.

To capture the commonality among some actions, it often is convenient to include operators as well as simple actions in our conceptualization. An *operator* is a function from objects to actions, which maps a group of objects into a common way of manipulating those objects. In the Blocks World, the generic act of moving a block from the top of one block to the top of another block can be conceptualized as an operator. It maps the three blocks involved into the corresponding *move* action. Similarly, the generic act of unstacking a block from another block and placing it on the table can be conceptualized as a binary function from the two blocks involved into the corresponding *unstack* action. The generic act of picking up a block from the table and stacking it on top of another block can be conceptualized as a binary function from two blocks into the corresponding *stack* action. The actions in the range of an operator are often called *instances* of the operator.

If we assume that all actions in our conceptualization of the Blocks World are instances of the *move*, *unstack*, and *stack* operators or the null action, then we need to add 19 more objects to our universe of discourse. There are six ways to move one block from a second block to a third. There are three choices for the block to be moved. Having made that choice, there are two choices for the block from which to move it. Having made that choice, the remaining block must be the destination. Similarly, there are six ways to unstack one block from another. There are also six ways to stack one block on top of another. Finally, there is only one null action.

To describe operators and actions, we first have to give them names. In what follows, we use the ternary function symbol M to designate the *move* operator, we use the binary function symbol U to designate the *unstack* operator, we use the binary function symbol S to designate the *stack* operator, and we use the constant Noop to designate the null action. With this vocabulary, we can name individual actions. For example, the term M(C,A,B) designates the action of moving block c from a to b. We call terms of this form *action designators*.

As with states, we express the fact that an object is an action with an appropriate unary relation constant. For example, the sentence Action(M(C,A,B)) states that the object denoted by the term M(C,A,B) is an action.

We can conceptualize the effects of actions in the form of a function *do* that maps an action (from the set A of all actions) and a state (from the set S of all states) into the state that results from the execution of the specified action in the specified state.

$$do : A \times S \rightarrow S$$

Figure 11.4 illustrates the *do* function for the nonnull actions and states in the Blocks World. The arrows indicate state transitions, and the labels on the arrows indicate the actions involved.

Note that Figure 11.4 does not present the effects of every action in every state. The reason for this is that, in some cases, those effects are not

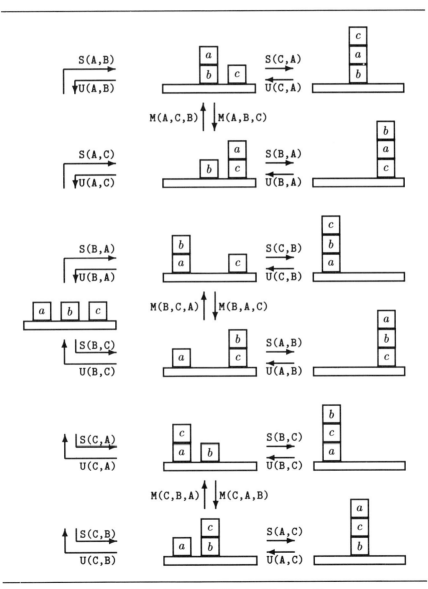

Figure 11.4   Effects of Blocks World actions.

well defined. For example, what is the result of trying to move block c from block a to block b when block c is not on block a? What is the result when block c is on block a but block b is on block c? In the following discussion, we simply treat *do* as a partial function and ignore such cases.

To characterize the results of actions performed simultaneously, we need to extend our *do* function to include all of the actions performed at the same time, since the effects of each action can depend on the execution of other actions. For example, if we try to lift a block with one hand while pressing down with another, the result may not be the same as in the single action case. We also ignore this possibility in the remainder of our discussion.

In characterizing the effects of actions and operators, we use the binary function constant Do to designate the *do* function. Thus, the term Do(M(C,A,B),S15) stands for the state that results from executing the M(C,A,B) action in state S15.

The primary effects of the M operator are described by the following sentence. The axiom is true for all blocks x, y, and z and all states s. (To simplify notation, we drop the universal quantifiers from here on.) If in state s block x is on block y, both x and z are clear, and x is not the same as z, then the action M(x,y,z) will have the effects indicated by the consequent of the implication. Block x will be on block z in the resulting state and block y will be clear.

$$T(\text{On}(x,y),s) \land T(\text{Clear}(x),s) \land T(\text{Clear}(z),s) \land x{\neq}z \Rightarrow$$
$$T(\text{On}(x,z),\text{Do}(M(x,y,z),s)) \land$$
$$T(\text{Clear}(y),\text{Do}(M(x,y,z),s))$$

The following sentence describes the U operator. If x is on y in state s and x is clear, then, after an *unstack* operation, x is on the table and y is clear.

$$T(\text{On}(x,y),s) \land T(\text{Clear}(x),s) \Rightarrow$$
$$T(\text{Table}(x),\text{Do}(U(x,y),s)) \land$$
$$T(\text{Clear}(y),\text{Do}(U(x,y),s))$$

Finally, we consider the S operator. If x is on the table, both x and y are clear, and x is not the same as y, then x is on y in the state resulting from the corresponding *stack* operation.

$$T(\text{Table}(x),s) \land T(\text{Clear}(x),s) \land T(\text{Clear}(y),s) \land x{\neq}y \Rightarrow$$
$$T(\text{On}(x,y),\text{Do}(S(x,y),s))$$

Using these operator descriptions and state constraints for the relations involved, we also can deduce which facts become false as a result of executing an action. For example, we can show that a *stack* action makes its second argument not clear, since no block is clear that has a block on top of it.

11.3 The Frame Problem

Unfortunately, these operator descriptions are not complete. They describe the facts that become true as a result of executing instances of each operator, and indirectly they describe the facts that become false. However, they do not specify anything about the facts that were true beforehand and that remain true afterward or about the facts that were false beforehand and that remain false afterward.

As an example, consider the Blocks World scene in Figure 11.1. Block *b* is on the table in this state, and it is on the table in the state resulting from moving block *c* from block *a* and to block *b*. However, we cannot prove this from the operator description for *move*.

The problem of characterizing the aspects of a state that are not changed by an action is called the *frame problem*. The name comes from a loose analogy with the world of animation. In creating a scene, most animators first draw a background that does not change throughout a scene. They then replicate it and superimpose the action in the foreground. The frame problem is to differentiate the background unchanged by an action from the changing foreground. One way of doing this is to write *frame axioms* that indicate the properties that remain unchanged after each action.

As an example, consider the following frame axioms for the U operator. The first axiom expresses that a block is clear after a U action if it is clear before the action. Similarly, the second axiom states that a block is on the table after a U action if it is on the table beforehand. The On case is slightly trickier, because a U action undoes an On relationship. The axiom states that one block is on another block after a U action provided that it is on that block beforehand *and* that it is not the block placed on the table.

$$T(Clear(u),s) \Rightarrow T(Clear(u),Do(U(x,y),s))$$

$$T(Table(u),s) \Rightarrow T(Table(u),Do(U(x,y),\varepsilon))$$

$$T(On(u,v),s) \wedge u{\neq}x \Rightarrow T(On(u,v),Do(U(x,y),s))$$

The following are frame axioms for the S operator. An object remains clear so long as it is not the destination of the S action. An object remains on the table so long as it is not the object that is stacked. An object that is on another object before the S action is on that object afterward.

$$T(Clear(u),s) \wedge u{\neq}y \Rightarrow T(Clear(u),Do(S(x,y),s))$$

$$T(Table(u),s) \wedge u{\neq}x \Rightarrow T(Table(u),Do(S(x,y),s))$$

$$T(On(u,v),s) \Rightarrow T(On(u,v),Do(S(x,y),s))$$

The frame axioms for M are as follows. An object remains clear after an M action unless it is the destination of the move. Any object that is on the table remains on the table. Any object that is on another object remains on that object, except for the object that is moved.

$$T(\text{Clear}(u),s) \land u{\neq}z \Rightarrow T(\text{Clear}(u),\text{Do}(M(x,y,z),s))$$

$$T(\text{Table}(u),s) \Rightarrow T(\text{Table}(u),\text{Do}(M(x,y,z),s))$$

$$T(\text{On}(u,v),s) \land u{\neq}x \Rightarrow T(\text{On}(u,v),\text{Do}(M(x,y,z),s))$$

Finally, there are the frame axioms for the null action. By definition, the null action changes nothing, and so anything true beforehand is true afterward.

$$T(\text{Clear}(u),s) \Rightarrow T(\text{Clear}(u),\text{Do}(\text{Noop},s))$$

$$T(\text{Table}(u),s) \Rightarrow T(\text{Table}(u),\text{Do}(\text{Noop},s))$$

$$T(\text{On}(u,v),s) \Rightarrow T(\text{On}(u,v),\text{Do}(\text{Noop},s))$$

Typically, the number of frame axioms is proportional to the product of the number of relations and the number of operators in our conceptualization. In this case, there are just 12 frame axioms. What makes the frame problem a problem is that, in worlds of realistic complexity, there are many more actions and relations, and so many more axioms are necessary. Furthermore, most actions change only a few of the facts about the world, so it seems a shame to write all those axioms simply to describe what is *not* happening. Dealing with the frame problem in an economic manner would seem to require nonmonotonic reasoning. The problem is subtle and is the subject of continuing research.

11.4 Action Ordering

Having treated individual actions, we turn now to multiple actions. For simplicity, we assume that actions take place successively and do not overlap. The key issue in analyzing situations of this sort is the ordering of actions; in this section, we examine two ways of formalizing action order: action blocks and sequential procedures.

An *action block* is a finite sequence of actions. Since there is no bound on the number of actions in an action block, we can form infinitely many such objects from any nonempty set of actions.

The overall result of executing an action block in some initial state is the state obtained by executing the constituent actions in order. The first action is performed in the initial state, the second action is performed in the state resulting from that action, and so forth. No other actions are performed between adjacent actions in the block.

The simplest way to denote an action block is with a list of terms in which each term denotes an action or another action block. For example, the following list denotes the action block consisting of the actions U(C,A), S(B,C), and S(A,B).

$$[U(C,A),S(B,C),S(A,B)]$$

To talk about the state resulting from the execution of an action block, we extend the Do function introduced in the Section 11.3 so that it applies to action blocks as well as to primitive actions, mapping an action block and a state into the state resulting from the execution of the entire block in the specified state. The state resulting from the execution of the empty block in state s is just s. The result of executing a nonempty block with initial action a and succeeding block 1 in a state s is the state obtained by executing 1 in the state that results from the execution of a in s.

$$Do([],s)=s$$

$$Do(a.l,s)=Do(l,Do(a,s))$$

Note that, in performing this reduction, we reverse the syntactic order of the action terms involved. For example, the term Do([a,b],s) designates the same state as does the term Do(b,Do(a,s)).

The preceding statements describe the effects of action blocks in terms of the states resulting from their execution. We also can describe their effects in terms of the properties of those states. The following sentences use the T relation in expressing the preceding definitions in this alternative form.

$$T(p,s) \Leftrightarrow T(p,Do([],s))$$

$$T(p,Do(l,Do(a,s))) \Leftrightarrow T(p,Do(a.l,s))$$

Of course, these sentences can be derived from the preceding sentences. The import of writing them this way is to emphasize that we can reduce questions about the effects of action blocks to questions about the effects of the actions contained in those blocks.

Now consider the problem of describing an infinite sequence of actions. Obviously, we cannot use list notation to denote such an object, since it is not possible to write down an infinite list. The solution is to use a different conceptualization of action order. A *sequential procedure* is a function from

positive integers to actions that maps each positive integer into the action
to be performed at the corresponding step of an infinite action sequence.

$$f : N \rightarrow A$$

By describing a sequential procedure, we implicitly characterize the
corresponding sequence of actions. For example, the following sentences
define the sequential procedure that dictates the three actions previously
listed followed by an unending string of Noop actions.

$$F(1) = U(C,A)$$

$$F(2) = S(B,C)$$

$$F(3) = S(A,B)$$

$$n>3 \Rightarrow F(n)=Noop$$

Although our motive for inventing the notion of sequential procedures is
the formalization of infinite action sequences, the conceptualization can be
used for finite sequences as well, provided that we generalize our definition
to include partial functions defined on initial segments of the positive
integers.

11.5 Conditionality

Another issue in characterizing actions is conditionality. We often want
to talk about actions that are executed only if certain conditions are met.
In this section, we discuss three approaches to formalizing conditionality:
conditional actions, production systems, and Markov procedures.

A *conditional action* consists of a condition (i.e., a state set) and two
actions. If the state in which the conditional action is executed satisfies
the condition (i.e., it is a member of the specified state set), then the first
of the two specified actions is performed; otherwise, the second action is
performed.

We denote a conditional action with a *conditional expression*; i.e., a
term of the form $\text{If}(\phi,\alpha,\beta)$, where If is a ternary function constant, ϕ
is a state descriptor, and α and β are actions. For example, the following
term is a conditional expression. The conditional action denoted by this
expression dictates the action M(A,B,C) if block A is on block B; otherwise,
it dictates the action S(A,C).

$$\text{If}(On(A,B),M(A,B,C),S(A,C))$$

We can describe the effects of executing a conditional action with the
sentences shown below. If the state in which the action is executed satisfies

the condition, the result is the state described in the consequent of the first alternative. Otherwise, it is the state described in the second alternative.

$$T(p,s) \Rightarrow Do(If(p,a,b),s)=Do(a,s)$$

$$T(\neg p,s) \Rightarrow Do(If(p,a,b),s)=Do(b,s)$$

By nesting conditional expressions, we can denote conditional actions involving more than one condition and more than two actions. For example, the following term describes a three-way conditional action based on the position of block A.

$$If(Table(A),S(A,C),If(On(A,B),M(A,B,C),Noop))$$

Although this approach to formalizing conditionality is quite general, it is inconvenient in situations involving many conditions and many actions. This inconvenience can be remedied in large measure by conceptualizing conditionality in terms of production systems.

A *production rule* is a pair consisting of a condition (i.e., a state set) and an action. A *production system* is a finite sequence of production rules.

Executing a production system in an initial state can involve many steps. On each step, the action performed is the action part of the first production rule in the sequence the condition of which is satisfied. The execution terminates if and only if there is no production rule with a satisfied condition.

We can designate any production rule with an expression of the form $\phi \to \alpha$, where ϕ is a state descriptor and α is an action designator. (The addition of the infix operator $\to$ here is not essential, but it is convenient and conforms nicely to the common notation for production rules.) Since the sequence of rules in a production system is finite in length, we can use list notation as our specification language.

To formalize the effects of executing a production system, we first define the relation denoted by Dictates, which holds of a production system, a state, and an action if and only if the production system dictates the specified action in the specified state.

$$T(p,s) \Rightarrow Dictates((p \to a).l,s,a)$$

$$\neg T(p,s) \wedge Dictates(l,s,b) \Rightarrow Dictates((p \to a).l,s,b)$$

Given this definition, we define the effects of a production system as shown in the following display. (We extend the Do function so that it applies to production systems.) If the system dictates no action for a state, the result is just the state itself. Otherwise, it is the result of executing the production system in the state obtained by executing the dictated action.

$$(\neg\exists a \text{ Dictates}(p,s,a)) \Rightarrow \text{Do}(p,s)=s$$

$$\text{Dictates}(p,s,a) \Rightarrow \text{Do}(p,s)=\text{Do}(p,\text{Do}(a,s))$$

As an example of a production system, consider the following list of rules. This particular system, when executed in any starting state, produces a final state in which block (denoted by) A is on block B and block B is on block C.

```
[Clear(C) ∧ On(C,z) → U(C,z),

 On(A,C) ∧ Clear(A) → U(A,C),

 On(B,C) ∧ On(C,A) → U(B,C),

 Clear(B) ∧ On(B,A) → U(B,A),

 Clear(A) ∧ On(A,B) ∧ Table(B) → U(A,B),

 Table(A) ∧ Table(B) ∧ Table(C) → S(B,C),

 Table(A) ∧ On(B,C) ∧ Table(C) → S(A,B)]
```

To see how this production system achieves its effect, consider what happens when the system is executed in the state S1 pictured in Figure 11.1. In the initial state, the antecedent of the first production rule is satisfied, so the corresponding action U(C,A) is dictated. Once this action is executed, all the blocks are on the table. In this state, only the sixth rule applies; therefore, the system dictates the action S(B,C). The seventh rule then applies, and the S(A,B) action is executed. Finally, we arrive at a state in which no rule applies. Therefore, no action is dictated, and the execution terminates.

Note that the conditions associated with the production rules in this system describe disjoint state sets; as a result, at most one rule applies in each state. Although this is a nice property, it is not essential. Recall that our definition of Dictates requires that we always take the *first* rule that applies, so any ambiguity due to overlapping state sets is eliminated. Although some production system interpreters use different strategies for *conflict resolution*, the policy described here is the most common.

One nice consequence of our conflict-resolution policy is that we can exploit rule order in simplifying the specification of a production systems. If we know that part of a condition in a rule must be true in order for the conditions in the preceding rules to have failed, then we can drop that part of the condition altogether.

As an example, consider the following production system. This system dictates the same actions as the preceding system, but it has fewer conjuncts. In particular, the condition that block C be on the table is unnecessary in the last two rules, since C must be on the table for the conditions in the preceding rules to have failed.

$$
\begin{array}{l}
\texttt{[Clear(C)} \wedge \texttt{On(C,z)} \rightarrow \texttt{U(C,z),} \\[4pt]
\texttt{On(A,C)} \wedge \texttt{Clear(A)} \rightarrow \texttt{U(A,C),} \\[4pt]
\texttt{On(B,C)} \wedge \texttt{On(C,A)} \rightarrow \texttt{U(B,C),} \\[4pt]
\texttt{Clear(B)} \wedge \texttt{On(B,A)} \rightarrow \texttt{U(B,A),} \\[4pt]
\texttt{Clear(A)} \wedge \texttt{On(A,B)} \wedge \texttt{Table(B)} \rightarrow \texttt{U(A,B),} \\[4pt]
\texttt{Table(A)} \wedge \texttt{Table(B)} \rightarrow \texttt{S(B,C),} \\[4pt]
\texttt{Table(A)} \wedge \texttt{On(B,C)} \rightarrow \texttt{S(A,B)]}
\end{array}
$$

Our final method for treating conditionality generalizes the notion of production systems. A *Markov procedure* f is a function from states to actions that dictates a single action to perform in each state of the world. (A production system is a special kind of Markov procedure.) Different Markov procedures dictate different actions in different states.

$$ f : S \longrightarrow A $$

Figure 11.5 illustrates a Markov procedure corresponding to the production system defined above. The key state for this procedure is the one in which all three blocks are on the table. From this state, the procedure prescribes the action of putting block B on block C; from there, it prescribes the action of putting A on B. In all other states, the procedure dictates appropriate actions to attain this key state.

Of course, this is not the only Markov procedure that solves the problem. For example, from the state in which block B is on block A and block C is on the table, we could move B directly to C rather than first putting it on the table.

On the other hand, there are some parts of the procedure that are not arbitrary. For example, every procedure that produces the final state prescribes the action of putting block A on block B whenever block B is on block C and block A is on the table.

A *Markov program* is a description of a Markov procedure in a formal programming language. In writing Markov programs, we use predicate calculus as our descriptive language, so a Markov program consists of a function constant π that designates the procedure and a set Δ of predicate-calculus sentences that describe that procedure.

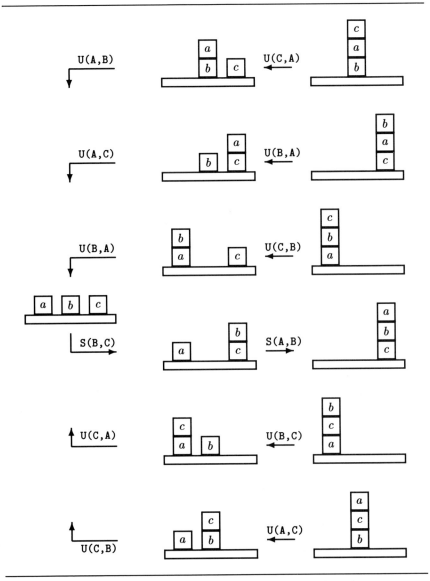

Figure 11.5   Procedure to stack up blocks *a*, *b*, **and** *c*.

A Markov program is *complete* if and only if it describes exactly one action for every state. Of course, not every Markov program is complete. Even though the procedure described by the program dictates a single action for each state, the description itself can be incomplete. In some cases, we may have a description that constrains the set of actions but does not pinpoint a particular action. In other cases, the program may specify actions for some states but not for others. Such *partial programs* are typical in AI applications.

The following sentences constitute a partial program (named P1) for the procedure pictured in Figure 11.5. In this case, the program is a simple syntactic variant of the production system presented earlier.

```
T(Clear(C),s) ∧ T(On(C,z),s)  ⇒  P1(s)=U(C,z)

T(On(A,C),s) ∧ T(Clear(A),s)  ⇒  P1(s)=U(A,C)

T(On(B,C),s) ∧ T(On(C,A),s)  ⇒  P1(s)=U(B,C)

T(Clear(B),s) ∧ T(On(B,A),s)  ⇒  P1(s)=U(B,A)

T(Clear(A),s) ∧ T(On(A,B),s) ∧ T(Table(B),s)  ⇒  P1(s)=U(A,B)

T(Table(A),s) ∧ T(Table(B),s) ∧ T(Table(C),s)  ⇒  P1(s)=S(B,C)

T(Table(A),s) ∧ T(On(B,C),s) ∧ T(Table(C),s)  ⇒  P1(s)=S(A,B)
```

A Markov program is *local* if and only if (1) each sentence contains at most one state-designating term or multiple occurrences of that term, and (2) that state designator, if it exists, is a universally quantified state variable. The presence of state descriptors (which designate sets of states) does not violate this definition. The significance of this property is that the action prescribed for a state by a local program can be determined solely from the features of that state. The preceding program is an example of a local program.

The preceding program is special in other ways as well. The conclusion in each implication is an equation dictating a specific action. The antecedents in each sentence are conditions on states written using the T relation.

When a program is local and has these additional properties, it is a simple matter to convert the program into a production system. We first form a list of the sentences in the program. Then, from each sentence we drop the name of the procedure, all occurrences of the T relation, and all state variables. Finally, we replace the implication operator ⇒ by the production rule operator →.

On the other hand, not every Markov program can be rewritten in this way. Problems arise when a program contains sentences that do not conclude with values for the procedure being defined, when the conclusion is not positive, and when multiple distinct state terms appear.

As an example of the first of these problems, consider the following program to stack block **A** on **B** in a world with any number of blocks. The first few sentences define the **Above** relation. The subsequent sentences use the relation in dictating appropriate actions to clear **A** and **B** before stacking

them. There is no simple way to convert this program to a production
system, because of the Above sentences.

$$T(On(x,y),s) \Rightarrow T(Above(x,y),s)$$

$$T(Above(x,y),s) \wedge T(Above(y,z),s) \Rightarrow T(Above(x,z),s)$$

$$T(\neg On(A,B),s) \wedge T(Above(x,A),s) \wedge T(On(x,y),s) \wedge \\ T(Clear(x),s) \Rightarrow P2(s)=U(x,y)$$

$$T(\neg On(A,B),s) \wedge T(Clear(A),s) \wedge T(Above(x,B),s) \wedge \\ T(On(x,y),s) \wedge T(Clear(x),s) \Rightarrow P2(s)=U(x,y)$$

$$T(On(A,y),s) \wedge T(Clear(A),s) \wedge T(Clear(B),s) \\ \Rightarrow P2(s)=M(A,y,B)$$

$$T(Table(A),s) \wedge T(Clear(A),s) \wedge T(Clear(B),s) \\ \Rightarrow P2(s)=S(A,B)$$

$$T(On(A,B),s) \\ \Rightarrow P2(s)=Noop$$

As another example of a Markov program that cannot be written as a
production system, consider the following simple constraint. It provides
only negative guidance about what should be done. The sentence asserts
that, whatever action is taken, it had better not be an instance of the
M operator.

$$P3(s) \neq M(x,y,z)$$

Finally, there are Markov programs involving multiple distinct state
terms. For example, the following Markov program asserts that, if an
action leads to a state in which block A is on block B, then that action
must be performed.

$$T(On(A,B),Do(k,s)) \Rightarrow P4(s)=k$$

The only way to convert such Markov programs to production systems
is to add additional information to our conceptualization of the state of the
world and to provide actions that modify this additional state.

11.6 Bibliographical and Historical Remarks

McCarthy [McCarthy 1963] proposed the idea of including states among
the objects that exist in one's conceptualization of the world. The idea was
discussed further in [McCarthy 1969]. Green [Green 1969a] was the first
person to develop a large, working program for reasoning about actions

and states. Kowalski [Kowalski 1979b] included *propositions* as objects and a *holds* relation on propositions and situations, which greatly simplifies writing frame axioms. Predicate-calculus formulations of actions and their effects on states has been called the *situation calculus*.

The frame problem has been thoroughly discussed in the literature. Some of the more important analyses are in [Hayes 1973a, Raphael 1971, Sandewall 1972]. Several different approaches have been pursued in attempting to deal with the frame problem. In their STRIPS system, Fikes and Nilsson [Fikes 1971] represented actions by a simple prescription for changing state descriptors, leaving unchanged those descriptors that are not specifically prescribed to be changed. Hayes [Hayes 1979b, Hayes 1985b] introduced the notion of *histories* in an attempt to define a conceptualization in which the frame problem does not arise. McCarthy [McCarthy 1986] and Reiter [Reiter 1980a] argued for the advantages of nonmonotonic reasoning in dealing with the frame problem. Hanks and McDermott [Hanks 1986] showed that a straightforward application of circumscription (using the usual situation-calculus formulation) does not produce results strong enough to solve the frame problem. Lifschitz [Lifschitz 1986c] introduced a variant called pointwise circumscription that is strong enough to do the job. He also proposed a reconceptualization of actions and their effects that permits the use of ordinary circumscription in solving the frame problem and the qualification problem [Lifschitz 1986d]. Shoham [Shoham 1986a] proposed an alternative minimization method related to circumscription, called *chronological ignorance*.

The classical state-action model described in this chapter can be generalized in three directions. First, we may want to reason about time directly. (The usual state formulations do not mention time explicitly, although there is obviously an implicit connection.) Second, assuming an underlying conceptualization involving time, we may want to consider continuous actions. Third, we may be concerned with simultaneous actions in addition to those that occur in strict sequence.

Several AI researchers have been concerned with reasoning with time. Some incorporate a time argument directly in their relations; others resort to a modal temporal logic. Shoham [Shoham 1986b] gave a clear overview of the field. Also see papers by McDermott [McDermott 1982b], Allen [Allen 1983, 1984, 1985a], Allen and Hayes [Allen 1985b], and Shoham [Shoham 1986c]. Van Benthem [Van Benthem 1983] wrote an excellent book on temporal logic.

Insufficient attention has been paid to the problem of continuous actions. Hendrix [Hendrix 1973] is an excellent early paper. Some of the work on "qualitative reasoning" [Bobrow 1984, deKleer 1984] dealt with continuous physical processes.

To deal with simultaneous actions, Georgeff and colleagues developed extended situation-calculus models [Georgeff 1984, 1985, 1987c]. The problem of modeling the effects of simultaneous actions also is, of course, a problem for parallel or concurrent programming. See, for example, [Filman 1984].

Exercises

1. *Side effects.* We can conceptualize a LISP s-expression as a composite object with two parts. The state-dependent function Car designates one part, and the state-dependent function Cdr denotes the other. The action Rplaca(x,y) changes the first part of x such that it is y. Similarly, the action Rplacd(x,y) replaces the second part of x with y. Write predicate-calculus sentences to describe the effects of these two operators.

2. *Simulation.* Give a resolution proof that block B is on block C after executing the action block [U(C,A),S(B,C),S(A,B)], starting in the state in which C is on A, A is on the table, and B is on the table.

3. *Nondeterminism.* Let us assume that our language includes terms of the form ND(α,β), where α and β are arbitrary actions. The idea is to use a term of this sort to designate a nondetermistic choice between the action designated by α and the action designated by β; i.e., executing this program is accomplished by executing one of α or β. Write a sentence that defines the semantics of ND in the manner of Sections 11.4 and 11.5.

4. *The waterpot problem.* You are given a 5-liter pot filled with water and an empty 2-liter pot, and are asked to obtain precisely 1 liter of water in the 2-liter pot. You can transfer water from one pot to the other, and you can discard water, but no additional water is available.

   a. What is the state space for this problem?

   b. What are the operators?

   c. Write operator descriptions and frame axioms for your operators.

   d. Describe an action block that solves the problem.

   e. Give a resolution proof that your program works.

5. *The 8-puzzle.* The 8-puzzle consists of a set of eight numbered tiles arranged in a 3 × 3 grid. Starting from a state in which the tiles are scrambled arbitrarily (as shown in the left box), the goal is to achieve a state in which the tiles are arranged in clockwise order (as shown in the right box). The only allowable state transitions are movements of the blank tile up, down, left, or right.

2	8	3
1		4
7	6	5

$\Longrightarrow$

1	2	3
8		4
7	6	5

a. What is the state space for this problem?

b. What are the operators?

c. Write operator descriptions and frame axioms for your operators.

d. Describe an action block that solves the puzzle.

e. Give a resolution proof that the tile numbered 8 is in the correct position after your composite action is executed.

6. *Thermostats.*   Write a production system for a thermostat controlling a furnace. The thermostat's external state includes a temperature setting (in degrees), a temperature reading (in degrees), and state sensor for the furnace (either on or off). The thermostat has three actions: It can turn on the furnace, turn off the furnace, or do nothing. It turns on the furnace whenever the ambient temperature is more than 5 degrees cooler than the setting. It turns off the furnace whenever the ambient temperature is more than 5 degrees warmer than the setting. Otherwise, it does nothing.

CHAPTER 12

Planning

THE ABILITY TO PLAN AHEAD is a key aspect of intelligent behavior. By knowing the consequences of our actions and exploiting that knowledge, we can achieve goals while avoiding danger and economizing on resources. For example, we know better than to rush out in front of a speeding car when trying to cross a busy street, and we can save time and energy in shopping if we think in advance about what we need to buy and plan an appropriate route.

In planning, we start with a set of desired properties and try to devise a plan that results in a state with the desired properties. We can picture this process as shown in Figure 12.1. The planner in this case takes as data an initial state designator σ, a goal designator ρ, a set Γ of action designators, and a database Ω of sentences about the initial state, the goal, and the available actions. The output is a term γ designating an action that, when executed in a state i satisfying the initial state description, produces a state g satisfying the goal description.

In this chapter, we first discuss the inputs to the planning process and the output. We then look at a method for planning action blocks and conditional plans. Finally, we discuss a variety of techniques for enhancing planning efficiency.

12.1 Initial State

The *initial state* in a planning problem is the state in which the executor is expected to begin operation. The initial state designator is our name for

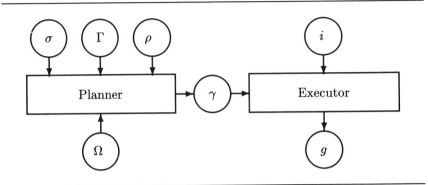

Figure 12.1   Planning and execution.

this state, and we use this state designator in writing sentences about the initial state.

As an example, consider the Blocks World state in which block C is on block A and blocks A and B are both on the table. If we call this state S1, then the following sentences constitute an initial state description.

$$T(Clear(C),S1)$$

$$T(On(C,A),S1)$$

$$T(Table(A),S1)$$

$$T(Clear(B),S1)$$

$$T(Table(B),S1)$$

Note that there is no requirement that the initial state description be complete. If some information is left out, it simply means that more than one state may satisfy the description and the planner must be sure to find a plan that is guaranteed to work in any of these states.

12.2 Goals

Generally speaking, a goal is any desirable state. In some planning problems, there is just a single goal state. For example, we may desire the Blocks World state in which all the blocks are on the table. In other problems, there can be more than one goal state. For example, we may desire that there be a stack of three blocks, but not care about the exact order. In a world with three blocks, this condition is true in any one of six states.

These possibilities lead to a conceptualization of goals as a unary relation on states. We say that a state is a *goal state* if and only if it satisfies this relation. In describing goals, we use the unary relation constant `Goal` to designate this goal relation. Consider the following examples.

The following sentence specifies that any state is a goal so long as block A is on block B and block B is on block C. There is just one state in which this is true.

$$T(On(A,B),t) \land T(On(B,C),t) \Leftrightarrow Goal(t)$$

In the following goal description, we allow any state in which block A is on block B. We do not care at all about block C; it could be on top of A, under B, or off to the side. There are three states that satisfy this goal relation.

$$T(On(A,B),t) \Leftrightarrow Goal(t)$$

Using variables, we can describe block configurations without naming individual blocks. For example, the following sentence describes a goal in which we desire a stack of three blocks without regard to order. In this case, there are six goal states.

$$T(On(x,y),t) \land T(On(y,z),t) \Leftrightarrow Goal(t)$$

For reasons of pedagogy, our examples here are extremely simple. Note, however, that in realistic domains, goal descriptions often are more complex.

12.3 Actions

The set of action designators in a planning problem includes a term for every primitive or composite action that can be used to convert the initial state into a state that satisfies the goal relation. Even though there are only finitely many primitive action designators, there can be infinitely many composite action designators in this set. When this is the case, we cannot pass the set itself as argument to our planner, and so instead we specify a computable metalevel relation that is true of every term in the set and only those terms that are in the set.

The reason for including this information as input to the planner is to restrict the plans it produces to those that can be used by the executor we have in mind. For example, it is inappropriate to allow the state descriptor `Color(A,Blue)` to be used in a conditional action if we know that the executor cannot determine the color of blocks. This is enforced by excluding from our action set all terms that involve this condition.

Corresponding to the elements in the action designator set in a planning problem, we have appropriate action descriptions. These include operator descriptions and frame axioms for primitive actions, the usual definitions of composite actions such as action blocks and conditional actions, and state constraints that must be true of every state; i.e., relationships that cannot be changed by any action.

For example, from Chapter 11, we know that the following sentences describe the effects of the U and S operators.

```
T(On(x,y),s) ∧ T(Clear(x),s) ⇒
  T(Table(x),Do(U(x,y),s))) ∧
  T(Clear(y),Do(U(x,y),s)))

T(Table(x),s) ∧ T(Clear(x),s) ∧ T(Clear(y),s) ∧ x≠y ⇒
  T(On(x,y),Do(S(x,y),s))
```

The state features not affected by these operators can be described with the following frame axioms. We also have added a frame axiom for the Noop action.

```
T(Table(u),s) ⇒ T(Table(u),Do(U(x,y),s))

T(Clear(u),s) ⇒ T(Clear(u),Do(U(x,y),s))

T(On(u,v),s) ∧ u≠x ⇒ T(On(u,v),Do(U(x,y),s))

T(Table(u),s) ∧ u≠x ⇒ T(Table(u),Do(S(x,y),s))

T(Clear(u),s) ∧ u≠y ⇒ T(Clear(u),Do(S(x,y),s))

T(On(u,v),s) ⇒ T(On(u,v),Do(S(x,y),s))

T(p,s) ⇒ T(p,Do(Noop,s))
```

From Chapter 11, we have the following axioms that define the effects of action blocks. The result of executing the empty sequence in a state is just the state itself, so any property true in the state is true in the state resulting from the execution of the empty sequence. If a property is true in the state that results from executing the sequence 1 in the state resulting from the execution of the action a, then the property is true of the state resulting from the execution of the sequence a.1.

```
T(p,s) ⇒ T(p,Do([],s))

T(p,Do(1,Do(a,s))) ⇒ T(p,Do(a.1,s))
```

From Chapter 11, we also have a definition for the effects of executing a conditional action. The first of the following sentences says that the result of executing a conditional is the result of executing the first alternative, if the condition is true. The second sentence says that the result is the result of executing the other alternative, if the condition is not true.

$$T(p,s) \land T(q,Do(a,s)) \Rightarrow T(q,Do(If(p,a,b),s))$$

$$\neg T(p,s) \land T(q,Do(b,s)) \Rightarrow T(q,Do(If(p,a,b),s))$$

Finally, we add to our database state constraints that express those properties that are true of every state. For the Blocks World, these include the following.

$$T(Table(x),s) \Leftrightarrow \neg \exists y \; T(On(x,y),s)$$

$$T(Clear(y),s) \Leftrightarrow \neg \exists x \; T(On(x,y),s)$$

$$T(On(x,y),s) \land y \neq z \Rightarrow \neg T(On(x,z),s)$$

Of course, none of these descriptions need be complete. As we shall see, it is sometimes possible to produce guaranteed plans without full information, although this may require the use of conditional actions.

12.4 Plans

As described in the introduction to this chapter, a *planning problem* consists of an initial state designator σ, a goal relation designator ρ, a set of action designators Γ, a database Ω that includes sentences that describe the initial state, the goal relation, and the available actions.

An action designator γ is a *plan* for a planning problem of this sort if and only if it satisfies the following conditions.

(1) The action designator must be a member of the action designator set; i.e., $\gamma \in \Gamma$.

(2) We must be able to prove from Ω that γ achieves a state satisfying ρ when executed in state σ; i.e., $\Omega \models (\rho(Do(\gamma,\sigma)))$.

As an example of these definitions, consider a planning problem in which S1 is the initial state designator and Coal is the name of the goal relation. We assume that Γ includes the names for all of our usual primitive Blocks World actions and all finite sequences thereof. Our initial state description states that the block named C is on the block named A and blocks A and B are on the table. Our goal description states that a state satisfies the goals if and only if block A is on block B and block B is on block C.

The term [U(C,A),S(B,C),S(A,B)] is a plan to solve this problem. It is clearly a member of Γ. Furthermore, using the information in Ω, we can easily prove that the plan works; i.e., we can derive the following sentence.

$$Goal(Do([U(C,A),S(B,C),S(A,B)],S1))$$

We encourage the reader at this point to find a derivation for this sentence.

After having seen that proof methods can be used to show that a given plan achieves a given goal, we now move to the problem of devising a plan to achieve a goal.

12.5 Green's Method

Green's method is a planning procedure based on resolution. It takes as arguments a term designating an initial state, a unary relation constant designating a goal relation, a predicate satisfied by executable plans and only executable plans, and a database of facts about the initial state, the goal relation, and the available operators.

The key to the method is the use of fill-in-the-blank resolution to derive a correct plan as a side effect of proving the existence of a correct plan. In particular, given an initial state term σ and a goal relation constant ρ, we try to derive the following *plan-existence* statement.

$$\exists \nu \; \rho(\text{Do}(\nu,\sigma))$$

We use the executability predicate to check every answer returned by this process. If we find an answer that satisfies the predicate, we return that term as answer to the overall planning problem. Otherwise, we continue enumerating solutions.

Since Green's method is based on resolution, it is possible to prove some strong properties about its planning abilities. The method is sound in that it produces only correct plans. It also is complete in that it is guaranteed to produce a correct plan whenever one exists. There is no restriction about the type of plan involved. The next two sections show how the method can be used in the creation of action blocks and conditional programs.

Unfortunately, Green's method, like all planning procedures, can be extremely inefficient. After our discussion of the use of Green's method in synthesizing action blocks and conditional actions, we look at some methods for improving efficiency.

12.6 Action Blocks

The simplest use of Green's method is in the design of action blocks. In the following examples, we use the sentences listed in Section 12.3. As our initial state, we take the state S1 in which block A is on block B and block B is on block C.

T(Clear(A),S1)

T(On(A,B),S1)

```
T(On(B,C),S1)

T(Table(C),S1)
```

We define our goal to be the achievement of a state in which block A is on the table.

$$T(\text{Table}(A),t) \Leftrightarrow \text{Goal}(t)$$

We start the planning process by negating the plan-existence statement, converting to clausal form, and adding an appropriate answer literal. This results in the clause shown in the first line of the following derivation.

1. $\{\neg\text{Goal}(\text{Do}(a,S1)),\text{Ans}(a)\}$
2. $\{\neg T(\text{Table}(A),\text{Do}(a,S1)),\text{Ans}(a)\}$
3. $\{\neg T(\text{On}(A,y),S1),\neg T(\text{Clear}(A),S1),\text{Ans}(U(A,y))\}$
4. $\{\neg T(\text{Clear}(A),S1),\text{Ans}(U(A,B))\}$
5. $\{\text{Ans}(U(A,B))\}$

First, we use the goal description to deduce the clause in line 2. Then, we use the description for the U operator to reduce this goal to the subgoal in line 3. The upshot of this reduction is that we know that, if we can find a block y in state S1 such that A is on y in S1 and A is clear, then executing U(A,y) in that state will achieve the goal. Of course, both of these conditions are true if we let y be B; therefore using the corresponding facts from the initial state description, we arrive at the final answer.

As a slightly more complicated example, imagine a planning problem with the same initial state and operators but a slightly more specific goal. Starting from the same initial state, we would like to achieve a goal state in which both A and C are on the table, as described by the following sentence. The previous solution works for this problem as well. We present the case because it shows how frame axioms are called into play.

$$T(\text{Table}(A),t) \wedge T(\text{Table}(C),t) \Leftrightarrow \text{Goal}(t)$$

We start the process as before, by negating the plan-existence axiom, converting to clausal form, and adding an answer literal. As before, we replace this clause with clause 2 using the goal description and reduce this goal to the subgoal in line 3 using the description for the U operator. In this case, the subgoal consists of two constraints on state S1 and an additional constraint on the state Do(U(A,y),S1). Using the first frame axiom for the U operator, we replace this by a constraint on state S1, as shown in line 4. Since C is on the table in the initial state, we can eliminate that condition. The rest of the derivation then proceeds as before.

1. {¬Goal(Do(a,S1)),Ans(a)}
2. {¬T(Table(A),Do(a,S1)),¬T(Table(C),Do(a,S1)),Ans(a)}
3. {¬T(On(A,y),S1),¬T(Clear(A),S1),
   ¬T(Table(C),Do(U(A,y),S1)),Ans(U(A,y))}
4. {¬T(On(A,y),S1),¬T(Clear(A),S1),
   ¬T(Table(C),S1),Ans(U(A,y))}
5. {¬T(On(A,y),S1),¬T(Clear(A),S1),Ans(U(A,y))}
6. {¬T(Clear(A),S1),Ans(U(A,B))}
7. {Ans(U(A,B))}

As a final example, consider a variation with the same initial state but with the goal of getting block B onto the table. This problem is more difficult than either of the preceding problems in that two actions must be performed to achieve the goal. The following sentence describes the goal.

$$T(Table(B),t) \Leftrightarrow Goal(t)$$

Lines 1 and 2 of the following derivation are obtained as before. The axioms defining action blocks are then used to produce lines 3 through 5, in which the action variable is expanded into a two-member action block. We then use the operator description for the U operator to reduce the goal to the subgoal of finding an action that produces a state in which B is on some block y and B is clear. Note that, in performing this reduction, we bind the second action in the answer literal. At this point, we can use the operator description for the U operator again to reduce the goal of clearing B to the two new subgoals of proving that there is a block x on B in state S1 and that block is clear. Using this axiom binds the other action in the answer literal. We then use a frame axiom for U to reduce the goal of proving that B is on y after this action to the subgoal of proving that it is true beforehand, in S1. The rest of the derivation follows easily.

1. {¬Goal(Do(a,S1)),Ans(a)}
2. {¬T(Table(B),Do(a,S1)),Ans(a)}
3. {¬T(Table(B),Do(l,Do(b,S1))),Ans(b.l)}
4. {¬T(Table(B),Do(m,Do(c,Do(b,S1)))),Ans(b.(c.m))}
5. {¬T(Table(B),Do(c,Do(b,S1))),Ans([b,c])}
6. {¬T(On(B,y),Do(b,S1)),¬T(Clear(B),Do(b,S1)),
   Ans([b,U(B,y)])}
7. {¬T(On(B,y),Do(U(x,B),S1)),¬T(On(x,B),S1),
   ¬T(Clear(x),S1),Ans([U(x,B),U(B,y)])}
8. {¬T(On(B,y),S1),¬T(On(x,B),S1),
   ¬T(Clear(x),S1),Ans([U(x,B),U(B,y)])}
9. {¬T(On(x,B),S1),¬T(Clear(x),S1),
   Ans([U(x,B),U(B,C)])}

10. $\{\neg \text{T}(\text{Clear}(\text{A}),\text{S1}),\text{Ans}([\text{U}(\text{A},\text{B}),\text{U}(\text{B},\text{C})])\}$
11. $\{\text{Ans}([\text{U}(\text{A},\text{B}),\text{U}(\text{B},\text{C})])\}$

In looking at the derivations in this chapter, it is important to bear in mind that they are resolution derivations, not resolution traces. The alternative deductions are not listed. This can give one the impression that planning is easy. In fact, there are usually numerous alternatives, and planning in general is an extremely expensive process.

12.7 Conditional Plans

When information is missing at planning time, it is sometimes impossible to devise an action block that is guaranteed to achieve a goal state. Fortunately, we can solve problems of this sort through the use of conditional actions.

As an example of using Green's method in generating a conditional plan, consider a planning problem in which we know that block A is clear in the initial state, but we do not know anything else. Thus, we have the following initial state description.

$$\text{T}(\text{Clear}(\text{A}),\text{S1})$$

Our goal is to get block A onto the table.

$$\text{T}(\text{Table}(\text{A}),\text{t}) \Leftrightarrow \text{Goal}(\text{t})$$

The problem is underconstrained in that block A may already be on the table or it may be on block B or on block C. Because of this uncertainty, there is no single action sequence that is guaranteed to solve the problem. On the other hand, we can devise a conditional program to solve the problem, as shown in the following derivation.

1. $\{\neg \text{Goal}(\text{Do}(\text{a},\text{S1})),\text{Ans}(\text{a})\}$
2. $\{\neg \text{T}(\text{Table}(\text{A}),\text{Do}(\text{a},\text{S1})),\text{Ans}(\text{a})\}$

3. $\{\neg \text{T}(\text{p},\text{S1}),\neg \text{T}(\text{Table}(\text{A}),\text{Do}(\text{a},\text{S1})),\text{Ans}(\text{If}(\text{p},\text{a},\text{b}))\}$
4. $\{\neg \text{T}(\text{p},\text{S1}),\neg \text{T}(\text{On}(\text{A},\text{y}),\text{S1}),\neg \text{T}(\text{Clear}(\text{A}),\text{S1}),$
   $\text{Ans}(\text{If}(\text{p},\text{U}(\text{A},\text{y}),\text{b}))\}$
5. $\{\neg \text{T}(\text{p},\text{S1}),\neg \text{T}(\text{On}(\text{A},\text{y}),\text{S1}),\text{Ans}(\text{If}(\text{p},\text{U}(\text{A},\text{y}),\text{b}))\}$
6. $\{\neg \text{T}(\text{On}(\text{A},\text{y}),\text{S1}),\text{Ans}(\text{If}(\text{On}(\text{A},\text{y}),\text{U}(\text{A},\text{y}),\text{b}))\}$

7. $\{\text{T}(\text{p},\text{S1}),\neg \text{T}(\text{Table}(\text{A}),\text{Do}(\text{b},\text{S1})),\text{Ans}(\text{If}(\text{p},\text{a},\text{b}))\}$
8. $\{\text{T}(\text{p},\text{S1}),\neg \text{T}(\text{Table}(\text{A}),\text{S1}),\text{Ans}(\text{If}(\text{p},\text{a},\text{Noop}))\}$
9. $\{\text{T}(\text{p},\text{S1}),\text{T}(\text{On}(\text{A},\text{K}),\text{S1}),\text{Ans}(\text{If}(\text{p},\text{a},\text{Noop}))\}$
10. $\{\text{T}(\text{On}(\text{A},\text{K}),\text{S1}),\text{Ans}(\text{If}(\text{On}(\text{A},\text{K}),\text{a},\text{Noop}))\}$

11. {Ans(If(On(A,K),a,Noop)),Ans(If(On(A,K),U(A,K),b)}
12. {Ans(If(On(A,K),U(A,K),Noop))}

First, we reduce the goal statement to its definition. Then, we resolve the result with the two axioms for conditionals, leading to clauses 3 and 7. The operator description for U allows us to reduce clause 3 to clause 4. We use the fact that A is clear in the initial state to produce clause 5. Then, by factoring, we get clause 6. Note that this fills in the condition in the answer. Similarly, we use the frame axiom for Noop to reduce clause 7 to clause 8. This time, however, we use one of the state constraints in producing clause 9, in particular the first state constraint listed in Section 12.3. Note that the symbol K is a Skolem constant for the existential variable in the state constraint. Once again, factoring collapses literals and fills in the condition. Resolving the results of these two threads of deduction and factoring once again gives us an answer. We then generalize the Skolem constant K in this answer to get the desired program.

Note that, in getting this answer, we needed factoring. The generation of conditional plans is one important area in which this rule of inference is virtually essential.

12.8 Planning Direction

One of the key determinants of planning efficiency is planning direction. In some cases, it is better to plan forward from the initial state. In other cases, it is better to work backward from the goal. In yet other cases, a mixed strategy is best.

In resolution-based planning, we can enforce directionality using a modified set-of-support restriction strategy in which we relax the assumption that the complement of the set of support be satisfiable. If we take the clause derived from the negated plan-existence statement as our set of support, the result is backward planning. If we take the sentences describing the initial state as our set of support, we get forward planning. If we take the union of these two sets as our set of support, we get a mixed strategy.

All of the derivations in the preceding sections are instances of backward planning. In each, we start with the negated goal statement, reduce this goal to subgoals, and so forth until we get to conditions on the initial state.

As an example of forward planning, consider the abbreviated derivation shown below. The problem is to get block B on the table from an initial state in which A is on B and B is on C. We have rewritten the initial state description here as clauses 1 through 4 to help visualize the derivation. As always, we have the negated plan-existence statement as well; however, in this case we do not use it until the very end of the derivation. We derive clauses 6 through 10 from clauses 1 through 5 using the operator description and frame axioms for the U(A,B) action. We derive clauses 11 through 16

from these clauses and the operator description and frame axioms for the
U(B,C) action. We then derive clauses 17 through 20 using the axioms
defining the effects of action blocks. Finally, we use the goal description to
derive clause 21, which resolves with the negated goal query to yield the
overall answer.

1. {T(Clear(A),S1)}
2. {T(On(A,B),S1)}
3. {T(On(B,C),S1)}
4. {T(Table(C),S1)}
5. {¬Goal(Do(a,t)),Ans(a)}

6. {T(Clear(A),Do(U(A,B),S1))}
7. {T(Table(A),Do(U(A,B),S1))}
8. {T(Clear(B),Do(U(A,B),S1))}
9. {T(On(B,C),Do(U(A,B),S1))}
10. {T(Table(C),Do(U(A,B),S1))}

11. {T(Clear(A),Do(U(B,C),Do(U(A,B),S1)))}
12. {T(Table(A),Do(U(B,C),Do(U(A,B),S1)))}
13. {T(Clear(B),Do(U(B,C),Do(U(A,B),S1)))}
14. {T(Table(B),Do(U(B,C),Do(U(A,B),S1)))}
15. {T(Clear(C),Do(U(B,C),Do(U(A,B),S1)))}
16. {T(Table(C),Do(U(B,C),Do(U(A,B),S1)))}

17. {T(Table(B),Do(U(B,C),Do(U(A,B),S1)))}
18. {T(Table(B),Do([],Do(U(B,C),Do(U(A,B),S1))))}
19. {T(Table(B),Do([U(B,C)],Do(U(A,B),S1)))}
20. {T(Table(B),Do([U(A,B),U(B,C)],S1))}

21. {Goal(Do([U(A,B),U(B,C)],S1))}
22. {Ans([U(A,B),U(B,C)])}

One problem with using the set-of-support strategy to implement
forward planning is that it need not be complete. Consider, as an example,
a planning problem in which there is no information about the initial state
and in which there is an action that achieves the goal in any state. Using
backward planning in this situation, we could derive a plan, but there
would be no forward deductions at all. Nevertheless, in many cases forward
planning and backward planning are equally competent.

On the other hand, there are situations in which backward planning
is impractical. Take, for example, the problem of winning a chess game.
We could, at least in principle, work backward from some known winning
position in deciding our next move. The problem is that in general this is
prohibitively expensive. The alternative is to search forward a few moves,
replacing the goal of a win with the goal of the value of an appropriate
evaluation function on states.

For situations in which both forward and backward planning make sense, the choice of direction in planning usually is based on efficiency. If the number of possibilities to be explored in the forward direction exceeds the number in the backward direction, backward planning is indicated. If the branching factor in the backward direction exceeds that in the forward direction, forward planning may be better.

For reasons of conformity with the bulk of the literature on planning, we assume backward planning in the next few sections.

12.9 Unachievability Pruning

One source of computational waste in backward planning is work on clauses that describe unachievable states. For example, it is not possible to create a state in which block A is on block B and block B is clear. Thus, if we ever produce the following clause during backward planning using resolution refutation, we can prune it from further consideration because it is valid (i.e., its negation is inconsistent).

$$\{\neg T(On(A,B),Do(a,S1)),\neg T(Clear(B),Do(a,S1))\}$$

One way to detect such cases is to set up a resolution subprocess to test clauses for validity. If this test reveals that a clause is valid, that clause is pruned from further consideration. This deletion strategy is sometimes called *unachievability pruning*. We test for validity by testing the negated clause for consistency.

The database for the consistency tests consists of (1) the state constraints in the planning problem, and (2) the clauses that result from negating the clause in question and converting to clausal form. Thus, for the preceding problem, we would use the state constraints from Section 12.3 with the following clauses. Note that the variable a is replaced by the Skolem constant K in the process.

$$T(On(A,B),Do(K,S1))$$

$$T(Clear(B),Do(K,S1))$$

In this case, it is fairly easy to find an inconsistency. The fact that A is on B means that B is not clear, contradicting the supposition that B is clear.

For many databases, we can show that this resolution process is guaranteed to terminate, with an indication of either consistency or inconsistency. There are cases, however, for which it is impossible to know whether this will happen, and this can spell problems if the original resolution process is waiting for the resolution process to complete. One way of dealing with such situations is to limit the amount of time spent in consistency checking. Another approach is to interleave the consistency-checking process with the planning process.

12.10 State Alignment

During the planning process, we sometimes encounter situations in which there are several conditions to be satisfied in a single state. When we use an operator description axiom to satisfy one of these conditions, we end up with a subproblem in which the operator's preconditions must be met in one state, whereas the remaining conditions must be met in the successor state.

In the following example, the first clause expresses the goal of getting block A onto block B and block B onto the table. After using the operator description axiom for U to reduce one of the conditions on the state designated Do(a,S1), we end up with a clause involving two conditions on state S1 and the remaining condition on state Do(a,S1). Obviously, this subgoal is unachievable; but we cannot use unachievability pruning, since the states are not aligned.

1. $\{\neg T(On(A,B),Do(a,S1)),\neg T(Table(B),Do(a,S1))\}$
2. $\{\neg T(On(A,B),Do(U(B,y),S1)),\neg T(On(B,y),S1),$
   $\neg T(Clear(B),S1)\}$

At this point, we have the choice of further reducing the conditions on state S1 or reducing the remaining condition on Do(U(B,y),S1).

State alignment is a restriction strategy that excludes any resolution on a literal containing a state term σ when there is another literal in the same clause containing the state term Do(α,σ). The intent is to avoid reductions of conditions on one state, while there are still conditions on a successor state to be reduced.

When used with unachievability pruning, state alignment can lead to substantial improvements in planning efficiency. By aligning the conditions in a clause on a single state, we sometimes discover inconsistent conditions that would not otherwise be found. As a result, we can eliminate the clause and save further work. For example, we can prune the second clause in the preceding deduction, since it is impossible to achieve a state in which B is clear and A is on B. This problem would not have been caught if we had applied unachievability pruning to the first clause.

It should be clear that the use of state alignment can destroy the completeness of Green's method when used on arbitrary axiom sets. However, if the axioms are all written in the form of operator descriptions and frame axioms like the ones in this and the previous chapters, this does not happen.

12.11 Frame-Axiom Suppression

During planning, it often is the case that we need to fill in an action variable in order to prove that a state satisfies a specified condition. In so doing, we can use an operator description axiom to suggest the action or we can use a frame axiom.

For example, in working with the first literal in the following clause, we can use an operator description axiom for U to reduce this condition to some conditions on state S1, thereby instantiating the action variable a to U(A,y). Alternatively, we can use a frame axiom for an action such as S(C,B), again reducing the condition to conditions on S1 and instantiating the variable.

$$\{\neg T(\texttt{Table(A)},\texttt{Do(a,S1)}),\neg T(\texttt{Table(B)},\texttt{Do(a,S1)})\}$$

The use of a frame axiom in this situation is a bad idea, since it merely reduces the problem of achieving that condition in one state to the problem of achieving it in an earlier state. Now, it is possible that the frame axiom chosen fills in just the action needed to achieve some other state condition in the clause. However, this is unlikely; in most applications, there are more ways to preserve a condition than there are to achieve it. In other words, the choice is more likely to be wrong than right, which will lead to a need to back up at a later point.

As an example, consider the following resolution trace in which we have shown all the reductions of the first literal in the preceding clause. The conclusion in the second line is derived from the operator description for U(A,y), and the other conclusions are derived from frame axioms. Of the three frame axiom reductions, only one works.

1. $\{\neg T(\texttt{Table(A)},\texttt{Do(a,S1)}),\neg T(\texttt{Table(B)},\texttt{Do(a,S1)}),\texttt{Ans(a)}\}$
2. $\{\neg T(\texttt{On(A,y)},\texttt{S1}),\neg T(\texttt{Clear(A)},\texttt{S1}),$
   $\neg T(\texttt{Table(B)},\texttt{Do(U(A,y),S1)}),\texttt{Ans(U(A,y))}\}$
3. $\{\neg T(\texttt{Table(A)},\texttt{S1}),\neg T(\texttt{Table(B)},\texttt{Do(U(x,y),S1)}),\texttt{Ans(U(x,y))}\}$
4. $\{\neg T(\texttt{Table(A)},\texttt{S1}),\texttt{A}{\neq}\texttt{x},$
   $\neg T(\texttt{Table(B)},\texttt{Do(S(x,y),S1)}),\texttt{Ans(S(x,y))}\}$
5. $\{\neg T(\texttt{Table(A)},\texttt{S1}),\neg T(\texttt{Table(B)},\texttt{Do(Noop,S1)}),\texttt{Ans(Noop)}\}$

Frame-axiom suppression is a resolution restriction strategy in which we disallow any resolutions in which a frame axiom is used to constrain an action variable; i.e., a resolution in which the literal resolved upon is a condition on a state designated by a term of the form $\texttt{Do}(\nu,\sigma)$, where ν is a variable.

Applying frame-axiom suppression to the preceding example allows the reduction in line 2 to take place while preventing the generation of the clauses in lines 3, 4 and 5. In a world with more actions and, therefore, more frame axioms, the savings would be more dramatic. Of course, once the reduction in the second line is made, it is permissible to use the frame axiom for U(A,y) to reduce the second literal, since the action variable has been filled in already.

As we saw in the discussion of conditional plans, it is occasionally useful to introduce the Noop action into plans, but this is prevented by frame-axiom suppression. To generate such plans, we need to make an exception to the rule and allow the use of frame axioms to introduce the Noop action, but we need not do this for any other actions. With this extension, we can show that frame-axiom suppression has no effect on completeness when used with axiom sets in the form used in this and the previous chapters.

12.12 Goal Regression

It is interesting to note that all the operator descriptions in our examples have had a particularly simple form. The effects of each operator are characterized by a single sentence (not counting frame axioms and state constraints). The sentence in each case is an implication in which the antecedents mention conditions on a state necessary for the operator to have the effects mentioned in the consequent. The upshot of this is that, whenever we have operator descriptions of this sort, we can use an extremely simple but powerful planning strategy known as *goal regression*.

First, we rewrite our operator descriptions in an equivalent but simpler form. In particular, each operator instance is characterized by a set of prerequisites, a set of positive effects, and a set of negative effects. The prerequisites Pre(a) of an action a are the conditions that must be true in order for a to have the desired effect. The positive effects Add(a) are the conditions that become true after the action is executed. The negative effects Del(a) are the conditions that become false.

As an example of this transformation, consider how we would rewrite our description for the U operator. Looking at the operator description, we note that the conditions on an instance of the form U(x,y) include the state descriptors Clear(x) and On(x,y). The positive effects include Table(x) and Clear(y). There is just one negative effect, On(x,y).

$$Pre(U(x,y)) = \{On(x,y), Clear(x)\}$$
$$Add(U(x,y)) = \{Table(x), Clear(y)\}$$
$$Del(U(x,y)) = \{On(x,y)\}$$

In this formulation, we define a *goal set* to be a set of state sets, such that any state in the intersection of those sets is satisfactory. For example, the following goal set describes the set of states in which blocks **A** and **B** are on the table.

$$\{\texttt{Table(A)},\texttt{Table(B)}\}$$

The basic step in goal regression is the reduction of one goal to a subgoal on the basis of an action description. The reduction must have the property that executing the described action in a state satisfying the subgoal will produce a state satisfying the goal. Given the preceding definitions, we can see that the subgoal `Reg(q,a)` resulting from the *regression* of q *through* the action a consists of the prerequisites of a together with the members in q that are not among the positive effects of a. Furthermore, for the action to work, there must be no overlap between the negative effects of the action and the conditions in the goal.

$$(\texttt{q} \cap \texttt{Del(a)}) = \{\} \;\Rightarrow\; \texttt{Reg(q,a)} = \texttt{Pre(a)} \cup (\texttt{q} - \texttt{Add(a)})$$

For example, regressing this goal set through the action `U(A,B)` leads to the following goal set. Neither of the original goals is a negative effect of this action, so our definition applies. The subgoal set consists of the prerequisites of `U(A,B)` (i.e., `Clear(A)` and `On(A,B)`) together with the one goal not contained in the action's positive effects.

$$\{\texttt{Clear(A)},\texttt{On(A,B)},\texttt{Table(B)}\}$$

Next, we define the ternary relation `Plan`, which is true of a goal set, a state, and an action sequence if and only if the state that results from executing the action sequence in the given state is in the goal set.

$$\texttt{Plan(q,s,l)} \;\Leftrightarrow\; \texttt{T(q,Do(l,s))}$$

Finally, we can use our definition of regression to give some conditions under which an action sequence is a plan. The empty sequence is a plan for goal set q in state s if s satisfies the elements of q. The sequence a.l is a plan for goal set q if (1) a is an action the positive effects of which include an element of q and (2) l is a plan that achieves the goal set obtained by regressing q through a.

$$\texttt{T(q,s)} \;\Rightarrow\; \texttt{Plan(q,s,}\{\}\texttt{)}$$

$$(\texttt{q} \cap \texttt{Add(a)}) \neq \{\} \;\wedge\; \texttt{Plan(Reg(q,a),s,l)} \;\Rightarrow\; \texttt{Plan(q,s,a.l)}$$

Now suppose we are given a planning problem with initial state descriptor σ and goal descriptor ψ. *Goal regression* can be viewed as the problem of finding γ such that `Plan(`ψ`,`σ`,`γ`)` is true.

As an example of goal regression, consider the following problem. In the initial state, block C is on block A and blocks A and B are on the table. The goal is to achieve the state in which block A is on block B and block B is on block C. Figure 12.2 presents a graphical view of a portion of the search space.

There are two actions with positive effects that include elements of our goal. The action S(A,B) achieves On(A,B), and the action S(B,C) achieves On(B,C). The subgoal sets that result from regressing the goal through these two actions are shown below the goal, and the relevant actions are indicated by the labels on the arcs.

The subgoal on the right can be abandoned. It requires that B be clear and that A be on B at the same time. Consequently, it is unachievable.

The subgoal on the left has four possible subgoals. The leftmost of these is unachievable. The variable y cannot be A, since a block cannot be on top of itself; it cannot be B, since B must be clear; and it cannot be C, since B is on C. Similarly, the second and third subgoals are inconsistent and can be pruned.

The final subgoal corresponds to the action S(B,C), and this goal is consistent. In fact, it has the subgoal shown (as well as several others), and that subgoal is true in the initial state, if we let x be C. At this point, we can find a correct plan by reading the actions off the tree in reverse order. First unstack C from A; then stack B onto C; finally, stack A onto B.

Although goal regression appears very different from the preceding planning strategies, a little analysis reveals that it is very similar. In fact, it is equivalent to Green's method when used in conjunction with state alignment and frame-axiom suppression.

12.13 State Differences

Although it is possible for a restriction strategy to eliminate all search, this result is extremely unlikely. We are left with the problem of deciding the order in which to perform the resolutions allowed by the strategy. One common way of making this choice is to use a measure of dissimilarity between states.

A *state-difference function* is a binary function on states that returns a number indicating the degree of similarity between the states. The higher the value, the more dissimilar the states. A value of zero indicates state identity.

As an example in the Blocks World, consider a state-difference function defined as follows. The overall value is a sum of a location difference and a clearness difference for each block. The location difference for a block is one if the block is in a different place in the two states; otherwise, the difference is zero. If the block is on one block in one state and on another block in the other state or on the table, the value is one. The clearness difference for a block is one if the two states disagree on whether or not

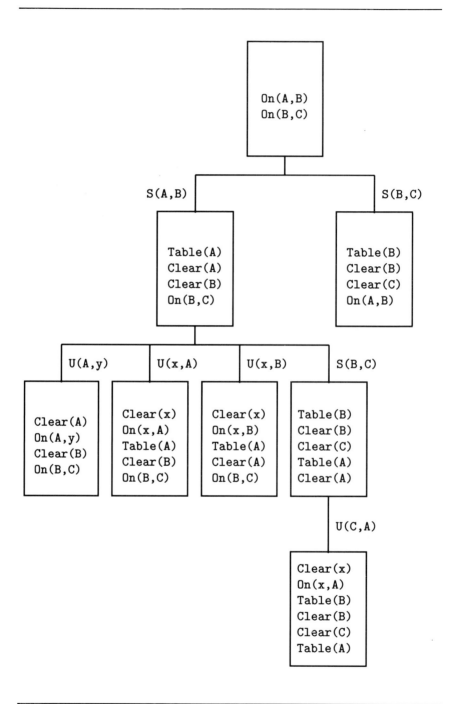

Figure 12.2   Planning by goal regression.

Figure 12.3   Two Blocks World states.

the block is clear. For a world with three blocks, the maximal value of the state difference function is six.

According to this function, the state pictured in Figure 12.3 is closer to the state in which block A is on block B and block B is on block C. In the state pictured on the left of the figure, block A is in the wrong place and should be clear; B is in the wrong place and should not be clear; and C is in the right place but should not be clear either. Thus, the difference value is five. In the state on the right, A is clear, as desired, but is in the wrong place; B is in the right place but should not be clear; and C is just right. Thus, the difference in this case is only two.

State ordering is a resolution strategy in which the order of resolutions on state-aligned clauses is determined by a difference function. In forward planning, resolution is done on the clause describing the state most similar to a goal state. In backward planning, resolution is done first on the clause describing the state most similar to the initial state.

As an example of state ordering in forward planning, consider a problem in which all the blocks are on the table in the initial state and in which the goal is to get block A onto block B and block B onto block C. Forward planning from the initial state in this problem yields both of the states shown in Figure 12.3 as well as four others. State ordering gives preference to the state on the right and leads quickly to the goal.

The strategy is of little use in the first step of backward planning on this problem, since there is only one state that can precede the goal: the state in which A is on the table and B is on C. However, there are three states that can precede this state: the initial state (difference zero), the goal state (difference four), and the state in which B is on A and both A and C are on the table (difference two). At this point, state ordering dictates that the clause describing the initial state be processed next.

For a state-difference function to be useful in improving planning efficiency, there must be a correlation between the difference function and the difficulty of devising a plan to convert one state into the other.

In the extreme case where the difference function is monotonic in planning difficulty, we can use hillclimbing as a search procedure. Note that the preceding difference function does not satisfy this condition. Suppose, for example, that we chose an initial state in which A is on B, B is on the table, and C is on the table; further suppose that we selected a goal state in which A is on B and B is on C. In this case, the difference between the initial state and goal state is two. To get to the goal state, it is necessary to remove block A from block B, thus going through an intermediate state with a difference of four.

When a difference function does not have this property of monotonicity in planning difficulty, we must fall back on a strategy that allows backup, such as best-first search. Even then, we must be careful, since it is possible for a bad ordering function on an infinite search space to prevent a planner from finding a solution.

Although we have talked only about planning difficulty here, it is common to sum state difference and a measure of plan cost to yield a more complicated ordering rule. Using this combined measure in a best-first search procedure leads to a search procedure called A^*.

One problem with the definition of state ordering given here is that it assumes each clause provides complete information about each state (either explicitly or after completion using state constraints). We can eliminate this deficiency by extending the notion of state difference to state sets. This can be done in various ways. We can define the difference based solely on properties shared by all elements of each state set, or we can define it on the basis of the size of the intersection between two state sets. The latter method seems better, but it is more expensive to compute than the former method is. At this point, it is not clear which of the methods is preferable or whether there is perhaps some other method that is superior to both of them.

12.14 Bibliographical and Historical Remarks

Green [Green 1969a] developed a resolution-based planner capable of constructing plans for a simulated robot. Fikes and Nilsson [Fikes 1971] proposed an approach to solving the frame problem in which the effects of an action were described by specifying how a theory should be changed so that it would describe the state of the world after the action is performed. Their planning system incorporating this idea was called STRIPS. A clear description of the STRIPS method also was described in [Nilsson 1980]. Later, formal accounts of STRIPS were given by Pednault [Pednault 1986] and by Lifschitz [Lifschitz 1987a]. STRIPS was used as the planning system in the SRI mobile robot, SHAKEY [Nilsson 1984]. The so-called PLANNER languages followed a similar approach to the problem of updating a theory to take account of actions [Hewitt 1969, Sussman 1970, Hewitt 1972, Bobrow 1974, Rulifson 1972]. Many of the advantages of the STRIPS approach can be achieved using the situation calculus employing strategies of state alignment and appropriate frame-axiom suppression. See, for example, [Warren 1974].

Sacerdoti showed how STRIPS could be modified (in a version he called ABSTRIPS) to generate plans in a hierarchical fashion, first computing the major actions in a plan and later filling in details [Sacerdoti 1974]. His later system, called NOAH, dealt with hierarchical planning more systematically and also generated *nonlinear plans*; i.e., plans consisting of partially ordered sequences of actions [Sacerdoti 1977]. Tate [Tate 1976, 1977] worked on similar hierarchical planning systems.

Stefik explored the idea of exploiting *constraints* in generating plans [Stefik 1981a]; he also described *metaplanning* techniques for reasoning about how to carry out the planning process more efficiently [Stefik 1981b]. Wilkins' SIPE system can be viewed as a hierarchical planner the reasoning of which is directed by explicitly taking into account the resources required to execute alternative plans [Wilkins 1983, Wilkins 1984, Wilkins 1985]. Following in this tradition, Chapman [Chapman 1985] developed an improved planning system called TWEAK.

Rosenschein used propositional dynamic logic to formalize planning [Rosenschein 1981] and to clarify problems in hierarchical and nonlinear planning. Waldinger introduced the idea of regression as a way of reordering linear plans to avoid conflicts in achieving conjunctive goals [Waldinger 1977]. McDermott [McDermott 1985] developed a planning system with a limited ability to reason about the planning process itself (in addition to its ability to reason about the effects of the planned actions). Feldman and Sproull [Feldman 1977] studied the problems caused by uncertainty in robot planning systems and recommended the use of decision-theoretic methods.

The A^* search procedure mentioned in this chapter in connection with best-first search over states was proposed in [Hart 1968] and described in [Nilsson 1980, Pearl 1984].

An interesting and potentially important application of planning is to the generation of "communicative acts." Like physical actions, actions of communication (such as requesting information, informing, asking for help) are deliberately planned to achieve specific goals. Cohen, Perrault, Allen, and Appelt have all done important work in this area [Cohen 1979, Perrault 1980, Appelt 1985a].

See [Georgeff 1987b] for a thorough survey of AI planning methods and a volume edited by Georgeff [Georgeff 1987a] for several papers on planning.

Exercises

1. *Goals.* Consider the game of ticktacktoe. We can describe the state of a game with a single 4-ary relation; Mark(i,j,z,s) means that the mark z

(either X or O) appears in row i and column j in state s. Obviously, only one mark can occupy a square in any given state. The X player's goal is to get three Xs in a row, horizontally, vertically, or diagonally. Formalize this by writing sentences that define X's Goal relation. In writing your description, it is okay to use standard arithmetic operators and to introduce new vocabulary.

2. *Conditional plans.* Consider a variation of the Blocks World in which the usual stacking and unstacking actions are replaced by two new actions. The action F(x,y) flips blocks x and y provided that x is on block y. The action L(x,y) linearizes x and y; i.e., it produces a state in which one is on top of the other. The hitch is that the outcome of an L action is uncertain. After executing L(x,y), block x may be on block y, or the blocks may be the other way around. Write sentences to describe the effects of these operators and use Green's method to devise a conditional plan to get block A onto block B from the state in which both blocks are on the table. Except for the relationship between A and B in describing the F operator, you can ignore the presence or absence of blocks on top of A and B.

3. *Waterpot problem.* Starting with your formalization of the waterpot problem from Chapter 11, use resolution to devise an action block that solves the problem.

CHAPTER 13
Intelligent-Agent Architecture

FOR A THEORY OF intelligence to be complete, it must provide an account of the internal structure (i.e., the architecture) of an intelligent agent as well as its external behavior. In this chapter, we define several types of intelligent agent architectures and discuss their properties.

Although much work in AI concerns multiple agents and their interactions, our treatment here presumes a world in which there is only one agent and which, therefore, does not change except through the actions of that one agent. This assumption dramatically simplifies the presentation of many key architectural issues. Although the resulting treatment is not completely general, it is nevertheless applicable in many situations, and many of the results apply even to worlds with multiple agents.

13.1 Tropistic Agents

A *tropism* is the tendency of an animal or plant to act in response to an external stimulus. In this section, we examine a class of agents, called *tropistic agents*, whose activity at any moment is determined entirely by their environments at that moment.

In our discussion of tropistic agents, we assume that the agent's world can be in any one of a set S of states. In the next section, we talk about agents with internal states (i.e., memory), but for now we ignore this possibility.

Of course, due to sensory limitations, not every agent can distinguish every external state from every other external state, and different agents can have different sensory capabilities. One agent may be able to sense the colors of blocks, while another agent may perceive weights but not colors. To characterize an agent's sensory capabilities, we partition the set S of external states into a set T of disjoint subsets such that the agent is able to distinguish states in different partitions but is unable to distinguish states in the same partition.

To relate the states in S with the partitions in T, we define a function *see*, which maps each state in S into the partition to which it belongs. We call a function of this sort a *sensory function*.

$$see : S \longrightarrow T$$

Just as with sensory capabilities, different agents can have different effectory capabilities. One agent may be able to paint blocks but not move them, whereas another agent may be able to move blocks but not change their colors. To characterize these effectory capabilities, we assume the existence of a set A of actions, all of which can be performed by the agent we are describing.

In order to characterize the effects of these actions, we define a function *do*, which maps each action and state into the state that results from the execution of the given action in the given state. We call a function of this sort an *effectory function*.

$$do : A \times S \longrightarrow S$$

In order to characterize the activity of an agent, we define a function *action* from state partitions to actions that maps each state partition into the action that the agent is to perform whenever it finds itself in a state in that partition.

$$action : T \longrightarrow A$$

Finally, we define a *tropistic agent* in an environment by a 6-tuple of the form shown below. The set S here includes all of the states of the external world, T is a set of partitions of S, A is a set of actions, *see* is a function that maps S into T, *do* is a function from $A \times S$ into S, and *action* is a function from T into A.

$$\langle S, T, A, see, do, action \rangle$$

We can summarize the operation of a tropistic agent as follows. On each cycle, the agent's environment is in a state s. The agent observes the partition t corresponding to $see(s)$. It uses *action* to find the action a appropriate to t. Then, it executes this action, thereby producing the state $do(a, s)$. Then the cycle repeats.

In illustrating these concepts, we use a problem area known as the Maze World. The Maze World consists of a set of cells interconnected by paths.

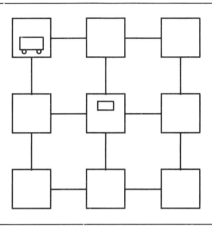

Figure 13.1   One state of the Maze World.

The cells are laid out on a rectangular grid, with each cell connected to its neighbors. There is a cart in one of the cells and some gold in another.

One state of the Maze World is shown in Figure 13.1. The cart is in the first cell in the first row, and the gold is in the second cell in the second row. Figure 13.2 illustrates a different state of the Maze World. The only difference is the location of the cart and of the gold. In this case, both are located in the third cell in the third row.

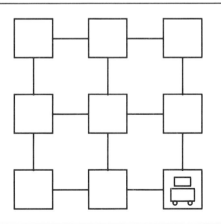

Figure 13.2   Another state of the Maze World.

For a Maze World with a 3 × 3 grid of cells, there are 90 possible states. The cart can be in any one of nine cells (9 possibilities), and the gold can be in any one of nine cells or in the cart (10 possibilities in all).

Given *our* point of view, we can distinguish every one of these states from every other state. By contrast, consider an intelligent agent with sensors mounted on the cart. It can tell its own location; but, as far as the gold is concerned, it can tell only whether the gold is in the cart, in the same cell, or elsewhere.

These sensory limitations divide the set of all 90 states into 27 subsets. The states in each subset agree on the position of the cart. They also agree on the position of the gold relative to the cart, but they disagree on the exact position of the gold when it is located in a different cell.

In addition to these sensory limitations, our agent has certain effectory limitations. For example, it cannot transform the state pictured in Figure 13.1 into the state pictured in Figure 13.2 in a single step. However, it can move the cart from cell to cell, and it can manipulate the gold whenever the latter is either in the cart or in the same cell.

We can conceptualize the agent's effectory capabilities in the form of seven actions. The agent can move the cart up, down, left, or right—one cell at a time. It can place the gold in the cart or remove the gold from the cart. The agent can also do nothing. We assume that *do* characterizes the usual effects of these actions. For example, moving the cart right from the cell in the upper-left corner leads to a state in which the cart is in the middle column of the upper row. Trying to put the gold in the cart in a state in which the gold is in the same cell results in a state in which the gold is in the cart. For simplicity, we assume that the attempt to perform any of these actions in an inappropriate state has no effect. For example, trying to move right from a cell in the rightmost column has no effect. Trying to move the gold into or out of the cart has no effect when the gold is elsewhere.

Now, consider the problem of designing an action function for an agent with these limitations. Let us assume that in the initial state the cart occupies the cell in the upper-left corner of the maze. Our goal is to get the gold to the exit—the cell in the lower-right corner—no matter where the gold starts out.

The basic idea of our definition is as follows. If the cart is at the exit and the gold is in the same cell, the agent does nothing. If the cart is at the exit and the gold is in the cart, the agent removes the gold. If the cart is anywhere else and the gold is in the same cell, the agent puts the gold in the cart. If the cart is not at the exit and the gold is in the cart, the agent moves the cart toward the exit. Otherwise, the agent moves the cart systematically through the maze until the gold is found. The agent first moves the cart across the first row, then down to the third cell in the second row, across the second row to the left, down again, and across the third row to the right.

Row	Column			
1	1	right	in	right
1	2	right	in	right
1	3	down	in	down
2	1	right	in	down
2	2	right	in	left
2	3	down	in	left
3	1	right	in	right
3	2	right	in	right
3	3	out	noop	

Figure 13.3   Action function for a tropistic agent.

The action function corresponding to this procedure is given by the table in Figure 13.3. The rows correspond to cart locations, and the columns correspond to relative gold locations. Each entry indicates the action for the state partition defined by the row and column. We have not supplied a value for the situation in which the cart is at the exit but the gold is elsewhere, since this situation is impossible.

Of course, this is not the only procedure that solves the problem. Instead of first moving the cart into the same column as the exit and then getting it into the same row, we could have first moved it into the same row and then gotten it into the same column.

On the other hand, there are some parts of this procedure that are not arbitrary. For example, every procedure that solves the problem must prescribe the unload action whenever the gold is in the cart and the cart is at the exit.

13.2 Hysteretic Agents

The agent introduced in the last section is extremely simple. Since it has no internal state, it is forced to select its actions solely on the basis of its observations—it cannot retain information about one external state for use in selecting an action to perform in any other state. While there is no need for internal state in this simple case, the ability to retain information internally is extremely useful in general. In this section, we specialize our definitions from the last section to cover agents with internal state, hereafter called *hysteretic agents*.

In order to characterize a hysteretic agent, we assume that the agent itself can be in any one of a set I of internal states. We assume that the agent can distinguish any internal state from any other state, and so there is no need to partition I into subsets or define sensory functions. We also assume that the agent can tranform I into any other member of I in a single step. (While it is interesting to consider agents with internal sensory and effectory limitations, these complications are unnecessary for our treatment of agents in this chapter.)

An important difference between a tropistic agent and a hysteretic agent is that the action function for a hysteretic agent considers internal state as well as observations in dictating actions.

$$action : I \times T \longrightarrow A$$

In a hysteretic agent, there is also a memory update function that maps an internal state and an observation into the next internal state.

$$internal : I \times T \longrightarrow I$$

We define a *hysteretic agent* in an environment by an 8-tuple of the form shown below. The set I here is an arbitrary set of internal states, S is a set of external states, T is a set of partitions of S, A is a set of actions, *see* is a function from S into T, *do* is a function from $A \times S$ into S, *internal* is a function from $I \times T$ into I, and *action* is a function from $I \times T$ into A.

$$\langle I, S, T, A, see, do, internal, action \rangle$$

As an illustration of the need for memory and a suitable hysteretic agent, consider a variation of the Maze World in which the agent can determine the relative location of the gold but cannot determine its own location at all. As before, we assume that the agent starts out in the cell in the upper-left corner of the maze.

The agent's sensory limitations divide the set of all 90 states into three subsets. The first partition consists of the nine states in which the gold is in the cart. The second partition consists of the nine states in which the gold is in the same cell but not in the cart. The third partition consists of the 72 states in which the gold is elsewhere (nine cart locations and eight gold locations for each of these). In what follows, we assume that the function *see* maps each state into the appropriate partition.

We can illustrate these three partitions graphically, as shown in Figure 13.4. The diagram shown on the left denotes the set of states in which the gold is in the cart. The middle diagram denotes the set of states in which the gold is in the same cell. The diagram on the right denotes the set of states in which the gold is elsewhere.

Since our agent is incapable of perceiving its own location, this information must be recorded in the agent's internal state. For this purpose, we define the set of internal states to be the set of integers from 1 to 9, each denoting a distinct cell in the Maze. Thus, the integer 1 denotes the first cell in the first row, 2 denotes the second cell in the first row,

Figure 13.4   Three partitions of the Maze World.

3 denotes the third cell, 4 denotes the first cell in the second row, etc. Since we know that the agent starts operation in the upper-left corner, we arrange that its initial internal state is 1.

The action function for this procedure is given by the table in Figure 13.5, and the internal state update function is given in Figure 13.6. The rows in each table correspond to internal states, and the columns correspond to observations. Each entry in the action table indicates the action to be performed, and each entry in the internal state update table indicates the new internal state. Again, we have not supplied values for the situation in which the cart is at the exit but the gold is elsewhere, since that situation is impossible.

13.3 Knowledge-Level Agents

The conceptualization of agents in the preceding section allows us to describe agents at an arbitrarily fine level of detail. The problem is that for the purposes of AI it is inappropriate to attempt a design at such a detailed level, e.g., a neural map of the human brain or a wiring diagram

Internal State			
1	right	in	right
2	right	in	right
3	down	in	down
4	right	in	down
5	right	in	left
6	down	in	left
7	right	in	right
8	right	in	right
9	out	noop	

Figure 13.5   Action function for a hysteretic agent.

Internal State			
1	2	1	2
2	3	2	3
3	6	3	6
4	5	4	7
5	6	5	4
6	9	6	5
7	8	7	8
8	9	8	9
9	9	9	

Figure 13.6   Internal state update function for a hysteretic agent.

for an electronic computer. Intelligence appears to be a phenomenon that transcends implementation technology, such as biology or electronics. Consequently, we want a design in which physical detail is abstracted away.

In this section, we examine a conceptualization of agents, called the *knowledge level*, in which all excess detail is eliminated. In this abstraction an agent's internal state consists entirely of a database of sentences in predicate calculus, and an agent's mental actions are viewed as inferences on its database. At this level, we do not specify how the beliefs are physically stored, nor do we describe the implementation of the agent's inferences.

The action function *action* for a knowledge-level agent maps a database Δ and a state partition t into the action to be performed by the agent in a state with database Δ and observed state partition t.

$$action : \mathcal{D} \times T \longrightarrow A$$

The database update function *database* maps a database Δ and a state partition t into the new internal database.

$$database : \mathcal{D} \times T \longrightarrow \mathcal{D}$$

A *knowledge-level agent* in an environment is an 8-tuple of the form shown below. The set $\mathcal{D}$ in this tuple is an arbitrary set of predicate calculus databases, S is a set of external states, T is a set of partitions of S, A is a set of actions, *see* is a function from S into T, *do* is a function from $A \times S$ into S, *database* is a function from $\mathcal{D} \times T$ into $\mathcal{D}$, and *action* is a function from $\mathcal{D} \times T$ into A.

$$\langle \mathcal{D}, S, T, A, see, do, database, action \rangle$$

Database			
{Cart(AA)}	right	in	right
{Cart(AB)}	right	in	right
{Cart(AC)}	down	in	down
{Cart(BA)}	right	in	down
{Cart(BB)}	right	in	left
{Cart(BC)}	down	in	left
{Cart(CA)}	right	in	right
{Cart(CB)}	right	in	right
{Cart(CC)}	out	noop	

Figure 13.7   Action function for a knowledge-level agent.

From this definition, it should be clear that every knowledge-level agent is a hysteretic agent. As it turns out, for any hysteretic agent (whether knowledge-level or not), we can define a knowledge-level agent with the same external behavior.

As an example, consider the hysteretic agent defined in the last section. By changing the internal states of the agent from integers to databases and modifying the action and internal state update functions accordingly, we can define a corresponding knowledge-level version.

Let us use the following vocabulary. We name the nine cells of the maze with the symbols AA, AB, AC, BA, BB, BC, CA, CB, and CC. We name the three possible state partitions IC (in the cart), SC (in the same cell), and EW (elsewhere). We let the relation symbol Cart denote the unary relation that holds of the cell in which the cart is located; and we let the relation symbol Gold denote the unary relation that holds of the state partition corresponding to the location of the gold.

Rather than starting off with the integer 1 as the initial internal state for our agent, we start off with the following singleton set.

$$\{Cart(AA)\}$$

Since the internal states have changed, we need to redefine the agent's action function so that it takes into account databases, rather than integers. Figure 13.7 illustrates the new definition.

We also need to define a database function that maps databases and state partitions into the databases corresponding to the integers in the internal states of the preceding agent. See Figure 13.8.

Database			
{Cart(AA)}	{Cart(AB)}	{Cart(AA)}	{Cart(AB)}
{Cart(AB)}	{Cart(AC)}	{Cart(AB)}	{Cart(AC)}
{Cart(AC)}	{Cart(BC)}	{Cart(AC)}	{Cart(BC)}
{Cart(BA)}	{Cart(BB)}	{Cart(BA)}	{Cart(CA)}
{Cart(BB)}	{Cart(BC)}	{Cart(BB)}	{Cart(BA)}
{Cart(BC)}	{Cart(CC)}	{Cart(BC)}	{Cart(BB)}
{Cart(CA)}	{Cart(CB)}	{Cart(CA)}	{Cart(CB)}
{Cart(CB)}	{Cart(CC)}	{Cart(CB)}	{Cart(CC)}
{Cart(CC)}	{Cart(CC)}	{Cart(CC)}	

Figure 13.8   Database function for a knowledge-level agent.

One thing to notice about this agent is that it is extremely limited in its abilities. Although its behavior varies according to the position of the gold, it performs a fixed search in finding the gold and follows a fixed path to the exit once the gold is found. In certain circumstances, it is desirable to modify an agent's behavior. For example, we might want to get the agent to search up and down columns rather than back and forth across rows, or we might want to modify the procedure to work when the cart starts out in a different cell.

Unfortunately, a modification of this sort is not possible without defining entirely new functions for the agent. If we want to modify a physical agent and these functions are implemented in the agent's hardware, the change can be quite expensive. The alternative is to define a more flexible agent, one that can be *programmed* by changing the sentences in the agent's database.

In order to illustrate this idea, we need to enlarge our vocabulary. We use the symbols R, L, U, and D stand for the actions of moving right, left, up, and down; the symbols I and O stand for the actions of placing the gold in the cart and taking it out; and the symbol N stands for the null action. Finally, we let Must denote the action we want our agent to take in a given situation.

With this vocabulary, we can describe the behavior of the preceding agent with sentences of the following sort. We could write a more succinct version by making our sentences a little more complicated; for now, let us assume that all our sentences are written in this simple form.

$$Cart(AA) \land Gold(IC) \Rightarrow Must=R$$

$$\texttt{Cart(AA)} \land \texttt{Gold(SC)} \Rightarrow \texttt{Must=I}$$

$$\texttt{Cart(AA)} \land \texttt{Gold(EW)} \Rightarrow \texttt{Must=R}$$

$$\vdots$$

$$\texttt{Cart(CC)} \land \texttt{Gold(IC)} \Rightarrow \texttt{Must=0}$$

$$\texttt{Cart(CC)} \land \texttt{Gold(SC)} \Rightarrow \texttt{Must=N}$$

As before, we assume that the initial internal state contains the following sentence, describing the location of the cart in the initial state, as well as the sentences of our program.

$$\texttt{Cart(AA)}$$

In order to specify our action and database functions, it is helpful to define a naming function e for state partitions and actions. The names for our three partitions are given on the left in the following definition, and the names of our actions are shown on the right.

$$e\left(\boxed{}\right) = \texttt{IC}$$

$$e\left(\boxed{}\right) = \texttt{SC}$$

$$e\left(\boxed{}\right) = \texttt{EW}$$

$$
\begin{aligned}
e(\textit{left}) &= \texttt{L}\\
e(\textit{right}) &= \texttt{R}\\
e(\textit{up}) &= \texttt{U}\\
e(\textit{down}) &= \texttt{D}\\
e(\textit{in}) &= \texttt{I}\\
e(\textit{out}) &= \texttt{0}\\
e(\textit{noop}) &= \texttt{N}
\end{aligned}
$$

With this naming function, we can define the action function for our programmable agent as follows. Whenever the database Δ contains the sentence $\texttt{Cart}(\sigma)$ and also the sentence $\texttt{Cart}(\sigma) \land \texttt{Gold}(e(t)) \Rightarrow \texttt{Must} = e(a)$, then the agent executes action a.

$$action(\Delta, t) = a$$

Under the conditions described in the last paragraph, the database function dictates a new database containing all of the sentences from the old database except for the one describing the cart location, which is updated (via the function $next$) to the new location.

$$database(\Delta, t) = (\Delta - \{\texttt{Cart}(\sigma)\}) \cup \{\texttt{Cart}(next(\Delta, t))\}$$

It is easy to see that this agent executes the procedure described in its initial database. Consequently, we can change the procedure simply by changing the database. Although the format for the sentences in the description is somewhat rigid, we can define an agent capable of dealing with a more flexible format, and we do so in a later section.

13.4 Stepped Knowledge-Level Agents

In looking at the agents in the last section, it is interesting to note that they are both nonmonotonic; sentences are occasionally removed from their databases as well as added. The reason for this is that our conceptualization of state-dependent relations does not mention state, e.g., in the location of the cart. Each database describes just one state; after each action is performed, the description must be altered so that it corresponds to the state resulting from that action.

This observation raises the question of whether it is possible to design a monotonic agent, in which new sentences are added to the internal database but no sentences are ever removed. As it turns out, it is indeed possible to build monotonic agents, but we need to make some changes.

The first step is to switch to a state-based conceptualization like the one employed in Chapters 11 and 12. In particular, we use the T relation to describe the properties of individual states. We convert relation symbols like Cart into function symbols; and we use the unary function symbol Ext to denote a function that maps each positive integer into the external state on the cycle of the agent's operation corresponding to that integer. Note that Ext maps an integer into an external state, not a state partition. (In this way, an agent has a name for its external state even if it does not know precisely which one it is.)

With this vocabulary, we can describe the initial external state seen by our Maze World agent, as follows. Of course, this description is not complete, since it says nothing about the location of the gold.

$$T(\text{Cart(AA)},\text{Ext(1)})$$

We also can use this vocabulary in rewriting the sentences describing the agent's procedure. In this case, we have had to use the variable n that ranges over the cycles of the agent's operation, and we have converted the object constant Must into a function constant.

$$T(\text{Cart(AA)},\text{Ext(n)}) \land T(\text{Gold(IC)},\text{Ext(n)}) \Rightarrow \text{Must(n)=R}$$

$$T(\text{Cart(AA)},\text{Ext(n)}) \land T(\text{Gold(SC)},\text{Ext(n)}) \Rightarrow \text{Must(n)=I}$$

$$T(\text{Cart(AA)},\text{Ext(n)}) \land T(\text{Gold(EW)},\text{Ext(n)}) \Rightarrow \text{Must(n)=R}$$

$$\vdots \qquad\qquad \vdots \qquad\qquad \vdots$$

$$T(\text{Cart(CC)},\text{Ext(n)}) \land T(\text{Gold(IC)},\text{Ext(n)}) \Rightarrow \text{Must(n)=O}$$

$$T(\text{Cart(CC)},\text{Ext(n)}) \land T(\text{Gold(SC)},\text{Ext(n)}) \Rightarrow \text{Must(n)=N}$$

Unfortunately, these changes alone are not enough to permit purely monotonic behavior. The agent still needs to know which cycle it is executing to use the information recorded in its database. It cannot keep information about the current cycle in its database, since that information changes after each action. The alternative is to define a new kind of knowledge-level agent in which the internal state includes a counter as well as its database of sentences.

A *stepped knowledge-level agent* in an environment is an 8-tuple of the form shown below. The set $\mathcal{D}$ in this tuple is an arbitrary set of predicate calculus databases, S is a set of external states, T is a set of partitions of S, A is a set of actions, *see* is a function from S into T, *do* is a function from $A \times S$ into S, *database* is a function from $\mathcal{D} \times N \times T$ into $\mathcal{D}$, and *action* is a function from $\mathcal{D} \times N \times T$ into A.

$$\langle \mathcal{D}, S, T, A, see, do, database, action \rangle$$

Notice that the only difference between a stepped knowledge-level agent and an ordinary knowledge-level agent is the dependence of the database and action functions on the agent's cycle number. Since the cycle number is kept outside the database, this information does not need to be stored in the database; and, therefore, the requirement described above is met.

It is a fairly simple matter to modify the action and database functions for the programmable agent in the preceding section so that they satisfy this definition and cause the desired behavior. They need to be a little more complicated in order to handle the variables in the database; but, otherwise, they are identical. We leave this modification as an exercise for the reader. In a later section, we define an even more flexible stepped knowledge-level agent, which is capable of working with arbitrary databases; but first we define some concepts to help formalize what we expect of such agents.

For the purposes of analysis, it is often useful to characterize how the internal states, external states, observations, and actions of a stepped knowledge-level agent vary with its cycle number. The function $int_{\Delta,s}$ maps an integer n into the internal state that results on the n-th cycle of activity of the knowledge-level agent with initial database Δ and initial external state s. The function $ext_{\Delta,s}$ maps an integer n into the external state that results on the n-th cycle of activity. The function $obs_{\Delta,s}$ maps an integer n into the state set observed by the agent on the n-th cycle of activity. The function $act_{\Delta,s}$ maps an integer n into the action taken by the agent on the n-th cycle of activity.

The initial values for these functions follow. The internal state on the first cycle of the agent's operation is the agent's initial database, and the external state on the first cycle is the initial external state. The agent's first observation is given by applying the *see* function to the initial external state, and the agent's first action is determined by its initial database, the cycle number 1, and the agent's initial observation.

$$int_{\Delta,s}(1) = \Delta$$
$$ext_{\Delta,s}(1) = s$$
$$obs_{\Delta,s}(1) = see(s)$$
$$act_{\Delta,s}(1) = action(\Delta, 1, see(s))$$

The definitions for these functions after the first cycle follow. The internal state on each cycle is the result of applying the agent's memory function to the preceding internal state, the preceding cycle number, and the agent's observations of the preceding external state. The external state is the result of executing the action determined on the preceding cycle to the preceding external state. The agent's observation is the state partition containing the external state. The action to be executed is determined by applying the function *action* to the current internal state, the current cycle number, and the agent's observations of the current external state.

$$int_{\Delta,s}(n) = database(int_{\Delta,s}(n-1), n-1, obs_{\Delta,s}(n-1))$$
$$ext_{\Delta,s}(n) = do(act_{\Delta,s}(n-1), ext_{\Delta,s}(n-1))$$
$$obs_{\Delta,s}(n) = see(ext_{\Delta,s}(n))$$
$$act_{\Delta,s}(n) = action(int_{\Delta,s}(n), n, obs_{\Delta,s}(n))$$

A knowledge-level agent with initial database Δ and initial external state s is *consistent* if and only if its database on every cycle is consistent.

$$int_{\Delta,s}(n) \not\models \{\}$$

A knowledge-level agent is *database retentive* if and only if its database on every cycle after the first logically implies the database on the preceding cycle.

$$int_{\Delta,s}(n) \models int_{\Delta,s}(n-1)$$

The simplest type of database retentive agent is one in which all the sentences in $int_{\Delta,s}(n-1)$ are contained in $int_{\Delta,s}(n)$. Our definition is phrased in terms of logical implication rather than set membership to allow for inferences that produce compressed databases with equivalent or greater implicational force.

13.5 Fidelity*

In looking at the agent described in the last section, it is interesting to note that, under the usual interpretation for the symbols in this agent's vocabulary, the database on each cycle correctly describes its external environment. Thus, after the agent moves right in the initial state, the cart is in cell AB, as specified in the database on that cycle.

The fact is that there is nothing in the definition of the agent that enforces this correspondence. If we were to permute the databases systematically and modify the agent's database and action functions accordingly, the agent would solve the problem equally well, but the sentences in the databases would be false under the usual interpretation.

On the other hand, in analyzing a knowledge-level agent, we often want to talk about its behavior with respect to some interpretation or partial interpretation for the sentences in its database. In general, we cannot expect an agent to abide by our interpretation for *all* of the symbols in its vocabulary. However, it is interesting to look at the agent's properties if we assume that it agrees with us on *some* of its vocabulary. The following correspondences are particularly useful.

The function *obsrecord* maps a positive integer n and a state partition t into a set of sentences asserting that the external state on cycle n is a member of partition t. In the previous example, the observation for the first cycle and the state partition in which the gold is elsewhere is the database consisting of the single sentence T(Gold(EW),Ext(1)).

$$obsrecord\left(1, \boxed{}\right) = \{\texttt{T(Gold(EW),Ext(1))}\}$$

To encode imperatives in an agent's database, we need some vocabulary that describes the actions the agent is *supposed* to do. The function *mustrecord* maps a positive integer n and an action a into a set of sentences asserting that the agent is supposed to perform action a on cycle n. For example, we might encode the fact that an agent is to move right on its first cycle as shown below.

$$mustrecord(1, right) = \{\texttt{Must(1)=R}\}$$

The function *mustnotrecord* maps a positive integer n and a state partition t into a set of sentences asserting that the agent is supposed to avoid action a on cycle n. For example, we might encode that fact that the agent is not to move right on its first cycle as shown below.

$$mustnotrecord(1, right) = \{\texttt{Must(1)} \neq \texttt{R}\}$$

The function *actrecord* maps a positive integer n and an action a into a set of sentences asserting that the agent *actually* performs action a on cycle n. We might, for example, encode the fact that an agent moves right on its first cycle with the sentence Act(1)=R.

$$actrecord(1, right) = \{\texttt{Act(1)=R}\}$$

As with other aspects of an agent's operation, it is convenient to conceptualize functions that define the records for an agent's observations and actions. We define $obsrec_{\Delta,s}$ to be a function that maps a cycle number into the observation record for the n-th cycle of activity of the knowledge-level agent with initial database Δ and initial external state s. The function $actrec_{\Delta,s}$ maps a cycle number into the corresponding action record. Using the terminology from the last section, we can define these functions as follows.

$$obsrec_{\Delta,s}(n) = obsrecord(n, obs_{\Delta,s}(n))$$
$$actrec_{\Delta,s}(n) = actrecord(n, act_{\Delta,s}(n))$$

We say that an agent is *observation retentive* if and only if it records its observations on each cycle in its database; i.e., on all cycles after the first the agent's database logically implies the observation record from the preceding cycle.

$$int_{\Delta,s}(n) \models obsrec_{\Delta,s}(n-1)$$

An agent is *action retentive* if and only if it records its action on each cycle in its database; i.e., on all cycles after the first the agent's database logically implies the action record from the preceding cycle.

$$int_{\Delta,s}(n) \models actrec_{\Delta,s}(n-1)$$

Given the correspondence functions defined above, we can determine whether or not an agent behaves in accordance with its database; i.e., whether it performs those actions that are prescribed by the database and avoids those actions that are forbidden.

We say that a database Δ *prescribes* an action a on cycle n of an agent's operation (written $P(\Delta, n, a)$) if and only if Δ logically implies that the action a must be executed on step n.

$$\Delta \models mustrecord(n, a)$$

Using this notation, we can also define what it means for an action to be forbidden. We say that Δ *forbids* action a on step n of an agent's operation (written $F(\Delta, n, a)$) if and only Δ logically implies that the action a must not be performed on step n.

$$\Delta \models mustnotrecord(n, a)$$

A knowledge-level agent is *locally faithful* if and only if on every cycle of its operation it acts in accordance with the database for that cycle; i.e., it satisfies the following conditions.

(1) The agent performs any action that is prescribed by its database and its observations of the current state.

$$P(int_{\Delta,s}(n) \cup obsrec_{\Delta,s}(n), n, a) \;\Rightarrow\; act_{\Delta,s}(n) = a$$

(2) The agent avoids every action that is forbidden by its database and its observations of the current state.

$$F(int_{\Delta,s}(n) \cup obsrec_{\Delta,s}(n), n, a) \;\Rightarrow\; act_{\Delta,s}(n) \neq a$$

Note that, for some knowledge-level agents, these conditions are redundant. Suppose, for example, that an agent's database has axioms asserting that there is only one prescribed action for every cycle, and suppose it also has axioms asserting the inequality of the agent's various actions. Then, if the database prescribes an action for a cycle, it forbids all other actions; and, if a database forbids all but one action, it necessarily prescribes the remaining action.

On the other hand, these conditions are not always redundant. We cannot drop the condition about forbidden actions, since there are databases that forbid actions but do not prescribe any actions and we want to be sure that the agent does not select a forbidden action. Similarly, we cannot do without the prescription condition, since there are databases that prescribe some actions but do not forbid all other actions, and we do not want the agent to perform just any non-forbidden action when there are some prescribed actions.

Local fidelity is a strong condition, and it is not guaranteed by any combination of consistency and retentiveness. However, we do have the following result.

THEOREM 13.1 *Consistency is a necessary condition for local fidelity.*

Proof If an agent introduces an inconsistency into its database on any cycle, then on that cycle every action is prescribed and every action is forbidden. Consequently, it is impossible for the agent to satisfy the definition of local fidelity on that cycle. $\square$

Even though local fidelity is stronger than conditions like consistency and retentiveness, it is weak in that it is based on information about an agent's current state only. Ideally, we would like a knowledge-level agent to take into account its initial database as well as information garnered in past states. This intuition underlies the notion of global fidelity.

A *history record* for a particular step of an agent's operation is the set of observation and action records for that step and all previous steps. The function *histrec* maps a step number into the corresponding history record.

$$histrec_{\Delta,s}(n) = \begin{cases} \{\} & n = 0 \\ histrec_{\Delta,s}(n-1) \cup obsrec_{\Delta,s}(n) \cup actrec_{\Delta,s}(n) & \\ & \text{otherwise} \end{cases}$$

Note the presence of information about history in an agent's database often permits the agent to draw conclusions that would not otherwise be possible. For example, after noticing that there is no gold in cell **AA** and moving to cell **AB**, our Maze World agent can conclude that the gold is not located in the cell **AA**, even though it can no longer observe that fact.

A deliberate agent is *globally faithful* if and only if on every cycle of its operation it acts in accordance with its initial database, its history, and its current observations; i.e., it satisfies the following conditions.

(1) The agent performs any action that is prescribed by its initial database, its history, and its observations of the current state.

$$P(\Delta \cup histrec_{\Delta,s}(n-1) \cup obsrec_{\Delta,s}(n), n, a) \;\Rightarrow\; act_{\Delta,s}(n) = a$$

(2) The agent avoids every action that is forbidden by its initial database, its history, and its observations of the current state.

$$F(\Delta \cup histrec_{\Delta,s}(n-1) \cup obsrec_{\Delta,s}(n), n, a) \;\Rightarrow\; act_{\Delta,s}(n) \neq a$$

It should be clear that retentiveness makes a locally faithful agent globally faithful as well.

THEOREM 13.2 *Database retentiveness, observation retentiveness, and action retentiveness and local fidelity imply global fidelity.*

Proof Consider cycle n. If the agent is observation retentive, action retentive, and database retentive, then the database $int_{\Delta,s}(n)$ must logically imply the agent's initial database and history. Consequently, if there is an action prescribed by the initial database and history, it is also prescribed by $int_{\Delta,s}(n)$; if the agent is locally faithful, it must execute that action. Similarly, if an action is forbidden by the initial database and history, it is forbidden by $int_{\Delta,s}(n)$, and the agent must avoid that action. $\square$

In thinking about the concept of global fidelity, it is important to keep in mind that the notion is based on histories, not complete knowledge. We do not require that an agent perform actions that are prescribed by full knowledge of its environment; it need perform only those actions prescribed by its observations, actions, and initial database. Similarly, we do not require that an agent avoid actions that are inconsistent with full knowledge of the environment; it need avoid only those actions that are forbidden by its observations, actions, and initial database.

Unfortunately, not taking full information into account can lead to peculiar results in some situations. In the absence of full information, an agent may have no prescribed action and, consequently, may select an action that is neither prescribed nor forbidden. In subsequent states, the agent may obtain information that bears on the earlier state, and this information together with the other sentences in the agent's database may prescribe a different action for the earlier cycle and thereby forbid the action the agent performed.

As an example, consider an agent that believes it should invest in bonds rather than stocks if the president is at the White House. If the agent does not know the president's whereabouts on a particular day, it may choose to invest in stocks. If on the next day the agent discovers that the president was at home the previous day, then it knows it should have invested in bonds instead.

This does not necessarily lead to inconsistencies nor imply global infidelity. It just means that the agent did not perform the action that, in light of further information, it should have done. Nevertheless, the possibility is somewhat disconcerting.

Of course, this sort of anomaly occurs only when an agent's database includes sentences that span different states, allowing it to draw conclusions about one state from information about other states. If the sentences in an agent's database are strictly local, as defined in Chapter 11, this cannot occur.

13.6 Deliberate Agents*

In this section, we define a class of somewhat specific knowledge-level agents that are globally faithful. The key idea in defining an agent in this class is the use of an automated inference method like resolution in deriving a sentence that indicates the required action on each cycle. An agent of this sort is *deliberate* in that it deliberates on every cycle about which external action to perform.

We can define the action function for a deliberate agent as follows. If on cycle n it is possible to prove $mustrec(n, a)$ from the current database and observation record using resolution or some other inference procedure, then the agent executes action a. The case in which no such sentence is provable is discussed later in this section.

$$action(\Delta, n, t) = a \text{ whenever } \Delta \cup obsrecord(n, t) \vdash mustrecord(n, a)$$

The agent's database is updated to include its observations and a record of its action on that cycle.

$$database(\Delta, n, t) = \Delta \cup obsrecord(n, t) \cup actrecord(n, a)$$

$$\text{whenever}$$

$$\Delta \cup obsrecord(n, t) \vdash mustrecord(n, a)$$

Figure 13.9 presents an alternative characterization of a deliberate agent in the form of a program in a traditional programming language. The

```
Procedure   CD (DB)
    Begin   CYCLE←1,
      Tag   OBS←OBSERVE(CYCLE),
            DB←APPEND([T(OBS,Ext(CYCLE))],DB),
            ACT←FIND(k,Must(CYCLE)=k,DB),
            EXECUTE(ACT),
            DB←APPEND([Act(CYCLE)=ACT],DB),
            CYCLE←CYCLE+1,
            GOTO Tag
      End
```

Figure 13.9   Deliberate agent.

program CD takes an initial database as argument. It manipulates four variables: CYCLE is the number of the current cycle, OBS is the state descriptor, DB holds the initial database and all observation and action records, and ACT is the name of the action to be executed.

The agent's sensory capability is implemented in the form of a primitive subroutine called OBSERVE. OBSERVE takes a cycle number n as argument and, when executed in a state s, returns $obsrecord(n, see(s))$ as a value. The agent's effectory vocabulary is implemented in the form of a primitive subroutine called EXECUTE. This subroutine takes as argument an action designator and, when invoked, executes the corresponding action. The code makes use of a theorem prover FIND, which returns a term that, when substituted for the variable supplied as its first argument in the sentence supplied as second argument, produces a sentence that is logically implied by the database supplied as its third argument.

The code defines a simple exit-free loop. Each time around the loop, the agent undergoes a single cycle of its history. First, the environment is observed and an appropriate sentence is added to the database. Then the agent performs inference on the database until it deduces an action to perform. It performs that action and updates its database and cycle number. Then the process repeats.

From this definition, it is easy to see that a deliberate agent is observation retentive, action retentive, and database retentive. Therefore, we have the following result.

THEOREM 13.3 *Every deliberate agent with a sound and complete theorem-proving procedure is globally faithful.*

One problem with the notion of deliberate agents as defined here is that it does not say what happens on cycles with no prescribed action. As mentioned earlier, we would like an agent to act in this situation, so long as it does not perform an action that is forbidden.

Fortunately, it is a simple matter to extend our definition in this way, at least for some databases. We simply have the agent use a theorem prover in an attempt to prove inconsistency of each of its actions in turn. If it proves inconsistency, then it goes on to the next action. If it fails in the attempt, as indicated by the inability of the procedure to find any new conclusions, then the corresponding action is consistent and can be executed safely. Of course, this has problems in the general case, since the proof of inconsistency may not terminate.

13.7 Bibliographical and Historical Remarks

A moderate amount of AI research has been devoted to the design of agents capable of complex reasoning. That topic is discussed extensively in earlier chapters of this book. By contrast, this chapter is concerned with the architectural issues involved in designing machines that interact with their physical environments.

Although there has been considerable work on planning, there has been relatively little work on the complications involved in connecting the planning process with the processes of making observations and performing actions. Early research concentrated on the techniques involved in monitoring the execution of plans [Fikes 1972]. The term *knowledge level* was first used by Newell [Newell 1982] to denote an implementation-independent account of an agent's knowledge. Rosenschein differentiated between two approaches in constructing an intelligent agent. According to the *grand tactic*, predicate-calculus sentences are used as data structures in an agent's memory. In the *grand strategy*, predicate calculus is used to describe the knowledge of an agent but may or may not be used in the implementation. Deliberate agents are thus compatible with both the grand strategy and the grand tactic. More recently, Brooks [Brooks 1985] and Rosenschein and Kaelbling [Rosenschein 1986] have proposed specific architectures for reactive intelligent agents. An approach to reasoning in real time as actions are performed is discussed in [Drapkin 1986]. The formalization of agents and their properties in this chapter are reported in [Genesereth 1987b].

Exercises

1. *Maze World.* Consider a Maze World agent with the ability to observe its own location exactly and the relative location of the gold (in the

cart, in the same cell, or elsewhere). Design an initial internal state, an action function, and an internal-state update function for a hysteretic agent that allows it to solve the Maze World problem when started in *any* external state.

2. *Turing machines.* Consider the class of Turing machines with a single head and a single tape. Each machine in the class is capable of sensing the bit written on the tape square under its head and is capable of writing a bit on that square and moving left, moving right, or remaining in place. Assuming that the head starts at the left-hand end of the tape, define the external state space, state partition, action set, sensory function, effectory function, internal state update function, and action function for a machine of this class that flips the bits on its tape. Obviously, the machine never halts when given an infinite tape.

3. *Planning.* Consider a knowledge-level agent in which the database consists of operator descriptions, frame axioms, state constraints, and goal descriptions like those described in Chapter 12. Define the action function for an agent of this sort that guarantees that agent achieves a goal state whenever possible. It is okay to define the agent's action function in terms of a semidecidable inference procedure.

Answers to Exercises

A.1 Introduction

1. *Structure and behavior.*

  a. Externally, we can think of a thermostat as a device with three inputs: a temperature setting, an ambient temperature, and power. The output is a power line, which is usually connected to a furnace. Current begins to flow down the line whenever the temperature, responding to heat loss, falls more than a few degrees lower than the setting. The current ceases to flow whenever the temperature, responding to the furnace, rises more than a few degrees higher than the setting.

  Internally, a thermostat contains a bimetallic coil that changes its position on the basis of ambient temperature. There are electrical contacts on the coil, which in certain positions allow current to flow out of the thermostat. The temperature-setting knob changes the position of the bimetallic coil.

  As the temperature falls, the bimetallic coil changes position, eventually making contact and sending power to the furnace. As the temperature rises, the coil changes position in the other direction, eventually breaking the contact.

  b. No, in general we cannot infer the purpose of an artifact from its behavior. The ticking of early clocks was a side effect of their mechanism and not part of their purpose.

c. An alarm clock knows what time it is and knows the hour for which its alarm is set. It desires to display the correct time on its face, and it desires to make a loud, irritating noise at the time for which the alarm is set.

2. *Missionaries and cannibals.*

a.

Step	Left	Boat	Right
1.	MMMCCC		
2.	MMMC	CC→	
3.	MMMC	←C	C
4.	MMM	CC→	C
5.	MMM	←C	CC
6.	MC	MM→	CC
7.	MC	←MC	MC
8.	CC	MM→	MC
9.	CC	←C	MMM
10.	C	CC→	MMM
11.	C	←C	MMMC
12.		CC→	MMMC
13.			MMMCCC

b. The number of assumptions is unbounded; e.g., the river has water in it, the boat floats, the river has finite width.

A.2 Declarative Knowledge

1. *Grain size.* We need a different relation for each way two devices can be connected; e.g., first input connected to first input, second input connected to second input, first output connected to first input, first output connected to first output, etc.

2. *Reification.* We conceptualize connections as objects in the universe of discourse. For the circuit in Figure 2.3, this introduces 12 new objects. We then conceptualize connectivity as a ternary relation that is true of two ports and a connection if and only if the specified connection exists between the two specified ports.

3. *Syntax.*

   a. Legal.

   b. Legal.

   c. Illegal. p and q are not sentences.

   d. Illegal. A sentence cannot be an argument to a relation.

   e. Legal.

   f. Legal.

g. Legal.

h. Legal.

i. Illegal. Variables may not occur in relational position.

j. Legal.

4. *Groups.* For simplicity, we assume that the universe of discourse contains the group elements and only the group elements. We use the symbol + to denote the function and the symbol 0 to denote the identity.

 a. ∀x∀y∃z x+y=z

 b. ∀x∀y∀z x+(y+z)=(x+y)+z

 c. ∀x x+0=x ∧ 0+x=x

 d. ∀x∃y x+y=0

5. *Lists.* The following definition uses the Append function defined in the text.

$$Reverse([])=[]$$

$$Reverse(x.l)=Append(Reverse(l),[x])$$

6. *Translation.*

 a. ¬∃x Male(x) ∧ Butcher(x) ∧ Vegetarian(x)

 b. ∀x∀y Male(x) ∧ ¬Butcher(x) ∧ Vegetarian(y)
    ⇒ Likes (x,y)

 c. ∀x Vegetarian(x) ∧ Butcher(x) ⇒ Female(x)

 d. ¬∃x∃y Male(x) ∧ Female(y) ∧ Vegetarian(y) ∧ Likes(x,y)

 e. ¬∃x∃y∃z Female(x) ∧ Male(y) ∧ Vegetarian(z) ∧
    ¬Likes(y,z) ∧ Likes(x,y)

7. *Reverse translation.*

 a. He who hesitates is lost.

 b. There's no business like show business.

 c. Not everything that glitters is gold.

 d. You can fool some of the people all of the time.

8. *Interpretation and satisfaction.*

 a. Let 2 be the World Trade Center, 3 be the Empire State Building, and > be the *taller than* relation.

b. Let P be the 0-ary relation meaning that it is sunny outside, and let Q be the 0-ary relation meaning that it is warm outside. The sentence then asserts that it is not warm outside if it is not sunny.

c. Let R be the empty relation. Then the left-hand side of the implication is never satisfied, and so the implication as a whole is always satisfied.

9. *Interpretation and satisfaction.* Consider a universe of discourse consisting of the three elements a, b, and c.

a. Let A be a, let B be b, and let P be the relation with the extension shown below. This relation is not transitive, so the first sentence is not satisfied. The second sentence is trivially satisfied, since there are no cases of two objects being related to each other and vice versa. The third sentence is satisfied, since P(x,B) is true for all objects in the universe.

$$\{\langle a, b\rangle, \langle b, b\rangle, \langle c, b\rangle\}$$

b. Let A be a; let B be b; and let P be the relation with the extension shown below. The relation is clearly transitive, so the first sentence is satisfied. Every element is related to b, so the third sentence is satisfied. However, there are distinct objects a and c that are related to each other, so the second sentence is not satisfied.

$$\{\langle a, a\rangle, \langle a, b\rangle, \langle a, c\rangle, \langle b, b\rangle, \langle c, a\rangle, \langle c, b\rangle, \langle c, c\rangle\}$$

c. Let A be a, let B be b, and let P be the relation with the extension shown below. The relation is clearly transitive, so it satisfies the first sentence. The only cases of commutativity occur between each object and itself, so the second sentence is satisfied. However, the third sentence is not satisfied, since there is an element to which a is related, but not every element is related to b. Incidentally, this interpretation is analogous to the *greater than or equal to* relation on the integers.

$$\{\langle a, a\rangle, \langle b, b\rangle, \langle c, c\rangle, \langle a, b\rangle, \langle b, c\rangle, \langle a, c\rangle\}$$

10. *Satisfiability.*

a. Valid.

b. Satisfiable.

c. Satisfiable.

d. Unsatisfiable.

e. Valid.

11. *Definability.*

$$\forall x \forall z \; \texttt{Above(x,z)} \Leftrightarrow (\texttt{On(x,z)} \lor \exists y \; \texttt{Above(x,y)} \land \texttt{Above(y,z)})$$

$$\forall x \forall z \; \texttt{On(x,z)} \Leftrightarrow (\texttt{Above(x,z)} \land \neg \exists y \; \texttt{Above(x,y)} \land \texttt{Above(y,z)})$$

12. *Tables.*   We cannot use the table language from the text to express the information in these two figures, since none of the relations is a binary function. However, we can define a slightly different table language that works.

    Each table designates a binary relation. The labels on the rows and columns represent objects in the universe of discourse. The difference is that, instead of placing the names of objects as entries in the table, either we write an X or we leave the space blank. The presence of an X signifies that the relation designated by the table holds for the corresponding objects. The absence of an X means that the relation does not hold.

    a. The table for the Isa relation follows. The other relations are handled similarly.

Isa	City	Country	Dialect
Paris	X		
France		X	
French			X

    b. The unary functions in the frames examples are also binary relations and can be handled the same as the semantic net examples.

13. *Frames.*

    a. The slots of frames designate unary functions, and the function in this case is binary.

    b. The following frame for Paris captures the information in the arcs emanating from the Paris node in the semantic net.

Paris	
Isa:	City
Part:	France

    The frames for the concepts of French, France, City, Country, and Dialect are similar.

14. *Pie charts and layered bar graphs.*

    a. A pie chart expresses the fractions of a total quantity assigned to each element of a decomposition of that total but does not convey the size of the total relative to other totals. The layered bar graph gives both kinds of information.

b. We can remedy this deficiency by using pies of various sizes in which the diameter or area conveys the size of the total, and the pie slices represent the fractions of this quantity.

A.3 Inference

1. *Derivability.* The sentence S(x,y,z) means that x sold y to z. The sentence U(y) means that y is an unregistered gun. The sentence C(x) means that x is a criminal. The sentence O(x,y) means that x owns y.

1. ∀x∀y∀z S(x,y,z) ∧ U(y) ⇒ C(x)   Δ
2. ∃y O(Red,y) ∧ U(y)   Δ
3. ∀y O(Red,y) ∧ U(y) ⇒ S(Lefty,y,Red)   Δ
4. O(Red,Gatling) ∧ U(Gatling)   2, EI
5. O(Red,Gatling) ∧ U(Gatling)   3, UI
   ⇒S(Lefty,Gatling,Red)
6. S(Lefty,Gatling,Red)   5, 4, MP
7. U(Gatling)   4, AE
8. S(Lefty,Gatling,Red) ∧ U(Gatling) ⇒ C(Lefty)   1, UI
9. S(Lefty,Gatling,Red) ∧ U(Gatling)   6, 7, AI
10. C(Lefty)   8, 9, MP

2. *Inference procedures.* We start by defining the function *concs*, which maps a sentence and a database into a list of the conclusions that can be formed from that sentence and an element of the database.

$$concs(\phi, \Delta) = \begin{cases} [] & \Delta = [] \\ append([\chi], concs(\phi, rest(\Delta))) & mp(\phi, first(\Delta), \chi) \\ concs(\phi, rest(\Delta)) & \text{otherwise} \end{cases}$$

Using *concs* we can define *fringe*, which maps an initial database and a positive integer into a list of sentences that have been derived but not yet "used." The initial value of *fringe* is just the set of all sentences in the initial database.

$$fringe(\Delta, n) = \begin{cases} \Delta & n = 1 \\ append(concs(first(fringe(\Delta, n - 1)), step(\Delta, n - 1)), \\ \quad rest(fringe(\Delta, n - 1))) & \text{otherwise} \end{cases}$$

On each step, the procedure adds the first element of the fringe to the database.

$$new(\Delta, n) = [first(fringe(\Delta, n))]$$

Finally, we define *step* in terms of *new*.

$$step(\Delta, n) = \begin{cases} \Delta & n = 1 \\ append(step(\Delta, n - 1), new(\Delta, n)) & \text{otherwise} \end{cases}$$

Note that, unlike the procedure in the text, each step of this procedure involves an entire scan of the database in order to collect the elements to add to the fringe.

3. *Distinctions and confusions.*

    a. P $\Rightarrow$ Q is a predicate-calculus sentence. It is satisfied by an interpretation and variable assignment if and only if P is not satisfied or Q is satisfied.

    b. P $\models$ Q is a statement about predicate calculus sentences. It states that P logically implies Q; i.e., every interpretation and variable assignment that satisfies P also satisfies Q.

    c. P $\vdash$ Q states that there is a formal proof of Q from P. As with b., it is a fact about predicate-calculus sentences P and Q, and it is not itself a sentence in predicate calculus.

4. *Proofs.* In the following proof, we write P for P(x), Q for Q(x), and R for R(x).

1.	$(\forall x \ (P\Rightarrow Q))$	Δ
2.	$(\forall x \ (Q\Rightarrow R))$	Δ
3.	$(\forall x \ ((Q\Rightarrow R)\Rightarrow(P\Rightarrow(Q\Rightarrow R))))$	II
4.	$(\forall x \ ((Q\Rightarrow R)\Rightarrow(P\Rightarrow(Q\Rightarrow R)))) \Rightarrow$	
	$\quad\quad ((\forall x \ (Q\Rightarrow R))\Rightarrow(\forall x \ (P\Rightarrow(Q\Rightarrow R))))$	UD
5.	$(\forall x \ (Q\Rightarrow R))\Rightarrow(\forall x \ (P\Rightarrow(Q\Rightarrow R)))$	3,4
6.	$(\forall x \ (P\Rightarrow(Q\Rightarrow R)))$	2,5
7.	$(\forall x \ ((P\Rightarrow(Q\Rightarrow R))\Rightarrow((P\Rightarrow Q)\Rightarrow(P\Rightarrow R))))$	ID
8.	$(\forall x \ ((P\Rightarrow(Q\Rightarrow R))\Rightarrow((P\Rightarrow Q)\Rightarrow(P\Rightarrow R)))) \Rightarrow$	
	$\quad\quad ((\forall x \ (P\Rightarrow(Q\Rightarrow R)))\Rightarrow(\forall x \ ((P\Rightarrow Q)\Rightarrow(P\Rightarrow R))))$	UD
9.	$(\forall x \ (P\Rightarrow(Q\Rightarrow R)))\Rightarrow(\forall x \ ((P\Rightarrow Q)\Rightarrow(P\Rightarrow R)))$	7,8
10.	$(\forall x \ ((P\Rightarrow Q)\Rightarrow(Q\Rightarrow R)))$	6,9
11.	$(\forall x \ ((P\Rightarrow Q)\Rightarrow(Q\Rightarrow R)))\Rightarrow((\forall x \ (P\Rightarrow Q))\Rightarrow(\forall x \ (P\Rightarrow R)))$	UD
12.	$(\forall x \ (P\Rightarrow Q))\Rightarrow(\forall x \ (P\Rightarrow R))$	10,11
13.	$(\forall x \ P\Rightarrow R)$	1,12

5. *Substitution.* The proof is a simple induction on the depth of nesting of ϕ in χ. If the depth is 0 (i.e., $\chi = \phi$), then $\chi_{\phi/\psi} = \psi$, and the result follows immediately. Now, let us assume that the result holds for all sentences with ϕ nested at levels less than or equal to n. Let χ be a sentence with ϕ nested at level $n + 1$. We can prove the result for each type of sentence in our language. Suppose, for example, that χ is a sentence of the form $\neg\theta$. By the induction hypothesis, we can prove that $\theta_{\phi/\psi} \Rightarrow \theta$. Therefore, we can prove $\neg\theta_{\phi/\psi}$. Now suppose that χ is a sentence of the form $\theta \Rightarrow \lambda$. By the induction hypothesis, we can prove $\theta_{\phi/\psi} \Rightarrow \theta$ and we can also prove $\lambda \Rightarrow \lambda_{\phi/\psi}$. But then, by transitivity,

we have $\theta_{\phi/\psi} \Rightarrow \lambda_{\phi/\psi}$. The proofs for sentences involving the other operators are similar.

6. *Generalization on constants.* If $\Delta \vdash \phi$, then there is a proof of ϕ from Δ. Let $\phi_1, \ldots, \phi_n$ be one such proof, where $\phi = \phi_n$. If we substitute ν for α in each of the ϕ_k to produce ϕ'_k, then the sequence $\phi'_1, \ldots, \phi'_n$ is a proof of ϕ'. The argument is simple. If $\phi_k \in \Delta$, then by the hypothesis, α does not appear in ϕ_k and so $\phi_k = \phi'_k$. If ϕ_k is a logical axiom, then so is ϕ'_k, as can be shown by an examination of the logical axiom schemata. Finally, if ϕ_k results from an application of modus ponens to ϕ_j and $\phi_j \Rightarrow \phi_k$, then ϕ'_k is obtained by modus ponens from ϕ'_j and $\phi'_j \Rightarrow \phi'_k$. Since ν does not appear in Δ and there is a proof of ϕ' from Δ, then by the generalization theorem there is a proof of $\forall\nu\phi'$ from Δ.

7. *Existential instantiation.* If $\Delta \cup \{\phi\} \vdash \psi$, then by the contraposition theorem it is the case that $\Delta \cup \{\neg\psi\} \vdash \neg\phi$. If α does not occur in Δ or ψ, then by the result in the previous exercise $\Delta \cup \{\neg\psi\} \vdash \forall\nu\neg\phi$ for some new variable ν. Of course, this is equivalent to $\Delta \cup \{\neg\psi\} \vdash \neg\exists\nu\phi$. But then, again by the contraposition theorem, $\Delta \cup \{\exists\nu\phi\} \vdash \psi$.

A.4 Resolution

1. *Clausal form.*

   a. $\{\neg P(x,y), Q(x,y)\}$

   b. $\{Q(x,y), \neg P(x,y)\}$

   c. $\{\neg P(x,y), \neg Q(x,y), R(x,y)\}$

   d. $\{\neg P(x,y), \neg Q(x,y), R(x,y)\}$

   e. $\{\neg P(x,y), Q(x,y), R(x,y)\}$

   f. $\{\neg P(x1,y1), Q(x1,y1)\}$
      $\{\neg P(x2,y2), R(x2,y2)\}$

   g. $\{\neg P(x1,y1), R(x1,y1)\}$
      $\{\neg Q(x2,y2), R(x2,y2)\}$

   h. $\{\neg P(x,F(x)), Q(x,F(x))\}$

   i. $\{\neg P(A,y), Q(A,y)\}$

   j. $\{\neg P(x), P(B)\}$

2. *Unification.*

   a. $\{x/Tweety, y/Yellow\}$.

   b. Not unifiable because x cannot have two different values.

c. {y/Postman,x/Blue}.

d. {y/F(x),z/B}.

e. {x/F(B),y/B}.

f. {x/F(F(A)),y/F(A),v/F(A)}.

g. {x/y}.

3. *Resolution.* The following axioms describe the situation. If the coin comes up heads, then I win. If it comes up tails, then you lose. If it does not come up heads, then it comes up tails. If you lose, then I win.

$$H \Rightarrow W(Me)$$

$$T \Rightarrow L(You)$$

$$\neg H \Rightarrow T$$

$$L(You) \Rightarrow W(Me)$$

Converting these to clausal form yields the first four axioms in the following proof. The fifth comes from the negation of the goal W(Me).

1. {¬H,W(Me)}	Δ	
2. {¬T,L(You)}	Δ	
3. {H,T}	Δ	
4. {¬L(You),W(Me)}	Δ	
5. {¬W(Me)}	Γ	
6. {¬T,W(Me)}	2,4	
7. {T,W(Me)}	1,3	
8. {W(Me)}	6,7	
9. {}	5,8	

4. *Resolution.* We start with the following axioms. For every course and every student, if the course has a final and the student is taking the course, then the student is not happy. For every course, if the course is easy, then there is a student taking the course who is not happy.

$$\forall c \forall s \ F(c) \land T(s,c) \Rightarrow \neg H(s)$$

$$\forall c \ E(c) \Rightarrow \exists s \ T(s,c) \land H(s)$$

The goal is expressed as follows.

$$\forall c \ F(c) \Rightarrow \neg E(c)$$

Converting the axioms to clausal form yields the first three clauses below. The Skolem function G designates a happy student in each easy course. The negated goal contributes the fourth and fifth axioms. Here, CS223 designates a course with a final that is hypothesized to be easy.

1. $\{\neg F(c), \neg T(s,c), \neg H(s)\}$ Δ
2. $\{\neg E(c), T(G(c),c)\}$ Δ
3. $\{\neg E(c), H(G(c))\}$ Δ
4. $\{F(CS223)\}$ Γ
5. $\{E(CS223)\}$ Γ
6. $\{T(G(CS223), CS223)\}$ 2,5
7. $\{H(G(CS223))\}$ 3,5
8. $\{\neg T(s, CS223), \neg H(s)\}$ 1,4
9. $\{\neg H(G(CS223))\}$ 6,8
10. $\{\}$ 7,9

5. *Resolution.* The key to this problem is to make the suspects' statements conditional on their innocence. The following axioms suffice. The first two axioms state that, if Arthur is innocent then Bertram was Victor's friend and Carleton did not like Victor, just as Arthur said. The third and fourth axioms capture Bertram's claims that he wasn't in town and that he didn't know Victor. The fifth and sixth axioms express Carleton's report about Arthur and Bertram having been with Victor on the day of the crime. The next three axioms encode the general facts that anyone who was with Victor on the day of the murder must have been in town, that a friend knows the person who is his friend, and that a person who likes someone must know him. The final three axioms capture the fact that only one of the suspects is guilty.

$$I(A) \Rightarrow F(B,V)$$

$$I(A) \Rightarrow \neg L(C,V)$$

$$I(B) \Rightarrow \neg T(B)$$

$$I(B) \Rightarrow \neg K(B,V)$$

$$I(C) \Rightarrow W(A,V)$$

$$I(C) \Rightarrow W(B,V)$$

$$W(x,V) \Rightarrow T(x)$$

$$F(x,y) \Rightarrow K(x,y)$$

$$L(x,y) \Rightarrow K(x,y)$$

$$I(A) \vee I(B)$$

I(A) ∨ I(C)

I(B) ∨ I(C)

Converting to clausal form leads to the first 12 axioms shown below. The goal ¬I(x) is negated, converted to clausal form, and combined with an answer literal, to yield the clause 13.

 1. {¬I(A),F(B,V)}   Δ
 2. {¬I(A),¬L(C,V)}   Δ
 3. {¬I(B),¬T(B)}   Δ
 4. {¬I(B),¬K(B,V)}   Δ
 5. {¬I(C),W(A,V)}   Δ
 6. {¬I(C),W(B,V)}   Δ
 7. {¬W(x,V),T(x)}   Δ
 8. {¬F(x,y),K(x,y)}   Δ
 9. {¬L(x,y),K(x,y)}   Δ
10. {I(A),I(B)}   Δ
11. {I(A),I(C)}   Δ
12. {I(B),I(C)}   Δ
13. {I(x),Ans(x)}   Γ
14. {¬I(A),K(B,V)}   1,8
15. {¬I(C),T(B)}   6,7
16. {¬I(A),¬I(B)}   4,14
17. {¬I(C),¬I(B)}   3,15
18. {I(C),¬I(B)}   11,16
19. {¬I(B)}   17,18
20. {Ans(B)}   13,19

6. *Logical axioms.*

   a. *Implication introduction.* P ⇒ (Q ⇒ P)

      1. {¬P}   Γ
      2. {¬Q}   Γ
      3. {P}   Γ
      4. {}   1,3

   b. *Implication distribution.*
      (P ⇒ (Q ⇒ R)) ⇒ ((P ⇒ Q) ⇒ (P ⇒ R))

      1. {¬P,¬Q,R}   Γ
      2. {¬P,Q}   Γ
      3. {P}   Γ
      4. {¬R}   Γ
      5. {¬P,R}   1,2

      6. {R}   3,5
      7. {}   4,6

c. *Contradiction realization.* $(Q \Rightarrow \neg P) \Rightarrow ((Q \Rightarrow P) \Rightarrow \neg Q)$

      1. $\{\neg Q, \neg P\}$ Γ
      2. $\{\neg Q, P\}$ Γ
      3. $\{Q\}$ Γ
      4. $\{\neg Q\}$ 1,2
      5. {}   3,4

d. *Universal distribution.*
   $(\forall x\ P(x) \Rightarrow Q(x)) \Rightarrow ((\forall x\ P(x)) \Rightarrow (\forall x\ Q(x)))$

      1. $\{\neg P(x), Q(x)\}$ Γ
      2. $\{P(x)\}$ Γ
      3. $\{\neg Q(A)\}$ Γ
      4. $\{Q(x)\}$ 1,2
      5. {}   3,4

e. *Universal generalization.* $P \Rightarrow \forall x\ P$

      1. $\{P\}$ Γ
      2. $\{\neg P\}$ Γ
      3. {}   1,2

f. *Universal instantiation.* $(\forall x\ P(x)) \Rightarrow P(A)$

      1. $\{P(x)\}$ Γ
      2. $\{\neg P(A)\}$ Γ
      3. {}   1,2

A.5 Resolution Strategies

1. *Deletion strategies.*

   a. Tautologies are marked as such and, of course, are not used in subsequent deductions.

      1. $\{P, Q\}$ Δ
      2. $\{\neg P, Q\}$ Δ
      3. $\{P, \neg Q\}$ Δ
      4. $\{\neg P, \neg Q\}$ Δ
      5. $\{Q\}$ 1, 2

$$
\begin{array}{lll}
\text{6.} & \{P\} & 1,3 \\
\text{7.} & \{Q,\neg Q\} & 2,3 \qquad \text{Tautology} \\
\text{8.} & \{P,\neg P\} & 2,3 \qquad \text{Tautology} \\
\text{9.} & \{Q,\neg Q\} & 1,4 \qquad \text{Tautology} \\
\text{10.} & \{P,\neg P\} & 1,4 \qquad \text{Tautology} \\
\text{11.} & \{\neg P\} & 2,4 \\
\text{12.} & \{\neg Q\} & 3,4 \\
\text{13.} & \{P\} & 3,5 \\
\text{14.} & \{\neg P\} & 4,5 \\
\text{15.} & \{Q\} & 2,6 \\
\text{16.} & \{\neg Q\} & 4,6 \\
\text{17.} & \{Q\} & 1,11 \\
\text{18.} & \{\neg Q\} & 3,11 \\
\text{19.} & \{\} & 6,11
\end{array}
$$

b. Each subsumed clause is marked by a number indicating the clause that subsumes it.

$$
\begin{array}{llll}
\text{1.} & \{P,Q\} & \triangle & \text{Subsumed by 5} \\
\text{2.} & \{\neg P,Q\} & \triangle & \text{Subsumed by 5} \\
\text{3.} & \{P,\neg Q\} & \triangle & \text{Subsumed by 6} \\
\text{4.} & \{\neg P,\neg Q\} & \triangle & \text{Subsumed by 6} \\
\text{5.} & \{Q\} & 1,2 \\
\text{6.} & \{\neg Q\} & 3,4 \\
\text{7.} & \{\} & 5,6
\end{array}
$$

2. *Linear resolution.*

$$
\begin{array}{lll}
\text{1.} & \{P,Q\} & \triangle \\
\text{2.} & \{Q,R\} & \triangle \\
\text{3.} & \{R,W\} & \triangle \\
\text{4.} & \{\neg R,\neg P\} & \triangle \\
\text{5.} & \{\neg W,\neg Q\} & \triangle \\
\text{6.} & \{\neg Q,\neg R\} & \triangle \\
\text{7.} & \{Q,\neg R\} & 1,4 \\
\text{8.} & \{Q\} & 2,7 \\
\text{9.} & \{\neg W\} & 5,8 \\
\text{10.} & \{R\} & 3,9 \\
\text{11.} & \{\neg Q\} & 6,10 \\
\text{12.} & \{\} & 8,11
\end{array}
$$

3. *Combination strategies.* It is possible to derive the empty clause from the following three clauses using unit resolution alone but not when ordered resolution is combined with unit resolution.

$$\{P,Q\}$$

$$\{\neg P,Q\}$$

$$\{\neg Q\}$$

4. *Combination strategies.* The following three clauses are unsatisfiable; but it is not possible to derive the empty clause from these clauses using ordered resolution combined with the set of support resolution, if we take the last clause as the sole element of the set of support.

$$\{P,\dot{Q}\}$$

$$\{\neg P\}$$

$$\{\neg Q\}$$

5. *Map coloring.* We can capture the constraint on colors with the following database. The symbols R, Y, G, and B stand for the colors red, yellow, green, and blue respectively. The relation named N holds of two colors if and only if they can occupy regions that are next to each other.

N(R,Y)	N(Y,R)	N(G,R)	N(B,R)
N(R,G)	N(Y,G)	N(G,Y)	N(B,Y)
N(R,B)	N(Y,B)	N(G,B)	N(B,G)

We phrase the goals as follows. Each of the variables here corresponds to one of the regions in the map, and the N literals capture its geometry.

$$N(r1,r2) \wedge N(r1,r3) \wedge N(r1,r5) \wedge N(r1,r6) \wedge$$
$$N(r2,r3) \wedge N(r2,r4) \wedge N(r2,r5) \wedge N(r2,r6) \wedge$$
$$N(r3,r4) \wedge N(r3,r6) \wedge N(r5,r6)$$

A.6 Nonmonotonic Reasoning

1. *Idempotence.* The following argument shows that the theories coincide not only in the sense that they have the same theorems, but even in the

sense that they have the same axioms. Every axiom of CWA[CWA[Δ]] that is not an axiom of CWA[Δ] is the negation of a ground atom A that is not provable in CWA[Δ]. But such an atom A is not provable in Δ either, so its negation is already in CWA[Δ].

2. *Insensitivity to negative clauses.* See [Reiter 1978]. Let Δ^- be Δ with an arbitrary negative clause, Ψ, removed. Let $\mathcal{A}[\Delta]$ be the set of ground atoms in $\mathcal{T}[\Delta]$. We first prove the following lemma.

LEMMA A.1 $\mathcal{A}[\Delta] = \mathcal{A}[\Delta^-]$.

Proof $\mathcal{A}[\Delta] \supseteq \mathcal{A}[\Delta^-]$ because anything derivable from Δ^- can be derived in the identical way from Δ.

Now consider an arbitrary $A \in \mathcal{A}[\Delta]$. Since A follows from Δ, there is a resolution proof of the empty clause from $\Delta \wedge \neg A$. The first clause in this proof has at most one positive literal, as $\Delta \cup \neg A$ is Horn. After that, the number of positive literals can never increase, because resolution with a negative Horn clause removes one positive literal, and resolution with any other Horn clause preserves the number of positive literals. It follows that at most one negative clause can be used in the proof. Moreover, this negative clause had better be $\neg A$; otherwise the proof shows that the empty clause can be derived from a consistent Δ. This means that no other negative clauses were used in the proof, including Ψ. Thus, the proof could be done identically from Δ^-, and so $\mathcal{A}[\Delta^-] \supseteq \mathcal{A}[\Delta]$. $\square$

Now observe that

$$\begin{aligned}
\text{CWA}[\Delta] &= \mathcal{T}[\Delta \cup \Delta_{asm}] \\
&= \mathcal{T}[\Delta^- \cup \Psi \cup \Delta_{asm}] \\
&= \mathcal{T}[\Delta^- \cup \Delta_{asm}] \text{ because } \Psi = \neg P_1 \vee \cdots \vee \neg P_n \text{ must be} \\
&\quad \text{subsumed by some negative literal } \neg P_i \text{ in } \Delta_{asm} \text{ (else} \\
&\quad \Delta \models P_i \text{ for all } i, \text{ contradicting } \Psi, \text{ and making } \Delta \\
&\quad \text{inconsistent)} \\
&= \mathcal{T}[\Delta^- \cup \Delta_{asm}^-] \text{ because } \Delta_{asm} = \Delta_{asm}^- \text{ by the lemma} \\
&= \text{CWA}[\Delta^-]
\end{aligned}$$

3. *Inconsistencies.* Since $\Delta \wedge \neg L_1 \wedge \neg L_2$ is Horn, there is an input resolution refutation showing the inconsistency of $\Delta \wedge \neg L_1 \wedge \neg L_2$. (This result is proved in [Chang 1973].) This refutation contains either $\neg L_1$ or $\neg L_2$ or both; otherwise there would be a refutation from Δ alone, and Δ is assumed consistent. Suppose the first (highest) occurrence of

either $\neg L_1$ or $\neg L_2$ in the refutation is $\neg L_1$. The resolvent resulting from this use of $\neg L_1$ contains only negative literals because the other parent of this resolvent has only one positive literal (Δ is Horn), the one cancelled by $\neg L_1$ in the resolution. Furthermore, none of the descendents of this resolvent in the refutation has any positive literals. Therefore none of them could resolve with $\neg L_2$, and $\neg L_2$ does not occur at all in the refutation. Thus, in this case, the same refutation shows that $\Delta \wedge \neg L_1$ is inconsistent. Similarly, if the first occurrence of either $\neg L_1$ or $\neg L_2$ were $\neg L_2$.

4. *Even and odd.* Replace the given formulas with the following equivalent formulas.

```
∀y (∃x Odd(x) ∧ x>0 ∧ y=Succ(x)) ⇒ Even(y))

∀y (∃x Odd(x) ∧ x>0 ∧ y=Pred(x)) ⇒ Even(y))
```

Rewriting these in normal form gives

```
∀y (∃x Odd(x) ∧ x>0 ∧ y=Succ(x)) ∨
    (∃x Odd(x) ∧ x>0 ∧ y=Pred(x)))
    ⇒ Even(y)
```

The completion of **Even** then is

```
Even(y) ⇔ (∃x Odd(x) ∧ x>0 ∧ (y=Succ(x) ∨ y=Pred(x)))
```

5. *Integers.* `Int(x) ⇔ (∃y x=Succ(y) ∧ Int(y)) ∨ x=0`.

6. *Delimited predicate completion.* Use the taxonomic hierarchy and the properties defined in our example about birds flying. State that Oswald is an ostrich. Do taxonomic completion to derive that Oswald cannot fly. Now say that Oswald has the (nontaxonomic) property of weightlessness (i.e., `Weightless(Oswald)`.) Then say (again nontaxonomically) that everything that is weightless can fly. This is not inconsistent with Δ because, after all, Oswald might have been a flying ostrich or might have had an abnormality of type 3.

7. *Completion.*

```
∀y P(y) ⇔
    (∃x y=F(x) ∧ Q1(x) ∧ Q2(x)) ∨ (∃x y=G(x) ∧ Q3(x))
```

8. *Is there a Q that is not a P?* Circumscribing Q in P < Q would limit the extension of Q such that there is exactly one object that satisfies the extension of Q that does not also satisfy the extension of P. (Can you also express this in predicate calculus?)

9. *Parallel.* Use Theorem 6.10 to write:

$$\text{CIRC}[(\forall x\ Q(x) \Rightarrow P1(x) \lor P2(x)); P1, P2]$$
$$\equiv \text{CIRC}[(\forall x\ Q(x) \Rightarrow P1(x) \lor P2(x)); P1]$$
$$\land\ \text{CIRC}[(\forall x\ Q(x) \Rightarrow P1(x) \lor P2(x)); P2]$$
$$\equiv (\forall x\ Q(x) \land \neg P2(x) \Leftrightarrow P1(x))$$
$$\land\ (\forall x\ Q(x) \land \neg P1(x) \Leftrightarrow P2(x))$$
$$\equiv \forall x\ Q(x) \land \neg P2(x) \Leftrightarrow P1(x)$$

10. *Knights and Knaves.*

    a. Write Δ as:

    $$N(\text{Liar}) \land \forall x\ (x = \text{Mork} \lor \text{Knave}(x)) \Rightarrow \text{Liar}(x)$$

    Where $N(\text{Liar}) \equiv$

    $$(\forall x\ \text{Knight}(x) \Rightarrow \text{Person}(x))\ \land$$
    $$(\forall x\ \text{Knave}(x) \Rightarrow \text{Person}(x))\ \land$$
    $$\text{Knave}(\text{Bork})\ \land$$
    $$(\exists x\ \neg \text{Liar}(x) \land \neg \text{Knave}(x))$$

    Use Theorem 6.5 to write CIRC[Δ; Liar] as:

    $$(\forall x\ \text{Knight}(x) \Rightarrow \text{Person}(x))\ \land$$
    $$(\forall x\ \text{Knave}(x) \Rightarrow \text{Person}(x))\ \land$$
    $$\text{Knave}(\text{Bork})\ \land$$
    $$(\exists x\ \neg(x = \text{Mork}) \lor \neg \text{Knave}(x))\ \land$$
    $$(\forall x\ x = \text{Mork} \lor \text{Knave}(x) \Leftrightarrow \text{Liar}(x))$$

    b. Write Δ as:

    $$N(\text{Liar}, \text{Knave}) \land (\forall x\ x = \text{Bork} \Rightarrow \text{Knave}(x))\ \land$$
    $$(\forall x\ x = \text{Mork} \lor \text{Knave}(x) \Rightarrow \text{Liar}(x))$$

    where $N(\text{Liar}, \text{Knave}) \equiv$

    $$(\forall x\ \text{Knight}(x) \Rightarrow \text{Person}(x))\ \land$$
    $$(\forall x\ \text{Knave}(x) \Rightarrow \text{Person}(x))\ \land$$
    $$(\exists x\ \neg \text{Liar}(x) \land \neg \text{Knave}(x))$$

Use Theorem 6.11 to write CIRC[Δ; Liar, Knave] as:

$$(\forall x \; \text{Knight}(x) \Rightarrow \text{Person}(x)) \wedge$$
$$(\forall x \; x=\text{Bork} \Rightarrow \text{Person}(x)) \wedge$$
$$(\exists x \; \neg(x=\text{Mork}) \vee (x=\text{Bork})) \wedge$$
$$(\forall x \; \text{Knave}(x) \Leftrightarrow x=\text{Bork}) \wedge$$
$$(\forall y \; \text{Liar}(x) \Leftrightarrow x=\text{Mork} \vee x=\text{Bork})$$

11. *AND gate.*

a. We can rewrite the formula involving Ab as $Q \wedge R \wedge \neg U \Rightarrow \text{Ab}(A)$. Putting this in normal form, we get:

$$Q \wedge R \wedge \neg U \wedge x=A \Rightarrow \text{Ab}(x)$$

By application of Theorem 6.5, the circumscription formula is

$$\forall x \; \text{Ab}(x) \Leftrightarrow Q \wedge R \wedge \neg U \wedge x=A$$

In this case, we are given that U is true; therefore, the right-hand side reduces to false, yielding $(\forall x \; \text{Ab}(x) \Leftrightarrow F)$, which is logically equivalent to $\neg(\exists x \; \text{Ab}(x))$, meaning that there is nothing that is abnormal.

b. In this case, we are given Q and R are true while U is false. Therefore, the formula reduces to $(\forall x \; \text{Ab}(x) \Leftrightarrow (x=A))$. In other words, A is the only abnormal thing.

12. *Both P and Q.*   Following the hint, we compute CIRC[Δ; Ab; (P, Q)] for the augmented database Δ consisting of the formulas

$$\forall x \; R(x) \Rightarrow P(x)$$
$$\forall x \; R(x) \Rightarrow Q(x)$$
$$\forall x \; P(x) \wedge Q(x) \Rightarrow \text{Ab}(x)$$

Δ can be written in the form $N(P, Q) \wedge (E_1 \leq P) \wedge (E_2 \leq Q)$, where

$$N(P, Q) \equiv \forall x \; P(x) \wedge Q(x) \Rightarrow \text{Ab}(x)$$
$$E_1 \equiv R$$
$$E_2 \equiv R$$

$N(P, Q)$ has no positive occurrences of P or Q, E_1 has no occurrences of P, and E_2 has no occurrences of Q. Thus, Theorem 6.12 can be used to compute

$$\text{CIRC}[\Delta; \text{Ab}; (P, Q)] \equiv \Delta \wedge \text{CIRC}[(\forall x \; R(x) \wedge R(x) \Rightarrow \text{Ab}(x)); \text{Ab}]$$

$$\equiv \Delta \wedge (\forall x\ \text{Ab}(x) \Rightarrow R(x))$$

Thus, using the definition of **Ab** and this circumscription, we can deduce

$$\forall x\ P(x) \wedge Q(x) \Rightarrow R(x)$$

A.7 Induction

1. *Concept formation.*

   a. Admissible.

   b. Characteristic.

   c. Discriminant.

   d. Characteristic.

   e. Discriminant.

2. *Boundary sets.* Without upper and lower bounds, it may not be possible to determine in finite time whether a given concept is in the version space.

3. *Independence.*

   a. Not independent, because the intersections of some of the rank relations with the *odd* and *even* relations are empty.

   b. Independent, because there is at least one even numbered card, at least one odd numbered card, at least one even face card, and at least one odd face card.

4. *Experiment generation.*

   a. Jack of spades.

   b. Two of spades.

A.8 Reasoning with Uncertain Beliefs

1. *Inequality.*

$$p(P) = p(P \wedge Q) + p(P \wedge \neg Q)$$
$$= p(P|Q)p(Q) + p(P \wedge \neg Q)$$

Thus, if $p(P|Q) = 1$, then

$$p(P) = p(Q) + p(P \wedge \neg Q) \geq p(Q)$$

since $p(P \wedge \neg Q) \geq 0$.

2. *Poker.*   C = Sam closes one eye. D = Sam drops out.

$$p(\text{C}|\text{D}) = 0.9$$
$$p(\text{D}) = 0.5$$
$$p(\text{C}) = 0.6$$
$$p(\text{D}|\text{C}) = p(\text{C}|\text{D}) \times p(\text{D})/p(\text{C})$$
$$= (0.9)(0.5)/(0.6) = 0.75$$

3. *Biology 15.*   Using the vocabulary

- A   means "Person gets an A"

- B   means "Person is a biology major"

- H   means "Person does all the homework"

We are given that

$$p(\text{A}) = 0.25$$
$$p(\text{H}|\text{A}) = 0.80$$
$$p(\text{H}|\neg\text{A}) = 0.60$$
$$p(\text{B}|\text{A}) = 0.75$$
$$p(\text{B}|\neg\text{A}) = 0.50$$

$$O(\text{A} \mid \text{H}) = \frac{p(\text{A} \mid \text{H})}{p(\neg\text{A} \mid \text{H})} = \frac{p(\text{H} \mid \text{A})p(\text{A})}{p(\text{H} \mid \neg\text{A})p(\neg\text{A})} = \frac{(0.8)(0.25)}{(0.6)(0.75)} = 0.4444$$

$$O(\text{A} \mid \text{B}\wedge\text{H}) = \frac{p(\text{A} \mid \text{B}\wedge\text{H})}{p(\neg\text{A} \mid \text{B}\wedge\text{H})} = \frac{p(\text{B}\wedge\text{H} \mid \text{A})p(\text{A})}{p(\text{B}\wedge\text{H} \mid \neg\text{A})p(\neg\text{A})}$$

$$= \frac{p(\text{B} \mid \text{A})p(\text{H} \mid \text{A})p(\text{A})}{p(\text{B} \mid \neg\text{A})p(\text{H} \mid \neg\text{A})p(\neg\text{A})} = \frac{(0.75)(0.8)(0.25)}{(0.5)(0.6)(0.75)} = 0.6667$$

4. *Manipulating probabilities.*

$$p(\text{P}\Rightarrow\text{Q}) = p(\neg\text{P}\vee\text{Q})$$
$$= 1 - p(\text{P}\wedge\neg\text{Q})$$
$$= 1 - p(\text{P} \mid \neg\text{Q})p(\neg\text{Q})$$
$$= 1 - 0.4p(\neg\text{Q})$$

also,

$$p(\text{P}) = p(\text{P}\wedge\text{Q}) + p(\text{P}\wedge\neg\text{Q})$$
$$= p(\text{P} \mid \text{Q})p(\text{Q}) + p(\text{P} \mid \neg\text{Q})p(\neg\text{Q})$$
$$= 0.2p(\text{Q}) + 0.4p(\neg\text{Q})$$

therefore,

$$p(\neg\text{Q}) = 5p(\text{P}) - 1$$

and

$$p(P \Rightarrow Q) = 1.4 - 2p(P)$$

5. *Another inequality.* The consistent truth values of the three sentences P, Q, and $\neg(P \Leftrightarrow Q)$ are as follows.

P	Q	$\neg(P \Leftrightarrow Q)$
0	0	0
0	1	1
1	0	1
1	1	0

Let the probability of the four worlds defined by the preceding rows of consistent truth values be p_1, p_2, p_3, and p_4 respectively. Then the matrix equation $\mathbf{\Pi} = \mathbf{VP}$ tells us that:

$$p(P) = p_3 + p_4$$
$$p(Q) = p_2 + p_4$$
$$p(\neg(P \Leftrightarrow Q)) = p_2 + p_3$$

From these equations, we have:

$$p(P) + p(Q) = p_2 + p_3 + 2p_4$$
$$p(\neg(P \Leftrightarrow Q)) = p_2 + p_3$$

Since $p_4 \geq 0$, it follows that $p(\neg(P \Leftrightarrow Q)) \leq p(P) + p(Q)$ as required.

6. *Entailment.* Use the semantic tree method and draw diagram.

7. *Independence.* Maximum entropy solution for this problem:

$$\mathbf{V}' = \begin{bmatrix} 1 & 1 & 1 & 1 \\ 1 & 1 & 0 & 0 \\ 1 & 0 & 1 & 0 \end{bmatrix} \qquad \mathbf{\Pi}' = \begin{bmatrix} 1 \\ \pi_2 \\ \pi_3 \end{bmatrix}$$

$$p_1 = a_1 a_2 a_3$$
$$p_2 = a_1 a_2$$
$$p_3 = a_1 a_3$$
$$p_4 = a_1$$

Using $\mathbf{\Pi}' = \mathbf{V}'\mathbf{P}$ we get

$$a_1 a_2 a_3 + a_1 a_2 + a_1 a_3 + a_1 = 1$$
$$a_1 a_2 a_3 + a_1 a_2 = \pi_2$$
$$a_1 a_2 a_3 + a_1 a_3 = \pi_3$$

Solving yields:

$$a_2 = \frac{\pi_2}{1 - \pi_2}$$

$$
\begin{aligned}
p(\mathsf{P}\wedge\mathsf{Q}) = p_1 &= a_1 a_2 a_3 \\
&= \frac{\pi_3 a_2 a_3}{a_2 a_3 + a_3} \\
&= \frac{\pi_3}{1 + \frac{1}{a_2}}
\end{aligned}
$$

Finally, $p(\mathsf{P}\wedge\mathsf{Q}) = \pi_2\pi_3 = p(\mathsf{P})p(\mathsf{Q})$. (Maximum entropy occurs when P and Q are independent!)

Projection approximation solution: The row-vector representation for P∧Q is $[1, 0, 0, 0]$. Its projection onto the subspace defined by the row vectors of $\mathbf{V'}$ is $[\frac{3}{4},\frac{1}{4},\frac{1}{4},-\frac{1}{4}]$ (i.e., $[1, 0, 0, 0]$ is the sum of the two orthogonal vectors $[\frac{3}{4},\frac{1}{4},\frac{1}{4},-\frac{1}{4}]$ and $[\frac{1}{4},-\frac{1}{4},-\frac{1}{4},\frac{1}{4}]$. $[\frac{3}{4},\frac{1}{4},\frac{1}{4},-\frac{1}{4}]$ is a linear combination of the row vectors of $\mathbf{V'}$, and $[\frac{1}{4},-\frac{1}{4},-\frac{1}{4},\frac{1}{4}]$ is orthogonal to all the row vectors of $\mathbf{V'}$). The coefficients c_i are given by: $c_1 = -\frac{1}{4}$, $c_2 = \frac{1}{2}$, $c_3 = \frac{1}{2}$. Using these, the "approximate value" for $p(\mathsf{P}\wedge\mathsf{Q})$ is $-\frac{1}{4}\pi_1 + \frac{1}{2}\pi_2 + \frac{1}{2}\pi_3$, which is equal to $\frac{1}{2}(p(\mathsf{P}) + p(\mathsf{Q}) - \frac{1}{2})$. The two values for $p(\mathsf{P}\wedge\mathsf{Q})$, maximum entropy and projection approximation are obviously not equal.

8. *Not necessarily the same.*

P	Q	$P{\Rightarrow}Q$	$P{\wedge}Q$	
0	0	1	0	$p1$
0	1	1	0	$p2$
1	0	0	0	$p3$
1	1	1	1	$p4$

$$
\begin{aligned}
p(P{\Rightarrow}Q) &= p1 + p2 + p4 \\
&= 1 - p3 \\
p(Q|P) &= p(P{\wedge}Q)/p(P) \\
&= p4/(p3 + p4)
\end{aligned}
$$

Thus, $p(P{\Rightarrow}Q) = p(Q|P)$ precisely when

$$
\begin{aligned}
1 - p3 &= p4/(p3 + p4) \\
(p3 + p4)(1 - p3) - p4 &= 0 \\
p3(1 - p4 - p3) &= 0
\end{aligned}
$$

$p3 = 0$ or $p3 + p4 = 1$. In other words, when $p(P{\Rightarrow}Q) = 1$ or $p(P) = 1$.

A.9 Knowledge and Belief

1. *One cannot both know ϕ and know $\neg\phi$.* Convert $\mathbf{K}_\alpha(\phi) \Rightarrow \neg\mathbf{K}_\alpha(\neg\phi)$ to $\neg\mathbf{K}_\alpha(\phi) \vee \neg\mathbf{K}_\alpha(\neg\phi)$. Now prove by refutation. Assume $\neg(\neg\mathbf{K}_\alpha(\phi) \vee \neg\mathbf{K}_\alpha(\neg\phi))$ or $\mathbf{K}_\alpha(\phi) \wedge \mathbf{K}_\alpha(\neg\phi)$. Using Axiom 9.2 (assuming reflexivity of the accessibility relation), we get $\phi \wedge \neg\phi$ or F. Thus, our original formula must be true.

2. *Resolution.* Use Rule 9.5 to infer $\mathbf{K}_\alpha(L_1 \vee L_2 \Rightarrow (\neg L_1 \Rightarrow L_2))$. Then use $\mathbf{K}_\alpha(L_1 \vee L_2)$ and Axiom 9.1 to deduce $\mathbf{K}_\alpha(\neg L_1 \Rightarrow L_2)$. Then use $\mathbf{K}_\alpha(\neg L_1)$ and Axiom 9.1 to deduce $\mathbf{K}_\alpha(L_2)$.

3. *Conjunction.* $\mathbf{K}(\alpha,\phi)$ and $\mathbf{K}(\alpha,\psi)$ imply that ϕ and ψ are true in all possible worlds accessible for α. Thus, $\phi \wedge \psi$ is true in all possible worlds accessible for α and $\mathbf{K}(\alpha,\phi\wedge\psi)$. $\mathbf{K}(\alpha,\phi\wedge\psi)$ implies that $\phi \wedge \psi$ is true in all possible worlds accessible for α. Thus, ϕ and ψ are both true in all possible worlds accessible for α. Thus, $\mathbf{K}(\alpha,\phi)$ and $\mathbf{K}(\alpha,\psi)$.

4. *Brouwer Axiom.* Using $P2$, we can show that the the Brouwer Axiom (symmetric) follows from Axiom 9.2 (reflexive) and Axiom 9.4 (Euclidean).

5. *Rule 9.7.* From $\phi \Rightarrow \psi$ being a theorem, we get $\mathbf{K}(\alpha, \phi \Rightarrow \psi)$ by necessitation. The inference then follows from the alternative form of Axiom 9.1.

6. *Sam and John.*

    1. $\mathbf{B}_J(\mathbf{B}_S(P) \vee \mathbf{B}_S(Q))$
    2. $\mathbf{B}_J(\mathbf{B}_S(P \Rightarrow R))$
    3. $\mathbf{B}_J(\mathbf{B}_S(\neg R))$

Part a. First prove $\mathbf{B}_J(\mathbf{B}_S(\neg P))$. Assume:

    $4'$. $\neg\mathbf{B}_J(\mathbf{B}_S(\neg P))$

2, 3, and $4'$ are contradictory (by resolution) if

$$\mathbf{B}_S(P \Rightarrow R) \wedge \mathbf{B}_S(\neg R) \vdash_J \mathbf{B}_S(\neg P)$$

If J has attachment and J, S has resolution, this deduction goes through, and thus:

    4. $\mathbf{B}_J(\mathbf{B}_S(\neg P))$

Now assume the negation of what we are trying to prove:

    $5'$. $\neg\mathbf{B}_J(\mathbf{B}_S(Q))$

1, 4, and 5' are contradictory (by resolution) if

$$(\mathbf{B_S}(P) \lor \mathbf{B_S}(Q)) \land \mathbf{B_S}(\neg P) \vdash_J \mathbf{B_S}(Q)$$

To prove $\mathbf{B_S}(Q)$ in J's system from $(\mathbf{B_S}(P) \lor \mathbf{B_S}(Q)) \land \mathbf{B_S}(\neg P)$, we set up, for J, the refutation problem:

$\mathbf{B_S}(P) \lor \mathbf{B_S}(Q)$
$\mathbf{B_S}(\neg P)$
$\neg \mathbf{B_S}(Q)$

These can be shown to be contradictory, for J, if J has attachment and if $\mathbf{B_S}(P)$ and $\mathbf{B_S}(\neg P)$ are contradictory for J. Assuming P and $\neg$P are contradictory for J, S, we have established $\mathbf{B_J}(\mathbf{B_S}(Q))$.

Part b.

4. $\mathbf{K_J}(\mathbf{K_S}(\neg R \Rightarrow \neg P))$	2
5. $\mathbf{K_S}(\neg R \Rightarrow \neg P)$	4, Axiom 9.2
6. $\mathbf{K_S}(\neg R)$	3, Axiom 9.2
7. $\mathbf{K_S}(\neg P)$	5, 6, Axiom 9.1
8. $\neg \mathbf{K_S}(P)$	7, exercise 1
9. $\mathbf{K_J}(\neg \mathbf{K_S}(P))$	2, 3, 5, 6, 8, Rule 9.6
10. $\mathbf{K_J}(\mathbf{K_S}(Q))$	1, 9, Axiom 9.1

7. *Properties of accessibility.* We prove the validity of each of the axioms in an arbitrary world, w_0.

  a. Given $k(\alpha, w_0, w_0)$ and assuming $\mathbf{K_\alpha}(P)$ in w_0, we infer (from possible-worlds semantics) that P is true in w_0 (since it is true in *all* worlds accessible for α from w_0). Therefore, $\mathbf{K_\alpha}(P) \Rightarrow P$ in w_0.

  b. Suppose, assuming $\mathbf{K_\alpha}(P)$ in w_0, it is *not* the case that $\mathbf{K_\alpha}(\mathbf{K_\alpha}(P))$ in w_0 (given the transitivity of k). Then, from possible-worlds semantics, there would be a world accessible for α from w_0 in which $\mathbf{K_\alpha}(P)$ is not true. Call this world w^*. From possible-worlds semantics, there must then be a world, w', accessible from w^* in which P is not true. But if k is transitive, w' is accessible from w_0, and since P is not true in w', it cannot be the case that $\mathbf{K_\alpha}(P)$ is true in w_0—contradicting our assumption and proving $\mathbf{K_\alpha}(P) \Rightarrow \mathbf{K_\alpha}(\mathbf{K_\alpha}(P))$.

  c. This part and part 7d are proved by methods similar to those used in part 7a and part 7b.

  e. We prove the validity of Axiom 9.1 for an arbitrary world, w_0. Assuming $\mathbf{K_\alpha}(\phi)$ and $\mathbf{K_\alpha}(\phi \Rightarrow \psi)$ in w_0, possible-worlds semantics ensures that ϕ and $\phi \Rightarrow \psi$ are true in all worlds accessible from w_0.

Ordinary propositional semantics then indicates that ψ is true in all of these worlds. Using the statement in the exercise then indicates that $\mathbf{K}_\alpha(\psi)$ is true in w_0.

8. *Brouwer and belief.*   Probably not, because, fundamentally, whether a fact ϕ is true is independent of an agent's beliefs.

9. *A visiting Swede.*
   de re: ∃x Swede(x) ∧ **B**(John, Willvisit(x))
   de dicto: **B**(John, ∃x Swede(x) ∧ Willvisit(x))

A.10 Metaknowledge and Metareasoning

1. *Syntax.*   First, we define negations, conjunctions, disjunctions, implications, reverse implications, and bidirectional implications.

$$∀p \; Sent(p) \Leftrightarrow Neg(["¬", p])$$

$$∀p∀q \; Sent(p) ∧ Sent(q) \Leftrightarrow Conj(["∧",p,q])$$

$$∀p∀q \; Sent(p) ∧ Sent(q) \Leftrightarrow Disj(["∨",p,q])$$

$$∀p∀q \; Sent(p) ∧ Sent(q) \Leftrightarrow Imp(["⇒",p,q])$$

$$∀p∀q \; Sent(p) ∧ Sent(q) \Leftrightarrow Rimp(["⇐",p,q])$$

$$∀p∀q \; Sent(p) ∧ Sent(q) \Leftrightarrow Bimp(["⇔",p,q])$$

These are all logical sentences and the only logical sentences.

$$∀p \; Logical(p) \Leftrightarrow$$
$$Neg(p) ∨ Conj(p) ∨ Disj(p) ∨ Imp(p) ∨ Rimp(p) ∨ Bimp(p)$$

Universal and existential sentences.

$$∀p∀v \; Sent(p) ∧ Variable(v) \Leftrightarrow Univ(["∀",v,p])$$

$$∀p∀v \; Sent(p) ∧ Variable(v) \Leftrightarrow Exist(["∃",v,p])$$

These are both quantified sentences and the only quantified sentences.

$$∀p \; Quant(p) \Leftrightarrow Univ(p) ∨ Exist(p)$$

Finally, we define general sentences.

$$∀p \; Sent(p) \Leftrightarrow Atom(p) ∨ Logical(p) ∨ Quant(p)$$

2. *Rules of inference.* We define modus ponens as a ternary relation on sentences as follows:

$$\forall p \forall q \ \text{MP}(["\Rightarrow",p,q],p,q)$$

3. *Restriction strategies.* All of the strategies share the following basic definitions.

```
∀d Step(d,1)=d

∀d∀n Step(d,n)=Append(Step(d,n-1),New(d,n))

∀d∀n∀p∀q∀r Res(d,n)=[p,q,r] ⇒ New(d,n)=[r]
```

a. Subsumption.

```
∀p∀q Subsumes(p,q) ⇔ ∃s Subset(Subst(p,s),q)

∀d∀n∀a∀b∀c (∃s Member(s,Step(d,n-1)) ∧ Subsumes(s,a))
  ⇒ (Res(d,n)≠[a,b,c] ∧ Res(d,n)≠[b,a,c])
```

b. Set of support.

```
Ansliteral("Ans".1)

∀c (∃p Member(p,c) ∧ Ansliteral(p)) ⇔ Ansclause(c)

¬Ansclause(a) ∧ ¬Ansclause(b) ⇒ Res(d,n) ≠ [a,b,c]
```

c. Linear resolution.

```
∀d∀n∀a∀b∀c Resc(d,n)=[a,b,c]
  ⇒ (Member(a,d) ∨ Anc(a,b,d,n) ∨
      Member(b,d) ∨ Anc(b,a,d,n))

∀b∀c∀d∀n Anc(b,c,d,n) ⇔
  (b=c ∧ (∃m m<n ∧ Res(d,m)=[s,t,c] ∧
      (Anc(b,s,d,m) ∨ Anc(b,t,d,m))))
```

4. *Ordering strategies.* The axioms from above, plus the following.

```
∀d∀n∀p∀q∀r Res(d,n)=[p,q,r] ⇒ Ordered(r)

Ordered([])

∀p Ordered([p])
```

$$\text{Ordered}(q.1) \wedge \text{Numsol}(p) \leq \text{Numsol}(q) \Rightarrow \text{Ordered}(p.q.1)$$

$$\text{Ordered}(p.1) \wedge \text{Numsol}(p) > \text{Numsol}(q) \Rightarrow \text{Ordered}(q.p.1)$$

5. *Reflection.*

$$[\text{Ans}("\Delta")] \in data(\Omega, 3)$$

implies

$$next(\Omega) = append(data(\Omega, 3) - answers(data(\Omega, 3)), newmeta(\Delta), \Delta)$$

A.11 State and Change

1. *Side effects.* The primary effects of these actions can be described as follows.

$$\text{T(Car(a)=y,Do(Rplaca(a,y),s))}$$

$$\text{T(Cdr(a)=y,Do(Rplacd(a,y),s))}$$

We also have the following frame axioms.

$$\text{T(Cdr(a)=x,s)} \Rightarrow \text{T(Cdr(a)=x,Do(Rplaca(a,y),s))}$$

$$\text{T(Car(b)=x,s)} \wedge \text{a}\neq\text{b} \Rightarrow \text{T(Car(b)=x,Do(Replaca(a,y),s))}$$

$$\text{T(Car(a)=x,s)} \Rightarrow \text{T(Car(a)=x,Do(Rplacd(a,y),s))}$$

$$\text{T(Cdr(b)=x,s)} \wedge \text{a}\neq\text{b} \Rightarrow \text{T(Cdr(b)=x,Do(Replaca(a,y),s))}$$

2. *Simulation.* We prove the result using the set-of-support strategy with the goal clause as the sole member of the initial set of support.

```
{T(Clear(C),S1)}
{T(On(C,A),S1)}
{T(Table(A),S1)}
{T(Clear(B),S1)}
{T(Table(B),S1)}
{¬T(On(B,C),Do([U(C,A),S(B,C),S(A,B)],S1))}
{¬T(On(B,C),Do([S(B,C),S(A,B)],Do(U(C,A),S1)))}
{¬T(On(B,C),Do([S(A,B)],Do(S(B,C),Do(U(C,A),S1))))}
{¬T(On(B,C),Do([],Do(S(A,B),Do(S(B,C),Do(U(C,A),S1)))))}
{¬T(On(B,C),Do(S(A,B),Do(S(B,C),Do(U(C,A),S1))))}
{¬T(On(B,C),Do(S(B,C),Do(U(C,A),S1)))}
```

```
{¬T(Table(B),Do(U(C,A),S1)),¬T(Clear(B),Do(U(C,A),S1)),
 ¬T(Clear(C),Do(U(C,A),S1)),B=C}
{¬T(Table(B),S1),¬T(Clear(B),Do(U(C,A),S1)),
 ¬T(Clear(C),Do(U(C,A),S1)),B=C}
{¬T(Clear(b),Do(U(C,A),S1)),
 ¬T(Clear(c),Do(U(C,A),S1)),B=C}
{¬T(Clear(B),S1),¬T(Clear(C),Do(U(C,A),S1)),B=C}
{¬T(Clear(C),Do(U(C,A),S1)),B=C}
{¬T(Clear(C),S1),B=C}
{B=C}
{}
```

3. *Nondeterminism.* We can characterize the state that results from the execution of a nondeterministic action as a disjunction.

$$\forall a \forall b \forall s \ (Do(ND(a,b),s)=Do(a,s) \lor Do(ND(a,b),s)=Do(b,s))$$

Describing the effects in terms of state descriptors is slightly more complicated.

$$\forall p \forall a \forall b \forall s \ T(p,Do(a,s)) \land T(p,Do(b,s)) \Rightarrow T(p,Do(ND(a,b),s))$$

$$\forall p \forall a \forall b \forall s \ T(p,Do(ND(a,b),s)) \Rightarrow (T(p,Do(a,s)) \lor T(p,Do(b,s)))$$

4. *The waterpot problem.*

   a. We conceptualize 18 states, six possible quantities in the large container and three in the small one. We cannot necessarily get to all of these states, but we can at least imagine them.

   b. There are four actions: emptying the small container E, emptying the large container F, pouring from the small container to the large container L, and *vice versa* S. The pouring action pours water from one container into another container until the second container is full or the first is empty, whichever comes first. The emptying action results in the loss of all water from container.

   c. The structure of this problem allows us to use an approach that obviates the need for separate frame axioms. We use a single state descriptor Quant(m,n) that gives the quantities of the two containers in a single term. The first two axioms below describe the effects of the emptying actions. The other two axioms describe the effects of pouring water from the large to the small container. The axioms for the reverse action are similar.

$$T(\text{Quant}(m,n),s) \Rightarrow T(\text{Quant}(0,n),\text{Do}(F,s))$$

$$T(\text{Quant}(m,n),s) \Rightarrow T(\text{Quant}(m,0),\text{Do}(E,s))$$

$$T(\text{Quant}(m,n),s) \wedge m{\geq}2\text{-}n \wedge p{=}m{+}n{-}2$$
$$\Rightarrow T(\text{Quant}(p,2),\text{Do}(L,s))$$

$$T(\text{Quant}(m,n),s) \wedge m{<}2\text{-}n \wedge q{=}2\text{-}n{-}m$$
$$\Rightarrow T(\text{Quant}(0,q),\text{Do}(L,s))$$

d. [L,E,L,E,L].

e. The proof goes as follows. We assume the presence of semantic attachments to handle the arithmetic.

```
{T(Quant(5,0),S1)}
{¬5≥2-0,¬p=5+0-2,T(Quant(p,2),Do(L,S1))}
{¬p=5+0-2,T(Quant(p,2),Do(L,S1))}
{T(Quant(3,2),Do(L,S1))}
{T(Quant(3,0),Do(E,Do(L,S1)))}
{¬3≥2-0,¬p=3+0-2,T(Quant(p,2),Do(L,Do(E,Do(L,S1))))}
{¬p=3+0-2,T(Quant(p,2),Do(L,Do(E,Do(L,S1))))}
{T(Quant(1,2),Do(L,Do(E,Do(L,S1))))}
{T(Quant(1,0),Do(E,Do(L,Do(E,Do(L,S1)))))}
{¬1<2-0,q=2-0-1,
 T(Quant(0,q),Do(L,Do(E,Do(L,Do(E,Do(L,S1))))))}
{¬q=2-0-1,
 T(Quant(0,q),Do(L,Do(E,Do(L,Do(E,Do(L,S1))))))}
{T(Quant(0,1),Do(L,Do(E,Do(L,Do(E,Do(L,S1))))))}
{T(Quant(0,1),Do([],Do(L,Do(E,Do(L,Do(E,Do(L,S1)))))))}
{T(Quant(0,1),Do([L],Do(E,Do(L,Do(E,Do(L,S1)))))))}
{T(Quant(0,1),Do([E,L],Do(L,Do(E,Do(L,S1))))))}
{T(Quant(0,1),Do([L,E,L],Do(E,Do(L,S1))))}
{T(Quant(0,1),Do([E,L,E,L],Do(L,S1)))}
{T(Quant(0,1),Do([L,ES,L,E,L],S1))}
```

5. *The 8-puzzle.*

   a. There are 9! states, one for each arrangement of tiles on the grid. It is interesting to note that these states can be partitioned into two subsets such that no arrangement in one subset can be converted into an arrangement in the other subset.

   b. We conceptualize four actions: moving the blank up, down, left, and right.

c. The following axiom describes the action U of moving the blank up one square. The axioms for the other actions are similar.

T(Loc(B,m,n),s) ∧ p=m-1 ⇒ T(Loc(B,p,n),Do(U,s))

T(Loc(t,m,n),s) ∧ p=m+1 ⇒ T(Loc(t,p,n),Do(U,s))

T(Loc(B,m,n),s) ∧ T(Loc(t,p,q),s) ∧ (m≠p+1 ∨ n≠q)
⇒ T(Loc(t,p,q),Do(U,s))

d. [U,L,D,R].

e. The proof goes as follows. We assume procedural attachments to handle the arithmetic.

{T(Loc(2,1,1),S1)}
{T(Loc(8,1,2),S1)}
{T(Loc(1,2,1),S1)}
{T(Loc(B,2,2),S1)}
{¬p=2-1,T(Loc(B,p,2),Do(U,S1))}
{T(Loc(B,1,2),Do(U,S1))}
{¬p=1+1,T(Loc(8,p,2),Do(U,S1))}
{T(Loc(8,2,2),Do(U,S1))}
{¬p=2-1,T(Loc(B,1,p),Do(L,Do(U,S1)))}
{T(Loc(B,1,1),Do(L,Do(U,S1)))}
{¬T(Loc(t,p,q),Do(U,S1)),
 1=p,T(Loc(t,p,q),Do(L,Do(U,S1)))}
{1=2,T(Loc(8,2,2),Do(L,Do(U,S1)))}
{T(Loc(8,2,2),Do(L,Do(U,S1)))}
{¬p=1+1,T(Loc(B,p,1),Do(D,Do(L,Do(U,S1))))}
{T(Loc(B,2,1),Do(D,Do(L,Do(U,S1))))}
{¬T(Loc(t,p,q),Do(L,Do(U,S1))),1=q,
 T(Loc(t,p,q),Do(D,Do(L,Do(U,S1))))}
{1=2,T(Loc(8,2,2),Do(D,Do(L,Do(U,S1))))}
{T(Loc(8,2,2),Do(D,Do(L,Do(U,S1))))}
{¬p=2-1,T(8,2,p),Do(R,Do(D,Do(L,Do(U,S1))))}
{T(8,2,1),Do(R,Do(D,Do(L,Do(U,S1))))}
{T(8,2,1),Do({},Do(R,Do(D,Do(L,Do(U,S1)))))}
{T(8,2,1),Do({R},Do(D,Do(L,Do(U,S1))))}
{T(8,2,1),Do({D,R},Do(L,Do(U,S1)))}
{T(8,2,1),Do({L,D,R},Do(U,S1))}
{T(8,2,1),Do({U,L,D,R},S1)}

6. *Thermostats.* The expression Setting=x describes the set of states in which the thermostat setting is x. The expression Temp=x describes states in which the ambient temperature is x. The expression On

describes states in which the furnace is on, and the expression Off describes states in which it is off. There are three actions: Start, Stop, and Noop.

$$\text{Off} \wedge \text{Setting=g} \wedge \text{Temp=t} \wedge \text{t<g-5 -> Start}$$

$$\text{On} \wedge \text{Setting=g} \wedge \text{Temp=t} \wedge \text{t>g+5 -> Stop}$$

$$\text{1=1 -> Noop}$$

A.12 Planning

1. *Goals.* We first define relations for the various ways to win the game and then disjoin them to define the goal.

$$\text{Mark(i,1,x,s)} \wedge \text{Mark(i,2,x,s)} \wedge \text{Mark(i,3,x,s)} \Leftrightarrow \text{Horiz(x,s)}$$

$$\text{Mark(1,j,x,s)} \wedge \text{Mark(2,j,x,s)} \wedge \text{Mark(3,j,x,s)} \Leftrightarrow \text{Vert(x,s)}$$

$$\text{Mark(1,1,x,s)} \wedge \text{Mark(2,2,x,s)} \wedge \text{Mark(3,3,x,s)} \Leftrightarrow \text{Nwse(x,s)}$$

$$\text{Mark(1,3,x,s)} \wedge \text{Mark(2,2,x,s)} \wedge \text{Mark(3,1,x,s)} \Leftrightarrow \text{Nesw(x,s)}$$

$$\text{Horiz(X,s)} \vee \text{Vert(X,s)} \vee \text{Nwse(X,s)} \vee \text{Nesw(X,s)} \Leftrightarrow \text{Goal(s)}$$

2. *Conditional plans.* The following axioms describe the effects of the two operators.

$$\text{T(On(x,y),s)} \Rightarrow \text{T(On(y,x),Do(F(x,y),s))}$$

$$\text{T(On(x,y),Do(L(x,y),s))} \vee \text{T(On(y,x),Do(L(x,y),s))}$$

In the initial state, both blocks are on the table and clear.

$$\text{T(Clear(A),S1)}$$

$$\text{T(Table(A),S1)}$$

$$\text{T(Clear(B),S1)}$$

$$\text{T(Table(B),S1)}$$

The goal is to get block A onto block B.

$$\text{T(On(A,B),s)} \Leftrightarrow \text{Goal(s)}$$

The derivation goes as follows.

```
{¬Goal(Do(a,S1)),Ans(a)}
{¬T(On(A,B),Do(a,S1)),Ans(a)}
{¬T(On(A,B),Do(1,Do(a,S1))),Ans(a.1)}
{¬T(On(A,B),Do(1,Do(b,Do(a,S1)))),Ans(a.(b.1))}
{¬T(On(A,B),Do(b,Do(a,S1))),Ans([a,b])}

{¬T(p,Do(a,S1)),¬T(On(A,B),Do(c,Do(a,S1))),
 Ans([a,If(p,c,d)])}
{¬T(p,Do(a,S1)),¬T(On(B,A),Do(a,S1)),
 Ans([a,If(p,F(B,A),d)])}
{¬T(On(B,A),Do(a,S1)),Ans([a,If(On(B,A),F(B,A),d)])}

{T(p,Do(a,S1)),¬T(On(A,B),Do(d,Do(a,S1))),
 Ans([a,If(p,c,d)])}
{T(p,Do(a,S1)),¬T(On(A,B),Do(a,S1)),
 Ans([a,If(p,c,Noop)])}
{T(p,Do(L(A,B),S1)),T(On(B,A),Do(L(A,B),S1)),
 Ans([L(A,B),If(p,c,Noop)])}
{T(On(B,A),Do(L(A,B),S1)),
 Ans([L(A,B),If(On(B,A),c,Noop)])}

{Ans([L(A,B),If(On(B,A),F(B,A),d)]),
 Ans([L(A,B),If(On(B,A),c,Noop)])}
{Ans([L(A,B),If(On(B,A),F(B,A),Noop)])}
```

3. *Waterpot problem.*   Although we could use backward plannning to solve this problem, we use forward planning in the following solution. This is not a bad strategy, since the forward branching factor for this problem is quite small.

```
{T(Quant(5,0),S1)}
{Goal(Do(a,S1)),Ans(a)}
{¬5≥2-0,¬p=5+0-2,T(Quant(p,2),Do(L,S1))}
{¬p=5+0-2,T(Quant(p,2),Do(L,S1))}
{T(Quant(3,2),Do(L,S1))}
{T(Quant(3,0),Do(E,Do(L,S1)))}
{¬3≥2-0,¬p=3+0-2,T(Quant(p,2),Do(L,Do(E,Do(L,S1))))}
{¬p=3+0-2,T(Quant(p,2),Do(L,Do(E,Do(L,S1))))}
{T(Quant(1,2),Do(L,Do(E,Do(L,S1))))}
{T(Quant(1,0),Do(E,Do(L,Do(E,Do(L,S1)))))}
{¬1<2-0,¬q=2-0-1,
 T(Quant(0,q),Do(L,Do(E,Do(L,Do(E,Do(L,S1))))))}
{¬q=2-0-1,T(Quant(0,q),Do(L,Do(E,Do(L,Do(E,Do(L,S1))))))}
{T(Quant(0,1),Do(L,Do(E,Do(L,Do(E,Do(L,S1))))))}
{T(Quant(0,1),Do([],Do(L,Do(E,Do(L,Do(E,Do(L,S1)))))))}
```

```
{T(Quant(0,1),Do([L],Do(E,Do(L,Do(E,Do(L,S1))))))}
{T(Quant(0,1),Do([E,L],Do(L,Do(E,Do(L,S1)))))}
{T(Quant(0,1),Do([L,E,L],Do(E,Do(L,S1))))}
{T(Quant(0,1),Do([E,L,E,L],Do(L,S1)))}
{T(Quant(0,1),Do([L,E,L,E,L],S1))}
{¬T(Quant(m,1),Do(a,S1)),Ans(a)}
{Ans([L,E,L,E,L])}
```

A.13 Intelligent-Agent Architecture

1. *Maze World.* There are two phases of the agent's operation. The first phase is concerned with getting the cart to the upper left corner to start searching for the gold, and the second is concerned with finding the gold and getting it to the exit. The internal state of the agent is a number corresponding to the phase. The *action* and *internal* functions are summarized in the following tables. Missing entries are impossible.

Row	Col	Phase=1		Phase=2		
---	---	Same Cell	Elsewhere	In Cart	Same Cell	Elsewhere
1	1	2	2	2	2	2
1	2	2	1	2	2	2
1	3	2	1	2	2	2
2	1	2	1	2	2	2
2	2	2	1	2	2	2
2	3	2	1	2	2	2
3	1	2	1	2	2	2
3	2	2	1	2	2	2
3	3	1	1	2	2	

Row	Col	Phase=1		Phase=2		
---	---	Same Cell	Elsewhere	In Cart	Same Cell	Elsewhere
1	1	in	noop	right	in	right
1	2	in	left	right	in	right
1	3	in	left	down	in	down
2	1	in	up	right	in	down
2	2	in	up	right	in	left
2	3	in	up	down	in	left
3	1	in	up	right	in	right
3	2	in	up	right	in	right
3	3	noop	up	out	noop	

2. *Turing machines.*   Underlining in a bit string denotes the location of the head.

$$I = \{0\}$$
$$S = \{b_1 \ldots b_{i-1}\underline{b_i}b_{i+1} \ldots\}$$
$$T = \{0,1\}$$
$$A = \{0L, 0R, 1L, 1R\}$$
$$see(b_1 \ldots b_{i-1}\underline{b_i}b_{i+1} \ldots) = b_i$$
$$do(0L, b_1 \ldots b_{i-1}\underline{1}b_{i+1} \ldots) = b_1 \ldots \underline{b_{i-1}}0b_{i+1} \ldots$$
$$action(0,0) = 1R$$
$$action(0,1) = 0R$$
$$internal(0,b) = 0$$

3. *Planning.*

$$action(\Delta, n, t) \in \{a | \Delta \cup obsrecord(n,t) \vdash \texttt{Goal}(\texttt{Do}(e(a), \texttt{Ext}(e(n))))\}$$

References

[AAAI 1980]   *Proceedings of the First Annual National Conference on Artificial Intelligence*, Stanford University, 1980. Los Altos, CA: Morgan Kaufmann, 1980.

[AAAI 1982]   *Proceedings of the National Conference on Artificial Intelligence*, Pittsburgh, PA, 1982. Los Altos, CA: Morgan Kaufmann, 1982.

[AAAI 1983]   *Proceedings of the National Conference on Artificial Intelligence*, Washington, DC, 1983. Los Altos, CA: Morgan Kaufmann, 1983.

[AAAI 1984]   *Proceedings of the National Conference on Artificial Intelligence*, University of Texas at Austin, 1984. Los Altos, CA: Morgan Kaufmann, 1984.

[AAAI 1986]   *Proceedings of the Fifth National Conference on Artificial Intelligence*, University of Pennsylvania, 1986. Los Altos, CA: Morgan Kaufmann, 1986.

[Adams 1975]   Adams, E. W. and Levine, H. F., "On the Uncertainties Transmitted from Premises to Conclusions in Deductive Inferences," *Synthese*, 30: 429–460, 1975.

[Allen 1983]   Allen, J., "Maintaining Knowledge About Tempo-
                    ral Intervals," *Communications of the Association
                    for Computing Machinery*, 26(11): 832–843, 1983.
                    (Also in Brachman, R. and Levesque, H. (eds.),
                    Readings in Knowledge Representation. Los Altos,
                    CA: Morgan Kaufmann, 1985.)

[Allen 1984]   Allen, J. F., "Towards a General Theory of Action
                    and Time," *Artificial Intelligence*, 23(2): 123–154,
                    1984.

[Allen 1985a]   Allen, J. and Kautz, H., "A Model of Naive Tem-
                    poral Reasoning," in Hobbs, J. R. and Moore, R. C.
                    (eds.), *Formal Theories of the Commonsense World*.
                    Norwood, NJ: Ablex, 1985, pp. 251–268.

[Allen 1985b]   Allen, J. and Hayes, P. J., "A Common-Sense The-
                    ory of Time," *Proceedings of the Ninth Interna-
                    tional Joint Conference on Artificial Intelligence*,
                    Los Angeles, CA, 1985. Los Altos, CA: Morgan
                    Kaufmann, 1985, pp. 528–531.

[Anderson 1973]   Anderson, J. and Bower, G., *Human Associative
                    Memory*. Washington, DC: Winston, 1973.

[Angluin 1983]   Angluin, D. and Smith, C., "Inductive Inference:
                    Theory and Methods," *Computing Surveys*, 15(3):
                    237–269, 1983.

[Appelt 1985a]   Appelt, D., "Planning English Referring Expres-
                    sions," *Artificial Intelligence*, 26(1): 1–33, 1985.
                    (Also in Grosz, B., Jones, K., and Webber, B.
                    (eds.), *Readings in Natural Language Processing*.
                    Los Altos, CA: Morgan Kaufmann, 1986, pp. 501–
                    517.)

[Appelt 1985b]   Appelt, D., *Planning English Sentences*. Cam-
                    bridge, UK: Cambridge University Press, 1985
                    (Ph.D. dissertation).

[Ballantyne 1977]   Ballantyne, A. M. and Bledsoe, W. W., "Auto-
                    matic Proofs of Theorems in Analysis Using Non-
                    Standard Techniques." *Journal of the Association
                    for Computing Machinery*, 24(3): 353–374, 1977.

[Barr 1982]   Barr, A. and Feigenbaum, E. (eds.), *The Handbook
                    of Artificial Intelligence*, Vol. I and II. Reading,
                    MA: Addison-Wesley, 1981 and 1982.   (Vol. I

reviewed by F. Hayes-Roth in *Artificial Intelligence*, 18(3): 369–371, 1982.)

[Bledsoe 1977] Bledsoe, W. W., "Non-Resolution Theorem Proving," *Artificial Intelligence*, 9(1): 1–35, 1977. (Also in Webber, B. L. and Nilsson, N. J. (eds.), *Readings in Artificial Intelligence*. Los Altos, CA: Morgan Kaufmann, 1981.)

[Bobrow 1974] Bobrow, D. and Raphael, B., "New Programming Languages for Artificial Intelligence Research," *Association for Computing Machinery Computing Surveys*, 6: 153–174, 1974.

[Bobrow 1977] Bobrow, D. and Winograd, T., "An Overview of KRL, a Knowledge Representation Language," *Cognitive Science*, 1(1): 3–46, 1977. (Also in Brachman, R. and Levesque, H. (eds.), *Readings in Knowledge Representation*. Los Altos, CA: Morgan Kaufmann, 1985.)

[Bobrow 1979] Bobrow, D. and Winograd, T., "KRL: Another Perspective," *Cognitive Science*, 3(1): 29–42, 1979.

[Bobrow 1980] Bobrow, D., *Special Volume on Non-Monotonic Reasoning. Artificial Intelligence*, 13(1–2), 1980.

[Bobrow 1984] Bobrow, D., *Special Volume on Qualitative Reasoning about Physical Systems. Artificial Intelligence*, 24(1–3), 1984. (Also published as Bobrow, D., *Qualitative Reasoning about Physical Systems*. Cambridge, MA: MIT Press, 1985.)

[Bobrow 1985] Bobrow, D. G. and Hayes, P. J., "Artificial Intelligence—Where Are We?" *Artificial Intelligence*, 25(3): 375–415, 1985.

[Boden 1977] Boden, M. A., *Artificial Intelligence and Natural Man*. New York: Basic Books, 1977.

[Boyer 1971] Boyer, R. S., *Locking: A Restriction of Resolution*. Austin, TX: University of Texas at Austin, 1971 (Ph.D. dissertation).

[Boyer 1979] Boyer, R. S. and Moore, J. S., *A Computational Logic*. New York: Academic Press, 1979.

[Brachman 1979] Brachman, R., "On the Epistemological Status of Semantic Networks," in Findler, N. (ed.), *Associative Networks: Representation and Use of Knowledge by Computers*. New York: Academic

Press, 1979, pp. 3–50. (Also in Brachman, R. and Levesque, H. (eds.), *Readings in Knowledge Representation*. Los Altos, CA: Morgan Kaufmann, 1985.)

[Brachman 1983a]   Brachman, R., Fikes, R., and Levesque, H., "KRYPTON: A Functional Approach to Knowledge Representation," *IEEE Computation*, 16(10): 67–73, 1983. (Also in Brachman, R. and Levesque, H. (eds.), *Readings in Knowledge Representation*. Los Altos, CA: Morgan Kaufmann, 1985.)

[Brachman 1983b]   Brachman, R., Fikes, R., and Levesque, H., "KRYPTON: Integrating Terminology and Assertion," *Proceedings of the National Conference on Artificial Intelligence*, Washington, DC, 1983. Los Altos, CA: Morgan Kaufmann, 1983, pp. 31–35.

[Brachman 1983c]   Brachman, R., "What Is-a Is and Isn't: An Analysis of Taxonomic Links in Semantic Networks," *IEEE Computation*, 16(10): 30-36, 1983.

[Brachman 1985a]   Brachman, R., Gilbert, V., and Levesque, H., "An Essential Hybrid Reasoning System: Knowledge and Symbol Level Accounts of KRYPTON," *Proceedings of the Ninth International Joint Conference on Artificial Intelligence*, Los Angeles, CA, 1985. Los Altos, CA: Morgan Kaufmann, 1985, pp. 532–539.

[Brachman 1985b]   Brachman, R. and Levesque, H. (eds.), *Readings in Knowledge Representation*. Los Altos, CA: Morgan Kaufmann, 1985.

[Brachman 1985c]   Brachman, R. and Schmolze, J., "An Overview of the KL-ONE Knowledge Representation System," *Cognitive Science*, 9(2): 171–216, 1985.

[Brooks 1985]   Brooks, R., "A Robust Layered Control System for a Mobile Robot," Memo 864. Cambridge, MA: Massachusetts Institute of Technology, Artificial Intelligence Laboratory, 1985.

[Brownston 1985]   Brownston, L., et al., *Programming Expert Systems in OPS5: An Introduction to Rule-Based Programming*. Reading, MA: Addison-Wesley, 1985.

[Buchanan 1976]   Buchanan, B. G., "Scientific Theory Formation by Computer," in Simon, J. C. (ed.), *Computer*

Oriented Learning Processes. Leyden: Noordhoff, 1976.

[Buchanan 1984] Buchanan, B. G. and Shortliffe, E. H., *Rule-Based Expert Systems: The* MYCIN *Experiments of the Stanford Heuristic Programming Project.* Reading, MA: Addison-Wesley, 1984. (Reviewed by W. R. Swartout in *Artificial Intelligence,* 26(3): 364–366, 1985.)

[Campbell 1982] Campbell, A. N., et al., "Recognition of a Hidden Mineral Deposit by an Artificial Intelligence Program," *Science,* 217(4563): 927–929, 1982.

[Carnap 1950] Carnap, R., "The Two Concepts of Probability," in Carnap, R., *Logical Foundations of Probability.* Chicago, IL: University of Chicago Press, 1950, pp. 19–51.

[Chang 1973] Chang, C. L. and Lee, R. C. T., *Symbolic Logic and Mechanical Theorem Proving.* New York: Academic Press, 1973. (Reviewed by R. B. Anderson in *Artificial Intelligence,* 4(3–4): 245–246, 1973.)

[Chang 1979a] Chang, C. L. and Slagle, J. R., "Using Rewriting Rules for Connection Graphs to Prove Theorems," *Artificial Intelligence,* 12(2): 159–178, 1979. (Also in Webber, B. L. and Nilsson, N. J. (eds.), *Readings in Artificial Intelligence.* Los Altos, CA: Morgan Kaufmann, 1981.)

[Chang 1979b] Chang, C. L., "Resolution Plans in Theorem Proving," *Proceedings of the Sixth International Joint Conference on Artificial Intelligence,* Tokyo, 1979. Los Altos, CA: Morgan Kaufmann, 1979, pp. 143–148.

[Chapman 1985] Chapman, D., "Planning for Conjunctive Goals," Technical Report 83–85. Cambridge, MA: Massachusetts Institute of Technology, Artificial Intelligence Laboratory, 1985 (M.S. thesis).

[Charniak 1979] Charniak, E., Riesbeck, C., and McDermott, D., *Artificial Intelligence Programming.* Hillsdale, NJ: Lawrence Erlbaum Associates, 1979.

[Charniak 1984] Charniak, E. and McDermott, D., *Introduction to Artificial Intelligence.* Reading, MA: Addison-Wesley, 1984.

[Cheeseman 1983]   Cheeseman, P., "A Method of Computing Generalized Bayesian Probability Values for Expert Systems," *Proceedings of the Eighth International Joint Conference on Artificial Intelligence*, Karlsruhe, 1983. Los Altos, CA: Morgan Kaufmann, 1983, pp. 198–202.

[Clancey 1983]   Clancey, W. J., "The Advantages of Abstract Control Knowledge in Expert System Design," *Proceedings of the National Conference on Artificial Intelligence*, Washington, DC, 1983. Los Altos, CA: Morgan Kaufmann, 1983, pp. 74–78.

[Clancey 1984]   Clancey, W. J. and Shortliffe, E. H. (eds.), *Readings in Medical Artificial Intelligence: The First Decade.* Reading, MA: Addison-Wesley, 1984.

[Clark 1978]   Clark, K., "Negation as Failure," in Gallaire H. and Minker J. (eds.), *Logic and Data Bases.* New York: Plenum Press, 1978, pp. 293–322.

[Clocksin 1981]   Clocksin, W. and Mellish, C., *Programming in PROLOG.* New York: Springer-Verlag, 1981.

[Cohen 1979]   Cohen, P. R. and Perrault, C. R., "Elements of a Plan-Based Theory of Speech Acts," *Cognitive Science*, 3(3): 177–212, 1979. (Also in Webber, B. L. and Nilsson, N. J. (eds.), *Readings in Artificial Intelligence.* Los Altos, CA: Morgan Kaufmann, 1981. Also in Grosz, B., Jones, K., and Webber, B. (eds.), *Readings in Natural Language Processing.* Los Altos, CA: Morgan Kaufmann, 1986, pp. 423–440.)

[Cohen 1982]   Cohen, P. R. and Feigenbaum, E. A. (eds.), *The Handbook of Artificial Intelligence*, Vol. III. Reading, MA: Addison-Wesley, 1982.

[Collins 1967]   Collins, N. L. and Michie, D. (eds.), *Machine Intelligence 1.* Edinburgh, UK: Edinburgh University Press, 1967.

[Colmerauer 1973]   Colmerauer, A., et al., "Un Système de Communication Homme-Machine en Français," Research Report. France: Université Aix-Marseille II, Groupe d'Intelligence Artificielle, 1973.

[Dale 1968] Dale, E. and Michie, D. (eds.), *Machine Intelligence 2*. Edinburgh, UK: Edinburgh University Press, 1968.

[Davis 1960] Davis, M. and Putnam, H., "A Computing Procedure for Quantification Theory," *Journal of the Association for Computing Machinery*, 7(3): 201–215, 1960.

[Davis 1976] Davis, R., "Applications of Meta-Level Knowledge to the Construction, Maintenance and Use of Large Knowledge Bases," Memo 283. Stanford, CA: Stanford University, Artificial Intelligence Laboraratory, 1976 (Ph.D. dissertation).

[Davis 1977] Davis, R. and Buchanan, B., "Meta-Level Knowledge: Overview and Applications," *Proceedings of the Fifth International Joint Conference on Artificial Intelligence*, Cambridge, MA, 1977. Los Altos, CA: Morgan Kaufmann, 1977, pp. 920–927. (Also in Brachman, R. and Levesque, H. (eds.), *Readings in Knowledge Representation*. Los Altos, CA: Morgan Kaufmann, 1985.)

[Davis 1980] Davis, M., "The Mathematics of Non-Monotonic Reasoning," *Artificial Intelligence*, 13(1–2): 73–80, 1980.

[DeFinetti 1974] De Finetti, B., *Theory of Probability*, Vol. I and II. New York: John Wiley and Sons, 1974.

[deKleer 1977] deKleer, J., et al., "AMORD: Explicit Control of Reasoning," *SIGPLAN Notices*, 12(8): 116–125, 1977.

[deKleer 1984] deKleer, J. and Brown, J. S., "A Qualitative Physics Based on Confluences," *Artificial Intelligence*, 24(1–3): 7–83, 1984. (Also in Hobbs, J. R. and Moore, R. C. (eds.), *Formal Theories of the Commonsense World*. Norwood, NJ: Ablex, 1985.)

[Deliyani 1979] Deliyani, A. and Kowalski, R., "Logic and Semantic Networks," *Communications of the Association for Computing Machinery*, 22(3): 184–192, 1979.

[Dempster 1968] Dempster, A. P., "A Generalization of Bayesian Inference," *Journal of the Royal Statistical Society*, Series B, 30(2): 205–247, 1968.

[Dennett 1986]   Dennett, D., "Cognitive Wheels: The Frame Problem of Artificial Intelligence," in Hookway, C. (ed.), *Minds, Machines, and Evolution*. Cambridge, UK: Cambridge University Press, 1986.

[Doyle 1980]   Doyle, J., "A Model of Deliberation, Action, and Introspection," Technical Report TR-581. Cambridge, MA: Massachusetts Institute of Technology, Artificial Intelligence Laboratory, 1980.

[Drapkin 1986]   Drapkin, J. and Perlis, D., "Step Logics: An Alternative Approach to Limited Reasoning," *Proceedings of the Seventh European Conference on Artificial Intelligence*, Brighton, UK. London, UK: Conference Services Limited, 1986, pp. 160–163.

[Dreyfus 1972]   Dreyfus, H. L., *What Computers Can't Do: A Critique of Artificial Reason*. New York: Harper & Row, 1972. (A revision of "Alchemy and Artificial Intelligence," Paper P-3244. The RAND Corporation, 1965.)

[Dreyfus 1981]   Dreyfus, H., "From Micro-Worlds to Knowledge Representation: AI at an Impasse," in Haugeland, J. (ed.), *Mind Design*. Cambridge, MA: MIT Press, 1981, pp. 161–204. (Also in Brachman, R. and Levesque, H. (eds.), *Readings in Knowledge Representation*. Los Altos, CA: Morgan Kaufmann, 1985.)

[Dreyfus 1986]   Dreyfus, H. L. and Dreyfus, S. E., *Mind Over Machine: The Power of Human Intuition and Expertise in the Era of the Computer*. New York: The Free Press, 1986.

[Duda 1976]   Duda, R. O., Hart, P. E., and Nilsson, N. J., "Subjective Bayesian Methods for Rule-Based Inference Systems," *Proceedings 1976 National Computer Conference*, Vol. 45. Arlington, VA: American Federation of Information Processing Societies, 1976, pp. 1075–1082. (Also in Webber, B. W. and Nilsson, N. J. (eds), *Readings in Artificial Intelligence*. Los Altos, CA: Morgan Kaufmann, 1981, pp. 192–199.)

[Duda 1978]   Duda, R. O., et al., "Semantic Network Representations in Rule-Based Inference Systems," in Waterman, D. and Hayes-Roth, F. (eds.), *Pattern-*

Directed Inference Systems. New York: Academic Press, 1978, pp. 203–221.

[Duda 1984] Duda, R. O. and Reboh, R., "AI and Decision Making: The PROSPECTOR Experience," in Reitman, W. (ed.), *Artificial Intelligence Applications for Business.* Norwood, NJ: Ablex, 1984, pp. 111–147.

[Elcock 1977] Elcock E. and Michie, D. (eds.), *Machine Intelligence 8: Machine Representations of Knowledge.* Chichester, UK: Ellis Horwood, 1977.

[Enderton 1972] Enderton, H. B., *A Mathematical Introduction to Logic.* New York: Academic Press, 1972.

[Erman 1982] Erman, L. D., et al., "The Hearsay-II Speech-Understanding System: Integrating Knowledge to Resolve Uncertainty," in Webber, B. L. and Nilsson, N. J. (eds.), *Readings in Artificial Intelligence.* Los Altos, CA: Morgan Kaufmann, 1981, pp. 349–389.

[Etherington 1985] Etherington, D., Mercer, R., and Reiter, R., "On the Adequacy of Predicate Circumscription for Closed-World Reasoning," *Computational Intelligence,* 1(1): 11–15, 1985.

[Etherington 1986] Etherington, D., *Reasoning with Incomplete Information.* Vancouver, BC: University of British Columbia, 1986 (Ph.D. Dissertation).

[Fagin 1985] Fagin, R. and Halpern, J., "Belief, Awareness and Limited Reasoning," *Proceedings of the Ninth International Joint Conference on Artificial Intelligence,* Los Angeles, CA, 1985. Los Altos, CA: Morgan Kaufmann, 1985, pp. 491–501.

[Feigenbaum 1963] Feigenbaum, E. and Feldman, J. (eds.), *Computers and Thought.* New York: McGraw-Hill, 1963.

[Feldman 1977] Feldman, J. A. and Sproull, R. F., "Decision Theory and Artificial Intelligence II: The Hungry Monkey," *Cognitive Science,* 1(2): 158–192, 1977.

[Fikes 1971] Fikes, R. E. and Nilsson, N. J., "STRIPS: A New Approach to the Application of Theorem Proving to Problem Solving," *Artificial Intelligence,* 2(3–4): 189–208, 1971.

372 References

[Fikes 1972]   Fikes, R. E., Hart, P. E., and Nilsson, N. J., "Learning and Executing Generalized Robot Plans," *Artificial Intelligence*, 3(4): 251–288, 1972. (Also in Webber, B. L. and Nilsson, N. J. (eds.), *Readings in Artificial Intelligence*. Los Altos, CA: Morgan Kaufmann, 1981.)

[Filman 1984]   Filman, R. E. and Friedman, D. P., *Coordinated Computing: Tools and Techniques for Distributed Software*. New York: McGraw-Hill, 1984.

[Findler 1979]   Findler, N. V. (ed.), *Associative Networks—The Representation and Use of Knowledge in Computers*. New York: Academic Press, 1979.

[Forgy 1981]   Forgy, C. L., "The OPS5 Users Manual," Technical Report CMU-CS-79-132. Pittsburgh, PA: Carnegie-Mellon University, Computer Science Department, 1981.

[Frege 1879]   Frege, G., "Begriffsschrift, a Formula Language Modelled upon that of Arithmetic, for Pure Thought," (1879), in van Heijenoort, J. (ed.), *From Frege to Gödel: A Source Book In Mathematical Logic, 1879–1931*. Cambridge, MA: Harvard University Press, 1967, pp. 1–82.

[Gallaire 1978]   Gallaire, H. and Minker, J. (eds.), *Logic and Databases*. New York: Plenum Press, 1978.

[Galler 1970]   Galler, B. and Perlis, A., *A View of Programming Languages*. Reading, MA: Addison-Wesley, 1970.

[Gardner 1982]   Gardner, M., *Logic Machines and Diagrams* (second edition). Chicago, IL: University of Chicago Press, 1982.

[Garvey 1981]   Garvey, T., Lowrance, J., and Fischler, M., "An Inference Technique for Integrating Knowledge from Disparate Sources," *Proceedings of the Seventh International Joint Conference on Artificial Intelligence*, Vancouver, BC, 1981. Los Altos, CA: Morgan Kaufmann, 1981, pp. 319–325. (Also in Brachman, R. and Levesque, H. (eds.), *Readings in Knowledge Representation*. Los Altos, CA: Morgan Kaufmann, 1985.)

[Geissler 1986]   Geissler, C. and Konolige, K., "A Resolution Method for Quantified Modal Logics of Knowledge and Belief," in Halpern, J. Y. (ed.), *Theoretical Aspects of Reasoning About Knowledge*. Los Altos, CA: Morgan Kaufmann, 1986.

[Gelfond 1986]   Gelfond, M., Przymusinska, H., and Przymusinski, T., "The Extended Closed World Assumption and Its Relationship to Parallel Circumscription," *Proceedings of the Association for Computing Machinery SIGACT-SIGMOD Symposium on Principles of Database Systems*. New York: Association for Computing Machinery, 1986, pp. 133–139.

[Genesereth 1979]   Genesereth, M. R., "The Role of Plans in Automated Consultation," *Proceedings of the Sixth International Joint Conference on Artificial Intelligence*. Los Altos, CA: Morgan Kaufmann, 1979, pp. 311–319.

[Genesereth 1982]   Genesereth, M. R., "An Introduction to MRS for AI Experts," Technical Report HPP-82-27. Stanford, CA: Stanford University, Department of Computer Science, Heuristic Programming Project, 1982.

[Genesereth 1983]   Genesereth, M. R., "An Overview of Metalevel Architecture," *Proceedings of the National Conference on Artificial Intelligence*, Washington, DC, 1983. Los Altos, CA: Morgan Kaufmann, 1983, pp. 119–123.

[Genesereth 1984]   Genesereth, M. R., "The Use of Design Descriptions in Automated Diagnosis," *Artificial Intelligence*, 24(1–3): 411–436, 1984.

[Genesereth 1987a]   Genesereth, M. R., "Introspective Fidelity," Technical Report Logic-87-1. Stanford, CA: Stanford University, Logic Group, 1987.

[Genesereth 1987b]   Genesereth, M. R., "Deliberate Agents," Technical Report Logic-87-2. Stanford, CA: Stanford University, Logic Group, 1987.

[Georgeff 1984]   Georgeff, M. P., "A Theory of Action for Multi-Agent Planning," *Proceedings of the National Conference on Artificial Intelligence*, Austin, TX. Los Altos, CA: Morgan Kaufmann, 1984, pp. 121–125.

[Georgeff 1985]   Georgeff, M. P. and Lansky, A. L., "A System for Reasoning in Dynamic Domains: Fault Diagnosis on the Space Shuttle," Technical Note 375. Menlo Park, CA: SRI International, Artificial Intelligence Center, 1985.

[Georgeff 1987a]   Georgeff, M. P. and Lansky, A. (eds.), *Reasoning About Actions and Plans.* Los Altos, CA: Morgan Kaufmann, 1987.

[Georgeff 1987b]   Georgeff, M. P., "Planning," in *Annual Review of Computer Science* (in press).

[Georgeff 1987c]   Georgeff, M. P., "Actions, Processes, and Causality," in Georgeff, M. P. and Lansky, A., (eds.), *Reasoning About Actions and Plans.* Los Altos, CA: Morgan Kaufmann, 1987, pp. 99–122.

[Gödel 1930]   Gödel, K., "Die Vollständigkeit der Axiome des Logischen Funktionenkalküls," *Monatshefte für Matheematik und Physik,* 37: 349–360, 1930.

[Gödel 19 31]   Gödel, K., "Über Formal Unentscheidbare Sätze der Principia Mathematica und Verwandter Systeme I," *Monatshefte für Mathematik und Physik,* 38: 173–198, 1931. (For a readable explanation, see Nagel, E. and Newman, J., *Gödel's Proof.* New York: New York University Press, 1958.)

[Goldstein 1979]   Goldstein, I. P. and Roberts, R. B., "Using Frames in Scheduling," in Winston, P. H. and Brown, R. H. (eds.), *Artificial Intelligence: An MIT Perspective,* Vol. I. Cambridge, MA: MIT Press, 1979, pp. 251–284.

[Green 1969a]   Green, C., "Application of Theorem Proving to Problem Solving," *Proceedings of the First International Joint Conference on Artificial Intelligence,* Washington, DC, 1981. Los Altos, CA: Morgan Kaufmann, 1969, pp. 219–239. (Also in Webber, B. L. and Nilsson, N. J. (eds.), *Readings in Artificial Intelligence.* Los Altos, CA: Morgan Kaufmann, 1981.)

[Green 1969b]   Green, C., "Theorem-Proving by Resolution as a Basis for Question-Answering Systems," in Meltzer, B. and Michie, D. (eds.), *Machine Intelligence 4.* Edinburgh, UK: Edinburgh University Press, 1969, pp. 183–205.

[Grosof 1984]   Grosof, B. N., "Default Reasoning as Circumscription," *Proceedings of the Workshop on Non-Monotonic Reasoning*, New Paltz, NY, 1984. Menlo Park, CA: AAAI, 1984.

[Grosof 1986a]   Grosof, B. N., "An Inequality Paradigm for Probabilistic Knowledge," in Kanal, L. N. and Lemmer, J. F. (eds), *Uncertainty in Artificial Intelligence.* New York: North-Holland, 1986, pp. 259–275.

[Grosof 1986b]   Grosof, B. N., "Evidential Confirmation as Transformed Probability," in Kanal, L. N. and Lemmer, J. F. (eds), *Uncertainty in Artificial Intelligence.* New York: North-Holland, 1986, pp. 153–166.

[Grosz 1986]   Grosz, B. J., Jones, K. S., and Webber, B. L., *Readings in Natural Language Processing.* Los Altos, CA: Morgan Kaufmann, 1986.

[Haas 1986]   Haas, A. R., "A Syntactic Theory of Belief and Knowledge," *Artificial Intelligence*, 28(3): 245–292, 1986.

[Halpern 1983]   Halpern, J. Y. and Rabin, M., "A Logic to Reason About Likelihood," Research Report RJ 4136 (45774). IBM Corporation, 1983. (Also in *Proceedings of the Fifteenth Annual ACM Symposium on Theory of Computing*, Boston, MA, 1983 (ACM Order No. 508830), pp. 310–319. Also in *Artificial Intelligence* (in press).)

[Halpern 1984]   Halpern, J. Y. and Moses, Y. O., "Knowledge and Common Knowledge in a Distributed Environment," *Proceedings of the Third Association for Computing Machinery Conference on Principles of Distributed Computing* New York: Association for Computing Machinery, 1984.

[Halpern 1985]   Halpern, J. Y. and Moses, Y., "A Guide to the Modal Logics of Knowledge and Belief," *Proceedings of the Ninth International Joint Conference on Artificial Intelligence*, Los Angeles, CA, 1985. Los Altos, CA: Morgan Kaufmann, 1985, pp. 479–490.

[Halpern 1986]   Halpern, J., (ed.), *Theoretical Aspects of Reasoning About Knowledge.* Los Altos, CA: Morgan Kaufmann, 1986.

[Halpern 1987]   Halpern, J., "Using Reasoning about Knowledge to Analyze Distributed Systems," *Annual Review of Computer Science* (in press).

[Hanks 1986]   Hanks, S. and McDermott, D., "Default Reasoning, Nonmonotonic Logics, and the Frame Problem," *Proceedings of the Fifth National Conference on Artificial Intelligence*, University of Pennsylvania, 1986. Los Altos, CA: Morgan Kaufmann, 1986.

[Hart 1968]   Hart, P. E., Nilsson, N. J., and Raphael, B., "A Formal Basis for the Heuristic Determination of Minimum Cost Paths," *IEEE Transactions on Systems Science and Cybernetics*, SSC-4(2): 100–107, 1968.

[Hayes-Roth 1978] Hayes-Roth, F. and McDermott, J., "An Interference Matching Technique for Inducing Abstractions," *Communications of the Association for Computing Machinery*, 21(5): 401–410, 1978.

[Hayes-Roth 1985] Hayes-Roth, B., "A Blackboard Architecture for Control," *Artificial Intelligence*, 26(3): 251–321, 1985.

[Hayes 1973a]   Hayes, P. J., "The Frame Problem and Related Problems in Artificial Intelligence," in Elithorn, A. and Jones, D. (eds.), *Artificial and Human Thinking*, San Francisco, CA: Jossey-Bass, 1973, pp. 45–49. (Also in Webber, B. L. and Nilsson, N. J. (eds.), *Readings in Artificial Intelligence*. Los Altos, CA: Morgan Kaufmann, 1981.)

[Hayes 1973b]   Hayes, P. J., "Computation and Deduction," *Proceedings of the Second Symposium on Mathematical Foundations of Computer Science*. Czechoslovakia: Czechoslovakian Academy of Sciences, 1973, pp. 105–118.

[Hayes 1977]   Hayes, P. J., "In Defense of Logic," *Proceedings of the Fifth International Joint Conference on Artificial Intelligence*, Cambridge, MA, 1977. Los Altos, CA: Morgan Kaufmann, 1977, pp. 559–565.

[Hayes 1979a]   Hayes, P. J., "The Logic of Frames," in Metzing, D. (ed.), *Frame Conceptions and Text Understanding*. Berlin: de Gruyter, 1979, pp. 46–61. (Also in Webber, B. L. and Nilsson, N. J. (eds.), *Readings in Artificial Intelligence*. Los Altos, CA:

Morgan Kaufmann, 1981. Also in Brachman, R. and Levesque, H. (eds.), *Readings in Knowledge Representation.* Los Altos, CA: Morgan Kaufmann, 1985.)

[Hayes 1979b]   Hayes, P. J., "The Naive Physics Manifesto," in Michie, D. (ed.), *Expert Systems in the Micro-Electronic Age.* Edinburgh, UK: Edinburgh University Press, 1979, pp. 242–270.

[Hayes 1979c]   Hayes, J. E., Michie, D., and Mikulich, L. I. (eds.), *Machine Intelligence 9: Machine Expertise and the Human Interface.* Chichester, UK: Ellis Horwood, 1979.

[Hayes 1985a]   Hayes, P., "Naive Physics I: Ontology for Liquids," in Hobbs, J. R. and Moore, R. C. (eds.), *Formal Theories of the Commonsense World.* Norwood, NJ: Ablex, 1985, pp. 71–107.

[Hayes 1985b]   Hayes, P., "The Second Naive Physics Manifesto," in Hobbs, J. R. and Moore, R. C. (eds.), *Formal Theories of the Commonsense World.* Norwood, NJ: Ablex, 1985, pp. 1–36. (Also in Brachman, R. and Levesque, H. (eds.), *Readings in Knowledge Representation.* Los Altos, CA: Morgan Kaufmann, 1985.)

[Heckerman 1986]   Heckerman, D., "Probabilistic Interpretations for MYCIN's Certainty Factors," in Kanal, L. N. and Lemmer, J. F. (eds), *Uncertainty in Artificial Intelligence.* New York: North-Holland, 1986, pp. 167–196.

[Hempel 1965]   Hempel, C. G., "Studies in the Logic of Confirmation," in Hempel, C. G., *Aspects of Scientific Explanation and Other Essays in the Philosophy of Science.* New York: The Free Press, 1965, pp. 3–51.

[Hendrix 1973]   Hendrix, G., "Modeling Simultaneous Actions and Continuous Processes," *Artificial Intelligence,* 4(3–4): 145–180, 1973.

[Hendrix 1979]   Hendrix, G., "Encoding Knowledge in Partitioned Networks," in Findler, N. (ed.), *Associative Networks.* New York: Academic Press, 1979, pp. 51–92.

[Herbrand 1930] Herbrand, J., "Recherches sur la Théorie de la Démonstration," *Travaux de la Société des Sciences et de Lettres de Varsovie, Classe III Sci. Math. Phys.*, 33, 1930.

[Hewitt 1969] Hewitt, C., "PLANNER: A Language for Proving Theorems in Robots," *Proceedings of the First International Joint Conference on Artificial Intelligence.* Los Altos, CA: Morgan Kaufmann, 1969, pp. 295–301.

[Hewitt 1972] Hewitt, C., "Description and Theoretical Analysis (Using Schemata) of PLANNER: A Language for Proving Theorems and Manipulating Models in a Robot," Report AI-TR-258. Cambridge, MA: Massachusetts Institute of Technology, Artificial Intelligence Laboratory, 1971 (Ph.D. dissertation).

[Hintikka 1962] Hintikka, J., *Knowledge and Belief: An Introduction to the Logic of the Two Notions.* Ithaca, NY: Cornell University Press, 1971.

[Hintikka 1971] Hintikka, J., "Semantics for Propositional Attitudes," in Linsky, L. (ed.), *Reference and Modality.* London, UK: Oxford University Press, 1971, pp. 145–167.

[Hobbs 1985a] Hobbs, J. R. (ed.), "Commonsense Summer: Final Report," Report CSLI-85-35. Stanford, CA: Stanford University, Center for the Study of Language and Information, 1985.

[Hobbs 1985b] Hobbs, J. R. and Moore, R. C. (eds.), *Formal Theories of the Commonsense World.* Norwood, NJ: Ablex, 1985.

[Hobbs 1985c] Hobbs, J. R., "Granularity," *Proceedings of the Ninth International Joint Conference on Artificial Intelligence*, Vol. I, Los Angeles, CA, 1985. Los Altos, CA: Morgan Kaufmann, 1985, pp. 432–435.

[Hoel 1971] Hoel, P. G., Port, S. C., and Stone, C. J., *Introduction To Probability Theory.* Boston, MA: Houghton Mifflin, 1971.

[Horvitz 1986] Horvitz, E. J. and Heckerman, D. E., "A Framework for Comparing Alternative Formalisms for Plausible Reasoning," *Proceedings of the Fifth National Conference on Artificial Intelligence*, University of Pennsylvania, 1986. Los Altos, CA: Morgan Kaufmann, 1986, pp. 219–214.

[Hughes 1968] Hughes, G. E. and Cresswell, M. J., *An Introduction to Modal Logic.* London, UK: Methuen and Co. Ltd., 1968.

[Hunt 1966] Hunt, E. B., Marin, J., and Stone, P. T., *Experiments in Induction.* New York: Academic Press, 1966.

[IJCAI 1969] *Proceedings of the First International Joint Conference on Artificial Intelligence,* Washington, DC, 1969. Los Altos, CA: Morgan Kaufmann, 1969.

[IJCAI 1971] *Advance Papers, Second International Joint Conference on Artificial Intelligence,* London, UK, 1971. Los Altos, CA: Morgan Kaufmann, 1971.

[IJCAI 1973] *Advance Papers, Third International Joint Conference on Artificial Intelligence,* Stanford, CA, 1973. Los Altos, CA: Morgan Kaufmann, 1973.

[IJCAI 1975] *Advance Papers of the Fourth International Joint Conference on Artificial Intelligence,* Vols. I and II, Tbilisi, Georgia, USSR, 1975. Los Altos, CA: Morgan Kaufmann, 1975.

[IJCAI 1977] *Proceedings of the Fifth International Joint Conference on Artificial Intelligence,* Vols. I and II, MIT, Cambridge, MA, 1977. Los Altos, CA: Morgan Kaufmann, 1977.

[IJCAI 1979] *Proceedings of the Sixth International Joint Conference on Artificial Intelligence,* Vols. I and II, Tokyo, 1979. Los Altos, CA: Morgan Kaufmann, 1979.

[IJCAI 1981] *Proceedings of the Seventh International Joint Conference on Artificial Intelligence,* Vols. I and II, Vancouver, BC, 1981. Los Altos, CA: Morgan Kaufmann, 1981.

[IJCAI 1983] *Proceedings of the Eighth International Joint Conference on Artificial Intelligence,* Vols. I and II, Karlsruhe, 1983. Los Altos, CA: Morgan Kaufmann, 1983.

[IJCAI 1985] *Proceedings of the Ninth International Joint Conference on Artificial Intelligence,* Vols. I and II, Los Angeles, CA, 1985. Los Altos, CA: Morgan Kaufmann, 1985.

[Imielinski 1985] Imielinski, T., "Results on Translating Defaults to Circumscription," *Proceedings of the Ninth International Joint Conference on Artificial Intelligence,* Los Angeles, CA, 1985. Los Altos, CA: Morgan Kaufmann, 1985, pp. 114–120.

[Israel 1983] Israel, D., "The Role of Logic in Knowledge Representation," *IEEE Computation,* 16(10): 37–42, 1983.

[Konolige 1982] Konolige, K. G., "An Information-Theoretic Approach to Subjective Bayesian Inference in Rule-Based Systems," Working Paper. Menlo Park, CA: SRI International, 1982. (A revision of "Bayesian Methods for Updating Probabilities," Appendix D in Duda, R. O., et al., "A Computer-Based Consultant for Mineral Exploration," Grant AER 77-04499 Final Report. Menlo Park, CA: SRI International, 1979.)

[Konolige 1984] Konolige, K., *A Deduction Model of Belief and Its Logics.* Stanford, CA: Stanford University, 1984 (Ph.D. dissertation). (Also "A Deduction Model of Belief and Its Logics," Technical Note 326. Menlo Park, CA: SRI International, Artificial Intelligence Center, 1984.)

[Konolige 1985] Konolige, K., "Belief and Incompleteness," in Hobbs, J. R. and Moore, R. C. (eds.), *Formal Theories of the Commonsense World.* Norwood, NJ: Ablex, 1985, pp. 359–404.

[Konolige 1986] Konolige, K., "Resolution and Quantified Modal Logics," draft paper, 1986.

[Konolige 1987] Konolige, K., "On the Relation Between Default Theories and Autoepistemic Logic," Working Paper. Menlo Park, CA: SRI International, Artificial Intelligence Center, 1987.

[Kowalski 1970] Kowalski, R., "Search Strategies for Theorem-Proving," in Meltzer, B. and Michie, D. (eds.), *Machine Intelligence 5.* Edinburgh, UK: Edinburgh University Press, 1970, pp. 181–201.

[Kowalski 1971] Kowalski, R., and Kuehner, D., "Linear Resolution with Selection Function," *Artificial Intelligence,* 2(3–4): 227–260, 1971.

[Kowalski 1972]   Kowalski, R., "AND/OR Graphs, Theorem-Proving Graphs, and Bidirectional Search," in Meltzer, B. and Michie, D. (eds.), *Machine Intelligence 7.* Edinburgh, UK: Edinburgh University Press, 1972, pp. 167–194.

[Kowalski 1974]   Kowalski, R, "Predicate Logic as a Programming Language," in Rosenfeld, J. L., (ed.), *Information Processing, 1974.* Amsterdam: North-Holland, 1974, pp. 569–574.

[Kowalski 1975]   Kowalski, R., "A Proof Procedure Using Connection Graphs," *Journal of the Association for Computing Machinery,* 22(4): 572–595, 1975.

[Kowalski 1979a]   Kowalski, R., "Algorithm = Logic + Control," *Communications of the Association for Computing Machinery,* 22(7): 424–436, 1979.

[Kowalski 1979b]   Kowalski, R., *Logic for Problem Solving.* New York: North-Holland, 1979.

[Kripke 1963]   Kripke, S., "Semantical Analysis of Modal Logic," *Zeitschrift für Mathematische Logik und Grundlagen der Mathematik,* 9: 67–96, 1963.

[Kripke 1971]   Kripke, S., "Semantical Considerations on Modal Logic," in Linsky, L. (ed.), *Reference and Modality.* London, UK: Oxford University Press, 1971, pp. 63–72.

[Kripke 1972]   Kripke, S., "Naming and Necessity," in Davidson, D. and Harmon, G. (eds.), *Semantics of Natural Language,* Dordrecht, Holland: Reidel, 1972, pp. 253–355.

[Laird 1986]   Laird, J. E., Rosenbloom, P., and Newell, A., *Universal Subgoaling and Chunking: The Automatic Generation and Learning of Goal Hierarchies.* Hingham, MA: Kluwer Academic Publishers, 1986.

[Laird 1987]   Laird, J. E., Newell, A., and Rosenbloom, P., "SOAR: An Architecture for General Intelligence," *Artificial Intelligence* (in press).

[Langley 1983]   Langley, P., Bradshaw, G. L., and Simon, H. A., "Rediscovering Chemistry with the Bacon System," in Michalski, R. S., Carbonell, J., and Mitchell, T. M. (eds.), *Machine Learning: An*

Artificial Intelligence Approach, Los Altos, CA: Morgan Kaufmann, 1983.

[Larson 1977]   Larson, J., *Inductive Inference in the Variable Valued Predicate Logic System VL21: Methodology and Computer Implementation.* Champagne-Urbana, IL: University of Illinois, 1977 (Ph.D. dissertation).

[Lee 1972]   Lee, R. C. T., "Fuzzy Logic and the Resolution Principle," *Journal of the Association for Computing Machinery*, 19(1): 109–119, 1972.

[Lehnert 1979]   Lehnert, W. and Wilks, Y., "A Critical Perspective on KRL," *Cognitive Science*, 3(1): 1–28, 1979.

[Lemmer 1982a]   Lemmer, J. F. and Barth, S. W., "Efficient Minimum Information Updating for Bayesian Inferencing in Expert Systems," *Proceedings of the National Conference on Artificial Intelligence*, Pittsburgh, PA, 1982. Los Altos, CA: Morgan Kaufmann, 1982, pp. 424–427.

[Lemmer 1982b]   Lemmer, J. F., "Generalized Bayesian Updating of Incompletely Specified Distributions," Working Paper. New Hartford, NY: Par Technology Corporation, 1982.

[Lemmon 1986]   Lemmon, H., "COMAX: An Expert System for Cotton Crop Management," *Science*, 233(4759): 29–33, 1986.

[Lenat 1976]   Lenat, D. B., "AM: An Artificial Intelligence Approach to Discovery in Mathematics as Heuristic Search," Report STAN-CS-76-570, Stanford, CA: Stanford University, Department of Computer Science, 1976.

[Lenat 1982]   Lenat, D. B., "The Nature of Heuristics," *Artificial Intelligence*, 19(2): 189–249, 1982.

[Lenat 1983a]   Lenat, D. B., "Theory Formation by Heuristic Search. The Nature of Heuristics, II: Background and Examples," *Artificial Intelligence*, 21(1–2): 31–59, 1983.

[Lenat 1983b]   Lenat, D. B., "EURISKO: A Program that Learns New Heuristics and Domain Concepts. The Nature of Heuristics, III: Program Design and Results," *Artificial Intelligence*, 21(1–2): 61–98, 1983.

[Lenat 1986]   Lenat, D. B., Prakash, M., and Shepherd, M., "CYC: Using Commonsense Knowledge to Overcome Brittleness and Knowledge Acquistion Bottlenecks," *AI Magazine*, 6(4): 65–85, 1986.

[Levesque 1984]   Levesque, H., "A Logic of Implicit and Explicit Belief," *Proceedings of the National Conference on Artificial Intelligence*, University of Texas at Austin, 1984. Los Altos, CA: Morgan Kaufmann, 1984, pp. 198–202.

[Levesque 1986]   Levesque, H., "Knowledge Representation and Reasoning," *Annual Review of Computer Science*, 1: 255–288, 1986.

[Lifschitz 1985a]   Lifschitz, V., "Computing Circumscription," *Proceedings of the Ninth International Joint Conference on Artificial Intelligence*, Los Angeles, CA, 1985. Los Altos, CA: Morgan Kaufmann, 1985, pp. 121–127.

[Lifschitz 1985b]   Lifschitz, V., "Closed-World Databases and Circumscription," *Artificial Intelligence*, 27(2): 229–235, 1985.

[Lifschitz 1986a]   Lifschitz, V., *Mechanical Theorem Proving in the USSR: The Leningrad School.* Falls Church, VA: Delphic Associates, 1986.

[Lifschitz 1986b]   Lifschitz, V., "On the Satisfiability of Circumscription," *Artificial Intelligence*, 28(1): 17–27, 1986.

[Lifschitz 1986c]   Lifschitz, V., "Pointwise Circumscription: Preliminary Report," *Proceedings of the Fifth National Conference on Artificial Intelligence*, University of Pennsylvania, 1986, Vol. I. Los Altos, CA: Morgan Kaufmann, 1986, pp. 406-410.

[Lifschitz 1986d]   Lifschitz, V., "Formal Theories of Action: Preliminary Report," Working Paper. Stanford, CA: Stanford University, Department of Computer Science, 1986.

[Lifschitz 1987a]   Lifschitz, V., "On the Semantics of STRIPS," in Georgeff, M. and Lansky, A. (eds.), *Reasoning About Actions and Plans.* Los Altos, CA: Morgan Kaufmann, 1987.

[Lifschitz 1987b]   Lifschitz, V., "Rules for Computing Circumscription," paper in preparation.

[Lindsay 1980]   Lindsay, R. K., et al., *Applications of Artificial Intelligence for Organic Chemistry: The Dendral Project*. New York: McGraw-Hill, 1980.

[Loveland 1978]   Loveland, D. W., *Automated Theorem Proving: A Logical Basis*. New York: North-Holland, 1978.

[Loveland 1983]   Loveland, D. W., "Automated Theorem Proving: A Quarter Century Review," in Bledsoe, W. W. and Loveland, D. W. (eds.), *Automated Theorem Proving: After 25 Years*. *Special Session on Automated Theorem Proving*, Denver, CO, 1983. Providence, RI: American Mathematical Society, 1984.

[Lowrance 1982]   Lowrance, J. D. and Garvey, T. D., "Evidential Reasoning: A Developing Concept," *Proceedings of the International Conference on Cybernetics and Society*. New York: IEEE, 1982, pp. 6–9.

[Lowrance 1983]   Lowrance, J. D. and Garvey, T. D., "Evidential Reasoning: An Implementation for Multisensor Integration," Technical Note 307. Menlo Park, CA: SRI International, Artificial Intelligence Center, 1983.

[Lucas 1961]   Lucas, J. R., "Minds, Machines, and Gödel," *Philosophy*, 36: 112–127, 1961. (Also in Anderson, A. R. (ed.), *Minds and Machines*. Englewood Cliffs, NJ: Prentice-Hall, 1964, pp. 43–59.

[Luckham 1971]   Luckham, D. C. and Nilsson, N. J., "Extracting Information from Resolution Proof Trees," *Artificial Intelligence*, 2(1): 27–54, 1971.

[Lukasiewicz 1970] Lukasiewicz, J., "Logical Foundations of Probability Theory," in Berkowski, L. (ed.), *Jan Lukasiewicz, Selected Works*. Amsterdam: North-Holland, 1970, pp. 16–43.

[Maes 1987]   Maes, P. and Nardi, D., *Metalevel Architectures and Reflection*. Amsterdam: North-Holland, 1987.

[Malone 1985]   Malone, T. W., et al., "Toward Intelligent Message Routing Systems," Working Paper, August, 1985.

[Manna 1979]   Manna, Z. and Waldinger, R., "A Deductive Approach to Program Synthesis," *Proceedings of the Sixth International Joint Conference on Artificial*

Intelligence, Tokyo, 1979. Los Altos, CA: Morgan Kaufmann, 1979, pp. 542–551. (Also in Webber, B. L. and Nilsson, N. J. (eds.), *Readings in Artificial Intelligence.* Los Altos, CA: Morgan Kaufmann, 1981. Also in Rich, C. and Waters, R. C. (eds.), *Readings in Artificial Intelligence and Software Engineering.* Los Altos, CA: Morgan Kaufmann, 1986.)

[Margenau 1956]   Margenau, H. and Murphy, G. M., *The Mathematics of Physics and Chemistry,* (second edition). New York: Van Nostrand, 1956.

[Markov 1954]   Markov, A., *A Theory of Algorithms.* USSR: National Academy of Sciences, 1954.

[McCarthy 1958]   McCarthy, J., "Programs with Common Sense," *Mechanisation of Thought Processes, Proceedings of the Symposium of the National Physics Laboratory,* Vol. I. London, UK: Her Majesty's Stationary Office, 1958, pp. 77–84. (Also in Minsky, M. (ed.), *Semantic Information Processing.* Cambridge, MA: MIT Press, 1968, pp. 403–410. Also in Brachman, R. and Levesque, H. (eds.), *Readings in Knowledge Representation.* Los Altos, CA: Morgan Kaufmann, 1985.)

[McCarthy 1960]   McCarthy, J., "Recursive Functions of Symbolic Expressions and Their Computation by Machine," *Communications of the Association for Computing Machinery,* 3(4): 184–195, 1960.

[McCarthy 1963]   McCarthy, J., "Situations, Actions and Causal Laws," Memo 2. Stanford, CA: Stanford University Artificial Intelligence Project, 1963. (Reprinted in Minsky, M (ed.), *Semantic Information Processing.* Cambridge, MA: MIT Press, 1968, pp. 410–418.)

[McCarthy 1969]   McCarthy, J. and Hayes, P., "Some Philosophical Problems from the Standpoint of Artificial Intelligence," in Meltzer, B. and Michie, D. (eds.), *Machine Intelligence 4.* Edinburgh, UK: Edinburgh University Press, 1969, pp. 463–502. (Also in Webber, B. L. and Nilsson, N. J. (eds.), *Readings in Artificial Intelligence.* Los Altos, CA: Morgan Kaufmann, 1981.)

[McCarthy 1979a]   McCarthy, J., "First Order Theories of Individual Concepts and Propositions," in Hayes, J., Michie, D., and Mikulich, L. (eds.), *Machine Intelligence 9*. Chichester, UK: Ellis Horwood, 1979, pp. 129–147. (Also in Brachman, R. and Levesque, H. (eds.), *Readings in Knowledge Representation*. Los Altos, CA: Morgan Kaufmann, 1985.)

[McCarthy 1979b]   McCarthy, J., "Ascribing Mental Qualities to Machines," Technical Report STAN-CS-79-725, AIM-326.   Stanford CA: Stanford University, Department of Computer Science, 1979.

[McCarthy 1980]   McCarthy, J., "Circumscription—A Form of Non-Monotonic Reasoning," *Artificial Intelligence*, 13(1–2): 27–39, 1980. (Also in Webber, B. L. and Nilsson, N. J. (eds.), *Readings in Artificial Intelligence*. Los Altos, CA: Morgan Kaufmann, 1981.)

[McCarthy 1986]   McCarthy, J., "Applications of Circumscription to Formalizing Commonsense Knowledge," *Artificial Intelligence*, 28(1): 89–116, 1986.

[McCorduck 1979]   McCorduck, P., *Machines Who Think*.   San Francisco, CA: W. H. Freeman, 1979.

[McDermott 1980]   McDermott, D. and Doyle, J., "Non-Monotonic Logic I," *Artificial Intelligence*, 13(1–2): 41–72, 1980.

[McDermott 1982a]   McDermott, D., "Non-Monotonic Logic II: Non-Monotonic Modal Theories," *Journal of the Association for Computing Machinery*, 29(1): 33–57, 1982.

[McDermott 1982b]   McDermott, D., "A Temporal Logic for Reasoning About Processes and Plans," *Cognitive Science*, 6(2): 101–155, 1982.

[McDermott 1985]   McDermott, D., "Reasoning About Plans," in Hobbs, J. R. and Moore, R. C. (eds.), *Formal Theories of the Commonsense World*. Norwood, NJ: Ablex, 1985.

[McDermott 1987a]   McDermott, D., "A Critique of Pure Reason," *Computational Intelligence*, (with open peer commentary) (in press).

[McDermott 1987b]   McDermott, D., "Logic, Problem Solving, and Deduction," *Annual Review of Computer Science* (in press).

[Meltzer 1969]   Meltzer, B. and Michie, D. (eds.), *Machine Intelligence 4*. Edinburgh, UK: Edinburgh University Press, 1969.

[Meltzer 1970]   Meltzer, B. and Michie, D. (eds.), *Machine Intelligence 5*. Edinburgh, UK: Edinburgh University Press, 1970.

[Meltzer 1971]   Meltzer, B. and Michie, D. (eds.), *Machine Intelligence 6*. Edinburgh, UK: Edinburgh University Press, 1971.

[Meltzer 1972]   Meltzer, B. and Michie, D. (eds.), *Machine Intelligence 7*. Edinburgh, UK: Edinburgh University Press, 1972.

[Mendelson 1964]   Mendelson, E., *Introduction to Mathematical Logic*. Princeton, NJ: Van Nostrand, 1964 (third edition, 1987).

[Michalski 1980]   Michalski, R. S., "Pattern Recognition as Rule-Guided Inductive Inference," *Transactions on Pattern Analysis and Machine Intelligence*, PAMI-2(2–4): 349–361, 1980.

[Michalski 1983a]   Michalski, R. S., Carbonell, J., and Mitchell, T. M. (eds.), *Machine Learning: An Artificial Intelligence Approach*. Los Altos, CA: Morgan Kaufmann, 1983.

[Michalski 1983b]   Michalski, R. S. and Stepp, R. E., "Learning from Observation: Conceptual Clustering," in Michalski, R. S., Carbonell, J., and Mitchell, T. M. (eds.), *Machine Learning: An Artificial Intelligence Approach*. Los Altos, CA: Morgan Kaufmann, 1983, pp. 331–363.

[Michalski 1983c]   Michalski, R. S., "A Theory and Methodology of Inductive Learning," in Michalski, R. S., Carbonell, J., and Mitchell, T. M. (eds.), *Machine Learning: An Artificial Intelligence Approach*. Los Altos, CA: Morgan Kaufmann, 1983, pp. 83–134.

[Michalski 1986]   Michalski, R. S., Carbonell, J., and Mitchell, T. M., *Machine Learning: An Artificial Intelligence Approach*, Vol. II. Los Altos, CA: Morgan Kaufmann, 1986.

[Michie 1968]   Michie, D. (ed.), *Machine Intelligence 3*. Edinburgh, UK: Edinburgh University Press, 1968.

[Minker 1973]   Minker, J., Fishman, D. H., and McSkimin, J. R., "The Q* Algorithm—A Search Strategy for a Deductive Question-Answering System," *Artificial Intelligence*, 4(3–4): 225–244, 1973.

[Minker 1979]   Minker, J. and Zanon, G., "Lust Resolution: Resolution with Arbitrary Selection Function," Research Report TR-736. College Park, MD: University of Maryland, 1979.

[Minker 1984]   Minker, J. and Perlis, D., "Protected Circumscription," *Proceedings of the Workshop on Non-Monotonic Reasoning*, New Paltz, NY, 1984. Menlo Park, CA: AAAI, 1984, pp. 337–343.

[Minsky 1975]   Minsky, M., "A Framework for Representing Knowledge," in Winston, P. H. (ed.), *The Psychology of Computer Vision*. New York: McGraw-Hill, 1975, pp. 211–277. (Also in Haugeland, J. (ed.), *Mind Design*. Cambridge, MA: MIT Press, 1981, pp. 95–128. Also in Brachman, R. and Levesque, H. (eds.), *Readings in Knowledge Representation*. Los Altos, CA: Morgan Kaufmann, 1985.)

[Minsky 1986]   Minsky, M., *The Society of Mind*. New York: Simon and Schuster, 1986.

[Mitchell 1978]   Mitchell, T. M., *Version Spaces: An Approach to Concept Learning*. Stanford, CA: Stanford University, 1978 (Ph.D. dissertation). (Also Stanford Technical Report STAN-CS-78-711, HPP-79-2.)

[Mitchell 1979]   Mitchell, T. M., "An Analysis of Generalization as a Search Problem," *Proceedings of the Sixth International Joint Conference on Artificial Intelligence*, Tokyo, 1979. Los Altos, CA: Morgan Kaufmann, 1979, pp. 577–582.

[Mitchell 1982]   Mitchell, T. M., "Generalization as Search," *Artificial Intelligence*, 18(2): 203–226, 1982.

[Mitchell 1986]   Mitchell, T. M., Carbonell, J. G., and Michalski, R. S., *Machine Learning: A Guide to Current Research*. Hingham, MA: Kluwer Academic Publishers, 1986.

[Moore 1975]   Moore, R. C., "Reasoning from Incomplete Knowledge in a Procedural Deduction System," Technical Report AI-TR-347. Cambridge, MA: Massachusetts Institute of Technology, Artificial Intelligence Laboratory, 1975. (Also published as Moore, R. C., *Reasoning from Incomplete Knowledge in a Procedural Deduction System*. New York: Garland Publishing, 1980.)

[Moore 1979]   Moore, R. C., "Reasoning About Knowledge and Action," Technical Note 191. Menlo Park, CA: SRI International, Artificial Intelligence Center, 1979 (Ph.D. dissertation).

[Moore 1982]   Moore, R. C., "The Role of Logic in Knowledge Representation and Commonsense Reasoning," *Proceedings of the National Conference of on Artificial Intelligence*, Pittsburgh, PA, 1982. Los Altos, CA: Morgan Kaufmann, 1982, pp. 428–433. (Also in Brachman, R. and Levesque, H. (eds.), *Readings in Knowledge Representation*. Los Altos, CA: Morgan Kaufmann, 1985.)

[Moore 1985a]   Moore, R. C., "A Formal Theory of Knowledge and Action," in Hobbs, J. R. and Moore, R. C. (eds.), *Formal Theories of the Commonsense World*. Norwood, NJ: Ablex, 1985.

[Moore 1985b]   Moore, R. C., "Semantical Considerations on Nonmonotonic Logic," *Artificial Intelligence*, 25(1): 75–94, 1985.

[Moore 1986]   Moore, R. C., "The Role of Logic in Artificial Intelligence," in Benson, I. (ed.), *Intelligent Machinery: Theory and Practice*. Cambridge, UK: Cambridge University Press, 1986.

[Moses 1986]   Moses, Y., *Knowledge in a Distributed Environment*. Stanford, CA: Stanford University, 1986 (Ph.D. dissertation).

[Newell 1972]   Newell, A. and Simon, H. A., *Human Problem Solving*. Englewood Cliffs, NJ: Prentice-Hall, 1972.

[Newell 1973]   Newell, A., "Production Systems: Models of Control Structures," in Chase, W. G. (ed.), *Visual Information Processing*. New York: Academic Press, 1973, pp. 463–526.

[Newell 1976]   Newell, A. and Simon, H. A., "Computer Science as Empirical Inquiry: Symbols and Search,"

Communications of the Association for Computing Machinery, 19(3): 113–126, 1976.

[Newell 1982]   Newell, A., "The Knowledge Level," *Artificial Intelligence*, 18(1): 87–127, 1982.

[Nilsson 1965]   Nilsson, N. J., *Learning Machines: Foundations of Trainable Pattern-Classifying Systems.* New York: McGraw-Hill, 1965.

[Nilsson 1971]   Nilsson, N. J., *Problem-Solving Methods in Artificial Intelligence.* New York: McGraw-Hill, 1971.

[Nilsson 1980]   Nilsson, N. J., *Principles of Artificial Intelligence.* Los Altos, CA: Morgan Kaufmann, 1980. (Reviewed by J. McDermott in *Artificial Intelligence*, 15(1–2): 127–131, 1980.)

[Nilsson 1984]   Nilsson, N. J., "Shakey the Robot," Technical Report 323. Menlo Park, CA: SRI International, Artificial Intelligence Center, 1984.

[Nilsson 1986]   Nilsson, N. J., "Probabilistic Logic," *Artificial Intelligence*, 28(1): 71–87, 1986.

[Nonmonotonic 1984]   *Proceedings from the Workshop on Non-Monotonic Reasoning*, New Paltz, NY, 1984. Menlo Park, CA: AAAI, 1984.

[Paterson 1968]   Paterson, M. and Wegman, M., "Linear Unification," *Journal of Computer and System Science*, 16, 1968.

[Pearl 1984]   Pearl, J., *Heuristics.* Reading, MA: Addison-Wesley, 1984.

[Pearl 1986a]   Pearl, J., "Fusion, Propagation, and Structuring in Belief Networks," *Artificial Intelligence*, 29(3): 241–288, 1986.

[Pearl 1986b]   Pearl, J., "On Evidential Reasoning in a Hierarchy of Hypotheses," *Artificial Intelligence*, 28(1): 9–15, 1986.

[Pearl 1987]   Pearl, J., "Search Techniques," *Annual Review of Computer Science* (in press).

[Pednault 1986]   Pednault, E., *Toward a Mathematical Theory of Plan Synthesis.* Stanford, CA: Stanford University, Department of Electrical Engineering, 1986 (Ph.D. dissertation).

[Perlis 1985]   Perlis, D., "Languages with Self-Reference, I: Foundations," *Artificial Intelligence*, 25(3): 301–322, 1985.

[Perlis 1986]   Perlis, D. and Minker, J., "Completeness Results for Circumscription," *Artificial Intelligence*, 28(1): 29–42, 1986.

[Perlis 1987]   Perlis, D., "Languages with Self-Reference, II: Knowledge, Belief, and Modality," *Artificial Intelligence* (to appear).

[Perrault 1980]   Perrault, C. R. and Allen, J. F., "A Plan-Based Analysis of Indirect Speech Acts," *American Journal of Computational Linguistics*, 6(3): 167–182, 1980.

[Pospesel 1976]   Pospesel, H., *Introduction to Logic: Predicate Logic*. Englewood Cliffs, NJ: Prentice-Hall, 1976.

[Post 1943]   Post, E. L., "Formal Reductions of the General Combinatorial Problem," *American Journal of Mathematics*, 65: 197–268, 1943.

[Prawitz 1960]   Prawitz, D., "An Improved Proof Procedure," *Theoria*, 26: 102–139, 1960.

[Przymusinski 1986]   Przymusinski, T., "A Decidable Query Answering Algorithm for Circumscriptive Theories," Working Paper. El Paso, TX: University of Texas, Department of Mathematical Sciences, 1986.

[Quillian 1968]   Quillian, M., "Semantic Memory," in Minsky, M. (ed.), *Semantic Information Processing*. Cambridge, MA: MIT Press, 1968, pp. 216–270.

[Quine 1971]   Quine, W. V. O., "Quantifiers and Propositional Attitudes," in Linsky, L. (ed.), *Reference and Modality*. London, UK: Oxford University Press, 1971, pp. 101–111.

[Quinlan 1983]   Quinlan, J. R., "Learning Efficient Classification Procedures and Their Application to Chess End Games," in Michalski, R. S., Carbonell, J., and Mitchell, T. M. (eds.), *Machine Learning: An Artificial Intelligence Approach*. Los Altos, CA: Morgan Kaufmann, 1983.

[Raphael 1971]   Raphael, B., "The Frame Problem in Problem Solving Systems," in Findler, N. and Meltzer, B. (eds.),

Artificial Intelligence and Heuristic Programming. New York: American Elsevier, 1971, pp. 159–169.

[Raulefs 1978] Raulefs, P., et al., "A Short Survey on the State of the Art in Matching and Unification Problems," *AISB Quarterly*, No. 32: 17–21, 1978.

[Reboh 1986] Reboh, R. and Risch, T., "Syntel™: Knowledge Programming Using Functional Representation," *Proceedings of the Fifth National Conference on Artificial Intelligence*, University of Pennsylvania, 1986. Los Altos, CA: Morgan Kaufmann, 1986, pp. 1003–1007.

[Reiter 1978] Reiter, R., "On Closed World Data Bases," in Gallaire, H. and Minker, J. (eds.), *Logic and Data Bases.* New York: Plenum Press, 1978, pp. 55–76. (Also in Webber, B. L. and Nilsson, N. J. (eds.), *Readings in Artificial Intelligence.* Los Altos, CA: Morgan Kaufmann, 1981, pp. 199–140.)

[Reiter 1980a] Reiter, R., "A Logic for Default Reasoning," *Artificial Intelligence*, 13(1–2): 81–132, 1980.

[Reiter 1980b] Reiter, R., "Equality and Domain Closure in First-Order Databases," *Journal of the Association for Computing Machinery*, 27(2): 235–249, 1980.

[Reiter 1982] Reiter, R., "Circumscription Implies Predicate Completion (Sometimes)," *Proceedings of the National Conference on Artificial Intelligence*, Pittsburgh, PA, 1982. Los Altos, CA: Morgan Kaufmann, 1982, pp. 418–420.

[Reiter 1983] Reiter, R. and Criscuolo, G., "Some Representational Issues in Default Reasoning," *International Journal of Computers and Mathematics. Special Issue on Computational Linguistics*, 9(1): 15–27, 1983.

[Reiter 1987a] Reiter, R., "A Theory of Diagnosis From First-Principles," *Artificial Intelligence*, 32(1): 57–95, 1987.

[Reiter 1987b] Reiter, R., "Nonmonotonic Reasoning," *Annual Review of Computer Science* (in press).

[Reitman 1984] Reitman, W. (ed.), *Artificial Intelligence Applications for Business.* Norwood, NJ: Ablex, 1984.

[Rich 1983]   Rich, E., *Artificial Intelligence*. New York: McGraw-Hill, 1983. (Reviewed by R. Rada in *Artificial Intelligence*, 28(1): 119–121, 1986.)

[Rich 1986]   Rich, C. and Waters, R. C. (eds.), *Readings in Artificial Intelligence and Software Engineering*. Los Altos, CA: Morgan Kaufmann, 1986.

[Roach 1985]   Roach, J. W., et al., "POMME: A Computer-Based Consultation System for Apple Orchard Management Using PROLOG," *Expert Systems*, 2(2): 56–69, 1985.

[Robinson 1965]   Robinson, J. A., "A Machine-Oriented Logic Based on the Resolution Principle," *Journal of the Association for Computing Machinery*, 12(1): 23–41, 1965.

[Robinson 1979]   Robinson, J. A., *Logic: Form and Function*. New York: North-Holland, 1979.

[Rosenschein 1981] Rosenschein, S., "Plan Synthesis: A Logical Perspective," *Proceedings of the Seventh International Joint Conference on Artificial Intelligence*, Vancouver, BC, 1981. Los Altos, CA: Morgan Kaufmann, 1981, pp. 331–337.

[Rosenschein 1986] Rosenschein, S. J. and Kaelbling, L. P., "The Synthesis of Machines with Provably Epistemic Properties," in Halpern, J. F. (ed.), *Proceedings of the 1986 Conference on Theoretical Aspects of Reasoning about Knowledge*. Los Altos, CA: Morgan Kaufmann, 1986, pp. 83–98.

[Rulifson 1972]   Rulifson, J. F., Derksen, J. A., and Waldinger, R. J., "QA4: A Procedural Calculus for Intuitive Reasoning," Technical Note 73. Menlo Park, CA: SRI International, Artificial Intelligence Center, 1972.

[Rumelhart 1986]   Rumelhart, D. E., et al., *Parallel Distributed Processing: Explorations in the Microstructure of Cognition*; Vol. I: *Foundations*, Vol. II: *Psychological and Biological Models*. Cambridge, MA: MIT Press, 1986.

[Sacerdoti 1974]   Sacerdoti, E. D., "Planning in a Hierarchy of Abstraction Spaces," *Artificial Intelligence*, 5(2): 115–135, 1974.

[Sacerdoti 1977]   Sacerdoti, E. D., *A Structure for Plans and Behavior.* New York: Elsevier, 1977.

[Sandewall 1972]   Sandewall, E., "An Approach to the Frame Problem and Its Implementation," in Meltzer, B. and Michie, D. (eds.), *Machine Intelligence 7.* Edinburgh, UK: Edinburgh University Press, 1972.

[Schubert 1976]   Schubert, L. K., "Extending the Expressive Power of Semantic Networks," *Artificial Intelligence,* 7(2): 163–198, 1976.

[Searle 1980]   Searle, J. R., "Minds, Brains, and Programs," *The Behavioral and Brain Sciences,* 3: 417–457, 1980 (with open peer commentary). (Reprinted in Hofstadter, D. R., and Dennett, D. C. (eds.), *The Mind's Eye: Fantasies and Reflections on Self and Soul.* New York: Basic Books, 1981, pp. 351–373.)

[Shafer 1979]   Shafer, G. A., *Mathematical Theory of Evidence.* Princeton, NJ: Princeton University Press, 1979.

[Shankar 1986]   Shankar, N., *Proof-Checking Metamathematics.* Austin, TX: The University of Texas at Austin, 1986 (Ph.D. dissertation).

[Shapiro 1987]   Shapiro, S. C. (ed.), *Encyclopedia of Artificial Intelligence.* New York: John Wiley and Sons, 1987.

[Shepherdson 1984]   Shepherdson, J. C., "Negation as Failure: A Comparison of Clark's Completed Data Base and Reiter's Closed World Assumption," *Logic Programming,* 1(1): 51–79, 1984.

[Shieber 1986]   Shieber, S., *An Introduction to Unification-Based Approaches to Grammar,* CSLI Lecture Notes No. 4. Stanford, CA: Stanford University, Center for the Study of Langauge and Information, 1986.

[Shoham 1986a]   Shoham, Y., "Chronological Ignorance: Time, Nonmonotonicity and Necessity," *Proceedings of the Fifth National Conference on Artificial Intelligence,* University of Pennsylvania, 1986. Los Altos, CA: Morgan Kaufmann, 1986, pp. 389–393.

[Shoham 1986b]   Shoham, Y., "Temporal Reasoning," in Shapiro, S. C. (ed.), *Encyclopedia of Artificial Intelligence.* New York: John Wiley and Sons, 1987.

[Shoham 1986c] Shoham, Y., *Reasoning About Change: Time and Causation from the Standpoint of Artificial Intelligence.* New Haven, CT: Yale University, 1986 (Ph.D. dissertation).

[Shortliffe 1976] Shortliffe, E. H., *Computer-Based Medical Consultations:* MYCIN. New York: Elsevier, 1976.

[Sickel 1976] Sickel, S., "A Search Technique for Clause Interconnectivity Graphs," *IEEE Transactions on Computers,* C-25(8): 823–835, 1976.

[Siekmann 1983a] Siekmann, J. and Wrightson, G. (eds.), *Automation of Reasoning: Classical Papers on Computational Logic,* Vol. I: 1957–1966. New York: Springer-Verlag, 1983.

[Siekmann 1983b] Siekmann, J. and Wrightson, G. (eds.), *Automation of Reasoning: Classical Papers on Computational Logic,* Vol. II: 1967–1970. New York: Springer-Verlag, 1983.

[Simmons 1973] Simmons, R. F., "Semantic Networks: Their Computation and Use for Understanding English Sentences," in Schank, R. and Colby, K. (eds.), *Computer Models of Thought and Language.* San Francisco, CA: W. H. Freeman, 1973, pp. 63–113.

[Simon 1983] Simon, H. A., "Search and Reasoning in Problem Solving," *Artificial Intelligence,* 21(1–2): 7–29, 1983.

[Smith 1982] Smith, B. C., *Reflection and Semantics in a Procedural Language.* Cambridge, MA: Massachusetts Institute of Technology, 1982 (Ph.D. dissertation).

[Smith 1985] Smith, D. E. and Genesereth, M. R., "Ordering Conjunctive Queries," *Artificial Intelligence,* 26(3): 171–215, 1985.

[Smith 1986] Smith, D. E., Genesereth, M. R., and Ginsberg, M. L., "Controlling Recursive Inference," *Artificial Intelligence,* 30(3): 343–389, 1986.

[Smullyan 1968] Smullyan, R. M., *First-Order Logic.* New York: Springer-Verlag, 1968.

[Stalnaker 1985] Stalnaker, R., "Possible Worlds," Chapter 3 in Stalnaker, R., *Inquiry.* MIT Press, Cambridge, MA, 1985.

[Stefik 1979]   Stefik, M., "An Examination of a Frame-Structured Representation System," *Proceedings of the Sixth International Joint Conference on Artificial Intelligence*, Tokyo, 1979. Los Altos, CA: Morgan Kaufmann, 1979, pp. 845–852.

[Stefik 1981a]   "Planning with Constraints (MOLGEN: Part 1)," *Artificial Intelligence*, 15(2): 111–140, 1981.

[Stefik 1981b]   Stefik, M., "Planning and Meta-Planning (MOLGEN: Part 2)," *Artificial Intelligence*, 16(2): 141–170, 1981. (Also in Webber, B. L. and Nilsson, N. J. (eds.), *Readings in Artificial Intelligence*. Los Altos, CA: Morgan Kaufmann, 1981.)

[Stefik 1986]   Stefik, M. and Bobrow, D., "Object-Oriented Programming: Themes and Variations," *AI Magazine*, 6(4): 40–64, 1986.

[Sterling 1986]   Sterling, L. and Shapiro, E., *The Art of PROLOG: Advanced Programming Techniques*. Cambridge, MA: MIT Press, 1986.

[Stickel 1982]   Stickel, M. E., "A Nonclausal Connection-Graph Resolution Theorem-Proving Program," *Proceedings of the National Conference on Artificial Intelligence* Pittsburgh, PA, 1982. Los Altos, CA: Morgan Kaufmann, 1982, pp. 229–233. (Also published as Stickel, M. E., "A Nonclausal Connection-Graph Resolution Theorem-Proving Program," Technical Note 268. Menlo Park, CA: SRI International, Artificial Intelligence Center, 1982.)

[Stickel 1985]   Stickel, M. E., "Automated Deduction by Theory Resolution," *Proceedings of the Ninth International Joint Conference on Artificial Intelligence* Los Angeles, CA, 1985. Los Altos, CA: Morgan Kaufmann, 1985, pp. 1181–1186. (Also in *Journal of Automated Reasoning*, 1(4): 333–355, 1985.)

[Stickel 1986]   Stickel, M. E., "Schubert's Steamroller Problem: Formulations and Solutions," *Journal of Automated Reasoning*, 2(1): 89–101, 1986.

[Subramanian 1986]   Subramanian, D. and Feigenbaum, J., "Factorization in Experiment Generation," in *Proceedings of the Fifth National Conference on Artificial Intelligence*, University of Pennsylvania, 1986. Los Altos, CA: Morgan Kaufmann, 1986.

[Suppes 1966]   Suppes, P., "Probabilistic Inference and the Concept of Total Evidence," in Hintikka, J. and Suppes, P. (eds.), *Aspects of Inductive Logic*. Amsterdam: North-Holland, 1966, pp. 49–65.

[Sussman 1970]   Sussman, G., Winograd, T., and Charniak, E., "Micro-Planner Reference Manual," Memo 203a. Cambridge, MA: Massachusetts Institute of Technology, Artificial Intelligence Laboratory, 1970.

[Tate 1976]   Tate, A., "Project Planning Using a Hierarchic Non-Linear Planner," Research Report 25. Edinburgh, UK: University of Edinburgh, Department of Artificial Intelligence, 1976.

[Tate 1977]   Tate, A., "Generating Project Networks," *Proceedings of the Fifth International Joint Conference on Artificial Intelligence*, Cambridge, MA, 1977. Los Altos, CA: Morgan Kaufmann, 1977, pp. 888–893.

[Trappl 1986]   Trappl, R. (ed.), *Impacts of Artificial Intelligence*. Amsterdam: North-Holland, 1986.

[Treitel 1987]   Treitel, R. and Genesereth, M. R., "Choosing Directions for Rules," *Journal of Automated Reasoning* (in press).

[Uncertain 1985]   *Proceedings of the Workshop on Uncertainty and Probability in Artificial Intelligence*, Los Angeles, CA. Menlo Park, CA: AAAI, 1985. (The papers in this *Proceedings* also appear, in revised form, along with other papers, in Kanal, L. N. and Lemmer, J. F. (eds.), *Uncertainty in Artificial Intelligence*. New York: North-Holland, 1986.)

[Uncertain 1986]   *Proceedings of the Workshop on Uncertainty in Artificial Intelligence*, University of Pennsylvania. Menlo Park, CA: AAAI, 1986.

[Van Benthem 1983] Van Benthem, J., *The Logic of Time*. Hingham, MA: Kluwer Academic Publishers, 1983.

[Vere 1975]   Vere, S. A., "Induction of Concepts in the Predicate Calculus," *Proceedings of the Fourth International Joint Conference on Artificial Intelligence*. Los Altos, CA: Morgan Kaufmann, 1975, pp. 281–287.

[Vere 1978]   Vere, S. A., "Inductive Learning of Relational Productions," in Waterman, D. A. and Hayes-

Roth, F. (eds.), *Pattern Directed Inference Systems.*
New York: Academic Press, 1978.

[Waldinger 1977]   Waldinger, R. J., "Achieving Several Goals Simultaneously," in Elcock, E. and Michie, D. (eds.), *Machine Intelligence 8: Machine Representations of Knowledge.* Chichester, UK: Ellis Horwood, 1977, pp. 94–136. (Also in Webber, B. L. and Nilsson, N. J. (eds.), *Readings in Artificial Intelligence.* Los Altos, CA: Morgan Kaufmann, 1981.)

[Walther 1985]   Walther, C., "A Mechanical Solution of Schubert's Steamroller by Many-Sorted Resolution," *Artificial Intelligence*, 26(2): 217–224, 1985.

[Warren 1974]   Warren, D. H. D., "WARPLAN: A System for Generating Plans," Memo 76. Edinburgh, UK: University of Edinburgh, School of Artificial Intelligence, Department of Computational Logic, 1974.

[Warren 1977]   Warren, D. H. D. and Pereira, L. M., "PROLOG— The Language and Its Implementation Compared with LISP," *Proceedings of the Symposium on Artificial Intelligence and Programming Languages, SIGPLAN Notices*, 12(8) and *SIGART Newsletter*, No. 64: 109–115, 1977.

[Webber 1981]   Webber, B. L. and Nilsson, N. J., *Readings in Artificial Intelligence.* Los Altos, CA: Morgan Kaufmann, 1981.

[Weizenbaum 1976]   Weizenbaum, J., *Computer Power and Human Reason: From Judgment to Calculation.* San Francisco, CA: W. H. Freeman, 1976. (Reviews by B. Kuipers and J. McCarthy with a response by Weizenbaum appear in *SIGART Newsletter*, No. 58: 4–13, 1976.)

[Weyhrauch 1980]   Weyhrauch, R., "Prolegomena to a Theory of Mechanized Formal Reasoning," *Artificial Intelligence*, 13(1–2): 133–170, 1980. (Also in Webber, B. L. and Nilsson, N. J. (eds.), *Readings in Artificial Intelligence.* Los Altos, CA: Morgan Kaufmann, 1981. Also in Brachman, R. and Levesque, H. (eds.), *Readings in Knowledge Representation.* Los Altos, CA: Morgan Kaufmann, 1985.)

[Wilkins 1983]   Wilkins, D. E., "Representation in a Domain-Independent Planner," *Proceedings of the Eighth*

International Joint Conference on Artificial Intelligence, Karlsruhe, 1983. Los Altos, CA: Morgan Kaufmann, 1983, pp. 733–740.

[Wilkins 1984] Wilkins, D. E., "Domain-Independent Planning: Representation and Plan Generation," *Artificial Intelligence*, 22(3): 269–301, 1984.

[Wilkins 1985] Wilkins, D. E., "Recovering from Execution Errors in SIPE," *Computational Intelligence*, 1(1): 33–45, 1985.

[Winker 1982] Winker, S., "Generation and Verification of Finite Models and Counterexamples Using an Automated Theorem Prover Answering Two Open Questions," *Journal of the Association for Computing Machinery*, 29(2): 273–284, 1982.

[Winograd 1975] Winograd, T., "Frame Representations and the Declarative/Procedural Controversy," in Bobrow, D. and Collins, A. (eds.), *Representation and Understanding: Studies in Cognitive Science.* New York: Academic Press, 1975, pp. 185–210. (Also in Brachman, R. and Levesque, H. (eds.), *Readings in Knowledge Representation.* Los Altos, CA: Morgan Kaufmann, 1985.)

[Winograd 1980] Winograd, T., "Extended Inference Modes in Reasoning by Computer Systems," *Artificial Intelligence*, 13(1–2): 5–26, 1980.

[Winograd 1986] Winograd, T. and Flores, F., *Understanding Computers and Cognition: A New Foundation for Design.* Norwood, NJ: Ablex, 1986. (Four reviews and a response appear in *Artificial Intelligence*, 31(2): 213–261, 1987.)

[Winston 1975] Winston, P., "Learning Structural Descriptions from Examples," in Winston, P. (ed.), *The Psychology of Computer Vision.* New York: McGraw-Hill, 1975, pp. 157–209. (Also in Brachman, R. and Levesque, H. (eds.), *Readings in Knowledge Representation.* Los Altos, CA: Morgan Kaufmann, 1985.)

[Winston 1977] Winston, P. H., *Artificial Intelligence.* Reading, MA: Addison-Wesley, 1977 (second edition, 1984). (Second edition reviewed by D. Reese in *Artificial Intelligence*, 27(1): 127–128, 1985.)

[Winston 1984]   Winston, P. H. and Prendergast, K. A. (eds.), *The AI Business: The Commercial Uses of Artificial Intelligence.* Cambridge, MA: The MIT Press, 1984. (Reviewed by L. B. Elliot in *Artificial Intelligence,* 26(3): 361–363, 1985. Also reviewed by M. J. Stefik in *Artificial Intelligence,* 28(3): 347–348, 1986.)

[Woods 1975]   Woods, W., "What's in a Link: Foundations for Semantic Networks," in Bobrow, D. and Collins, A. (eds.), *Representation and Understanding: Studies in Cognitive Science.* New York: Academic Press, 1975, pp. 35–82. (Also in Brachman, R. and Levesque, H. (eds.), *Readings in Knowledge Representation.* Los Altos, CA: Morgan Kaufmann, 1985.)

[Wos 1984a]   Wos, L., et al., *Automated Reasoning: Introduction and Applications.* Englewood Cliffs, NJ: Prentice-Hall, 1984.

[Wos 1984b]   Wos, L., et al., "A New Use of an Automated Reasoning Assistant: Open Questions in Equivalential Calculus and the Study of Infinite Domains," *Artificial Intelligence,* 22(3): 303–356, 1984.

[Wos 1985]   Wos, L., et al., "An Overview of Automated Reasoning and Related Fields," *Journal of Automated Reasoning,* 1(1): 5–48, 1985.

[Zadeh 1975]   Zadeh, L. A., "Fuzzy Logic and Approximate Reasoning," *Synthese,* 30: 407–428, 1975.

[Zadeh 1983]   Zadeh, L. A., "Commonsense Knowledge Representation Based on Fuzzy Logic," *IEEE Computation,* 16(10): 61–66, 1983.

Index

This book employs the Computer Modern family of fonts, generated in METAFONT by Donald Knuth. The manuscript of this book was entered into DEC20 computers of the Computer Science Department at Stanford University and formatted with markup commands for the LaTeX macro package under TeX. Special LaTeX .sty files implemented the book design.

Xerox and Imagen laser printers produced the copies used in proof, and camera-ready films were prepared on the Autologic APS-μ5 printer at the CSD. Chapter heads and two figures in Chapter 8 required hand layout work.

Printing was done by R. R. Donnelley and Sons onto Patina matte paper and cased with Hollingston Kingston Linen in a perf/notch binding.